MARKETING FASHION:
A GLOBAL PERSPECTIVE

MARKETING FASHION:
A GLOBAL PERSPECTIVE

Patricia Mink Rath
Marketing Education Consultant

Richard Petrizzi
Illinois Institute of Art

Penny Gill
PWG Communications Inc.

FAIRCHILD BOOKS
NEW YORK

Executive Director & General Manager: **Michael Schluter**
Executive Editor: **Olga T. Kontzias**
Assistant Acquisitions Editor: **Amanda Breccia**
Development Editor: **Rob Phelps**
Assistant Art Director: **Sarah Silberg**
Production Director: **Ginger Hillman**
Associate Production Editor: **Jessica Katz**
Ancillaries Editor: **Amy Butler**
Associate Director of Sales: **Melanie Sankel**
Copyeditor: **Joanne Slike**
Cover Design: **Erin Fitzsimmons**
Text Design: **Alicia Freile, Tango Media**
Page Layout: **Alicia Freile, Tango Media**
Back Cover Credits: **(Top to Bottom)**
Courtesy of WWD/Donato Sardella
Courtesy of WWD/Pasha Antonov
Courtesy of WWD/Stefanie Keenan

Library of Congress Catalog Card Number: 2011940997

978-1-60901-078-2
GST R 133004424
Printed in Canada
CH16, TP14

Dedication

For Phil, Eric, Kiyomi, Dana, Stefani, and Justin

Contents

Extended Contents

PART II:
BUILDING A FASHION
MARKETING STRATEGY   97

PART IV:
COMMUNICATING FASHION'S
VALUE THROUGH PROMOTION   372

Preface

The vibrant field of fashion marketing contributes frequently and heavily to society's swiftly changing moods. Marketers of fashion navigate customer whims and continually develop new offerings as they strive to persuade customers to take part in their latest innovations. In accomplishing its objective, fashion marketing provides a range of opportunities and challenges for dedicated students. Careers in product design and development, research and trend forecasting, retail buying and merchandising, sales, advertising, and promotion, among other areas of expertise, all make up the field of fashion marketing—a field replete with many creative and rewarding occupations.

The fashion marketing process, while following traditional marketing in theory, has many unique applications. Up until now, no textbook firmly anchored in marketing theory and practice has existed to specifically cover the fashion universe. *Marketing Fashion: A Global Perspective* accurately and engagingly presents theories and best practices current among fashion marketing businesses today.

ORGANIZATION OF THE TEXT

The premise of this book is based on a definition of fashion goods that includes all currently popular designed products from apparel to automobiles and from cosmetics to kitchen equipment. Further unifying elements include a focus on how marketers find their customers and determine their fashion needs, and how they then center their strategies on reaching their twin goals of maintaining consumer satisfaction and corporate profitability. The overarching themes of globalization and ethics as they apply to all aspects of fashion marketing are discussed in every chapter.

Marketing Fashion: A Global Perspective is organized in four parts to guide the reader in a logical way through the processes and practices of marketing.

PART I: DEFINING FASHION MARKETING AND HOW IT WORKS

The first chapter opens with an overview of marketing and fashion marketing, explains the marketer's long-term goals and the basic elements of the marketing process, and outlines the direction fashion marketing is moving in the global economy. Chapter 2 examines the various internal and external elements that impact fashion marketers today, and describes how those entities and forces influence the way fashion businesses operate in the global marketplace. The third chapter explores the topic of consumer behavior from the fashion marketer's point of view. It explains how a customer's level of involvement with a product or buying situation influences the purchase process, and looks at the internal and external influences that have an effect on both consumer and business buyer behavior.

PART II: BUILDING A FASHION MARKETING STRATEGY

The fourth chapter describes the purpose of the marketing planning process and the mission statement. It then explains how to formulate a competitive analysis, develop a marketing strategy and a marketing mix, and measure the results. Chapter 5 explores fashion organizations' need for marketing information in order to create their strategies. This chapter details the available research sources, the marketing research process, and the uses of research findings. Creating the right relationship with fashion customers is the topic of Chapter 6, which describes market segmentation, targeting, and positioning, and the resulting application of the marketing mix.

PART III: FOCUSING MARKETING MIX ELEMENTS ON THE FASHION CONSUMER

Chapter 7 describes the importance of branding and building brand loyalty with consumers. It differentiates among various types of brands including designer, private label, and generic, and discusses how fashion marketers make decisions about product lines and mixes and branding strategies. Fashion marketers continually need to develop new goods and services, and the product development process is the topic of Chapter 8. The many factors that fashion marketers must consider in establishing prices for their products is the subject of Chapter 9. This chapter looks at aspects of pricing including the customer's estimate of the product's value, production and marketing costs, and various pricing strategy options. Chapter 10 covers marketing channel activities and supply chain management practices in marketing fashion goods. Channel organization, distribution intensity, and international marketing strategies are all explored. Fashion wholesaling and retailing are the topics of Chapter 11. Included is description of the marketing practices of fashion wholesalers, organizational characteristics of global fashion retailers, and activities of Internet fashion businesses.

PART IV: COMMUNICATING FASHION'S VALUE THROUGH PROMOTION

Fashion promotion objectives, making customers aware and persuading them to buy, are the topics of Part IV. The promotion mix is defined in Chapter 12, with an overview of how the five major promotional elements work separately and together in an integrated marketing communications strategy to convey a marketing message to target customers. Chapter 13 delves more deeply into the promotional elements of direct marketing and personal selling, describing their use and effectiveness in marketing fashion products. How fashion marketers create awareness and stimulate customer demand through advertising, sales promotion, and public relations is the subject of the final chapter, which details the goals and activities involved in developing advertising campaigns, sales promotions, and public relations plans.

KEEPING AN EYE ON GLOBALIZATION AND ETHICS

Increasingly today, consumers demand fashions from throughout the world, while fashion businesses seek out products and expanded customer markets across the globe. The importance and application of global marketing, therefore, is woven into each chapter throughout the text. In addition, because consumers prefer to patronize businesses they recognize as ethical and socially responsible, examples of the way fashion marketers demonstrate social responsibility and ethical business practices are also an integral part of every chapter.

LEARNING RESOURCES AND ACTIVITIES

Marketing Fashion: A Global Perspective contains a wealth of color illustrations, case studies, and other current examples of fashion marketing practices that create for students a vivid portrayal of fashion marketing theories, concepts, and real-life applications. The text contains a number of engaging special features designed to actively involve students in the learning process. Many of these features may be used for class discussion, research, and individual and group projects. They include:

▶ *Opening Statement.* Each chapter begins with a brief statement regarding its contents. It is suitable for quick reading as an overview and also as a class topic for preliminary discussion.

▶ *What Do I Need to Know about …?* A list at the start of each chapter presents the major concepts that students will find covered therein, laying a roadmap for their study and an easy reference to ensure they have met the objectives upon completing the chapter.

▶ *Fashion Marketing in Focus.* Each chapter begins with a fashion marketing observation or scenario that pertains to the chapter's content and leads into its introductory topics. As a basis for opening class discussion, students may be asked to introduce similar examples they've encountered from their own experiences.

▶ *Marketer's Insight.* Boxed sidebar features in each chapter bring the chapter's content to life and offer further enrichment, often through real-world examples that help illustrate key concepts. Some may be a basis for additional research and individual and group reports to the class.

▶ *What's Your Point of View?* Select boxed features include questions that ask readers to consider the sidebar content as it applies to their own experience.

▶ *What Do You Think?* Questions for classroom discussion or individual consideration are scattered throughout each chapter to offer readers the opportunity to pause and reflect on key concepts fresh in their minds.

▶ *Summary and Review.* Each chapter contains a brief summary of the chapter contents, giving students an opportunity to synthesize and internalize what they have studied and reflect back on the questions posed at the chapter's introduction. A list of the chapter's Key Terms provides an opportunity for increasing fashion marketing vocabulary. Review Questions reflect the chapter objectives, while Discussion Activities and Projects encourage students to explore the chapter's topics more broadly, offering opportunity for hands-on projects or further research related to what they have just learned.

▶ *Fashion Marketing Case Study.* Each chapter contains a fashion marketing case study related to the content of the chapter. Students may respond to the questions posed about the case and do further research as the instructor deems suitable.

▶ *References.* The references cited apply directly to the chapter content and may serve as sources for additional student research on particular related topics.

DEVELOPING YOUR MARKETING PLAN

Each chapter contains instructions for a course-long project in which students develop their own marketing plan for a business they have selected, using what they have learned in the chapter to build each segment of their overall plan. Included as an appendix is an example of a marketing plan, which the students will be encouraged to use as a reference but not as a model, since it is emphasized throughout the book that every marketing plan must be created to target its own set of goals.

INSTRUCTOR'S GUIDE AND POWERPOINT

The instructor's manual contains an assortment of useful resources. These include general teaching suggestions as well as suggestions specific to each chapter. Outlines for each of the chapters are provided, as are answers to the Review Questions, Discussion Activities and Projects, and tips on how to help students develop their Marketing Plans. A test bank and answers are also provided, along with additional activities and resources. In addition, PowerPoint lectures have been developed for each chapter.

Acknowledgments

The authors wish to express deep appreciation to our many colleagues in academia and business whose interest and enthusiasm helped move this text toward its goal. In particular, we thank Fairchild's Executive Editor, Olga Kontzias, who imagined this text and propelled it along to production, plus the entire group who helped convert our manuscript to final text, including Executive Director and General Manager Michael Schluter, Development Editor Rob Phelps, Production Director Ginger Hillman, Production Editor Jessica Katz, Assistant Art Director Sarah Silberg, Graphic Designer Vanessa Han, and Ancillaries Editor Amy Butler.

Our special appreciation goes to Dr. Stewart Husted, who, as expert reviewer, guided us through some of the subtleties of marketing with patience and enthusiasm. His focus and attention to detail significantly enrich the outcome. We also express appreciation to Fairchild's peer reviewers: Emily Davis, Woodbury University; Beth Hinckley, FIDM; and Kate Schaefer, Columbia College Chicago.

Among the business and academic communities, we are grateful to Wilma Kozar for her original suggestion for the text, and to Sandra Henderson-Williams for her contributions to the development of its early outline and chapters. We also appreciate the interest and contributions of the following: Dr. Alexxis Avalon, Dr. Karen Janko, Judy Aronson, Lee Collingwood, Philip R. Nielsen, Margot A. Wallace, Inese Apale, and Nicholas Braggo.

Part I

DEFINING FASHION MARKETING AND HOW IT WORKS

BEFORE YOU CAN understand the process and practices of marketing fashion, you need to understand the fashion marketer's long-term goals, the basic elements of the fashion marketing process, and the direction fashion marketing is moving in the global economy. This includes the various internal and external elements that impact fashion marketers today, and involves how those entities and forces influence the way fashion businesses operate in the global marketplace. Fashion marketers must be alert to the many ways potential customers may behave in the marketplace. They must also develop a keen sense of the level of involvement the customer has with a product or buying situation that influences the purchase process; then they can begin to explore the internal and external influences that have an effect on both consumer and business buyer behavior.

CHAPTER 1

Developing and Maintaining Profitable Customer Relationships

This chapter offers an overview of marketing and fashion marketing, explains marketers' long-term goals and the basic elements of the marketing process, and outlines the directions fashion marketing is moving in our global economy.

WHAT DO I NEED TO KNOW ABOUT DEVELOPING AND MAINTAINING PROFITABLE CUSTOMER RELATIONSHIPS?

* How to define marketing and fashion marketing
* What the long-term goal of marketing is, and some of the ways fashion marketers build customer loyalty
* What the basic fashion marketing process encompasses
* The components of the marketing mix and their function
* Major trends that impact fashion marketing in the twenty-first century
* The importance of ethics and social responsibility in fashion marketing

FASHION MARKETING IN FOCUS:
A World of Fashion and Marketing

Whoever you are and wherever you live, if you are like the vast majority of people inhabiting our planet, there are two things that have an influence on you virtually every single day—fashion and marketing.

Fashion surrounds you constantly in the things you see, use, wear, watch, and do. There is fashion not only in the clothes you put on this morning, but in everything from the sheets on your bed, to the iPhone you may be carrying, to the new film all your friends are buzzing about or the trendy café where you like to meet after class to relax over the latest flavor of cappuccino.

Marketing is equally pervasive. It's what catches your eye as you walk past a department store window. It pops up on the screen when you surf to a favorite Web site. It's an integral part of why your best friend just bought those stylish boots and how your parents decided on the particular flat-panel TV they mounted on the family room wall. It's what persuades you to go shopping when you receive a 15 percent discount offer in the mail or by e-mail, and what gets you to purchase the same well-fitting brand of jeans over and over again ... or maybe tempts you to try on a new brand that promises to fit even better and whose maker donates a portion of profits to fight world hunger.

There is no question that both fashion and marketing influence many facets of our daily life, even when we're not directly aware of that influence. Fashion adds newness and freshness to the clothes we wear, the products we use, the cars we drive, and the activities we enjoy. Marketing not only informs us about the existence of those fresh new offerings, but it is also a driving force behind how new products are conceived and designed, how they are presented and sold to us, and at what point they make way for even newer versions.

Put the concepts of fashion and marketing together, and you've got one of the most dynamic, exciting segments of business—and the subject we will explore in depth in this text. Let's begin with some definitions.

FIGURE 1.1 Fashion and marketing surround and influence us virtually every day and everywhere.

What Are Marketing and Fashion Marketing?

The term "marketing" brings to mind different things to different people. Some may think of marketing as a dirty word: businesses foisting things off on people who don't really want or need them. Others think of marketing as simply television commercials and ads in magazines or on Web sites—which is indeed an aspect of marketing, but hardly the whole picture.

In reality, marketing is a complex system that, when well planned and effectively executed, makes customers the central focus and builds long-term relationships that are rewarding both to customers and to the marketer. Like fashion, marketing is constantly evolving ... as customers change their minds about what they want, as technology advances, as global markets emerge, and as concepts of ethics and social responsibility mature. Each of these conditions contributes challenges and compensations to the vibrant field of fashion marketing today.

MARKETING DEFINED

According to the American Marketing Association (AMA), an international association of professionals and organizations involved in the practice, teaching, and development of marketing, "**Marketing** is an organizational function and a set of processes for creating, communicating, and delivering value to customers and for managing customer relationships in ways that benefit the organization and its stakeholders."[1] Another way of stating it is that marketing is "the process by which companies create value for customers and build strong customer relationships in order to capture value from customers in return."[2]

Let's look more closely at elements within those definitions. Both mention value. The value that marketers provide to customers is derived from the product they are offering, whether it's something to fill a need (like food or shelter) or something to satisfy a want (like a videogame or a motorcycle). In the AMA's definition, there are three specific components relating to that value: creating, communicating, and delivering. Creating a product involves inventiveness and design skills, but marketing is what directs the creative process to ensure

that the product has value for customers. Once a product is developed, it requires a coordinated plan of advertising and other forms of marketing communication to get the word out to customers about its features and benefits so they will understand its value. Determining the best retail stores or other channels for delivering the product into customers' hands is also an important function of marketing because it helps to reinforce the marketer's value message.

The other key concept in both definitions cited above is that of building and managing customer relationships so that both customer and marketer benefit. This final component involves an **exchange**—or in marketing terms, any activity, such as buying and selling, in which one party receives something by voluntarily giving something in return. The exchange activities in marketing are what provide value back to the marketer, allowing the company to earn profits, and sometimes foster goodwill, as well.

To illustrate how those aspects might manifest themselves within a total marketing plan, consider the Tommy Hilfiger brand.

- ▶ *Creating.* For nearly three decades, Tommy Hilfiger has designed high-quality fashions that have been proven to appeal to customers the designer wants to reach.
- ▶ *Delivering.* In 2008, the Hilfiger company made a strategic decision to partner with Macy's as the exclusive U.S. department store to sell its men's and women's sportswear lines.
- ▶ *Communicating.* The retailer and designer began working together to promote the availability of the sportswear at Macy's to consumers, not only through advertising and other communications

FIGURE 1.2 In marketing, exchange activities are what provide value to consumers as well as returning value to the marketer.

but also via special events, such as an appearance by Hilfiger himself at Macy's Union Square store in San Francisco to celebrate his company's twenty-fifth year in business.

▶ *Exchanging.* As part of the event, customers who purchased $75 worth of Hilfiger apparel received priority seating at a free concert by alternative rock band Third Eye Blind, held in Union Square the same day as Hilfiger's appearance—providing value to customers (desired apparel plus better concert seats) and value back to Hilfiger (profits from the apparel sale plus goodwill from attendees at the free concert).

Later chapters will discuss in more detail how activities and processes such as these are developed and incorporated into a company's comprehensive marketing plan. But whatever specific plan a marketer establishes, the marketing process generally begins with the company looking at itself from the consumer's point of view and determining its capabilities to supply something the customer needs or wants. It then creates, prices, delivers, and promotes a product that it believes customers will deem valuable to their lifestyle. If the item is well conceived and timely, and more important, if customers buy it, then the process is successful—and ideally, satisfied customers will reward the marketer with loyalty and future purchases. In short, the ultimate goal of marketing is to bring continuing satisfaction to the customer and ongoing profits to the marketer. Or, as Tom Asacker puts it in *A Clear Eye for Branding,* the purpose of marketing is "to create and maintain a strong feeling with customers so they are mentally predisposed to continually choose and recommend you."[3]

FASHION MARKETING DEFINED

Adding a focus on fashion does not change the basic marketing concept, but it may introduce new elements in how a marketing plan is executed, since fashion goods require a somewhat different marketing approach from that of many non-fashion products and services. First, let's define what is meant by fashion: A **fashion** is any designed product that is currently popular, that is of the moment and subject to change, and that people consider desirable and appropriate at a given time.[4]

Clearly, our definition of fashion encompasses apparel and accessories, including footwear, jewelry, cosmetics, and fragrances, which tend to be the first categories most people think of when they think "fashion." But the concept of fashion extends much further than that. Fashion plays an important role in home furnishings, including textiles (microplush throws, animal print bolster pillows), furniture (clean-lined minimalist tables, Mission-style futons), and appliances (electric cooktops, gourmet coffeemakers). There is also fashion in toys, in cars, in consumer electronics, and in architecture. Fashion even exists in films, music, television programs, food, vacation hot spots—anything that is in favor at a given time. We will use that broad definition of fashion throughout the text, with a primary focus on designed goods, which we'll describe further in a moment.

Fashion marketing, then, can be defined as the application of marketing processes and activities to currently popular designed products. It encompasses everything that goes into the creation and development of a fashion product, through its presentation and promotion to customers, through

FIGURE 1.3 Fashion can be found not only in clothing and accessories but in home furnishings, automobiles, consumer electronics, architecture, food, films, and other currently popular designed products.

its purchase and support after the sale. Fashion marketing employs the same general concepts, activities, and processes as the marketing of other products, but it has its own challenges and opportunities that arise from the continually changing nature of fashion. Think of it this way: How often are you inspired to buy a new brand of corn flakes or laundry detergent? But in the past six months, how many new items of apparel did you buy? Did you upgrade your MP3 player because you liked the color offered in a newer model? Fashion marketers, more than marketers of basic or commodity-type items, must work to address that consumer desire for newness, stay ahead of fast-moving trends, and apply creative marketing to capture the attention and interest of often fickle but also savvy customers.

Putting the Fashion Marketing Process into Action

The process works like this: Say that a fashion marketer learns that more people are taking up skiing, so it decides it would like to offer a collection of practical yet fashionable skiwear. First, the company determines exactly who its customers will be and what kinds of garments they would prefer and find useful. For example, what features and styling do customers want in a ski jacket? Using market research, the company determines the number of potential customers for its ski apparel, where/how they prefer to shop, and what types of ski jackets are already being sold by other companies; then, also through research, it learns about the details customers might want in a ski jacket and the price they're willing to pay. Armed with this information, the company designs a ski jacket in a fresh style, color, and fabric it believes customers will like.

It oversees production of the jacket, determines where it will be sold, and communicates information about the new garment through a variety of media it thinks will reach the right customers. As a result of these activities, skiing enthusiasts become aware of the jacket through a Web site or an ad in a ski magazine, learn where they can purchase the jacket and how much it costs, try it on in the store or order it online to try at home, and decide to buy. After wearing it on their next ski trip, some of those customers are so pleased with the style, fit, comfort, and other features of the jacket that they return to the marketer to find out what additional products are offered that they might want to buy.

In this scenario, the marketer has approached potential customers with an integrated marketing plan. It identified what customers want that the company can best provide. It reached out to selected customers with information about its product and made the product readily available at an acceptable price. Customers responded with a purchase, were satisfied with the product, and rewarded the marketer with repeat business. These are fundamental marketing elements in action, where the customer's point of view is a marketer's primary consideration and both parties benefit from the exchange. Figure 1.4 illustrates the basic steps in the marketing process.

Fashion Marketers' Long-term Goal: Customer Loyalty

As stated, the ultimate goal of fashion marketers is to gain and keep customers over time. Long-term customer loyalty is important because returning

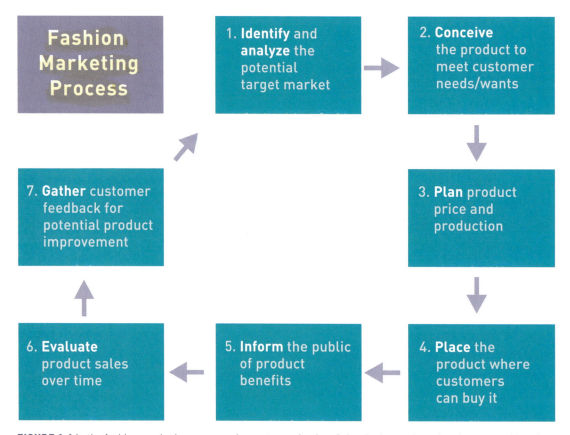

FIGURE 1.4 In the fashion marketing process, the customers' point of view is the marketer's primary consideration and both parties benefit from the exchange. BY VANESSA HAN AND ALICIA FREILE

customers tend to generate more profits for a company—so much so that in describing customer loyalty, marketers often refer to the *80/20 rule*: A company obtains 80 percent of its business from 20 percent of its customers.

In order to identify the customers most likely to become loyal purchasers, marketers learn all they can about the needs and wants of customers they hope to attract. A **need** is something a person cannot do without, whereas a **want** is something a person craves or desires, influenced by his or her personality, culture, and society. For example, you need clothing, but you want 7 For All Mankind jeans; you need food, but you want a Taco Bell burrito. For the most part, marketers of fashion address consumers' wants more than their needs. In addition, to achieve the long-term goal of customer loyalty, marketers must appeal to their customers by creating products that offer the right value, as well as by nurturing relationships with customers to keep them coming back for more.

IDENTIFYING CUSTOMERS

With any product, fashion marketers must know to whom they want to sell. This means identifying the

MARKETING BEAUTY PRODUCTS TO CHINESE WOMEN

Understanding the needs and wants of target customers is always crucial to successful marketing, but perhaps especially so in the category of cosmetics and skin care. Even though the definition of "beauty" has become homogenized by the globalization of media, there are distinct cultural and societal differences that affect the way women in different countries view and use beauty products, especially in China.

Beauty treatments are still relatively new to Chinese women since Mao Tse-tung forbade the use of cosmetics until the 1980s. As a result, while today's western women generally are initiated into the beauty ritual by their mothers, Chinese women are dependent on outside sources for their beauty information. So education is a valuable tool for consumers—and an opportunity for skin care and cosmetics marketers. Many companies have stepped in to fill the void and offer training programs to their consultants at department store counters, where well over half of all beauty products are purchased. The payoff of that investment in education is that Chinese women are more likely to use all the products recommended to them.

Of course, those products still must meet their needs and wants; and the Pao Principle, a New York-based global business consulting firm, conducted a study of more than 1,000 Chinese women ages 20 to 29 to help marketers better understand these customers. Among the findings were that Chinese women—unlike many American women—understand that using effective products early in life can positively impact their skin. However, while skin care use starts at an early age, color and fragrance usage normally is delayed until after a Chinese woman finishes high school. In addition, when they find something that works, Chinese women are generally loyal to that product.

Unlike western women, who like to experiment with small, indie brands, the Chinese beauty consumer prefers to use big, well-known global brands. Shiseido was the most-used skin care brand cited by the panelists, who believe that Japanese technology is the most cutting-edge, and also that, because Japanese skin is close to theirs, Shiseido has the best understanding of their skin care needs. For color cosmetics, however, Maybelline was the favored brand—an unsurprising finding since L'Oréal Group (the parent company of Maybelline) has aggressively focused resources on all elements of the marketing mix in China, including sharp pricing, creative promotions, and heavy ad campaigns featuring global and local celebrities and models.

Adapted from: Patricia Pao, "Why Shiseido Beats Western Beauty Marketers," Advertising Age, September 1, 2010, http://adage.com/china/article/viewpoint/why-shiseido-beats-western-beauty-marketers-in-china/145645/ (accessed March 8, 2012).

market, or the group of actual and potential customers who have both an interest in and the ability to buy the company's product. The market for athletic shoes, for instance, is all of the people who buy or might buy athletic shoes.

The market for any given product or for any particular marketer is never the entire universe of consumers. A customer who buys athletic shoes as everyday footwear will not be as likely to buy a pair of high-tech, feature-laden running shoes—and a serious runner might not take a second look at basic sneakers designed more for fashion than for function. So marketers go further and undertake **market segmentation**, defining smaller, more homogeneous customer groups based on similar customer characteristics. A single **market segment**, then, is a group of consumers displaying like needs, wants, values, and buying habits. Different market segments within the athletic shoe market might be kids, basketball players, joggers, or casual wearers. (See Chapter 6 for more detail on choosing and segmenting markets.)

When they select one or more segments on which to concentrate, marketers are identifying their **target market**, the group of customers deemed most likely to purchase a given product and on whom the company's marketing efforts will be focused. Depending on their offerings, fashion companies often have different target markets for different portions of their product lines. Donna Karan, for instance, targets a different group of consumers for her sophisticated Donna Karan New York collection than for her hipper DKNY fashions.

CREATING FASHION PRODUCTS

Knowing the consumers they are trying to reach is the critical first step for fashion marketers in order to create the right offerings for their target customers. That understanding of who their customers are and what they want, coupled with the mission and capabilities of the company, forms the foundation for development of the company's products.

In marketing terms, any offering that marketers create and present to target markets is called a **product**. Products include **goods**, tangible items such as coats and hats, iPods, or a Louis XV ormolu mirror. Products also include **services**, helpful or professional activities provided to another, such as hair styling, wardrobe consulting, a concert, or an airplane ride. Some products are a combination of goods and services, such as a meal in a restaurant, a manicure, automobile detailing, or the work of a personal shopper. Products can also be ideas, such as views on social issues like climate change and sustainability, or the views of a political candidate.

WHAT DO YOU THINK?

What goods are fashionable today among college students? What combinations of goods and services are in fashion? Which fashion services seem to be popular?

Miniskirts, Flat-Panel TVs, and Social Media

Like other marketers, fashion marketers develop their products influenced by knowledge of the wants of their target market—but the nature of fashion adds a twist: A new fashion product can actually influence customers' wants. The inherent creativity and innovation that bring about changes in fashion mean that marketers often anticipate what their customers want even before those customers know it themselves. So in creating products, fashion marketers must not only be on top of the latest trends, but sometimes a step or two ahead of them. Back in the 1960s, for example, British designer Mary Quant was making a dramatic break from the styles of the day when she introduced her famous miniskirts. But young women worldwide quickly validated her vision and marketing savvy by snapping up the ultra-short skirts.

Similarly, up until recent years, most consumers were satisfied with their traditional televisions; but once they experienced the high-definition picture quality and slim styling of the newer flat-panel sets, most were eager to own the fashionable new technology. In turn, as flat-panel televisions grew in popularity, furniture companies began phasing out heavy wall units and armoires designed for the bulkier tube models and introduced new styles of stands and mounts that complement the sleekness of the thin TVs. Going further, furniture companies targeting the more affluent end of the market added desirable but more costly features such as motorized lifts that raise or lower the panel at the touch of a button, discreetly hiding the television in a stylish cabinet when not in use. These marketers understood that the higher-end market segment did not necessarily want the television to be a focus of their décor, so they created a product designed with those customers' desires in mind.

FIGURE 1.5 Fashion marketers' products can include goods, services, or a combination of the two. Boots are goods. A professional wardrobe consultation that leads a customer to buy the boots is a service. If the customer gets the boots resoled, the shoe repair shop is offering a combination of goods (new soles) and service (putting the soles on the boots).

At the same time, some fashion marketers are taking advantage of the two-way communication made possible by the Internet via blogs, social communities, and other sites, and are using direct customer feedback to help shape their products. At Threadless.com, for instance, the entire premise is to have users submit original T-shirt designs and other users vote on their favorites, with the most popular designs getting made and sold on the site. Other fashion marketers may not take consumer input to quite that level. But virtually all are using or exploring the use of social media as a way to gain deeper insight into how customers feel about their products, in order to continue to create products that meet customer needs and wants.

BUILDING CUSTOMER RELATIONSHIPS

Attracting customers and keeping them are two different matters. With so many businesses competing for consumers' attention and dollars, marketers can never rest on their laurels, assuming that success today will automatically translate to success tomorrow. Especially in today's world, where information about people and products travels around the globe in an instant, it takes continuous effort—and a willingness to adapt quickly to new trends and new customer demands—for fashion marketers to sustain strong relationships with their customers. For that reason, an increasingly important aspect of marketing is **customer relationship management** (**CRM**), the overall process of building and maintaining profitable customer relationships through providing superior customer value and

FIGURE 1.6 Fashion products are influenced by marketers' knowledge—and sometimes anticipation—of target customers' needs and wants. Sony met customer needs by taking an existing product (cassette player) and transforming it into the stylish, easily portable Walkman; then later updated it as consumers trended to CDs. MP3 players were a completely new concept to most consumers when first introduced, but Apple knew its customers would be eager to transport all their music in one device when it launched the iPod.

satisfaction.[5] (See Chapter 6 for more discussion of this topic.)

Managing customer relationships and building customer loyalty is a multifaceted effort. As discussed above, it is based in part on understanding target customers' wants and needs and creating products that meet or exceed customers' expectations—in other words, delivering a product with a high **perceived value**, a customer's internal calculation as to whether or not a product is worth its cost (both in money and in effort to obtain it). In deciding on a purchase—whether it's a Starbucks Frappaccino, a silk shirt, or a BMW sedan—consumers weigh the actual cost of the product against the benefits they believe they will gain from it. If the product's benefits equal or exceed its cost in a consumer's mind, the perceived value makes the purchase worth the money and effort.

Wherever they fall in the price range, fashion marketers' aim is to communicate to customers how their products' benefits exceed their cost—in other words, to enhance the perceived value of their offerings for their target customers. When Walmart, for example, touts its "always low prices," cost-conscious customers perceive value in the fact that they're paying less than they would elsewhere for the same or similar goods. At the other end of the spectrum, when Hermès has its artisans layer each color on separate screens and then hand-roll the hem of its designer silk scarves, it hopes that customers will perceive that the quality and uniqueness of the scarves offer value to match or exceed the lofty price tag. Or when the now-defunct Filene's Basement held its renowned periodic bridal gown sales, customers would line up long before the doors opened and were willing

FIGURE 1.7 For luxury goods consumers, the perceived value outweighs the cost of the item.

MARKETER'S INSIGHT:
ZAPPOS MAKES CUSTOMER SERVICE AN OBSESSION

When Zappos first began selling shoes on the Internet, consumers were skeptical about buying footwear that they couldn't first try on. So how did the company overcome that hesitation? It made customer service a cornerstone of its marketing strategy—a strategy that remains solidly in place even after Zappos' sale to Amazon.com. And its customer-centric approach runs the gamut from everyday free shipping and free returns to directing consumers to competitors if the company doesn't have a style or size available.

Zappos pays close attention to all details of customer service. Its customer service center is staffed 24/7 with 500 employees answering 5,000 calls a day. The service reps do not rely on scripts, but rather engage in regular conversations with customers, and are given latitude to go the extra mile to address customer needs. For example, when the payment deadline for shoes a customer had ordered came and went, a Zappos rep e-mailed the woman to remind her the money was due. The woman told the rep the reason: She had meant to send back the shoes, which were for her ailing mother, but in the meantime, her mother had died. The company rep arranged to have UPS pick up the shoes; then actually sent the woman a flower arrangement and condolence card. A blog the customer wrote about the event, "I Heart Zappos," bounced around the Web, with other customers contributing their own good experiences with the company.

That culture and philosophy starts at the top with Zappos' CEO, Tony Hsieh, who once announced a surprise happy hour on Twitter and bought drinks for the 200 people who showed up with "Zappos" written on their hands. To make sure the customer obsession permeates the entire organization, Hsieh requires each new hire—everyone from the chief financial officer to the children's footwear buyer—to go through four weeks of customer loyalty training. Customer service reps are trained to look on at least three rival Web sites if a shopper asks for specific shoes that Zappos doesn't have in stock.

"My guess is that other companies don't do that," Hsieh states. "For us, we're willing to lose that sale, that transaction in the short term. We're focused on building the lifelong loyalty and relationship with the customer." Does his philosophy work? No question about it: Some 75 percent of Zappos' sales come from repeat customers.

Adapted from: Natalie Zmuda, "Zappos: Customer Service First—and a Daily Obsession," *Advertising Age*, October 20, 2008, p. 36; Brian Morrissey, "These Brands Build Community: How These Web 2.0 Companies Build Good Relationships to Build Their Brands," Adweek.com, May 12, 2008, www.adweek.com/aw/content_display/news/digital/e3i5e732e045deaaba3f3762d92cf386637?pm=1 (accessed March 8, 2012).

to scramble for the merchandise because the perceived value of a designer gown at a discounted price made the search well worth the effort.

WHAT DO YOU THINK?

What has a fashion marketer done recently to attract your interest and loyalty? A fashion show? Discount coupons? Gifts-with-purchase? Did that effort win you over? Why or why not?

Enhancing a product's perceived value is just one component of building strong customer relationships. Nurturing those relationships also involves developing trust and ensuring customer satisfaction. Both of those aspects may be influenced by what a marketer does that goes above and beyond the product itself. When cosmetics companies offer a gift-with-purchase, or when electronics marketers bundle free movies with a Blu-ray player, they are hoping that the extras will please customers and cause them to think of their company the next time. On the flip side, customer trust and satisfaction can be undermined when there is a problem with a product. If the heating element on an espresso maker stops working after a month or the seam on an expensive new jacket rips the second time it's worn, consumers will think twice about buying the brand again—unless the marketers respond in a way that overrides customers' negative feelings. The company offering the espresso maker might offer a replacement and also give the customer a coupon for free coffee; or the marketer of the jacket might offer an immediate exchange with a handwritten note of apology for the customer's inconvenience. Marketers need to build trust with their customers by ensuring that their products perform as expected, and they need to ensure satisfaction by listening to consumers and offering excellent customer service if something should go wrong. These are important aspects of the overall marketing process that we'll explore further later in the text.

Developing a Fashion Marketing Strategy

We've seen some of the basic steps that fashion marketers must take on the road to their long-term goal of customer loyalty. Now let's look at how they go about developing a marketing approach that fits their business, and the elements that go into a marketing plan.

As part of their strategy, fashion marketers need to decide in what ways they will serve their customers, how they stand out from the competition, and how they want consumers to see their unique features. The sum of all benefits that marketers offer customers is known as the company's **value proposition**. For example, when Sean "Diddy" Combs launched his Sean John sportswear, he differentiated his apparel by designing it to "fill a void in the market for well-made, sophisticated fashion forward clothing that also reflected an urban sensibility and style." He also stated that the company would "use all of our resources to ensure that quality in both design and production of Sean John always exceeds your expectation."[6] From those statements, you could glean that distinctive

FIGURE 1.8 The value proposition of Sean John apparel includes its fashion-forward styling, urban sensibility, high-quality construction, and customer satisfaction.

styling, high quality, and dedication to customer satisfaction are all part of the value proposition of Sean John apparel. The value proposition is often proclaimed in a marketer's slogan. Consider tag lines such as American Airlines' "We know why you fly," L'Oréal's "Because you're worth it," or Nike's "Just do it." Each of these slogans underscores the companies' value proposition and why consumers should believe their products will offer greater benefits than those of the competition.

CHOOSING A MARKETING POINT OF VIEW

No two organizations are the same, so every company has to approach marketing in a way that makes sense for its specific mission and capabilities, and for its goals regarding profitability and customer relationships. But there are five basic points of view, or marketing orientations, that marketers can adopt: the *production concept*, the *product concept*, the *selling concept*, the *marketing concept*, and the *societal marketing concept*.[7] In most cases, fashion marketers will focus on the final two, but let's look at all five and how they differ.

The Production Concept

One of the earliest guiding concepts used in marketing, the production concept is one in which marketers operate under the principle that customers want products that are inexpensive and readily available. This orientation focuses less on the changing wants and needs of consumers and more on creating efficiencies in production and distribution in order to keep volume high and costs low. A company making plain, solid-color baseball caps or basic toys like beach balls or jacks probably follows the production concept.

The Product Concept

The product concept is based on the idea that customers want high-quality products that offer performance and innovative features. Under this orientation, a marketer's product development is based less on acting on its customers' desires than operating from its own design capabilities. An example of a company using the product concept might be the

DeLorean Motor Company, whose single product, the DMC-12 sports car, featured a striking stainless-steel design and gull-wing doors (you may remember it from the *Back to the Future* movies). Despite its innovations, the car did not generate the necessary interest and sales, causing the company to go out of business after just a few years.

The Selling Concept

The selling concept works under the theory that goods will not be purchased widely enough unless they are aggressively sold and promoted. Most frequently used with products that consumers are not actively seeking, such as extended service plans, the selling concept may be employed for some fashion goods, such as the accessories or cosmetic "as seen on TV" items that are the subject of seemingly constant commercials. Some new fashion looks may also be at least partially marketed via the selling concept if they are too different to be accepted right away, such as an unusual new combination of plaids and prints. The marketer might arrange to have celebrities wear the look, have it featured in fashion magazines, give it prominent placement on the home page of its Web site, and offer incentives to store salespeople to persuade customers of the benefits of the fashion. The emphasis of the selling concept is on pushing the new look or product to customers and not primarily listening to what it is that customers want, so its effectiveness in marketing fashion is limited.

The Marketing Concept

Probably the most widely followed marketing philosophy today, the marketing concept begins with the customer as the focus. Rather than simply trying to sell what the company has produced, companies operating by the marketing concept determine what customers want and then supply it. The rationale is that by satisfying customers, the marketer will achieve profits.

Eileen Fisher offers an example of the marketing concept in action. The designer originally offered stylish but comfortable apparel for more

FIGURE 1.9 Marketers operating under the production concept, product concept, and selling concept do not have customer wants as their primary focus.

mature women, such as loose-fitting jackets, long skirts, and wide-leg pants. Over time (and with some strong "hints" from her teenage daughter), Fisher realized that younger women appreciated the timeless look of the apparel but wanted a greater selection of styles to match their lifestyle. As a result, the company began taking younger looks, like skinny jeans, and translating them into apparel in keeping with the company's overall signature design—being careful not to alienate its core customers as it updated its look for new customers. Eileen Fisher was responding to the desires of a new target market while not losing sight of what the company's loyal customers wanted. In the process, the company satisfied both its established and new customers, as proven by the fact that the company's sales have shown solid growth since the new designs were introduced.[8]

Companies using the marketing concept are often called *customer driven,* because they look at the desires of their target customers, rather than just their own capabilities, when developing and marketing their products. Fashion marketing is customer driven even when companies anticipate what customers will want before the customers know themselves, since it is based on the marketer's knowledge and understanding of its customer base.

The Societal Marketing Concept

A marketing philosophy that is seeing increasingly wider adoption, the societal marketing concept goes beyond satisfying immediate consumer needs by questioning whether or not a product is good for the general welfare of all of society. Marketers who follow the societal marketing concept work to balance satisfying consumer wants and the company's need for profits with the long-term well-being of society as a whole. Developers of electric cars, for example, are addressing a consumer desire for vehicles that cost less to run because they don't need gasoline, but they are also offering a solution to improve the environment through the cars' zero emissions. Another example is sportswear manufacturer and marketer Patagonia, whose mission includes sourcing materials and using processes that are less harmful to the earth, without compromising the quality of its products. As the company's Web site notes, "To us, quality is not only how well a product performs and holds up, but also how it's made." Among the "e-fibers"—as it calls environmentally friendlier fibers—the company uses are recycled polyester, organic cotton, hemp, chlorine-free wool, and recycled nylon; and when customers no longer plan to wear a piece of apparel, many Patagonia garments can be returned to the company to be recycled into new clothing.[9] We'll discuss social responsibility more later in this chapter and throughout the book.

WHAT DO YOU THINK?

What do you think of the societal marketing concept? Which fashion businesses can you cite that are using this concept? In your opinion, what motivates them to do so? Profits? Societal welfare? Other reasons?

CREATING A MARKETING MIX

With their direction chosen regarding target markets, intended value proposition, and marketing point of view, companies are ready to develop a

FIGURE 1.10 Patagonia is one of a growing number of fashion marketers that use the societal marketing concept as their philosophy.

specific marketing plan by which to carry out their strategy. They do this through the **marketing mix**, or the combination of marketing tools that a firm uses to offer its customers value and to pursue its own sales and profitability goals.

The marketing mix is composed of four basic elements: *product*, *price*, *place*, and *promotion*.

Product

As we've discussed, a fashion marketer needs to design and develop products that address the needs and wants of its target customers. Since fashion and fashion customers constantly change, products must evolve with the times to remain in demand.

For example, the Burberry trench coat was originally created by the British apparel company in the late nineteenth century and adopted by the military; but before long, Burberry realized that consumers appreciated the garment's sturdy construction and timeless style, and adapted the trench coat for the consumer market. Over the years, the company has continued to introduce new design adaptations of its classic trench coat to reflect changing consumer tastes. In the fall of 2010, for instance, when Angela Ahrendts, Burberry's CEO, announced plans to visit the company's 50-some stores in China, she wore a current version of the coat. In addition, Burberry has built on the reputation and popularity of its

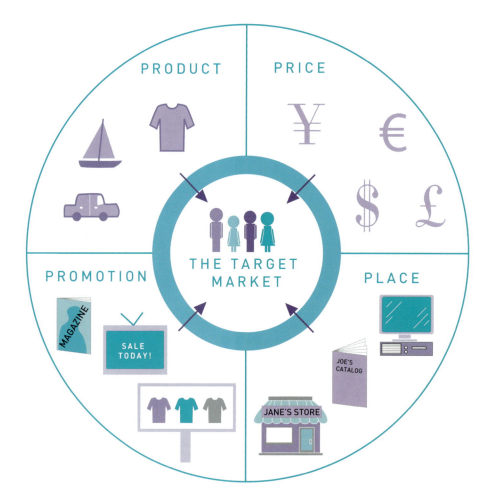

FIGURE 1.11 The target customer is the focus of each of the four marketing mix elements. BY VANESSA HAN AND ALICIA FREILE

outerwear by expanding its offerings into men's wear, women's wear, children's apparel, and more, as it recognized additional opportunities to meet its customers' product needs and wants.

Price

Looking at the second element of the marketing mix, clearly any product a marketer introduces has to be available at a price customers are willing to pay. So in the marketing process, companies must look at a variety of expenses—including the raw materials and labor that go into production, shipping, advertising, and so on—to know the base cost of a product before they add on a suitable margin for profit. If the resulting price is higher than they believe their customers will pay, they must reexamine all the cost components and try to revise the price to an amount that offers customers the right perceived value. The target customers for a Burberry trench coat are more than willing to pay its designer price because they value the quality construction, details, and mystique. Other companies, targeting less affluent customers, have created their own versions of the trench coat at a lower cost, putting the price within the reach of a different market segment.

Place

The third element of the marketing mix refers to ensuring that products are available to customers when and where it is convenient for them to make a purchase. Fashion marketers' knowledge of their target customers helps them determine the best places for selling their products, including the appropriateness of selling them online. For instance, Burberry sells its high-priced coats primarily in cities, which have a greater number of consumers with the taste level and means to purchase them, and sells them in its own stores or in other high-end stores, such as Saks Fifth Avenue, frequented by its target customers. Other considerations go into choosing appropriate places to sell fashion products. Winter coats are not heavily marketed in warmer climates, for example, whereas in regions that have cold winters, swimwear is sold mostly in spring and early summer.

Promotion

The final element involves all the ways in which marketers communicate information to consumers about their products, including advertising, personal selling, sales promotion, fashion shows, blogs, and more. Integrating and coordinating the four elements of the marketing mix becomes the basis for the implementation of a company's marketing strategy. How each element of the marketing mix is developed and used will be covered fully in Chapters 7 to 14.

Fashion Marketing in the Twenty-First Century

Marketing in the twenty-first century still serves the same basic purpose that it did in the past. But its tools and implementation have changed dramatically in the past decade—and continue to change, as technology "shrinks" the world and enables unprecedented innovation, and as global issues such as climate change and fair trade move front and center in the public consciousness.

As a result, fashion marketers face greater opportunities and challenges than ever before as they work to keep pace with new trends and new markets. Three broad areas having perhaps the most impact are *globalization*, *social media and mobile communications*, and *ethics and social responsibility*. Later chapters will address these influences as they relate to the specific marketing topics being discussed, but let's look briefly at each one for a basic understanding of its role and impact on fashion marketing today.

GLOBALIZATION

Selling their products in other countries is nothing new for fashion marketers. Consumers in the United States, for example, have long had access to a range of fashion goods produced by companies around the world, including apparel and accessories (Benetton, Chanel), home furnishings (IKEA, Royal Doulton), automobiles (Volkswagen, Porsche), electronics (LG, Samsung), and more. At the same time, American companies such as Guess, Apple, Ralph Lauren, and Walmart have long sold their goods to customers outside the United States.

In recent years, however, there has been an acceleration in the number and types of products whose market has been expanded to include even larger portions of the globe. A number of factors are contributing to the increased globalization of fashion marketing, not the least of which is rising income levels in some regions and countries, giving more consumers the means to purchase a broader range of fashion goods. In addition, when marketers believe they have reached as many target customers as they can in their existing markets, they may look to new markets in other countries as a way to increase their sales. What's more, there is growing interest in fashion products on a worldwide scale thanks to the Internet and mobile communications, which enable faster and wider communication of fashion news to virtually all corners of the globe. We'll take a more detailed look at the global fashion marketplace in Chapter 2.

SOCIAL MEDIA AND MOBILE COMMUNICATIONS

As stated earlier, communication is a key component of marketing, but in the past, most of the communication between marketers and customers flowed

FIGURES 1.12A–B The increased globalization of fashion marketing is reflected in these recently opened Gap stores in (a) Poland and (b) Japan.

MARKETER'S INSIGHT:
TURNING SOCIAL NETWORKING INTO CUSTOMER LOYALTY

Whether they take advantage of communities such as Facebook, tools like Twitter, or the power of apps, savvy marketers know that social media can help their customer relationship management efforts. And as social and mobile technologies continue to experience explosive growth, marketers are transforming them into high-performance loyalty tools by not only participating in digital communities, but by organizing and promoting their own programs that cultivate a brand's loyal following of friends.

Take Victoria's Secret Pink. With more than 6 million "friends" and counting in its Facebook community, Pink maintains an ongoing conversation with its loyal fans, providing tools that help manage the brand's identity as well as opportunities for customers to win gift cards, receive special offers, enter contests, and much more. For one special "Pinkapalooza" event in Los Angeles, featuring the band Fall Out Boy, Facebook friends could download an invitation online, participate in games and contests via mobile, and afterward received an mCoupon on their mobile device for in-store specials on merchandise.

Similarly, marketers ranging from Best Buy and Barneys to designers Diane von Furstenberg and Nicole Miller are turning to Twitter to communicate with target customers about anything from up-to-the-minute inventory information from the sales floor, to special sales and contests, to troubleshooting a problem product. Gap Outlet, for instance, sent its Twitter followers an offer for 15 percent off purchases of $75 or more; and Mall of America used its Twitter page one holiday season to alert consumers that two of its parking areas were at capacity, and their best bet was to park near IKEA. Said Greg Ahearn, senior vice president of marketing and e-commerce for Toys "R" Us, "It's one of the greatest emerging communication channels out there. This is a way people can stay connected with the brand in a way they've never been able to before."

Adapted from: "Social Media Can Boost Customer Loyalty," *DM News*, January 26, 2009, www.dmnews.com/Social-media-can-boost-customer-loyalty/article/126250 (accessed March 8, 2012); Stephanie Rosenbloom and Karen Ann Cullotta, "Buying, Selling and Twittering All the Way," *New York Times*, November 28, 2009, www.nytimes.com/2009/11/28/technology/28twitter.html?th&emc=th (accessed March 8, 2012).

in just one direction, with companies pushing their message out to consumers. The growth of social media and mobile communications, however, has altered that pattern radically, turning marketing into a two-way street where consumers are active participants in responding to, and sometimes actually shaping, the message.

As a result, marketers are scrambling to keep up with the rapidly changing landscape, which includes media tools—and therefore requires media strategies—that did not exist just a few years ago. Fashion marketers realize that staying up-to-date on these new marketing techniques is critical if they want to maintain a competitive edge. As one expert stated, "Studying how shoppers use social media not only provides an understanding of shoppers, but it also represents a vehicle for getting relevant information to shoppers when and where they need it."[10] From what are now relatively standard company Web sites and e-mail marketing programs, companies have expanded their efforts to include blogging, creating Facebook and Twitter accounts, and developing mobile marketing strategies that send up-to-the-minute information to consumers' smartphones and other handheld devices, all in order to convey their marketing message to consumers where they are most likely to see it and respond to it. Marketers are also monitoring blogs and social media sites to learn what consumers are saying about their products so they can themselves respond or adjust their own marketing messages. And by the time you are reading this, technology applications that impact marketing strategies will very likely be evolving even further.

ETHICS AND SOCIAL RESPONSIBILITY

Other major influences on fashion marketing in the twenty-first century are ethics and social responsibility. **Ethics** is a system of moral values, or a set of principles that define right and wrong. Both businesses and consumers engage in ethical or unethical behavior. Purchasing an outfit with the intent to wear it to a special party and then return it to the store is unethical consumer behavior. A business that realizes it produced flawed merchandise and immediately alerts customers to arrange an exchange is acting in an ethical manner. Ethics are not always so clear-cut. To some consumers, the use of fur in clothing or the testing of cosmetics products on animals signifies unethical behavior on the part of marketers, while other consumers may see nothing wrong with those practices.

Companies are only as ethical as the people who run them, and most businesses recognize that sound ethics engenders trust among a company's **stakeholders**—that is, those people and organizations that have an investment or other interest in the business, including its customers, employees, stockholders, suppliers, and government. A business that is trustworthy is one that customers tend to return to time and again. On the other hand, poor ethics discourages customers from repeat purchasing. Say that a design company intentionally orders inferior fabric for its upholstered furniture, or purposely cuts corners in its manufacturing process in order to make a bigger profit for itself. When customers buy and use the chairs and sofas and find that the products don't hold up as expected, they lose confidence in that

TABLE 1.1 Sample Ethical Issues Related to the Marketing Mix

Marketing Mix Element	Potential Issue	Unethical Activity
Product	Manufacturing flaws	Intentionally using materials or production techniques inferior to what the price reflects; covering up defects that could cause harm to a consumer
Price	Price manipulation	Raising the regular price on an item in advance of a sale in order to claim a reduced price for the sale period
Distribution (Place)	Counterfeiting	Using the Internet to sell counterfeit products, such as apparel, handbags, or jewelry, knowing that consumers cannot examine the goods prior to purchase
Promotion	False advertising	Using deception or misleading statements in advertising or personal selling situation; withholding key product information that could affect a purchase decision

Adapted from: William M. Pride and O.C. Ferrell, *Marketing*, 14th Edition (Boston: Houghton Mifflin, 2008), p. 97.

marketer's goods. Table 1.1 describes sample ethical issues related to the marketing mix.

Closely related to ethics is the issue of social responsibility. **Social responsibility** refers to the principle that everyone is responsible for making the world a better place for all its inhabitants. Among the areas in which fashion marketers may exercise social responsibility include protecting the environment, ensuring that their workers have safe conditions and receive a fair wage, and giving back through community service and charitable donations.

Fashion organizations that practice the social marketing concept build their marketing efforts on a foundation of striving to maintain society's well-being while satisfying customers' needs and wants. For example, Gap and Nike, among others, carefully oversee the manufacture of their goods in developing nations to verify that factory employees are paid fairly and have a safe workplace. In addition, many fashion companies donate certain profits or hold events to raise funds for charitable causes, such as Banana Republic's fashion show to benefit the Leukemia and Lymphoma Society.

Environmental Responsibility and Fashion Marketing

The environment is among the most prominent issues of social responsibility that fashion marketers are addressing today, whether through adopting more ecologically sound manufacturing practices, reducing their waste and carbon footprint, or practicing sustainability through recycling and use of renewable resources. Creating a more

FIGURE 1.13 Many fashion companies are now involved in green marketing, and some, like Fashion & Earth, offer nothing but green fashions.

not use pesticides or chemicals in the growing process, or using renewable materials such as bamboo, which is plentiful and replenishes itself quickly. In addition, because dyeing fabrics such as denim can be a harmful source of water pollution, some cotton farmers have begun growing cotton in shades of green, gray, and beige to be woven into fabrics that need no dyeing.

One apparel marketer, Fashion & Earth, sells nothing but "green fashions"—that is, apparel made from organic and sustainable textiles including bamboo, organic cotton, hemp, and soy. The company states that it is "championing a new kind of business model that makes doing good for the earth second nature, starting with the products we offer."[11] Retailers such as Lululemon, H&M, and Target are demonstrating social responsibility by responding to consumers' requests for green fashions and providing garments clearly labeled "sustainable" or "organic." These goods appeal to an increasing number of customers who are concerned with protecting the environment for today and for the future.

WHAT DO YOU THINK?

Which fashion businesses stand out in your mind as demonstrating social and environmental responsibility? How are they doing this?

environmentally friendly business operation has been dubbed **green marketing**, a business approach that protects the environment throughout the development and marketing of a company's products. For example, a growing number of marketers are designing their products with organic textiles, which are produced from crops that do

summary

The purpose of marketing is to create, communicate, and deliver value to customers and build strong customer relationships so that marketers receive value in return. Fashion marketing applies marketing processes and activities to currently popular designed products. Because of the changing nature of fashion, fashion marketing is dynamic and must constantly evolve to keep pace with trends and address consumers' desire for newness. The long-term goal of any marketer is customer loyalty.

Marketing begins with identifying the customers the company can serve best and then working to build strong customer relationships. The fashion marketing process involves researching customer needs and wants and selecting appropriate target markets; creating a product that offers a high perceived value to target customers; developing a customer-driven marketing plan that communicates the product's benefits to customers; and building trust and satisfaction with customers for long-term loyalty and profitability.

Most fashion organizations use either the marketing concept or the societal marketing concept as the approach to their marketing strategy, since both focus on the desires of target customers. Under the marketing concept, companies determine what customers want and then supply it, knowing that if they satisfy their customers, they'll achieve profits. With the societal marketing concept, fashion marketers focus not only on what customers want but also on what is good for society as a whole. To carry out their chosen strategy, companies develop marketing plans that incorporate the elements of the marketing mix: product, price, place, and promotion.

In the twenty-first century, several major trends are having a strong impact on fashion marketing. Globalization is opening new opportunities for more companies than ever to seek out additional markets for their products around the world. Social media and mobile communications are dramatically changing the way marketers communicate with customers. And ethics and social responsibility are playing an ever-greater role in fashion companies' marketing strategy, as consumers seek products from marketers they trust to act in the best interest of both customers and society, including by protecting the environment.

Macy's New Marketing Strategy Makes Customers the Focus

The overriding importance of putting customers first is not news to anyone in the business of fashion marketing. But it is news when a leading fashion marketer undertakes a major overhaul of its marketing strategy in order to better address its target customers' needs and wants—which is precisely what Macy's recently did.

It began with an intense research project aimed at better understanding Macy's current customers. The company conducted dozens of focus groups and talked with nearly a thousand people walking out of its stores. It leveraged research data from The NPD Group, a leading market research firm, for a holistic understanding of its customers, and combed through all their transactional data to discover themes in buying patterns and shopping habits. From all those efforts, the company identified one overwhelming finding. As stated by Peter Sachse, chief marketing officer, "What we don't need to do is get new customers. We realized that all we need to do is take care of those who already love us."

Operating with a new customer-centric focus, Macy's set out on a goal to encourage each existing customer to visit the store one more time each year. "Half the battle is won if we can get them to walk into our store," Sachse said. "And if we convert them [to a sale] during that visit, our [same] store sales will explode."

To accomplish that goal, there are a number of customer-focused marketing tactics Macy's is employing. These include the following:

- *Making merchandising decisions with the customer in mind.* Macy's used to let buyers make merchandising decisions based strictly on profit and loss statements. Now the company layers customer insight over the sales data, which helps buyers make more holistic decisions about how pulling a product might impact customer behavior and overall sales. The product is no longer king, Sachse said. Instead, the customer is queen.
- *Starting all meetings by asking, "What will our customer get out of this discussion?"* As Sachse noted, "If there's no answer, the meeting is over."
- *Creating a customer-champion team.* At Macy's, Chairman and CEO Terry Lundgren calls himself the "chief customer officer."
- *Using the Web site as the hub of the brand.* "Anything and everything a customer should ever want to do, they should be able to do on Macys.com," Sachse said. "There isn't anything more powerful that I have in my hands than Macys.com as a marketing tool."
- *Finding a campaign and a cause that customers—and employees—will rally around.* For Macy's, with its long, storied history, one such program was its "Believe" campaign, where for each letter to Santa brought into Macy's, the company would donate $1 to the Make-A-Wish Foundation. As an impetus to bring people to the stores, the campaign was very successful. "We had classrooms that used the Santa letter as a writing lesson—then they came as a field trip to bring them all in," Sachse said. What's more, the company received thousands of e-mails from its own employees about how proud they were of Macy's commitment to give back to communities. And employees feeling good about their company ultimately leads to a better customer experience.

Adapted from: Ellen Davis, "Macy's CMO Takes Unconventional Approach: 'We Don't Need to Get New Customers,'" Retail's BIG Blog, March 3, 2010, http://blog.nrf.com/2010/03/03/macy's-cmo-takes-unconventional-approach-"we-don't-need-to-get-new-customers"/ (accessed March 8, 2012).

QUESTIONS

1. Why do you think Macy's undertook the dramatic overhaul of its marketing strategy?
2. Why was it important for Macy's to use the knowledge it had gained about its target customers when making decisions about its merchandise assortments?
3. Macy's "Believe" campaign showed social responsibility, as well as building customer and employee loyalty. What would you suggest as a future campaign for Macy's that would build further on those goals? What cause would it benefit, and how would it engage customers and employees?

KEY TERMS

customer relationship management (CRM)

ethics

exchange

fashion

fashion marketing

goods

green marketing

market

market segment

market segmentation

marketing

marketing plan

marketing mix

need

perceived value

product

services

social responsibility

stakeholders

target market

value proposition

want

REVIEW QUESTIONS

1. Write a comprehensive definition of the term "marketing." Explain fashion marketing and describe the meaning of the term "fashion."

2. Explain the long-term goal of marketing and, using examples, describe how fashion marketers build customer loyalty.

3. Citing an example, explain the fashion marketing process.

4. Draw a diagram showing the components of the marketing mix and state their function.

5. How are social media and mobile communications affecting fashion marketing? Give an example.

6. Explain the importance of ethics and social responsibility to fashion marketers and to society.

DISCUSSION ACTIVITIES AND PROJECTS

1. As you go through the day, make note of ten examples of fashion marketing that you observe or hear, and record what they were and where you noticed them. Report your results to the class.

2. Select a fashion product or company that you feel loyal to, and describe how the elements of the marketing mix are influencing your loyalty.

3. Search your closet and identify five items that were each produced in a different foreign country. What similarities did you find? Share your findings with other class members.

4. Go to the Web site of a fashion marketer, and look for two or three examples of how that company incorporates social responsibility in its business. Write a brief report giving your opinion of how effective the company's efforts are in improving society or protecting the environment.

YOUR MARKETING PLAN

A **marketing plan** is a written document that indicates the tasks that are to be accomplished in order to reach an organization's objectives; it is the foundation of the company's marketing strategies. The marketing plan charts the course of the product or company and provides direction and control in reaching its goals. Every company that sells products develops (or should develop) a marketing plan for the company itself, as well as for its goods and services. Other types of organizations, such as universities, museums, and charities, also create and utilize marketing plans in order to accomplish their

TABLE 1.2 Components of a Marketing Plan

Plan Component	Component Purpose
Executive Summary	Offers a brief overview of the total marketing plan for easy reference to key points
Analysis of Market Environment	Examines the current market situation for the company and its products, including research on target markets and competition, as well as on external factors influencing the market, such as economic trends, technology advancements, new legislation
Strengths, Weaknesses, Opportunities, and Threats (SWOT) Analysis	Analyzes the company or product in relation to competitors, and assesses areas that could open beneficial avenues to pursue or create stumbling blocks to avoid
Marketing Objectives	Sets forth the specific, measurable goals the company wants to achieve through the marketing plan, usually within a specified time frame
Marketing Strategies	Outlines the methods that will be used to attain the company's marketing objectives, describing strategy for each element of the marketing mix and how the strategy addresses opportunities, threats, and other issues raised previously in the plan
Marketing Implementation	Details how the marketing strategies will be put into action, including specific activities, timeline, budget, and assignment of responsibilities for each activity
Evaluation and Control	Explains how results of the plan will be measured and evaluated for effectiveness, allowing management to review results and make any necessary adjustments to the plan

objectives. Many individuals have developed useful marketing plans for themselves as guides toward attaining their career objectives.

A course project for you as a student is to develop a marketing plan for a company or product, according to your instructor's directions, creating each part as you study it throughout the course. You will note at the end of each chapter this section entitled "Developing Your Marketing Plan," which will indicate the activities you are expected to complete to build your plan. Please look over the sample marketing plan outline in Table 1.2, and refer back to it as you develop your own with each chapter in this book. Every marketing plan is, of course, unique; however, it will also be useful for you to review Appendix A: Sample Marketing Plan at the back of this book.

Best wishes to you as you set out on this fashion marketing endeavor!

REFERENCES

1. American Marketing Association, "Dictionary," http://www.marketingpower.com/_layouts/Dictionary.aspx?dLetter=M (accessed March 8, 2012).

2. Gary Armstrong and Philip Kotler, *Marketing: An Introduction*, 10th ed. (Upper Saddle River, NJ: Pearson Prentice Hall, 2011), p. 5.

3. Tom Asacker, *A Clear Eye for Branding* (Ithaca, NY: Paramount Market Publishing, Inc., 2005), p. 29.

4. Patricia Mink Rath, Stefani Bay, Richard Petrizzi, and Penny Gill, *The Why of the Buy: Consumer Behavior and Fashion Marketing* (New York: Fairchild Books, 2008), p. 5.

5. Armstrong and Kotler, *Marketing: An Introduction*, 10th ed. (Upper Saddle River, NJ: Pearson Prentice Hall, 2011), p. 8.

6. Sean John, www.seanjohn.com/#/about/ (accessed March 6, 2012).

7. Op. cit.

8. Wendy Donahue, "Making a Fashion Statement—On Her Terms," *Chicago Tribune*, October 10, 2010, pp. 4, 5.

9. Patagonia Web site, http://www.patagonia.com/us/patagonia.go?assetid=10097 (accessed March 8, 2012).

10. Jim Lucas, "The Time Is Now to Take Shopper Marketing beyond the Store," *Advertising Age*, http://adage.com/article/cmo-strategy/marketing-taking-shopper-marketing-store/145430/ (accessed March 8, 2012).

11. Fashion & Earth, "About Fashion & Earth," http://www.fashionandearth.com/us/about-us (accessed March 8, 2012).

CHAPTER 2

Participating in the Global Fashion Marketplace

This chapter examines the various internal and external elements that impact fashion marketers today, and describes how those entities and forces influence the way fashion businesses operate in the global marketplace.

WHAT DO I NEED TO KNOW ABOUT THE GLOBAL FASHION MARKETPLACE?

* The importance of the global marketplace to fashion marketers today

* The elements that make up a fashion organization's microenvironment and how they can influence its marketing goals

* The components of the macroenvironment and the effect of each on a fashion marketer's operations

* The meaning of the concept of corporate social responsibility (CSR)

* How a fashion organization makes the decision to market on a global scale

FASHION MARKETING IN FOCUS:
The Global Nature of Today's Marketplace

Whether or not you are consciously aware of it, every action you take relates in some way to something or someone around you—that is, to elements of your environment.

When you got dressed this morning, did you put on boots or perhaps a pair of sandals instead? Whatever your choice of footwear, it was influenced in part by an aspect of your environment that you cannot control, namely, the weather. Maybe you were planning to meet your significant other for lunch and made a point of wearing a gold chain that he or she had given you. That decision was also influenced by your environment, but a part over which you do have control—in this case, another person with whom you choose to interact and whose attention and feelings you value.

The same concept holds true for fashion marketers but on a much broader scale, especially in light of the global nature of today's marketplace. In order to plan and carry out a marketing strategy, fashion companies must first recognize all the elements and influences of their environment, then work to adapt successfully to the forces they can't control while optimizing the forces they can.

A hundred years ago, fashion marketers operated in a far more limited environment than they do in the twenty-first century. There were no jets to whisk people to New York or Paris for the weekend if they wanted to shop in the tony designer boutique they'd just read about, and there were no televisions or Internet to quickly spread news and images of the latest products or looks. Even getting fashion goods from the producer to the consumer was a far lengthier process without the automated production techniques and speedy shipping methods now available.

By contrast, today's modern transportation and advanced communications technology have had the effect of diminishing distances between countries and cultures, so that the entire world now lies within the reach of marketers and consumers alike. As a result, fashion companies are faced with unprecedented opportunities to present their products to a global audience—but also the unprecedented challenges of dealing with an even wider range of influences that can have an impact, positive or negative, on their marketing efforts.

FIGURE 2.1 Modern technology has placed the entire world within the reach of fashion marketers and consumers alike.

Among the opportunities marketers enjoy from this expanded environment is an increasing international demand for fashion as emerging nations become more prosperous and develop a greater appetite for fashion goods. Contributing further to that demand is the ability for information about new fashions to be communicated to all corners of the globe with the click of a mouse or a "tweet" on a smartphone, raising instant awareness of a new style or trend. The challenges center on the fact that marketers who want to operate on a global scale now have to identify their target customers from among a vast number of countries and cultures, and build a marketing strategy and marketing mix that meet customers' needs—wherever in the world they are.

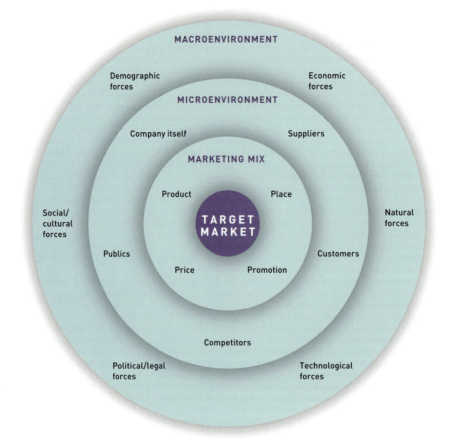

FIGURE 2.2 The macroenvironment and microenvironment exert a constant force on a fashion company's marketing mix.
BY VANESSA HAN AND ALICIA FREILE

The Fashion Marketing Environment

Every fashion company interacts with a variety of people and entities and faces diverse forces that can affect the way it reaches its marketing goals. Taken together, these players and forces represent the company's **marketing environment**. Some are internal within the company and some are external; some are elements that the company has the power to influence, and some are completely out of the company's control. A fashion marketer's objective is to understand all the forces in its environment and address them in a way that best satisfies customer wants and builds long-term relationships with customers.

To put it another way, when a company develops its marketing mix—the product, its price, where it is offered, and how it is promoted—it must plan the mix based on factors in its marketing environment that it can control, but with knowledge and anticipation of those it cannot. In preparation for a new season, for example, Marc Jacobs and his staff decide which designs are ready to be produced and select the items to be included in the upcoming collection. Knowing the costs for fabric, labor, and other expenses, the company is able to set the price of each product. It can then verify production schedules with the factory in order to establish expected delivery dates to Marc Jacobs retail store customers, such as Bloomingdale's, and namesake boutiques in the United States, as well as in Paris, London, and other world cities. Finally, the company develops an appropriate promotion campaign that might feature advertisements in *Vogue* and fashion shows at local retailers.

Fashion marketing would be relatively simple if that's all there was to it and marketers could manage all the aspects predictably. The marketing environment, however, is constantly shifting and there are always some elements that marketers cannot influence or sometimes even foresee. The cost of a particular fabric might go up unexpectedly, or a natural disaster might prevent a shipment from arriving at its destination. A competitor might introduce a similar product at a lower price, or a magazine that was planning to feature the product on its cover might suddenly fold. The entire world could plunge into an economic crisis, as it did in 2008, bringing consumer and business spending to a virtual standstill. These and other types of changes in the marketing environment can occur both in a company's immediate business surroundings, or microenvironment, and in the broader universe, or macroenvironment. Let's explore both in more detail.

The Microenvironment

A company's **microenvironment** is defined as the set of forces close to an organization that have direct impact on its ability to serve its customers.[1] The microenvironment includes the company itself, as well as its suppliers and intermediaries, its customers, its competitors, and various publics.

THE COMPANY

Within any company, the marketing function does not operate independently. It must work under the direction of top management, and it must work in cooperation with other departments, including research and development, production, accounting, and others involved in the overall operation of the business. In principle, all segments of the company support each other in meeting the ultimate goal of achieving customer satisfaction and loyalty.

Because a company's internal environment is capable of contributing to or detracting from its success, some organizations go the extra mile to create a positive and rewarding atmosphere for employees. Recall Threadless.com from Chapter 1—the T-shirt company that allows users of its Web site to submit and vote on original T-shirt art and then produces and sells the winning designs. The sense of community that the company nurtures online extends to its Chicago headquarters, where employees are encouraged to take breaks or work off stress by playing pool, ping-pong, or arcade and other games located on site. What's more, Threadless has established specific times when regular work shuts down and employees can dive into do-it-yourself projects that may or may not be related to company business. In one case, a team found a way to improve the company's Web site, while another group printed some popular T-shirt designs on different color shirts, which ended up boosting sales. As Threadless management recognizes, an atmosphere of flexibility and fun can result in more productive workers who truly care about the company, are more passionate about their work, and therefore work harder, helping the company better meet its marketing goals.[2]

SUPPLIERS AND INTERMEDIARIES

Suppliers are the life blood of the fashion business. At the manufacturing level, fashion companies depend on their suppliers for everything from fabric, thread, and zippers, to sewing and other production equipment, to packaging, tags and labels, and more. At the retail level, fashion marketers rely on their suppliers not only for the apparel and other fashion goods they sell to consumers but also for shopping bags, display units, and more run-of-the-mill necessities such as cash register paper and hangers, among other products. Because having the items they need—when they need them—is so critical to producing and selling their products, most companies view their relationship with their suppliers as a partnership, knowing that a disruption in the supply of needed goods can impact their marketing effort. If a fashion product is not available when customers want it, they will likely seek out a different item or marketer, no matter how exclusive or in demand the designer or the product might be.

One reason for the success of fast-fashion marketers, such as Zara, is that they control the product from its conception to the time it reaches the store, including its stated and actual delivery date. Virtually all companies now use technology known as **electronic data interchange** (**EDI**), through which they are able to share real-time information with their suppliers that can help in production planning and ensure timely delivery of needed goods. A related technology called **Quick Response** (**QR**)

FIGURE 2.3 Fashion marketers rely on their suppliers to provide needed goods and services on a timely basis.

TABLE 2.1 Types of Customer Markets in the Microenvironment

Market	Description
Consumer markets	Individuals or businesses buying fashion goods for themselves or others to use as purchased
Business markets	Organizations buying products either for use in their operation, or to process further or incorporate into their own final product
Reseller markets	Retailers, e-tailers, wholesalers, and others buying products to resell at a profit
Government markets	Local, state, and national agencies buying goods for internal use or for use in providing public services
International markets	Combination of all the above markets located in a country other than that of the marketer

ensures that retailers such as Bon-Ton or Dillard's are never out of certain brands of hosiery, intimate apparel, or jeans. The moment these goods pass through the electronic cash register, the QR system sends data about the sale to both the retailer and the manufacturer, alerting them when the store's supply needs to be replenished, and automatically initiating a new shipment of goods from the manufacturer.

Besides their suppliers, fashion marketers also build relationships with various intermediaries that provide services and assistance in the company's sales and marketing efforts. Among these may be wholesalers or other resellers, logistics organizations that provide warehousing and shipping services, and marketing services firms, such as advertising agencies and market research companies.

CUSTOMERS

Customers are the most important part of a company's microenvironment. They can be divided into several different types of markets, and a fashion organization may well target more than one of them. *Consumer markets* include individuals and others who buy fashion goods for personal use or for the use of another, as in a gift. When you buy any new fashion goods—a raincoat, a dining room table and chairs, or a new automobile—you are part of the consumer market.

Business markets, on the other hand, buy goods and services that will be used in the operation of their enterprise, or that they plan to process further or use in the production of their own final product. A luggage manufacturer purchasing zippers and wheels to incorporate into its suitcases is a business market; so is a law firm purchasing new window treatments or carpeting for its office space. Business markets can include companies and other for-profit businesses, as well as nonprofit and institutional customers. French designer Christian Lacroix was selling to the business market when he designed railcar interiors for the French National Railway's TGF, or bullet, trains. Similarly, Eddie Bauer and Pierre Cardin, among other fashion organizations, have designed automobile interiors for manufacturers to incorporate into certain models of their cars. Another example of a business market is a furniture company that purchases upholstery fabric and trims to use in manufacturing a sofa or chair.

Reseller markets buy goods in order to resell them to others at a profit. This group encompasses a broad range of traditional brick-and-mortar retailers, including Charlotte Russe, JCPenney, J.Crew, Crate & Barrel, and Neiman Marcus, among many others. It also includes non-store intermediaries such as the HSN and QVC television networks, catalogue retailers such as Frontgate and Newport News, and fashion e-tailers such as Shopbop, Zappos, and Gilt. Interior decorators and custom installers are other examples of resellers in the home fashions segment; and for some fashion goods, the reseller market also comprises distributors or wholesalers, companies that purchase from manufacturers and resell to retailers, often providing additional services such as warehousing and financing.

Government markets include local, state, and national government agencies that buy goods for their internal use or for use in providing public services. In the fashion arena, this would include products such as uniforms for police, firefighters, park service employees, and the military, among other goods.

The final type of customer market is *international markets*—which are a combination of the consumer, business, reseller, and government markets as described, but in countries other than where the marketer is based. International markets would encompass college students buying sweaters at Abercrombie & Fitch in London or Gap in Paris, high-end Italian sportswear company Fila purchasing Invista's Lycra Sport fabric for use in a line of women's body toning apparel, as well as retailers in countries around the world that import a variety of fashion goods to sell to consumers.

COMPETITORS

One very influential force in a fashion marketer's microenvironment, and one over which it clearly does not have control, is its competition. You'll recall from Chapter 1 that a key element of a company's marketing strategy is creating a value proposition that tells consumers how its product offers greater benefits than those of its competitors. That means fashion marketers need to know as much as possible about competitors' products and how they're being marketed, and be prepared to adjust their own marketing mix as necessary, based on changes in the competitive landscape. Have you seen the classic film *Miracle on 34th Street*? It offers a perfect example of the power of competitors in a company's microenvironment. When Macy's "Santa Claus," Kris Kringle, begins sending customers to other stores to find toys not available at Macy's, it's not long before rival

MARKETER'S INSIGHT:
MAX AZRIA—GLOBAL FASHION MARKETER

"I will be the merchant," declared designer Max Azria, describing the role he would play in the German department store chain Karstadt, which he and a partner had just purchased.

As if he weren't busy enough: Azria's company, BCBGMAXAZRIAGROUP, already operates nearly 1,000 stand-alone and partner stores on six continents. Not to mention that Azria is the creator and driving force behind a diversified group of collections including BCBG (named for the French phrase "bon chic, bon genre," Parisian slang meaning "good style, good attitude"), BCBG Max Azria, Hervé Léger by Max Azria, BCBGeneration, and a Miley Cyrus & Max Azria apparel line that retails exclusively at Walmart, among others.

Being an international businessman seems to come easily to Azria, who has been described as a very astute and superb merchant. He was born in Tunisia and grew up in France, where he spent 11 years designing women's wear before relocating to Los Angeles. Once in the United States, he first launched a series of new-concept boutiques before establishing his own design house in 1989. Over the years, he made some key acquisitions and built a portfolio of international brands—including Hervé Léger, the first time a French couturier had been absorbed by an American company. More recently, Azria acquired the French retail chain Alain Manoukian, which now has 115 stores worldwide, and G+G Retail, which was renamed Max Rave and operates 200 stores in the United States.

Regarding the Karstadt acquisition, Azria said, "I felt that it was fantastic for an American company to take it over." Indeed, there appears to be no end in sight for Azria's voracious appetite for acquisitions and atypical ways to expand his global fashion marketing empire.

Sources: Lisa Lockwood, "Max's Growing World: Azria Expands Empire with Karstadt," *Women's Wear Daily*, September 7, 2010, pp. 1 and 6; and BCBGMAXAZRIAGROUP, "About BCBGMAXAZRIA." From http://www.bcbgmaxazriagroup.com/spring2011/index.php?fc=about&lnt=bmF2 (accessed August 16, 2011).

department store Gimbels sees the need to follow suit in order to maintain customer loyalty.

To lessen the impact of competitors' marketing plans on their own, many fashion retailers employ a strategy of offering products that are theirs exclusively. Retailers such as Gap, Banana Republic, and Old Navy market unique products under their own store names, as do Talbots and Forever 21. Department and specialty stores create private-label goods that are not sold elsewhere, such as Nordstrom's Brass Plum and JC Penney's Arizona Blue. Sometimes retailers enter into partnerships with designers and celebrities to feature goods that are exclusive to their stores,

FIGURE 2.4 Many fashion retailers use private-label goods to lessen the impact of competitors' marketing activities on their own.

such as the Jaclyn Smith collection at Kmart and Isaac Mizrahi's fashions at Target. These topics are covered in more detail in Chapter 7, Branding Strategies for Fashion Goods and Services.

PUBLICS

Various types of publics are also part of a fashion marketer's microenvironment. A **public** is any group that has an actual or possible interest in or impact on the company's efforts to achieve its goals. One public is the *government*, which enforces laws regarding product safety, such as the flammability of fabrics for clothing, and labor practices, such as fair wages and proper working conditions, among others. *Financial publics*, such as banks and investors, are concerned with a company's financial stability and can affect its ability to maintain the capital needed to reach its marketing goals.

Television, the Internet, newspapers, and magazines are the *media publics*, which can impact a company in either a positive or negative way, depending on the information they disseminate. Additional publics include neighborhood organizations and local residents in the community where a company is located, which might support or oppose the construction of a nearby shopping mall, for example, and citizen action and political activist groups, such as PETA (People for the Ethical Treatment of Animals), which might call for a boycott of a company if it conducts product testing on animals. A final public is the *general public*, since any marketer will benefit from maintaining a positive image and reputation among the greater population, whether or not they are target customers.[3]

The Macroenvironment

While fashion marketers can control, or at least influence, many elements of their microenvironment, there's a much bigger picture that must come into focus for marketers to successfully participate in the global fashion marketplace. That is the **macroenvironment**, which is the collection of uncontrollable forces and conditions that face a company.[4] The macroenvironment includes *social*, *technological*, *economic*, *political and legal*, and *natural forces*, all of which a company must be aware of and ready to adapt to when conditions change.

SOCIAL FORCES

For a company to be able to identify and market to the customers in its microenvironment, it must first have a clear understanding of the population at large—including how that population is shifting and evolving. This includes such basics as the actual numbers of people in a market, their age and gender breakdown, ethnicity, and other key statistics. It also includes less easily measured information such as people's beliefs, attitudes, and view of themselves and others, since all those things can have a major effect on the goods and services they acquire.

These **social forces** within the macroenvironment encompass the elements of demographics and cultural values.

Demographics

Demographics is the statistical analysis of a population, especially with reference to its size and density, distribution, and vital statistics. Marketers can access demographic information on a local, national, and international level, helping them to pinpoint growing (or shrinking) segments of the population by age, region, marital status and family size, and a host of other criteria.

Population Growth   Nearly 7 billion people live in the world today, and projections are that the world's population will grow to more than 9 billion by 2050.[5] Most of the increase is occurring in developing nations of Asia, Central and South America, and Africa. China is currently the most populous country on the planet, but by 2025, India's population is expected to pass that of China. Those two nations together account for roughly a third of the world's total population, and their populations are projected to continue rising, to more than 1.6 billion for India and more than 1.3 billion for China by 2050.[6]

In the United States, the 2010 Census found that the population today consists of more than 308.7 million people—and it is growing larger, older, and more diverse. By 2050, the size of the U.S. population is predicted to top 439 million,[7] a number that will lend itself to market segmentation along highly refined niches based on age, income, family composition, geographic location, and ethnicity.

Income Another demographic item of key concern to marketers is the amount of income consumers have available to spend for all goods, including fashion merchandise. Incomes have been rising globally, although there is still a tremendous disparity between the wealthiest and the poorest nations. The country with the highest *per capita income* (a country's total income divided by the number of citizens) is Luxembourg. Its per capita income is $54,430, whereas per capita income for the United States, ranked third, is $37,500—numbers that dwarf those of third-world countries such as Tanzania, where per capita income is a mere $610.[8]

Throughout the world, fashion marketers are paying close attention to emerging countries that are experiencing a growing middle class. They recognize that as income rises, so does interest in fashion goods. As a result, companies including Levi Strauss, Estée Lauder, and Walmart are all increasing their presence in China, Latin America, and other locales where consumers find themselves with more money to spend on fashion.

Age Statistics Advances in medicine and a focus on improving living conditions in the world's poorest areas are contributing to another demographic trend: increased longevity and the overall aging of the population. Statistical projections indicate that in 2050 there will be 2 billion people worldwide over the age of 60, a fact that most fashion marketers

FIGURE 2.5 The world's population is expected to reach 9 billion people by 2050.

TABLE 2.2 Age Cohorts

Cohort Group	Age Range	Characteristics/ Interests	Fashion Preferences
Seniors	Born before 1946	Active; enjoy travel	Comfortable but stylish apparel
Baby Boomers	Born 1946–1964	Diverse interests; focus on fitness, appearance, retirement planning	Fashionable looks in choice of products
Generation X	Born 1965–1980	Self-reliant; well-educated; independent; pragmatic	Designer and brand names somewhat important
Generation Y and Millennials	Born 1981–2000+	Tech-savvy; self-confident; natural multitaskers; like to socialize in groups	Celebrity-influenced

have yet to fully recognize and address. Information such as this is important to marketers because the fashion wants and needs of an older population are different from those of younger groups.

As you can tell from Table 2.2, various age groups (or cohorts) have different outlooks on life and different fashion preferences. While many aging baby boomers and seniors are looking for comfortable style, others are seeking out adventure and exploring new travel destinations. Meanwhile, Millennials are experts in scoping out favorite celebrities and following their fashion lead, as well as being in total sync with the latest fashions in personal electronics. For any age group, however, income constraints and family obligations may create barriers to pursuing fashion interests.

Geographic Location Looking at another demographic element, marketers must take into account consumers' geographic location, since that can influence their fashion purchases, particularly the type and style of clothing they buy. Climate is clearly one factor, with parkas and snow boots being core wardrobe items in northern locales, while swimwear and flip-flops are year-round staples for warmer or tropical regions.

There are also differences in consumers' fashion needs and wants based on whether they live in an urban, suburban, or rural area. Consumers in New York or Los Angeles (not to mention Paris or Rome) will likely choose higher-style apparel than those living in a farming community in Kansas or mountain region of West Virginia. Also, because most city dwellers live in smaller apartments with elevator access, they generally need to fill their homes with less bulky furniture and smaller décor than they would in a single-family home in the suburbs—a factor that home fashions marketers need to consider when determining the "place" element of their marketing mix.

Ethnicity and Diversity The population of the United States is made up of many backgrounds and cultures, as you'll see in Table 2.3. In addition to people of Native American descent and descendants of the early settlers from Europe, millions of immigrants from around the globe have settled in America since its founding, creating one of the most racially and ethnically diverse populations in the world. What's more, each of these groups is not a single entity. Hispanics, for example, represent a variety of countries and cultures from throughout Central and South America, as well as from Spain, Cuba, and Puerto Rico. Asians might have their roots in Japan, Korea, Vietnam, China, India, or other nations. Each of these cultures has its own traditions, and fashion marketers that recognize the diverse tastes and traditions of the different groups

can work to anticipate their needs with appropriate products and marketing support.

African Americans are another group that marketers often target with tailored fashion products and promotions, particularly in the beauty category with specially formulated hair and skincare products. Yet another segment that contributes to population diversity is the LGBT (lesbian, gay, bisexual, and transgender) community. Marketers are increasingly focusing their attention on this influential group, which is generally considered to be more affluent than many other segments, as well as early adopters of new fashions.

Cultural Values

Culture is defined as the set of learned values, norms, and behaviors that are shared and practiced by members of a group or society.[9] Most Americans, regardless of their heritage or individual circumstances, share certain core cultural values such as

TABLE 2.3 U.S. Population by Race and Ethnicity

Race/Ethnicity	Percentage of U.S. Population
Caucasian	72.4%
Hispanic/Latino*	16.3%
African American	12.6%
Asian	4.8%
Native American	0.9%
Two or more races	2.9%

* Hispanics may be of any race, so also are included in applicable race categories, resulting in a total of greater than 100%.
Source: U.S. Census Bureau, USA QuickFacts. Accessed on August 16, 2011, from http://quickfacts.census.gov/qfd/states/00000.html.

MARKETER'S INSIGHT:
L'ORÉAL SPEAKS TO HISPANICS

It's been said that in America, a minority group has not truly arrived into the mainstream until it has been marketed to. That was true for African Americans, gay men and lesbians, and most recently, consumers who speak Spanish.

It took a while for many advertisers to recognize the growing economic power of Hispanic America, but census figures are persuading the laggards of their need to address this fast-growing demographic group. According to data from the 2010 Census, Hispanics accounted for more than half the growth of the total American population in the previous decade.

L'Oréal USA is one marketer that is taking the numbers seriously. The giant cosmetics, fragrance, and beauty products company recently joined forces with the Telemundo Communications Group to sponsor Club de Noveleras, the first official club for fans of Telemundo's popular serialized dramas, or telenovelas. The club was launched with the introduction of a Web site, clubdenoveleras.com, which includes video clips, photographs, articles, and a beauty blog. Visitors can interact with other ardent fans of telenovelas, as well as join a loyalty program that gives out points for activities like watching videos and clicking on the L'Oréal USA product ads on the site.

"We see it as a growth opportunity for the future," said Marc Speichert, L'Oréal USA's chief marketing officer, noting that the company was increasing its spending for ads in Spanish. "For us, Hispanic consumers are a very, very important target."

Adapted from: Stuart Elliott, "Pretty as a (Census) Picture," *The New York Times*, March 28, 2011. www.nytimes.com/2011/03/29/business/media/28adnewsletter1.html?src=busln (accessed March 28, 2011).

hard work, love of country, and equal opportunity for all. Beyond those universal beliefs, there are any number of other cultural values that Americans hold, based on their upbringing and surroundings. Attitudes based on religion are one example; loyalty to a particular political party is another. Because beliefs and behaviors grounded in culture are very difficult to change, marketers must recognize the cultural values of their target customers—and often the general public as well—when developing the elements of their marketing mix.

For instance, a large segment of the American population tends to be socially conservative, which means that marketers of certain fashion products have to walk a fine line in order not to offend portions of the public. Abercrombie & Fitch angered parents across the board when it promoted a bikini top initially described as a padded "push-up triangle" to girls as young as seven. After a public outcry, the company continued to market the top but renamed it simply a "striped triangle."[10] Of course, many leading fashion designers purposely try to push the envelope in creating shocking designs or risqué advertisements to set themselves apart and capture attention. In many cases, the target audience for these over-the-top creations is not fazed—particularly if the audience is in Europe, which tends to be more liberal than the United States—and the designs or ads serve their marketing purpose. In general, however, fashion companies are taking a risk if they go too far or ignore the cultural forces in action in their target markets.

A different type of cultural force that is emerging among fashion consumers is the desire to own luxury goods without having to pay the luxury prices associated with them. Sensing this trend, a number of designers have developed lower-priced products bearing their names to be sold in popularly priced stores. The term **masstige marketing**—popularized by Michael Silverstein and Neil Fiske in their book *Trading Up* and *Harvard Business Review* article "Luxury for the Masses"—refers to this process of designers creating goods specifically to be made available to the public at lower prices and in more accessible locations than their prestige lines. A classic example is Vera Wang, whose designer bridal gowns are sold at high-end stores like Bergdorf Goodman and whose lower-priced line, called Simply Vera Vera Wang, is carried by Kohl's.

While there is some risk that a designer could lose prestige status due to masstige marketing, this has not happened to Wang or many other designers, who take pains to ensure that the mass-market

FIGURE 2.6 Masstige marketing gives consumers high-fashion looks and designer name goods at more affordable prices.

designs are not overexposed or too closely connected to their high-end line. As a result, designers such as Missoni, Zac Posen, Anna Sui, Rodarte, and Jean Paul Gaultier, among others, have at times created lower-priced collections for Target; and H&M contracted for a short term with Karl Lagerfeld, Jimmy Choo, and others. Concerning masstige fashion, Stella McCartney noted, "I think it's really important and modern and contemporary if you can make clothes that are affordable and accessible." Jil Sander, who at one time teamed up with the Japanese fast-fashion organization Uniqlo, also commented on the changing values, saying, "There is a strong tendency toward a less frivolous lifestyle. You find people of style on all levels of income: quality and attractiveness wins over snobbism."[11]

WHAT DO YOU THINK?

Do you recall seeing a fashion ad that you or a friend found offensive or shocking? What kind of image, words, or other element in an ad would make you think less of a brand? Would your parents or older relatives be more sensitive to certain ads than you might be?

TECHNOLOGICAL FORCES

Even if you feel as though there has always been a world with iPhones and Facebook, if you really stop and think about it, the technological advances of the past 25 years can only be described as breathtaking in their speed and scope. All aspects of life and of business, from entertainment to communications,

have been revolutionized by technology. And the pace of innovation may only increase going forward, creating opportunities for marketers in the way of more efficient and effective operations, but also presenting the challenge of staying on top of the latest trends.

Already, marketers are not only able to target customers more accurately but also to ascertain more specifically what consumers want and then provide it more rapidly. In many ways, it is helping to change the paradigm, as consumers increasingly demand fast delivery of fashion goods that they themselves may have had a part in creating.

Advanced Production Techniques

First, let's look at how the fashion industry is able to meet consumer needs more rapidly and efficiently. In addition to the previously mentioned Quick Response replenishment systems that enable retailers never to be out of stock on certain items, new methods of design and manufacturing technology have greatly shortened the production process. This technology includes **computer-aided design** (**CAD**), which permits designers to create and change designs easily on their computer screen via special software; **computer-aided manufacturing** (**CAM**), which incorporates the power of computer processing into production equipment including patternmaking, cutting, and sewing machines; and **computer-integrated manufacturing** (**CIM**), which links many computers within a manufacturing company in order to streamline and coordinate production from design through finished product.

For example, using CAD technology, a designer in New York can create a sketch of a denim jacket for Gap. The digital sketch can then be transmitted instantaneously to Gap's factory affiliate in Asia, where production staff follows the specifications and submits a sample garment back to New York. When the design specifications are tweaked or approved, the final specifications are input into the CAM or CIM system, enabling the factory to automatically create patterns, cut the fabric, and sew the garment. With these and other new technologies, fashion goods can be designed, created, and delivered to retailers halfway around the world in a matter of weeks—perhaps days—instead of what used to be months.

Electronic Communications

More rapid availability of fashion products goes hand in hand with the fact that fashion consumers are demanding the goods *right now*. Thanks to streaming video, smartphone cameras, and platforms like Twitter, consumers are able to learn about new designer collections before they even leave the runway—or see the fabulous new jeans their friend bought on vacation (and which they have to have, too!) long before the friend arrives back home.

Fashion companies are now tapping into these technologies to enhance their marketing efforts. Burberry, for example, live-streamed the 2011 spring fashion show for its Prorsum line in London to viewers in 25 of its stores throughout the world, as well as online to its fans via Facebook. In the stores, the company provided iPads to sales clerks, enabling customers to place orders on the spot. The garments were also available for order from the company Web site, with delivery promised in just seven weeks.[12]

In addition to wanting fashions immediately, some consumers go further: They want to design their own goods and have them manufactured. A number of Web sites and blogs contain offers to turn a consumer design into a product. Jeff Silverman Creations at www.jeffsilverman.com, for example, lets consumers design their own shoes or handbags and have them made for between $100 and $200. In some cases, consumers might send a

FIGURE 2.7 Advanced communications technologies enable fashion marketers to reach customers around the world instantly and simultaneously.

MARKETER'S INSIGHT:
ADIDAS CONNECTS WITH A WORLD OF CONSUMERS

When adidas launched its "all adidas" global brand campaign, it was not only the brand's largest marketing campaign in history, but it was also the first time the company featured its adidas Sport Performance, adidas Originals, and adidas Sport Style sub-brands in a single campaign—with ad spots debuting the same day in more than 100 countries.

The campaign was designed to showcase adidas' distinctive presence across different cultures and lifestyles, fusing the world of sports, music, and fashion. Highlighted was an eclectic group of celebrities including NBA star Derrick Rose, soccer stars David Beckham and Lionel Messi, pop icon Katy Perry, hip hop artist B.o.B., University of Notre Dame football, and skateboarders Silas Baxter-Neal, Lem Villemin, and Jake Donnelly. The 30- and 60-second TV commercials and two-minute extended online version were directed by French film and music video director Romain Gavras and featured the song "Civilization" by French electronic band Justice. Fans could also go to Facebook and YouTube for additional in-depth content.

To develop a single, overarching approach that would cover footwear and apparel from both its athletic and fashion groups, as well as address customers from all over the world, was not a small task. But as Patrik Nilsson, president of adidas America, said, "Today's consumers are not one-dimensional. They live across the cultural spectrum and that's where adidas has its edge. The new campaign allows us to create stronger, truer connections with the consumer by encouraging and celebrating a mix of interests and passions central to their lives."

Source: "Adidas Launches Biggest Marketing Campaign in Brand's History," news release, March 14, 2011.

photo of an existing shoe that they'd like to have in a different color or material, or they could request a shoe that combines the overall style of one sample with the heel of another. Customers of the site can also place a widget on their Facebook page or blog, and if another customer orders their design, they receive a reward. As Silverman himself put it, "There's a new sheriff in town—it's called the consumer."[13]

Another aspect of technology having enormous impact on fashion marketing is social media, including Facebook, Foursquare, and Twitter, which represent a way for marketers to communicate inexpensively with target customers and, in some cases, to interact with them. If you own a smartphone, you've probably used an app that directs you to a store that carries an item you're looking for, or maybe that offers you points or coupons when you view store windows and go inside to see the merchandise. Brooks Brothers is developing a plan for a customer to shop and receive personalized attention—remotely through an app. When the customer accesses the store on his phone, he will see the actual site, his sales associate, and a virtual closet. The salesperson will recommend new looks, using the customer's past buying history as a guide. According to the company, the fact that the store associate and the customer can work directly with each other through this medium builds sales as well as customer satisfaction and loyalty.[14]

ECONOMIC FORCES

Economic forces have an effect on both fashion marketers and consumers. In today's global economy, an economic ripple halfway around the world can create an impact that is felt by companies and customers right here at home. For example, the rise or fall in the value of the U.S. dollar against another country's currency can instantly alter the cost of goods being bought from or sold to that other country. The fluctuating cost of oil is another economic force that has a direct impact on fashion marketers that rely on oil-based energy not only for their facilities and for shipping their goods but also for many production and packaging materials that are made of petroleum-based plastics.

Let's look at how other economic forces—the business cycle and consumer income—influence the way fashion marketers conduct their businesses and how consumers spend their money.

The Business Cycle

The economic conditions in every country are constantly shifting and are increasingly tied to the economy of other nations around the world. These movements are influenced by factors such as supply and demand, competition, willingness to spend, and even political stability. Typically, movement in an economy follows a **business cycle** that has four stages: *prosperity, recession, depression*, and *recovery*.[15]

Prosperity is identified as a time of stable income, low unemployment, and substantial buying power. The last part of the twentieth century and the beginning of this century were mostly periods of prosperity. In 2008, however, the United States (along with most of the world) entered a period of *recession* where production and employment declined, along with incomes and consumer spending. Through government financial incentives such as stimulus plans for highways, building construction, and other projects, the nation managed to avoid slipping deeper into a depression.

FIGURE 2.8 Fashion marketers such as Ross Stores retained customers during the recent recession by emphasizing high value and low cost.

Not seen in the United States since the 1930s, a *depression* occurs when unemployment is rampant, wages are low, and consumers have no confidence in the economy. Depressions can last for quite a while; the Great Depression of the 1930s began with the 1929 stock market crash and didn't completely end in the United States until 1941 when the country entered World War II. When a recession or depression ends, the nation enters a period of *recovery* characterized by gradual growth in employment and income, and a revival of consumer confidence.

Although there are often warning signs of impending economic downturns, no one can predict the depth or length of a recessionary period—or predict with certainty when a period of prosperity may start to fade. That means that marketers must be nimble and prepared to adjust their marketing strategy when changing economic conditions warrant it. During the most recent recession, the fashion marketers that suffered least from the drop-off in consumer spending were those that emphasized high value for the prices charged, including Ross Stores, Kohl's, and Walmart.

Consumer Income

The amount of money consumers are willing and able to spend is called **buying power**, and it depends on three things: available income, credit, and wealth. For most people, the main source of income is from salary or wages. Some people may also receive income from pensions, rent received, or investments. The median household income in the United States—meaning half of all households make more and half make less—is just over $49,700.[16] Over the past few decades, the wealthiest Americans have seen the biggest increases in their total income, while income for the middle and lower classes has been stagnant, effectively reducing the buying power of a large segment of the population.

Marketers know that consumers have certain obligations they must meet before using their income for purchases they desire. The first obligation is to pay federal and state taxes. The amount left over after taxes is called **disposable income**, but consumers must still allocate much of that amount to necessities such as food, shelter, utilities, and transportation. What is left after those necessities are paid for is the sum that consumers may spend or save as they wish; this amount is known as **discretionary income**. Discretionary income represents the funds that consumers can use for fashion apparel and accessories, home furnishings, entertainment, vacations, and other optional items.

When they do not have sufficient money available to make a purchase, many consumers use credit to obtain goods and services immediately, paying the total over time. Buying on credit can be a practical way to make expensive purchases such as a home, automobile, or major appliance. But for lesser purchases, consumers need to realize that with interest charges added in, they can end up paying a significantly higher price by the end of the repayment period.

POLITICAL AND LEGAL FORCES

The political environment is a major force in the macroenvironment, because governments at all levels pass laws that can impact how marketers do business. Although companies generally cannot

TABLE 2.4 Selected U.S. Laws Affecting Fashion Marketers

Name of Law and Date Enacted	Purpose
Sherman Antitrust Act (1890)	Prohibits contracts, combinations, or conspiracies to restrain trade; establishes as a misdemeanor monopolizing or attempting to monopolize
Clayton Act (1914)	Prohibits specific practices such as price discrimination, exclusive dealer arrangements, and stock acquisitions whose effect may noticeably lessen competition or tend to create a monopoly
Robinson-Patman Act (1936)	Prohibits price discrimination that lessens competition among wholesalers or retailers; prohibits producers from giving disproportionate services or facilities to large buyers
Lanham Act (1946)	Provides protections for and regulation of brand names, brand marks, trade names, and trademarks
Fair Packaging and Labeling Act (1966)	Prohibits unfair or deceptive packaging or labeling of consumer products
Trademark Counterfeiting Act (1980)	Imposes civil and criminal penalties against those who deal in counterfeit consumer goods or any counterfeit goods that can threaten health or safety
Digital Millennium Copyright Act (1996)	Refines copyright laws to protect digital versions of copyrighted materials, including music and movies

Adapted from: William M. Pride and O.C. Ferrell, *Marketing*, 14th Edition (Boston: Houghton Mifflin, 2008), p. 67.

prevent a law from taking effect, they can sometimes influence a law's final provisions through negotiations with legislators, an activity called *lobbying*. Few fashion companies are big enough to lobby effectively on their own, but they can do so by combining strength with others in their industry, often as part of an industry association.

There are a number of laws that have an impact on fashion marketing in the United States, some of which are shown in Table 2.4. Enacted by Congress over the years, laws that affect businesses generally have the purpose of maintaining fairness in business operations, such as forbidding a single company from monopolizing a market, maintaining equitable pricing for consumers, and safeguarding consumers' confidential information. In addition, the federal government contains a number of agencies that regulate different aspects of marketing activity, including some that have an influence on fashion marketing. (See Table 2.5.) The most notable agency that impacts fashion marketers is the Federal Trade Commission, which concerns itself with upholding laws regarding deceptive pricing, packaging, and advertising.

Sometimes laws may be challenged or enforced through court proceedings. For example, the United States Supreme Court recently upheld a previous ruling that found Costco liable in a case of copyright infringement. The warehouse club retailer had been selling Swiss-made Omega watches at a deep discount but was not authorized by the manufacturer to do so. Imports obtained this way, at lower-than-normal prices by avoiding the original manufacturer or its authorized U.S. distributors, are called *gray market goods*. The court ruling will likely serve to encourage other manufacturers to pursue legal remedies against unauthorized distribution of their goods, and could discourage other mass marketers from obtaining imported fashion goods in this way.[17]

A good grasp of the political and legal environment is perhaps even more important when

TABLE 2.5 Major Federal Regulatory Agencies That Influence Fashion Marketing

Agency	Main Areas of Responsibility
Federal Trade Commission (FTC)	Enforces laws and guidelines regarding business practices; takes action to stop false and deceptive advertising, pricing, packaging, and labeling
Food and Drug Administration (FDA)	Enforces laws and regulations to prevent distribution of adulterated or misbranded foods, drugs, medical devices, cosmetics, veterinary products, and potentially hazardous consumer products
Consumer Product Safety Commission (CPSC)	Ensures compliance with the Consumer Product Safety Act; protects the public from unreasonable risk of injury from any consumer product not covered by other regulatory agencies
Federal Communications Commission (FCC)	Regulates communication by wire, radio, and television in interstate and foreign commerce
Environmental Protection Agency (EPA)	Develops and enforces environmental protection standards and conducts research into the adverse effects of pollution

Adapted from: William M. Pride and O.C. Ferrell, *Marketing*, 14th Edition (Boston: Houghton Mifflin, 2008), p. 70.

companies are operating on a global scale. Fashion marketers must have solid knowledge of the laws in the countries and regions where they are doing business in order both to enter the market and to successfully maintain a presence there.

Sometimes, foreign government regulations can inhibit trade. This happens when a country establishes quotas on the quantities of certain items it will accept from another country or places a tax (called a *duty*) on some imported goods. In some cases, nations set up quotas and duties to protect the pricing of similar goods produced domestically. For years, the United States has imposed quotas and duties on many apparel items being imported from China and other nations, in order to maintain competition. One of the jobs of the **World Trade Organization** (**WTO**)—an international organization that deals with the rules of trade between nations—is to work toward lowering and eliminating such trade barriers among its member countries, which include most of the world's trading nations.

NATURAL FORCES

Anyone who experienced or saw video of the earthquake and tsunami that devastated Japan in 2011 can't help but have a profound appreciation for the forces of nature and their impact on all aspects of people's businesses and lives. Marketers certainly cannot predict when a natural catastrophe will occur, but they can have emergency plans in place for some of the more common or likely natural events they could envision affecting them or others in their microenvironment. When hurricane Katrina ravaged New Orleans, some national retailers with stores in the area quickly set out to ensure that their employees were safe, and began shipping needed water, blankets, and other supplies to residents. Once rebuilding was under way, many businesses reopened as quickly as possible to meet the needs of their customers in the region.

WHaT DO YOU THINK?

The United States imports a vast quantity of goods from China. What are several macroeconomic factors that encourage this trade? Imports of luxury goods such as designer apparel, leather goods, and fine jewelry tend to come from Europe. What are two or three of the macroeconomic factors contributing to this business?

Ethics and Social Responsibility

For a growing number of companies, there is one overriding strategy that guides them not only in how they approach their own marketing goals but also in how they deal with all the diverse elements of their marketing environment. Some of the most forward-thinking companies in the fashion industry are crafting their marketing decisions based on their ethical standards, and conducting their marketing activities within a framework of social responsibility. Known as **corporate social responsibility** (**CSR**), this strategy focuses on including public interest into corporate decision making, with the belief that responsible labor and environmental practices will benefit both the company and society as a whole. This concept is sometimes referred to as the "triple bottom line" of people, planet, and profit.

CSR strategies span a broad range of issues, from eliminating child labor in foreign factories and improving working conditions throughout the supply chain to promoting environmental sustainability through use of renewable resources. Gap, for example, has a strong commitment to social responsibility that includes not only a Code of Vendor Conduct governing the working conditions it requires at its factories around the world but a wide range of additional initiatives, such as offering educational programs for workers. The company's sustainability efforts encompass not only water and energy conservation at its facilities but extend to the consumer level as well, with events such as "Recycle Your Blues," during which consumers get a discount on a new pair of jeans when trading in an old pair. What happens to the old jeans? Gap has them converted to cotton insulation, which is donated to needy communities.[18]

Patagonia and Eileen Fisher are among a number of companies that have even created a corporate position to oversee their CSR strategy. Patagonia's Cara Chacon, whose title is director of social and environmental responsibility, stated, "We have fully integrated the CSR system into our sourcing production process. What that means is that people from sourcing, quality control, and social responsibility all sit at the table and make decisions together and

FIGURE 2.9 For fashion marketers, corporate social responsibility extends from enforcing safe working conditions to reducing their overall carbon footprint.

report to the same vice president." Among the results are that fair wages are included from the outset as the company determines costs and streamlines the supply chain.[19] Many other fashion companies are applying CSR throughout their operations, from their choice of "green" office supplies to their support for charitable organizations.

Global Fashion Marketing

As you've seen in this chapter, the world today has shrunk and its economies and marketplaces are increasingly intertwined. As a result, many fashion companies—if they haven't already done so—are considering expanding on an international scale. Before taking the plunge, however, they must look at all the elements of their marketing environment, assess their capabilities and marketing goals, and undertake careful research and planning in order to successfully establish a global presence.

As "Steps in Deciding to Market Globally" shows, getting started begins by evaluating the macroenvironment and the external forces that are impacting the global fashion marketplace. Walmart operates in some 15 international markets, and before it enters each new country, the company looks carefully at the forces in play there. Even then, a specific international venture may not work out as planned: After opening stores in Germany and South Korea, Walmart later withdrew from those nations because it didn't fully grasp aspects of the local culture and underestimated the strength of the competition.

The second step is to make a decision about entering the international marketplace, which means the company must evaluate its own resources to determine whether it has all the necessary capabilities to take on global markets. Deciding which fashion markets to enter is the next step in the process. Williams-Sonoma decided to begin by opening a store in Canada, since many Canadians were already customers of its West Coast stores. Phillip Lim chose to place stores in Japan because many Japanese customers loyally purchased his designs in the United States. Michael Kors has flagship stores for his chic sportswear in New York City, Beverly

FIGURE 2.10 In making the decision to expand internationally, Michael Kors chose London as the market to open his first European flagship store.

STEPS IN DECIDING TO MARKET GLOBALLY

1. Scanning the global fashion marketing environment
2. Determining the company's ability to market globally
3. Deciding which global markets to enter
4. Evaluating how best to enter a chosen market
5. Creating a global fashion marketing program

Hills, Palm Beach, and Chicago, so the similarly cosmopolitan cities of London, Milan, and Paris were logical locales for his initial expansion of flagship stores into the European market.

Evaluating how to enter the market is the fourth step. Ralph Lauren thought it best to sign licensing agreements with local companies in various countries throughout the world because these companies knew the potential customers and local marketing environment, and were eager to participate financially in the business. Timing is also a consideration, since the company may want to capitalize on other planned marketing activities that can help draw consumer (and media) attention. Elie Tahari, for example, opened his first international flagship store in Istanbul just before showing his spring collection during New York Fashion Week.[20]

The final step in the process is to create a global marketing program, coordinating the company's products, promotion, pricing, and distribution across international borders. While individual elements of the marketing mix almost always need to be adapted in some way to fit individual international markets, the overall goal remains to persuade consumers of the product's value and to earn long-term customer loyalty.

WHAT DO YOU THINK?

Describe a fashion business you have learned about that recently decided to begin or expand its global marketing activities. State two reasons for the company's choice of specific locations for expansion.

Summary

Every fashion company is influenced by people, entities, and forces within its marketing environment, which can affect the way it reaches its marketing goals. Some elements of the marketing environment represent conditions or situations that the company can control or influence, but others are out of the company's control. With advances in technology and communications having the effect of shrinking the world, the fashion marketing environment has expanded globally, presenting both opportunities and challenges.

A company's marketing environment consists of its microenvironment, or forces close to it that have direct impact on its ability to serve its customers, and the macroenvironment, the collection of uncontrollable forces and conditions that face a company. The microenvironment includes the company itself, its suppliers and intermediaries, its customers, competitors, and various publics. The macroenvironment includes social, technological, economic, political and legal, and natural forces. To successfully reach its marketing goals, a company must optimize the forces it can control while being aware of and ready to respond to shifts and changes in the forces it cannot control.

A growing number of fashion companies are approaching their marketing environment and making marketing decisions based on the concept of corporate social responsibility (CSR). This concept centers on the belief that being socially and environmentally responsible in all aspects of their business will benefit not only the company, but also the planet and society as a whole.

An assessment of all elements within the marketing environment is crucial to a fashion business that is considering entering the global marketplace. Key steps include scanning international markets for opportunities, evaluating the company's resources and capabilities, deciding which fashion markets to enter, determining how and when to enter them, and creating a marketing plan appropriate for each market and the company's overall marketing goals.

Nike Shifts with Its Environment

Nike, one of the world's most iconic brands, raised concept selling to a whole new level when it first rolled out its Niketown stores back in the early 1990s. Fast forward 20 years and Nike is once again incorporating new ideas into its retail concept—but this time it goes further than the brand "experience" and zooms in on its customer relationships.

The redesigned stores are smaller than the traditional Niketowns, while still hooking customers with a broad range of products covering its key categories of basketball, football, running, soccer, training, and action sports. But that's just the beginning. Responding to evolving technology, customer values, and other aspects of its marketing environment, the stores offer additional innovative components that are at the heart of the interaction with customers.

One is called Nike+, a $29 device developed in partnership with Apple that connects running shoes to wearers' iPods and iPhones, and gives users feedback on distance, pace, calories burned, and other data. A Nike+ station is positioned next to running shoe displays, and running enthusiasts can join the Nike+ Run Club to take part in organized runs, get expert training advice, and even try out new Nike footwear.

Another interactive component is Nike iD, which lets customers personalize apparel, shoes, and equipment to individual or team specifications. Using the Nike iD in-store computers, customers can select their desired colors, materials, and other elements for more than 115 styles of goods. The customized products are sent to consumers in about three weeks, although customers who want only logos, names, or numbers applied can have this done while they're in the store. This customization lets Nike stand out from competitors, and has proven to drive consumer sales.

Participating in the community is another aspect of Nike's aligning with its environment. Its debut store redesign in Santa Monica, California, for example, features mannequins sporting the uniforms of local high school teams, and a schedule of local runs is featured on a chalkboard in the dressing room area. In its revamped flagship store in London, where football (soccer) is king, it added a state-of-the-art football boot fitting machine that allows players to steam-mold boots to their feet, as well as an embroidery service for customizing football boots with names, flags, and numbers.

Nike expects the concept of the new store with its more personalized approach to customer demand to be the wave of the future and an important portion of its retail network, which is set to increase with 250 to 300 additional stores by 2015. Noted Tim Hershey, Nike's vice president and general manager of retail, "The difference here are the experiences. It is beyond just the product and the transaction. It is about how we can create relationships with the customer."

Sources: Rachel Brown, "New Nike Concept Focuses on Customer Interaction," *Women's Wear Daily*, August 12, 2010, p. 18; and "Niketown London Unveiled as the World's Largest Nike Store Following Striking New Redesign," press release, November 8, 2010.

QUESTIONS

1. From what you can tell by reading the case plus other information you know about Nike, how has each element of the company's microenvironment contributed to its development of the new stores and their innovative features?

2. What is the influence of the various components of the macroenvironment on the company's present situation?

3. Concerning current social attitudes and values, do you believe Nike is on the right track in its approach? Why or why not? What additional suggestions would you offer the company?

KEY TERMS

business cycle

buying power

computer-aided design (CAD)

computer-aided manufacturing (CAM)

computer-integrated manufacturing (CIM)

corporate social responsibility (CSR)

culture

demographics

discretionary income

disposable income

electronic data interchange (EDI)

macroenvironment

marketing environment

masstige marketing

microenvironment

public

Quick Response (QR)

social forces

World Trade Organization (WTO)

REVIEW QUESTIONS

1. Explain the importance of the global market-place to fashion marketers today.
2. Describe the elements of a fashion organization's microenvironment and their influence on its business.
3. Name the forces that are part of the macroenvironment, and explain the effects each has on a fashion marketer.

4. Explain the concept of corporate social responsibility (CSR) and cite an example of a fashion organization implementing a CSR program.
5. Construct a five-step plan for a fashion organization to follow in deciding whether to enter the global marketplace.

DISCUSSION ACTIVITIES AND PROJECTS

1. Consult the business news section of a local newspaper, the *Wall Street Journal*, or a fashion trade paper such as *Women's Wear Daily* to locate an article announcing the decision of a fashion business to enter an overseas market. From the article, try to determine why the company selected this particular location for its business. From your knowledge, what else indicates the suitability of that location for expanding the fashion business? Write a brief report on your findings and share it with the class.

2. In conducting an analysis of a fashion company's microenvironment, what are some of the things you would want to know about each of its elements? For each of the following elements of a company's microenvironment, write two questions that need to be answered in planning for global expansion: the company itself, its suppliers and intermediaries, its customers, its competitors, and key publics. Compare your questions with those of your classmates. What useful information would the answers yield about the company's microenvironment?

3. Look in your closet and among your personal effects and locate ten fashion items that were produced in another country. (Note: All apparel items must be labeled as to country of origin.) List each of the items and where it was made. Select one item and name all the macroenvironmental forces you can think of that might have facilitated (or hindered) that company's exporting to the United States.

4. Visit a social media site such as Facebook or Twitter. Locate a fashion marketing organization and explain how that organization responds to consumer inquiries. Prepare an oral report for your class describing how customers influence the types of communications that fashion marketers generate using social media.

5. Visit the Web site of a reputable fashion marketer such as Gap, Patagonia, or Nike, and determine how this organization is exercising CSR. Write your findings as a report that you will give on this evening's television news broadcast.

DEVELOPING YOUR MARKETING PLAN

Now you can start thinking about developing your own marketing plan. With your instructor's approval, select a real or imagined fashion product or company and begin your plans for it. To create a logical framework, you may use the Marketing Plan Outline, Table 1.2, provided in Chapter 1, as a guide.

For this first section of your marketing plan, you are working on an Analysis of the Marketing Environment. Based on your study of Chapter 2, write a few paragraphs on the marketing environments as they apply to your product or company. Be sure to consider the following topics:

▸ The elements that make up your product or company's microenvironment and how each influences your marketing goal

▸ The components of your product or company's macroenvironment and how they affect your marketing mix

▸ Ways that your product or company incorporates or reflects CSR

▸ How you envision your product or company's position in the global marketplace

By analyzing the marketing environments, you have started your own marketing plan. Share your work with your instructor and your classmates. You're off on a marketing discovery! Best wishes as you proceed with your plan.

REFERENCES

1. American Marketing Association, "Dictionary," http://www.marketingpower.com/_layouts/ Dictionary.aspx?dLetter=M (accessed August 16, 2011).

2. Ann Meyer, "For T-Shirt Company's Work Place: Loose Fits," *Chicago Tribune*, sec. 1, September 20, 2010, pp. 19, 21.

3. Gary Armstrong and Philip Kotler, *Marketing: An Introduction*, 10th ed. (Upper Saddle River, NJ: Pearson Prentice Hall, 2011), p. 69.

4. American Marketing Association, "Dictionary," http://www.marketingpower.com/_layouts/ Dictionary.aspx?dLetter=M (accessed August 16, 2011).

5. U.S. Census Bureau, International Data Base, "World Population: 1950–2050," http://www.census.gov/ipc/www/idb/worldpopgraph.php (accessed August 17, 2011).

6. U.S. Census Bureau, International Data Base, "Country Rankings," http://www.census.gov/ipc/www/idb/rank.php (accessed August 17, 2011).

7. Ibid.

8. Success-and-Culture.net, "Per Capita Income around the World," www.success-and-culture.net/articles/percapitaincome.shtml (accessed October 7, 2011).

9. American Marketing Association, "Dictionary," http://www.marketingpower.com/_layouts/Dictionary.aspx?dLetter=C (accessed August 16, 2011).

10. "Parents Angered by Abercrombie's New Swimsuit for Girls," WTAE.com, March 28, 2011, http://www.wtae.com/r/27343758/detail.html (accessed August 17, 2011).

11. Miles Socha, "A Bigger Crowd: In a Fashion Shift, Designers Go Masstige," Women's Wear Daily, October 5, 2010, pp. 1, 4.

12. Cate T. Corcoran, "Consumers Want It Now and Fashion World Adapts," Women's Wear Daily, September 15, 2010, pp. 1, 26; Michelle Dalton Tyree, "Burberry Spring/Summer 2011 Gets an Early Sales Boost through Limited iPad and Online Orders," Fashion Trends Daily, September 23, 2010, http://fashiontrendsdaily.com/spring-fashion-trends/burberry-springsummer-2011-gets-an-early-sales-boost-through-limited-ipad-and-online-orders (accessed August 17, 2011).

13. Cate T. Corcoran, "Consumers Want It Now and Fashion World Adapts," Women's Wear Daily, September 15, 2010, pp. 1, 26.

14. "Mobile Commerce Comes into Fashion," Women's Wear Daily, June 30, 2010, pp. 8, 9.

15. William M. Pride and O. C. Ferrell, Marketing, 14th ed. (Boston: Houghton Mifflin, 2008), p. 62.

16. U.S. Department of Commerce, "Income, Poverty, and Health Insurance Coverage in the United States: 2009," issued September 2010, http://www.census.gov/prod/2010pubs/p60-238.pdf (accessed August 16, 2011).

17. Kristi Ellis, "Omega Beats Costco: Court Upholds Copyright Law," Women's Wear Daily, December 14, 2010, pp. 1, 10.

18. Mary Hall, "Gap's Recycle Your Blues Campaign Returns: Donate Your Old Denim, Get 30% Off on New 1969 Blues," The Recessionista, October 4, 2010, http://therecessionista.blogspot.com/2010/10/gaps-recycle-your-blues-campaign.html (accessed August 17, 2011).

19. Liza Casabona, "Taking Social Responsibility to the Next Level," Women's Wear Daily, Textile and Trade Report, December 7, 2010, p. 10.

20. Marc Karimzadah, "Elie Tahari Raising Global Profile," Women's Wear Daily, September 15, 2010, p. 6.

Understanding Fashion Consumer and Business Buyer Behavior

This chapter explores the variety of internal and external factors that influence consumer behavior, and discusses how fashion marketers use knowledge of those factors to sway the purchasing decisions of consumers and business buyers.

WHAT DO I NEED TO KNOW ABOUT FASHION CONSUMER AND BUSINESS BUYER BEHAVIOR?

* The definition of the term "consumer behavior" and why interpreting it is of vital concern to fashion marketers

* How the level of a consumer's involvement with the purchase process relates to decision making and how fashion marketers address that challenge

* The effect of the buying situation and other external influences on fashion consumer behavior

* The range of internal influences on consumer behavior and how fashion marketers appeal to them

* What influences fashion business buyer behavior and some ways marketers target the trade

* How ethics and social responsibility relate to buyer behavior

Why Fashion Customers Buy

"People want to feel good about what they're acquiring, and we know this from being intimately in touch with our customers and shop owners," said Heather Perch, CEO of Nanette Lepore, an upscale New York fashion apparel organization, in an interview with *Women's Wear Daily.* Her remark strikes precisely the outcome fashion consumers seek when buying something new. And that feeling isn't limited to consumers alone. Businesses catering to fashion consumers also want to experience the positive feeling that comes from a lift in their sales (and profits) when they purchase successfully on behalf of their customers.

To attract and keep business, fashion marketers systematically reach out to customers, typically increasing this effort even more when business slows down. In an economic downturn, most stores tend to tout discounts to attract thrifty consumers. Many top-notch fashion marketers, however, actually double up on services to their customers—offering coffee or bottled water in the fitting rooms, hosting special events, and providing perks for their best customers in order to maintain loyalty. Some specialty stores hold favorite designer trunk shows, perhaps giving attendees small gifts, such as the sample bottle of nail polish that Rebecca Taylor customers received after the color had appeared in the designer's spring runway show. Efforts to influence consumer behavior occur early in the marketing of fashion. According to Abbey Samet of the fashion merchandising and consulting organization, the Doneger Group, "Designers should be in the stores, talking to as many customers as they can. That can only help business and strengthen a partnership between a designer and store owner."

Source: Julee Kaplan, "Designers Zero In on Shoppers' Needs," *Women's Wear Daily,* January 15, 2009, p. 9.

Businesses exist to fulfill customer needs. As you can tell from "Why Fashion Customers Buy," strengthening the partnership among designer, store owner, and consumer is an essential goal of marketing, that is, securing positive buying behavior. In fact, the focus of a successful marketing mix—product, place, price, promotion—is the customer because the purpose of marketing is to satisfy customer needs at a profit, thus creating goodwill and a win-win situation: The consumer is pleased with the purchase, and the company is able to grow its business. To reach that goal, fashion marketers need to know what influences consumer buying behavior.[1]

What Is Consumer Behavior and What Do Marketers Do about It?

Precisely what determines how consumers behave in the marketplace, and how do marketers influence consumer behavior? According to accepted definitions, **consumer behavior** consists of the decision-making processes and actions of buyers as

FIGURE 3.1 Marketers study consumer behavior in order to develop marketing strategies they hope will influence the behavior of their target customers.

they recognize their desire or need for a product or service, and engage in the search, evaluation, use, and disposal of a particular item.[2] Deciphering consumer behavior is complex and, today more than ever, a challenge. For example, today's consumers have diverse buying options. For one thing, instead of waiting to receive a sales approach, they initiate a product search themselves, obtaining information from periodicals or more likely from the Internet and often concluding the transaction electronically. Also, many consumers shop both ends of the price range: upscale at Prada for a billfold and downscale at Costco for socks. It takes marketing savvy to supply what the marketplace demands, and fashion marketers do this only when they understand what it is that customers want. By studying customer behavior and conducting market research (see Chapter 5), marketers learn how to target consumers more closely and determine more precisely what to provide.

This chapter covers consumer and customer behavior on two levels: first, the influences on the ultimate consumer or final user of a product, and second, the influences on professional fashion business buyers as they go about the business of obtaining goods for customers. The importance of the purchase, the effect of the buying situation, and some of the common external and personal influences on the purchasers of fashion goods are also covered.

FIGURE 3.2 The fashion industry introduces new looks every season, from two to five times a year.

FOCUSING THE MARKETING MIX ON THE CUSTOMER

Every consumer and every business buyer is unique, and what each seeks is constantly changing. Sometimes consumers know exactly what they want to buy, but many times they can't say what has led them to a certain purchase. It may be a desire to have an iPhone like the rest of the crowd. Or it may be a scarf that is too hard to resist on display in the store and thus becomes an **impulse item**, something purchased without previous thought. On occasion, it's just a replacement for a worn out pair of athletic shoes. To compound the many marketplace offerings, manufacturers introduce new products regularly and systematically. The automobile industry brings out its latest models once a year, as do many electronics manufacturers; fashion businesses such as the garment industry may offer new products every season, sometimes two to five times a year.

Consumers who are thinking about making an important purchase, then, are actually attempting to solve a problem. The process they use to resolve the problem becomes the basis for consumer behavior. For these combined reasons, fashion marketers need to possess a keen sense of what customers will want next.

It is here that marketing research becomes indispensable. Through research, marketers seek out individuals with similar characteristics who would tend to be their best customers, that is, the best target markets for their particular goods and services. They then coordinate and focus each element of the marketing mix—product, place, price, and promotion—on meeting the needs of those customers. By coordinating the marketing mix, fashion marketers create a unified impact on target customers. Keep in mind, however, that the marketing mix is most productive only when marketers understand what goes into buyer behavior and how to influence it. This section describes how companies gear elements of the marketing mix to specific target consumers.

Product

People buy goods and services because they need or want them. The reasons may be many, for instance, physiological (new automobile tires for safe driving) or psychological (text messaging capabilities to connect with friends). Marketers study consumer behavior in order to satisfy customer desires.[3] For example, fashion retailer Saks Fifth Avenue was one of the first upscale American specialty businesses to open stores in the Middle Eastern city of Dubai, a center for a significant number of wealthy, fashion-conscious customers. Already successful in Riyadh, Saudi Arabia, Saks' management knew that United Arab Emirates customers would recognize and want the European brands the retailer offers (Chanel, Dolce & Gabbana, Hermès, and more) and would patronize the new locations.[4]

To delve more deeply into meeting consumer product desires, marketers create personalities for their products, in a process known as **branding**, carefully building and matching the personality of the product to the characteristics of a specific target market. For example, Levi Strauss describes its 501 button fly jeans as strong, resourceful, independent, and sexually attractive, just the thing for men everywhere who seek to portray that image.[5] For more information on branding, see Chapter 7.

Place

Where customers buy is important to marketers in order to have goods available. For customers frequenting retail stores, maintaining an appealing environment is basic to a store's success; customers are drawn to intriguing merchandise displays and attractive merchandise assortments. To build on its physical accessibility to customers, the Swedish fast-fashion retailer Hennes and Mauritz (H&M) decided to expand its stores even when the world was experiencing an economic downturn. Bucking the global trend, H&M's sales went up, and its management realized that it could grow because fashion customers in many underserved markets relate to its trendy, reasonably priced goods.[6]

FIGURE 3.3 Television has the advantage of showing products in action, such as these outfits and accessories being modeled on a QVC program.

In addition to retail stores, marketers offer a variety of ways for consumers to buy new fashions, such as by phone, through catalogues, and increasingly over the Internet. And let's not forget television. During a recent Mercedes-Benz fashion week held in New York for fashion businesses, editors, buyers, and other related organizations, QVC held a two-hour TV selling program for consumers based on garments selected from the runway, creating a "runway to reality." This meant that spring merchandise could arrive in consumers' homes in a few days, and fall merchandise months before reaching the stores.[7]

Another example of offering consumers merchandise in the right place is the Las Vegas-based retailer Zappos. Maintaining a strictly virtual presence on the Web, Zappos' tremendous growth and success reflects consumers' increasing comfort with online shopping. Many brick-and-mortar stores such as Nordstrom, JCPenney, Victoria's Secret, and others have added e-commerce Web sites as another sales avenue along with their physical stores and catalogues—while further supplementing their exposure to consumers via print and online advertising and social media marketing including blogs and Facebook.

Price

Knowing how customers view price is essential to marketers as they develop pricing plans. When times are slow, many businesses lower prices to meet customer needs, yet others find ways to show their prices in a positive light. McDonald's, world leader in fast-food trends and an expert in keeping up with changing tastes (drive-through breakfasts for commuters in a hurry; salads for calorie counters) uses price to reach budget-conscious consumers. One way is by selling lattes and similar sophisticated beverages at a lower price than competitors. More than that, the company emphasizes its traditionally low-cost meals, and in a slow economy is able to boost sales, which enabled it to open 1,000 new outlets in 2009.[8]

Promotion

In order to make the best decisions on how to promote, marketers need to know the media and promotional vehicles that customers prefer. When Macy's took over a number of stores throughout the country in order to consolidate as a nationwide department store, it changed the names of some long-established regional retailers (such as Marshall Field's, Dayton's, and J. L. Hudson), distressing those stores' loyal customers. Nor was Macy's as familiar with local shopping habits as it might have been. In the Midwest, it seems that customers follow newspaper advertising and specifically look for and use the store coupons they contain. This practice wasn't nearly as common in the East, and it took a while for Macy's to catch on to the coupon practice, but when it did, coupons began appearing regularly as promotions in local papers. More recently, reaching out to local markets in certain parts of the country, Macy's set up a "My Macy's" campaign focusing on particular target customers. The campaign emphasis is to offer specific products and promotions geared to local tastes.[9]

FIGURE 3.4 Gwyneth Paltrow appeared in a series of ads for Tod's, an exclusive handbag line.

One way that marketers appeal to fashion consumers, particularly young and middle-aged, is through celebrity endorsements. Seeing a celebrity promoting a product or idea can give a viewer the feeling that he or she may become a little like that person by purchasing that product. Celebrities work under contract with fashion marketers in many price ranges. Examples include Madonna for Miu Miu, Victoria Beckham for Emporio Armani, LL Cool J for Sears, and Ellen DeGeneres for Olay.[10]

Analyzing customers even more closely, Paco Underhill, consumer behavior author and head of the consulting firm Envirosell, says that many times customers do not make up their minds to buy until they are in the store. For that reason, he calls for store signs that are clear, are strategically placed, and can be read by customers in 15 seconds, about 30 words maximum.[11] These and other promotional efforts are executed to attract target customers.

When all four elements of the marketing mix are planned, coordinated, and targeted, and a marketing organization has continuous sharing of ideas and strategies to reach customers, the result becomes an **integrated marketing system (IMS)**. Tied in with customer and employee feedback, IMS can lead to the highest levels of customer satisfaction.[12]

HOW MUCH DOES THE CUSTOMER CARE? THE BUYER'S LEVEL OF INVOLVEMENT

The amount of effort a customer wants to put into buying a product has a direct effect on the buying process the customer will go through, and therefore on the strategy a company selects to market that product. The level of a customer's interest in the process of buying a product as seen in that person's need for the product is known as **purchase involvement** and is temporary, ending with the purchase decision and evaluation. Purchase involvement differs from product involvement, which can be long-term ("Susie's mother wore Chanel No. 5 all of her adult life," or "The only soda Jeff will drink is Coca-Cola.")

As you can tell from Figure 3.5, the purchase decision-making process occurs as a continuum, with consumers' involvement with the purchase process ranging from a low level of involvement to a very high one.[13] A customer selecting a product such as shampoo, toothpaste, or a favorite lotion without seeming to think about it is engaged in a **routine problem-solving** process. Routine problem solving is often accompanied by the consumer's *low involvement* in the process itself, although the product sought—shampoo—may be one the customer insists on, that is, a high involvement product for that particular consumer who believes, say, "No other shampoo makes my hair so soft and silky." Often, low involvement purchase situations mean that the customer automatically selects a favorite brand, looking to repeat the successful performance of the previous choice. ("Neutrogena lotion works well for me," or "Everybody liked those M&Ms in fashion colors; let's get some more.")

A somewhat more complex purchase situation leads a consumer to consider a new brand ("I'm tired of my old jeans; I think I'll try 7 For All Mankind or maybe Lucky."); look for the least expensive ("Let's see what Walmart has in T shirts."); or perhaps find something to please a friend ("Ron might like a subscription to *GQ*."). These buying situations that

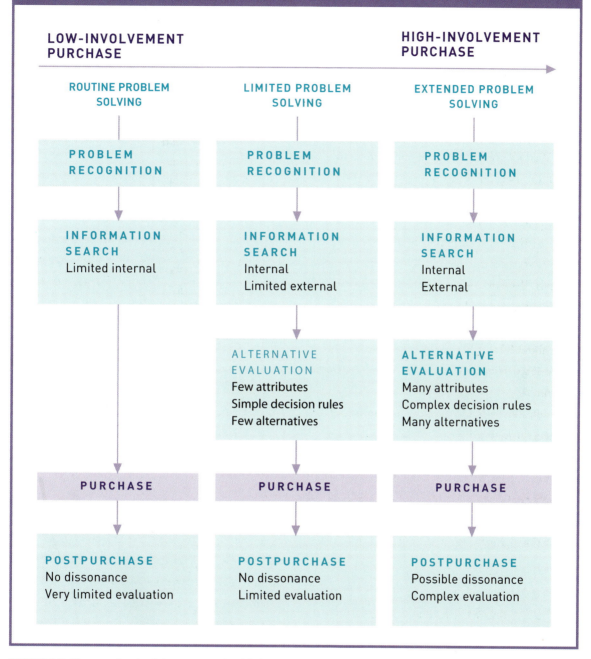

LEVELS OF CONSUMER INVOLVEMENT

LOW-INVOLVEMENT PURCHASE → **HIGH-INVOLVEMENT PURCHASE**

ROUTINE PROBLEM SOLVING

PROBLEM RECOGNITION

INFORMATION SEARCH
Limited internal

PURCHASE

POSTPURCHASE
No dissonance
Very limited evaluation

LIMITED PROBLEM SOLVING

PROBLEM RECOGNITION

INFORMATION SEARCH
Internal
Limited external

ALTERNATIVE EVALUATION
Few attributes
Simple decision rules
Few alternatives

PURCHASE

POSTPURCHASE
No dissonance
Limited evaluation

EXTENDED PROBLEM SOLVING

PROBLEM RECOGNITION

INFORMATION SEARCH
Internal
External

ALTERNATIVE EVALUATION
Many attributes
Complex decision rules
Many alternatives

PURCHASE

POSTPURCHASE
Possible dissonance
Complex evaluation

FIGURE 3.5 The more involved the customer is with the purchase, the more complex the decision-making process.
BY VANESSA HAN AND ALICIA FREILE

call for some additional consideration fall into the **limited problem-solving** purchase involvement category.[14] Perhaps a college student is looking for a jacket and searches the Web sites of Abercrombie, L.L.Bean, and Columbia to evaluate styles and prices. Then he recalls what a friend said about his own North Face jacket. Searching externally and reflecting internally are frequently part of limited decision making involvement.

When heavy-duty purchasing occurs, such as buying a car, finding an apartment, or choosing a college, most people engage in a lengthy and thorough or **extended problem-solving** process, seeking in-depth information, carefully weighing alternatives, reaching a decision, and evaluating the choice. Usually a high-involvement purchase situation involves a product that is expensive, has deep meaning to the buyer, or might somehow indicate one's social image.[15] Students selecting a college may visit several, learn about the programs each offers, consider the appropriateness of each one as it relates to their goals, select one college that seems to best suit their needs, and after settling in and attending classes, evaluate the outcome of that choice.

IMPLICATIONS FOR FASHION MARKETERS

A consumer's level of involvement with the purchase process and with the product each influence a company's marketing mix. Consider a couple planning to furnish a new home and deciding to work with an interior designer—a high-involvement purchase situation that can encompass a number of high-involvement products. The designer will learn as much as possible about the couple's tastes and lifestyles, and then will select colors, fabrics, furniture, and installations (product) specifically for them. The designer gives them detailed information, written descriptions, brochures, and even videos about the characteristics of recommended paints, fabrics, and flooring (promotion). The clients are then equipped to reach a decision after studying each suggestion as it relates to their particular needs (product, place, and price).

In contrast, low-involvement purchase situations mean that a consumer usually reaches a decision in a very short time, perhaps only after going to the store, as Paco Underhill described earlier. Stores can help prompt swift consumer decision making by providing convenient departments, prominently placed signage, and appealing displays with clearly labeled products, frequently accompanied by advertising and perhaps coupons or other price promotions, all backed by the manufacturer. These tactics make it easy for consumers to identify and select products quickly, essential factors in a low-involvement purchase situation.

WHAT DO YOU THINK?

Recall a product you obtained requiring a high level of purchase involvement, perhaps a winter coat, electronics such as a television, or an apartment. What strategies and/or tactics did the marketer use to engage your interest? When you buy a low-involvement product, such as a basic sweater or shampoo, how do marketers gain your attention?

THE BUYER'S DECISION-MAKING PROCESS

Consumers may have many reasons for buying. Some remain mysterious both to themselves and to marketers, but others are obvious. When buyers go through a rational decision-making process, consciously or unconsciously they follow a sequence of steps that remains constant. These are *recognizing a problem*, *seeking information*, *weighing alternatives*, *making a decision*, and *evaluating that decision*. As you can tell from Figure 3.6, many influences—including the marketing mix, social-cultural and personal influences, plus the buying situation itself—come into play as customers work toward purchase decisions. Let's look at each step of the decision-making process as it occurs to consumers.

Recognizing a Problem

Deciding what to buy is a problem-solving process that arises from a discomfort, that is, a feeling that something is lacking and that a purchase will restore a state of comfort. The need to purchase can show itself in many forms. Perhaps your cousin lost a glove and is looking for a replacement pair. Or, a friend may be attending a formal event and needs to buy or rent an outfit. Possibly you're starting a new job and want the right clothes to fit in with the organization. Fashion marketers anticipate these and other needs and promote their offerings to solve those buying problems. For example, skin care marketers know that in harsh climates, men as well as women look for a soothing way to treat their skin. The Old Spice ad in Figure 3.7 promotes a possible solution to this problem.

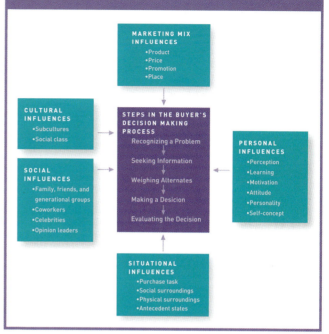

FIGURE 3.6 As consumers work toward a buying decision, they are subject to a number of influences, including the marketing mix, social and psychological influences, plus the buying situation itself. BY VANESSA HAN AND ALICIA FREILE

Seeking Information

Once consumers recognize a problem or need, they begin to seek out information about a solution. Suppose your cell phone is getting old and you want a new one that will have the features you use most but also be good-looking. You search *internally*, recalling the features of various cell phones with which you are familiar; then, you look *externally*, to friends and family, the ads or Web sites of various manufacturers, brochures highlighting different phones' functions and appearance, salespeople, and product demonstrations.

Weighing Alternatives

After collecting information from internal and external sources, you determine which phone has the best features for your purposes, is most user-friendly, and fits within your budget.

Making a Decision

At this point, you arrive at a decision. Do you want to be easy on your budget and go for the lowest price? Is there a special feature such as a built-in camera or Internet access that you must have? Maybe you want a BlackBerry to show your high-tech prowess to your friends, or because your work or lifestyle requires its capabilities. Or you may decide that your present phone is good enough for now, and so you defer your purchase.

Evaluating the Decision

Even after making a decision, consumers often continue to weigh the positive and negative factors of their choice. You may realize that you wouldn't really use many of the features on the new cell phone you were considering, and you may be quite pleased with your decision not to buy. Or you may have gone ahead and selected a cell phone that lets you contact friends by text and e-mail even when you take a trip abroad, and you find that feature a worthwhile reward for the expense. Whatever your purchase decision, the marketer keeps you informed about the attributes and features of the product, giving you information that you can process as you evaluate your purchase decision. In some cases, you may not be satisfied with your purchase and sense a feeling of discomfort, known as **cognitive dissonance**, which can occur when reevaluating the features of the product you bought. Suppose you really wanted a full keyboard for texting, a feature your new phone does not have, and now you are disappointed in your choice. Cognitive dissonance, also called *buyer's remorse*, is a common occurrence, and marketers handle it with reassuring information, in this case, perhaps a reminder of the features your new phone does possess. Fashion salespeople at Nordstrom deal with potential cognitive dissonance by sending customers handwritten notes assuring them of the good feelings they will experience from owning the new outfit, shoes, or jewelry they just purchased.

FIGURE 3.7 Deciding what to buy is a problem-solving process arising from a discomfort due to the consumer's sense of lacking something. Marketers know this and present solutions they hope will appeal to their target customers.

MARKETER'S INSIGHT:
WHAT DO PURCHASES SAY ABOUT US—AND WHO CARES?

Melissa emerged from the store triumphant. "I just had to have those designer earrings," she exclaimed to her friend Carla. "They are absolutely awesome and will look fabulous with my new outfit!" Some consumer researchers studying Melissa's buying behavior might just chalk up the earring purchase decision to the product's emotional appeal. Geoffrey Miller, an evolutionary psychologist at the University of New Mexico, however, believes that marketers could delve much deeper into consumer decision making by focusing on consumer intelligence and traits. According to Dr. Miller's theory, Melissa's statement probably could be translated into "the style of those earrings will show that I recognize and can afford the newest looks, and the fact that they complement my latest outfit will indicate that I'm a fashion leader."

The theory behind Dr. Miller's view is that the good feelings we gain from our purchases are based on the beliefs that they indicate to others our competence and suitability by revealing our intelligence, and some of what he terms are our major personality traits. The five traits are openness (to new ideas, people, products), conscientiousness (diligence), agreeableness, stability, and extroversion.

The results of some experiments revealed that at the end of the session, the consumers studied were open to spending more money. For example, after a group of men had been shown some pictures of women or told stories about dating, they were willing to consider indulging in purchases of higher-priced items such as designer sunglasses and watches. Possibly interest in these upscale items could be attributed to an appeal to each participant's traits such as openness, agreeableness, and extroversion.

And, according to the research, after various prestige items are acquired, how useful are they to their owners? Not very, according to Dr. Miller, because the basic flaw in consumer thinking, he maintains, is that what we buy influences how others treat us. (Think of how many people—teens in particular—buy brand-name products intending to impress others.) Therefore, according to Dr. Miller's research, appealing to an individual's self-centeredness as revealed through his or her traits can be an effective (though admittedly manipulative) way of reaching certain groups of consumers.

WHAT'S YOUR POINT OF VIEW?

1. What purchases has someone you know made that could be attributed in part to that person's desire to impress other people? By purchasing a particular item, what would seem to be the exact message that its owner wants to convey?

2. What fashion goods have you purchased with the intent of enjoying them yourself and possibly impressing others? Explain which one or two of the five traits mentioned could have played a part in your purchase decision. How useful is that purchase to you today?

Adapted from: Geoffrey Miller, *Spent: Sex, Evolution, and Consumer Behavior*. New York: Penguin Group, 2009; John Tierney, "Message in What We Buy, But Nobody's Listening," *New York Times*, May 18, 2009, D1 and D4.

When you shopped most recently for a significant fashion reason, perhaps to purchase an outfit for a job interview or formal social event, describe the decision-making process you went through as you determined whether or not you were going to buy the item you chose. How did the marketer attempt to influence your decision making? Was that influence successful? Why or why not?

The Buying Situation

The buying situation can have an effect on consumer purchase behavior, enhancing, detracting, or negating the buying process. Fashion marketers are aware of these influences and do what they can to make them positive. According to marketing experts, situational influences exist in five categories: the purchase task, social surroundings, physical surroundings, time constraints, and antecedent states. [16, 17]

The purchase task influences are different when you are choosing a grill for yourself than when you are choosing one for your cousin's wedding present. Fashion marketers reinforce the benefits of the product, reassuring you that the one for you is functional and practical, whereas your cousin's has the latest features and is worth the additional cost. Many people enjoy the social experience of shopping with others, for their company, for their opinions, or both. Trained salespeople know how to appeal to customers and those with them. Physical surroundings can make a shopping trip pleasant or the opposite. Upscale fashion merchants create attractive merchandise displays, clear lighting, wide aisles, well-planned assortments, and attentive staff to assist customers in buying. Fashion marketers in a bargain atmosphere build excitement through bright signs, overflowing racks, and goods piled on tables, encouraging customers to dig hands-on into the merchandise.

Time has an influence on consumers, too. Catalogues and the Internet provide shopping opportunities 24/7, allowing customers to browse for as long or as short a time as they wish. In stores, customers appreciate it when they can check out quickly if they're in a hurry or perhaps browse at their leisure if they prefer. Antecedent states include influences on the customer's mood when shopping. Perhaps it's been a long day, the customer is tired, and he wants to finish an errand quickly and get home. Or perhaps the customer has just gotten good news of a promotion at work and is eager to treat herself to something special. These conditions, while temporary, have an effect on the amount of information searching, weighing of alternatives, and decision making a customer feels like undertaking on a shopping trip.

Fashion marketers are aware of the pressures inherent in the shopping situation and create a marketing mix designed to lead to a successful purchasing experience.

Cultural Influences

Culture, as defined in Chapter 2, is perhaps one of the most significant elements influencing fashion buying decisions. We are all immersed in our culture, which includes the shared beliefs, values, and traditions learned and practiced by people who may live close to each other and who have a common quest.[18] As Americans, our culture shares many values. Some of these include freedom; youth; the right to choose one's own goals, and the right to keep the rewards of hard work; materialism and the right to own goods such as fashionable apparel, automobiles, and homes; and independence, or the right to change our minds and move in a new direction. Not all cultures have similar values. For example, some Asian cultures hold that the group is more important than the individual, and that the common welfare takes precedence over the rights of the individual. In order to live harmoniously in a given culture, members react to the influences of that culture on their buying behavior. As one example, notice how the ad for Lucky Brand jeans depicted in Figure 3.8 appeals to the American devotion to youth.

SUBCULTURES

Within each culture are many subcultures. These may be based on race or ethnicity, religion, occupation, intellectual, political, philanthropic, or leisure interests.

FIGURE 3.8 The breezy casual look in this advertisement illustrates American society's absorption with youth culture and staying young.

A **subculture** is a smaller group within a large society/culture (such as persons of the same age, political ideology, ethnicity, social class, sexual orientation) who possess distinct beliefs, goals, interests, and values that differentiate them from the dominant culture.[19] Hispanic Americans are a subculture, as are mountain skiers, jazz musicians, NASCAR devotees, serious Barbie doll collectors (some of whom are older than Barbie herself, who was "born" March 9, 1959), and many others.

The largest subcultures in the United States are based on race and ethnicity, accounting for the great diversity in the country's population. Projections for 2050 estimate that Caucasians will number 203 million, or 46 percent of the population; Hispanics, 132 million, or 30 percent of the population; African Americans, 65 million, or 15 percent of the population; and Asians, 41 million, or 9 percent of the population.[20]

Each subculture has its own values and shared beliefs, although the groups are not necessarily homogeneous. For example, Hispanics may trace their origins to Mexico, Central and South America, Cuba, or Puerto Rico, and while each of those regions has its own customs, some buying patterns are similar. Hispanics are young, with an average age of 28, versus the average age of the U. S. population as a whole of 36. Hispanics tend to be concerned with how they look, are fashion-aware, catch on easily to a trend, spend more time in stores than African Americans and Caucasians, and are more likely to shop online. Bright colors are a favorite, as are lace and beads. They seek out all price ranges and patronize Hispanic designers such as Carolina Herrera, Narciso Rodriguez, Daisy Fuentes, and Louis Verdad.[21]

African Americans have been called the most fashion-conscious racial group. Concerned with fashion trends, they spend more than other groups on apparel and personal care items. They look for quality and for the best value at the price. African Americans are brand-loyal, seeing designer brands as status symbols, indications of success. As a group, they are young, heavy consumers of media, particularly television and magazines such as *Ebony, Jet, Essence,* and *O*.[22] They also tend to recall advertising more often than other ethnic groups.[23] African-American designers such as Sean John Combs and Beyoncé have a large following, and the fashion influence of First Lady Michelle Obama (who shops a range of price lines including Thuyskens and J.Crew) is followed by many Americans.

Asian Americans are of diverse backgrounds, coming from Japan, Taiwan, the Philippines, Vietnam, and India, among other places. Each of these countries has its own traditions and customs that account in part for the diverse shopping preferences of this subculture. Some Asians (those with money) prefer designer apparel and accessories bearing names such as Gucci, Louis Vuitton, and Rolex, while others (with or without money) are frugal and spend more modestly. According to research done by a California mall, these Asians, such as those from the Philippines, are fashion conscious but also sensitive to price and will shop stores such as Uniqlo, Zara, and H&M, which offer trendy items at low prices. Many affluent Asians, including those from China and Japan, tend to shop at upscale stores such as Nordstrom and Guess.[24]

Marketers study subcultures in order to be able to market effectively to these groups, many of which

FIGURE 3.9 Fashion marketers group target consumers by subculture to address similar product and purchase preferences, and often try to appeal to more than one group.

represent significant buying power. As you can tell from the Totes ad (Figure 3.9), the retailer is looking to appeal to a culturally diverse target market.

Consumers worldwide have diverse tastes and wants, often stemming from the values within their distinct cultures. For example, the growing ranks of consumers in India, largely women, do not have wide access to credit cards, thus hindering their purchase of big-ticket items. In China, the most influential group of consumers tends to be under age 40, female, and with voracious appetites for travel, beauty products, and apparel.[25] It is up to the fashion marketers serving each market to accurately discern the fashion interests of their target customers and to provide the goods and services these consumers seek.

SOCIAL CLASS

Although many Americans like to think of the country as a classless society, that is not really the case. Most experts define **social class** as groups of individuals belonging to different levels of society.[26] The groups are hierarchical and are often based on income, education, occupation, and accumulated wealth. The members within each class tend to maintain similar interests and values, and—of particular use to marketers—similar behaviors. Unlike some European and Asian countries, membership in a particular social class in the United States need not be permanent; people may move upward or downward, and in times of prosperity, many families have moved to a higher level, while economic hardships may send others in a different direction.

The Chart of Social Class (Figure 3.10) shows four major hierarchical segments, each divided into two parts. The upper class consists of those who have inherited wealth and those who have high (sometimes excessively high) incomes, such as the chief executives of large corporations. This group also includes the *nouveau riche,* or those whose wealth has been accumulated more recently, often within the current generation. Fashion marketers have learned that the old money class tends to conserve, using what it has but (when the occasion arises) purchasing high quality. The more newly rich are avid collectors of high-status items: unique and expensive automobiles, art, and

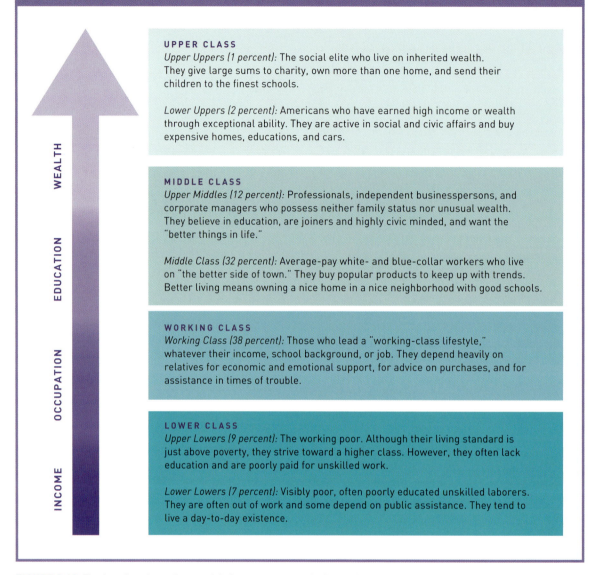

SOCIAL CLASS MEMBERSHIP

WEALTH · EDUCATION · OCCUPATION · INCOME

UPPER CLASS
Upper Uppers (1 percent): The social elite who live on inherited wealth. They give large sums to charity, own more than one home, and send their children to the finest schools.

Lower Uppers (2 percent): Americans who have earned high income or wealth through exceptional ability. They are active in social and civic affairs and buy expensive homes, educations, and cars.

MIDDLE CLASS
Upper Middles (12 percent): Professionals, independent businesspersons, and corporate managers who possess neither family status nor unusual wealth. They believe in education, are joiners and highly civic minded, and want the "better things in life."

Middle Class (32 percent): Average-pay white- and blue-collar workers who live on "the better side of town." They buy popular products to keep up with trends. Better living means owning a nice home in a nice neighborhood with good schools.

WORKING CLASS
Working Class (38 percent): Those who lead a "working-class lifestyle," whatever their income, school background, or job. They depend heavily on relatives for economic and emotional support, for advice on purchases, and for assistance in times of trouble.

LOWER CLASS
Upper Lowers (9 percent): The working poor. Although their living standard is just above poverty, they strive toward a higher class. However, they often lack education and are poorly paid for unskilled work.

Lower Lowers (7 percent): Visibly poor, often poorly educated unskilled laborers. They are often out of work and some depend on public assistance. They tend to live a day-to-day existence.

FIGURE 3.10 The fact that the various social classes are more similar in the ways they spend their leisure time and money as opposed to the size of their incomes is key to fashion marketers in planning strategy. BY VANESSA HAN AND ALICIA FREILE

designer fashions. Fashion marketers such as name interior and fashion designers, the media, and socialites have an influence on the fashion choices of this group. When Gucci, Tod's, or Hermès offer a new handbag design, affluent fashionistas want to be the first to own it. The upper middle class also has expensive tastes, buying high-quality apparel, home furnishings, and vacations. Their buying behavior may emulate that of fashion innovators from the upper classes. Fashion followers from the middle class seek recognizable, dependable brands and so are targeted by established fashion brands such as Tommy Hilfiger, Jones New York, Clinique, Ethan Allen, KitchenAid, and Chevrolet. Consumers in the working class buy goods that are serviceable and of good value for the money, and patronize retailers such as Kohl's and Walmart, and moderately priced fashion chains such as Forever 21, Dress Barn, and Claire's. Retailers reach these customers through mailers, newspaper ads, the Internet, and television. In England, members of the working class tend to attain their peak earnings early in their lives, doubtless influencing the timing of their purchases of clothing and accessories.[27] Social classes are alike in the ways they spend their money as opposed to the amount of money they possess. Because social classes each tend to have similar buying behaviors, segmenting markets by class provides direction to fashion businesses on how to create, price, promote, and place their products to reach these specific target groups.

FIGURE 3.11 In choosing a vacation destination, consumers are often influenced by the social groups to which they belong.

Social Influences

Social class is a rather arbitrary division of society; other groups, some of which are more voluntary, can influence buying behavior also. "Consumers are social creatures, who form groups and interact in relation to social goals," states fashion marketing professor Mike Easey. People belong to groups for a number of reasons: to meet social needs, to check attitudes, and to protect themselves. Belonging to a group has a price: A member must generally conform to **social norms,** that is, the group's expectations of behavior.[28] Among

the groups that often influence fashion consumer behavior are family, friends, co-workers, celebrities, and opinion leaders.

FAMILY

From the beginning, the core influence on consumer behavior stems from the family. Parents select fashion goods such as apparel, room furnishings, and toys for their offspring. More and more, however, children are making their own buying decisions at an early age, and marketers are encouraging buying curiosity. Television ads and colorful in-store merchandise displays attract and acquaint even the youngest with brand names such as Disney and Nike. Family guidance sets the realistic boundaries of what is appropriate and affordable.

FRIENDS AND REFERENCE GROUPS

Individually and in social groups, friends have an influence on buying behavior. Some consumers prefer the company and advice of others when they buy. Others want to look as though they belong to a certain group (based on age, gender, income, and/or other demographics) and so follow

FIGURE 3.12 American Express has built a high-status reputation for its charge cards and related services, making them appealing to consumers seeking the approval of their peers.

its norms in their fashion purchases. Fashion advertisers often proclaim the appropriateness of the goods and services they provide to a targeted group, as you can tell from the American Express message in Figure 3.12.

Co-Workers

Fitting into the work environment is a requisite, and appearance is a primary indicator. The environment, such as a fast-food restaurant or beauty salon, may require a uniform or it may leave fashion choices up to the individual. In such cases, determining the norms by observing what others are wearing is the first step. (Think of Andrea in *The Devil Wears Prada* and how her look transformed after a few weeks at *Runway* magazine.)

Celebrities

Many fashion followers are influenced by their favorite celebrities. Scouring the Internet, television, and fashion magazines to see how their favorite celebrities look and what they are wearing each season becomes a source of new fashion inspiration. And if their favorite happens to have his or her own fashion line (think Jennifer Lopez, Victoria Beckham, and Jay-Z), the opportunity to emulate that person's fashion choices in apparel, accessories, and fragrances becomes a reality.

Opinion Leaders

In reaching a buying decision, many people seek out the advice of opinion leaders. You may want a new outfit to wear to a club, and so you leaf through the pages of your favorite fashion magazine. A friend may plan on decorating her apartment but is hesitant to choose colors and fabrics herself, and so consults with a store's interior designer. Opinion leaders have specific areas of expertise. The tennis pro might know precisely the best racquet for your game but probably wouldn't be up on the latest looks in tennis apparel from Stella McCartney. Fashion marketers want to move goods from the producer to consumer, and so work to inform opinion leaders, as you saw in the chapter's opening vignette.

WHAT DO YOU THINK?

Think of a fashion purchase that you made largely due to the influence of your family, friends, or of celebrities. What was the effect of these influencers on your final purchase decision? If you bought the product, did it meet your expectations? Why or why not?

Personal Influences

In addition to the extent of a consumer's involvement with the product, the influences of the buying situation, the culture, the external influences of family, friends, and other groups and individuals, internal influences are at work on each of us as we deal with buying decisions. Internal influences are personal; that is, the strength of each of these influences is different for each of us. Internal or personal influences include how we perceive and learn, what motivates us, our attitudes toward products, our individual self-concepts and personalities, and our lifestyles.

PERCEPTION

Perception reaches us though our senses (vision, hearing, touch, taste, and smell). A stimulus must reach our senses in order for us to perceive and react. Notice some of the ways that fashion businesses stimulate our senses: brightly colored full-page ads in fashion magazines; cheery television commercials depicting models wearing the latest looks in jeans and casual wear while dancing at a club; furniture displayed in room settings at a store, encouraging shoppers to touch the surfaces and sit on the chairs. In a grocery store, an employee offers a sample of the newest cheese dip or salsa; standing at a cosmetics counter, a salesperson provides you with a paper wand containing the most recent designer fragrance, enabling you to see how the scent releases its various fragrance notes over time. These are all examples of ways fashion marketers reach out to influence consumer perception.

LEARNING

There are two main ways we learn: conditioning and cognitive learning. Fashion marketers use techniques from both of these to influence our consumer behavior. Conditioning theory states that we learn through repeated exposure; hence, the many, many repeats of television commercials that we're subjected to, or the same Ralph Lauren or Juicy Couture fashion ad displayed in four different fashion magazines the same month. Conditioning theory also tells us that we will react positively when presented a reward. This is one of the reasons cosmetics manufacturers such as Clinique, Lancôme, and others periodically offer gifts with a purchase. The purpose of the gift is to create good will and encourage consumers to buy the product. Cognitive learning is based on problem solving, as we saw earlier in the chapter. Fashion marketers appeal to cognitive learning by fully describing the features of a product, such as a shirt's fiber content and characteristics, care, and appropriateness. For example, a salesman working with a client purchasing a Hickey Freeman suit will note that the fabric is a comfortable-weight Italian silk and wool blend, the construction features durable and elegant hand-sewn details, and the tailoring is impeccable and timeless.

MOTIVATION

Individuals are motivated in different degrees. Some buying needs are emotional: A customer sees a high-definition 3D television and it becomes a "must-have." Some buying needs are rational: Worn brakes on an automobile must be replaced. For far too many people in the world, the act of survival is the main motivator. Half of the world's population lives on less than two dollars a day, and their motivation centers on finding enough to eat and a safe place to live. Those people who are fortunate enough to have some discretionary spending power are the targets of fashion marketers. These consumers are motivated to buy fashion goods for a number of reasons: wanting to belong to a group and buying fashions to fit in (appropriate apparel for work); wanting to find a fashion item for a loved one (an engagement ring); or wanting to impress others (through their Louis Vuitton handbag, Movado watch, or new Camaro). Still others seek to maximize their potential by selecting the most effective musical instruments or sports equipment. Marketers study these human motivations and create messages to influence specific behavior.

FIGURE 3.13 In buying a new Camaro, would you say a customer's motivation is more emotional or rational?

ATTITUDE

Attitudes indicate what we feel and believe about something, in this case, fashion goods and services. Three parts make up our attitudes: the *affective*, that is, how we feel about something such as a fashion item; the *cognitive*, what we know or believe about it; and the *behavioral*, how we act toward the product, that is, whether we buy it or not. Obviously, fashion marketers want their target customers to like and want their products, so they showcase them through promotions such as apparel runway and trunk shows. They want target customers to be as informed as possible about their goods, so they train salespeople, print brochures, enlarge their Web site, and create labels or packaging describing the characteristics and performance of their latest cell phones, laptops, kitchen appliances, automobiles, and other designed products. The purpose is to help consumers acquire knowledge and form positive feelings about their products, which in turn can influence consumers' behavior and lead them to buy the products.

PERSONALITY AND SELF-CONCEPT

Personality consists of the psychological characteristics that influence the way people react to their surroundings.[29] Closely related to personality is one's self-concept, that is, how an individual feels about him or herself. Actually, each person is made up of **multiple selves** because of his or her various roles in life.[30] Think about yourself; you are a student, a son or daughter, perhaps a sibling and/or a cousin, a niece or nephew, an employee, and

FIGURE 3.14 The message in this ad indicates to consumers the advertiser's way for them to achieve their ideal—complexion, at least.

possibly a parent. All of these selves react differently when you are a fashion goods consumer. One aspect of self-concept is concerned with self-esteem, that is, our positive and negative views of ourselves and our estimates of self-worth.[31] Fashion marketers are particularly adept at persuading us that by purchasing certain fashion goods we will come closer to an ideal version of ourselves. Note Figure 3.14, the Estée Lauder ad claiming outright that its product leads toward the ideal self.

Each of our personalities contains certain **traits**, distinct characteristics (such as agreeableness or extroversion) that differentiate us from others and contribute to our behavior. Although researchers tend to pay only passing attention to traits and consumer behavior, a new theory offers some deeper explanations as to the usefulness of trait study to marketers. For more information, see the Marketer's Insight feature, "What Do Purchases Say About Us—and Who Cares," on page 77.

Through appeals to fashion buyers based on how important the product is to them, the buying situation, cultures and subcultures, external influences such as family and various groups, and personal perceptions, learning, motivation, attitudes, and personality, fashion marketers work to present a positive and convincing influence on buyer behavior.

Read the Fashion Marketing in Focus feature, "What Do Foreign Consumers Like to Buy When Visiting the United States?," to see how foreign consumers choose U.S. products when traveling in the States, and then consider the questions that follow, including selecting the external and internal consumer influences that might come into play in these consumers' buying decisions.

Next, we will look at business fashion buyers and see the ways in which they differ from fashion consumers in their buying behavior.

WHaT DO YOU THINK?

Recall a fashion item you liked because you were attracted to its style. You then studied it and realized that it seemed to express your personality. What specific appeals did the fashion marketer use to attract your attention and interest?

Business Fashion Buyer Behavior

The buying behavior of professional buyers for business differs from consumer behavior in some respects and is quite similar in others. The business market contains fewer buyers than the consumer market, but their purchases are much, much larger and typically more regular, for example, each season in the fashion industry.

KINDS OF BUSINESS MARKETS

There are four kinds of **business-to-business (B2B) markets**, or companies and organizations that buy from or sell to other businesses or organizations as opposed to consumers. These are producers, resellers, governments, and institutions. An example of a *producer market* in the fashion industry would be the fiber and fabric manufacturers that sell their output to apparel manufacturers to make clothes and accessories. A *reseller* is a company that buys finished goods and resells them to another business. Resellers in the fashion field include retailers and wholesalers. Macy's, for example, may buy directly from manufacturers such as Donna Karan or through wholesalers and agents (see Chapter 11). College bookstores buy sportswear from manufacturers such as Champion and Adidas. *Governments* are a huge market that includes the federal government as well as governments of states, cities, townships, counties, and other localities. They may buy uniforms from apparel manufacturers and office décor from furniture, carpeting, and other companies. *Institutions* include hospitals, universities, and nonprofit organizations such as the Red Cross.

WHAT DO FOREIGN CONSUMERS LIKE TO BUY WHEN VISITING THE UNITED STATES?

The Golden Gate Bridge, Disneyland, and the White House are important, but they are not the only reasons foreign visitors like to travel to the United States. Most come for the shopping—or at least they make a point of finding a few favorite items in U.S. stores to take back home when they return.

A recent survey of 1,800 foreign visitors by Mandela Research & Consulting, commissioned for an organization made up of 200 shopping destinations and supported by the U.S. Department of Commerce, revealed some interesting facts about these shoppers. In addition to the favorable exchange rate in relation to their domestic currency, a number of things made U.S. shopping a real joy for travelers. Value for the price ranked first, followed by wide product assortments including luxury items, helpful sales personnel, and special travelers' discounts.

Among the visitors, the most sought-after labels were Nike, Levi's, Gap, Polo Ralph Lauren, Tommy Hilfiger, Abercrombie & Fitch, Calvin Klein, and Coach. The Mandela organization suggested that these companies could expand sales further by focusing on visiting consumers and building them into their marketing strategies.

The greatest numbers of international visitors came from Canada, Mexico, the United Kingdom, Japan, and Germany, according to the research. Typically, visitors spent a minimum of $250, with average purchases amounting to $1,063. What's more, the research indicated that half of the travelers surveyed said they would be returning to the United States within the next 12 months.

Another interesting discovery revealed by the research was that many of the survey respondents said that they would plan future trips to include attending a city-wide shopping festival in a major location, such as New York, where they could take advantage of the cultural attractions as well as the shopping. Such festivals appeal to tourists and retailers alike, and are already quite successful in places such as China, Japan, Thailand, India, Singapore, and Dubai.

WHAT'S YOUR POINT OF VIEW?

1. How might fashion consumers in the United States react to shopping festivals? Should they be held only for foreign visitors or open to everyone?

2. Cite three or four external and internal influences on consumers as described in this chapter that might be a focus of marketers targeting international shoppers.

Adapted from: Cecily Hall, "Shopping Looms Large for U. S. Visitors," *Women's Wear Daily,* June 17, 2009, p. 9.

An interesting point about the B2B market is that the demand for its products often stems from the demand existing in the consumer market. Take jeans, for example. A high consumer demand for jeans creates a business market demand for denim fabric, thread, zippers, and so on, as well as increased demand from resellers for the finished products. When consumer demand for jeans declines, so does the business demand for raw materials (denim), components (thread, zippers), and the jeans themselves.

THE NATURE OF BUSINESS BUYING

A professional business buyer of fashion goods is interested in moving the product from the manufacturer to the consumer or end user as smoothly and rapidly as possible, thus enabling the buyer's business to flourish, and enhancing his or her standing in the company. This task is not always easy to accomplish, because professional buying is a complex process, often requiring a number of people to reach a buying decision. For example, a fashion store buyer—before placing an order—may need the approval of his or her divisional or group manager, plus possibly the general merchandise manager (usually a corporate vice president), as well as a nod from the company fashion coordinator. The term used when a company creates a permanent group of people who must approve purchase orders is **buying center**.

The fashion goods buying process is complex for a number of reasons:

▸ The buyer must always keep in mind for whom the goods are being purchased. Losing sight of the customer or ultimate user can happen easily, as when one tony New York specialty chain started buying goods for a younger age group, ignoring the fact that its best customers were older women. It took a while for the store to do an about-face and cater again to its true customers.

▸ The buyer needs to be assured of the quality of the product in relation to its price and obtain the best quality for the money. Price is important because a government or institutional buyer must work within an allotted budget, and a reseller must know what price its customers are willing to pay, and if it is enough for the company to earn a profit. The prominence of sky-high-priced accessories, such as designer handbags and shoes, illustrates that high-end retail buyers know there is a sufficiently affluent market to pay the high prices and enable the company to make a profit.

▸ Fashion buyers also want to work with suppliers that are reliable and supportive. Reliability exists when the buyer is assured that the orders will arrive complete and on time. A fashion retailer has little use for outfits with jackets that arrive three weeks after the matching skirts and pants, or for a dress shipment containing only size eight. A supportive supplier is one that provides information on fashion trends and fabrics, helps with advertising, or presents a trunk show at which consumers may see a designer's entire line and order from it.

▸ Fashion marketers are interested in maintaining long-term relationships with profitable suppliers in order to provide customers with consistent fashion looks that they can count on. While it is important for buyers to know the range of suitable suppliers in the market and to always be on the lookout for new styles or goods, it is the long-term relationships that provide the steadiest profit for a company.

BUYING METHODS

Looking specifically at the reseller market, fashion goods are bought in a number of ways. For high-priced designer imports, buyers inspect the goods at the designer's showroom before or after the seasonal runway showings, or fashion shows. The showings take place during regularly held market weeks. (See Chapter 11.) Retail store buyers attend these shows and order goods on-site or after returning home and conferring with the buying center members. Large fashion retailers such as Macy's may go directly to the headquarters of a manufacturer, such as Vanity Fair, to see entire lines. Because of Walmart's size and clout in the marketplace, its vendors must go directly to the retailer's Arkansas headquarters to show their lines.

TYPES OF BUYING

Some buying tasks for resellers are easier than others. Of the three types of buying, the least complicated is the **straight rebuy**, which is exactly as it sounds: a reorder of the same merchandise in the same quantities and colors as the original order. Posing a little more of a challenge is the **modified rebuy**, where the second order may call for a change in fabric, color, or size distribution. For example, a corduroy jacket sold well in the fall, and the buyer wants the same look in linen for spring-summer. The most complex form is **new task buying**, where the buyer is selecting new styles, dealing with a new vendor, or offering a new classification of goods, such as adding accessories to casual and

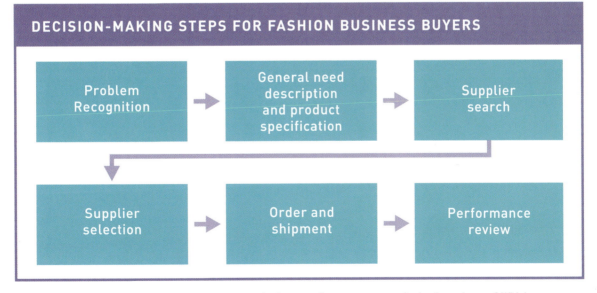

FIGURE 3.15 Which decision-making steps are nearly the same for consumers as for business buyers? Which ones are different? BY VANESSA HAN AND ALICIA FREILE

dress apparel. Here the business decision making (Figure 3.15) varies only somewhat from consumer decision making that we saw in Figure 3.6.

WHAT DO YOU THINK?

From what you have read about the work of a fashion buyer, how does the job appeal to you? What do you think you would like best about being a buyer? Why? What would you find less satisfying? Why?

Ethics and Social Responsibility

Sadly, each year illegal and unethical activities on the part of a small number of consumers and businesses add billions of dollars in marketing costs. In one recent year the total cost of worldwide retail theft amounted to the hefty sum of $119 billion, an amount that consumers must ultimately pay through higher prices for the goods they buy.[32] Consumer theft such as shoplifting and fraudulent returns, and business dishonesty through buyer greed and worker exploitation—in addition to raising prices—taint society's image of the marketing process. Fortunately, many consumers and business buyers are working to increase efficiency, lower costs, and create a more cooperative marketing environment by practicing sound ethics and social responsibility. And many individuals and businesses are doing this in a number of ways: through recycling, energy conservation, and careful financial management. All of these efforts lower costs and increase sustainability for individuals and society. Doing the right thing pays off.

Summary

Fashion marketers study consumer behavior in order to create and offer the products consumers want, when and where they wish to buy them. To effectively reach the appropriate consumers (the target market), fashion marketers coordinate the product, pricing, promotion, and place to meet consumers' needs. The amount of attention a consumer gives to reaching a fashion buying decision depends on how much the consumer cares about the product and the buying situation. Marketers must use different techniques when customers are not involved with the decision than when they are heavily involved. In a low-involvement situation, bright ads and convenient product placement can draw the consumer's attention; in a high-involvement situation, usually a significant purchase, fashion marketers often appeal to reasoning.

Making a significant consumer buying decision is a problem-solving process involving several steps: recognizing the problem, searching for information, weighing alternatives, reaching a decision, and evaluating that decision. A number of influences can have an effect on fashion buying decisions. These include the buying situation; one's culture, subculture, and social class; external influences from family, friends, co-workers, celebrities, and opinion leaders; and internal influences including perception, learning, motivation, attitude, personality, and self-concept.

Fashion buyers tend to be engaged in producer markets such as fabric and fiber marketers, or reseller markets such as wholesalers and retailers. There are fewer business buyers than consumer buyers, and they deal regularly in large purchases. Fashion business buyers are professionals who are concerned with supplying appropriate goods to their markets, obtaining the best quality for the price, and finding reliable and supportive suppliers with whom they can maintain a long-term relationship. To do their purchasing, retail fashion buyers attend market weeks in major cities, visit manufacturers' headquarters, or sometimes receive suppliers in their store headquarters. Fashion buying tasks include a straight rebuy, modified rebuy, or new task buying.

While a few individuals and businesses skirt the issues of ethics and social responsibility, resulting in higher merchandise prices and a poor public image, most consumers and businesses practice conservation and careful financial management in order to keep prices down and to create a more trusting marketing environment.

Zeroing in on Consumer Needs at IKEA

The Swedish furniture and home furnishings retailer IKEA, with some 267 stores in 25 countries and 590 million visitors in recent years, has studied its customers thoroughly and seeks to meet their shopping needs in a number of innovative ways.

IKEA's main target markets are young, middle-income, urban and suburban families, in their thirties and early forties. They are looking to furnish their homes with good-looking, modern, inexpensive furniture. To help its global customers stay within their budgets, IKEA cuts costs wherever possible. For example, tables, desks, and dressers are packed in flat containers, saving both assembly costs for customers and transportation costs for the company, resulting in lower retail prices. To make shopping easier for its global markets, the company also prints nearly 200 million catalogues each year in 27 languages and maintains a Web site featuring its complete product assortments of living room, dining room, bedroom, and kitchen furniture and furnishings.

One innovation for customers visiting IKEA stores is Småland play center, where—in the care of an IKEA employee—children can read books, watch television, or even bounce around in a bin with plastic balls. They can play with IKEA toys or dabble with arts and crafts projects while their busy, time-poor, and often stressed parents purchase dining room furniture, select a mattress, or just have a cup of coffee unencumbered. Children may stay at the play center up to an hour and a half, and parents are asked not to leave the store. When the time is up, a buzzer sounds on a handheld device supplied to parents when dropping off children at the center.

The company believes that providing a kind of escape for both parents and children is useful: for parents, relieving some of the stress that accompanies big-ticket purchase decisions, and for children, offering time for unstructured play. In fact, for some families an outing to the center becomes a regular event; children enjoy the activities while the parents take a breather just browsing through the various departments or sitting to read a newspaper. For IKEA, in addition to serving as an inducement to increase sales, the play centers contribute to the company's public image.

Adapted from: http:www.ikea.com/us/en/ (accessed January 18, 2010), and Michelle Higgins, "A Cheap Date, With Child Care by IKEA," *New York Times*, June 11, 2009, D3 and D6.

QUESTIONS

1. From what you have read in this chapter, what are three or four influences on consumer behavior that IKEA is attempting to tap into?
2. What is the company offering that appeals to consumers' motivation, attitude, and self-image?
3. If you were a parent, what would interest you about your child's using the play center? What questions would you want the staff there to answer before dropping off your child? How do these questions relate to consumer behavior?
4. As a marketing expert, what two or three additional customer services would you suggest that the company offer consumers?

KEY TERMS

branding

business-to-business (B2B) markets

buying center

cognitive dissonance

consumer behavior

extended problem solving

impulse item

integrated marketing system (IMS)

limited problem solving

modified rebuy

multiple selves

new task buying

purchase involvement

routine problem solving

social class

social norms

straight rebuy

subculture

traits

REVIEW QUESTIONS

1. What is meant by consumer behavior and why is it important to fashion marketers?
2. What is the relationship of the level of a consumer's purchase involvement to the consumer decision-making process, and how might fashion marketers deal with the challenge?
3. Describe the effects the buying situation and cultural and social influences can have on fashion consumer behavior.

4. Name a few personal influences on consumer behavior, and explain how fashion marketers appeal to these influences.
5. Describe fashion business buyer behavior, and cite three ways marketers target these customers.
6. How do ethics and social responsibility relate to buyer behavior?

DISCUSSION ACTIVITIES AND PROJECTS

1. Recall an instance when you were in a hurry but needed to make a fashion purchase. In what ways did time pressure affect your purchase decision regarding (a) your merchandise selection, (b) your encounter with the salesperson, and (c) the efficiency and smoothness of the sales transaction?
2. Think of a fashion item you purchased and describe each of the steps in the decision-making process that you went through in reaching your buying decision. Did you encounter the feeling of cognitive dissonance? If so, what did you do about it?
3. In a group with a few classmates, determine several beneficial ways to dispose of a usable fashion product you no longer need. Is there one preferred method? If so, what makes it preferable?
4. Go to the Web site www.myvirtualmodel.com or any other (such as www.landsend.com) that gives you an opportunity to select apparel and fit it to your silhouette. Choose two outfits, one for work and one for leisure activities. For each

of these outfits, describe the cultural, social, and personal influences that had an effect on your selection. Write an illustrated report on your findings, and hand it in to your instructor.

5. When executives of the New York Weatherproof Garment Company, maker of men's outerwear, saw a photograph of the President of the United States wearing one of the company's jackets as he toured the Great Wall of China, they jumped at the chance to publicize the event. Without obtaining permission, the image appeared on the company's Web site and went up on a billboard in New York's Times Square, as if to say the President endorsed the jacket. What is your opinion as to the ethics and social responsibility behind these acts on the part of Weatherproof Garment Company?

DEVELOPING YOUR MARKETING PLAN

For the next task in your marketing plan, you'll use what you've learned in this chapter about how consumers make buying decisions and try to identify the factors that might influence them as they weigh a purchase of your company's product. To do this:

1. Select three advertisements of your company's products.
2. For each one, determine two or three social, cultural, and/or personal influences on consumers that your company is seeking to target through its advertising messages.
3. Why did the company choose to emphasize those particular consumer influences in its

messages? If you had been creating the ads, would you have focused on a different consumer behavior influence?

4. Write a paragraph stating how these ads contribute to the company's total marketing strategy.

Refer to the Marketing Plan Outline, Table 1.2, provided at the end of Chapter 1, as well as Appendix A: Sample Marketing Plan.

REFERENCES

1. Mike Easey, ed., *Fashion Marketing,* 3rd ed. (Chichester, U. K.: John Wiley & Sons, 2009), p. 64.
2. Patricia Mink Rath, Stefani Bay, Richard Petrizzi, and Penny Gill, *The Why of the Buy: Consumer Behavior and Fashion Marketing* (New York: Fairchild Books, 2008), pp. 4, 5.
3. Op cit., pp. 67, 68.
4. Brenda Lloyd, "Saks Looking Overseas for Growth, Opens Men's Boutique In Dubai," *Women's Wear Daily,* June 5, 2008, p. 6.
5. IndiaCo, www.indiaco.com/resource-center/building-brands-personality. html (accessed April 15, 2009).
6. Miles Socha, "Karl-Johan Persson Next H&M CEO," *Women's Wear Daily,* February 12, 2009, p. 3.
7. Mark Karimzadah, "QVC to Launch Exclusive Line on the Catwalk," *Women's Wear Daily,* February 4, 2009, p. 8.
8. "Let Them Eat Big Mac," News You Need to Know column, *BusinessWeek,* February 9, 2009, p. 8.

9. Stefani Rosenbloom, "Macy's Cuts 7,000 Jobs in Overhaul," *New York Times*, February 3, 2009, pp. B1, B2.

10. Cecily Hall, "Crafting an Image for Hard Times," *Women's Wear Daily,* February 4, 2009, p. 10.

11. "Getting the Most out of Every Shopper," *BusinessWeek*, February 9, 2009, p. 45.

12. Op cit., pp. 6, 7.

13. Del I. Hawkins, David Mothersbaugh, and Roger J. Best, *Consumer Behavior*, 10th ed. (New York: McGraw-Hill Irwin, 2007), pp. 511–512.

14. Ibid.

15. Roger A. Kerin, Stephen W. Hartley, and William Rudelius, *Marketing: the Core,* 2nd ed. (New York: McGraw-Hill Irwin, 2007), pp. 102, 103.

16. Op cit., Chapter 13.

17. Op cit., pp. 103, 104.

18. Op cit., p. 17.

19. Ibid., p. 446.

20. U.S. Census Bureau, press release, http://www.census.gov/newsroom/releases/archives/population/cb08-123.html (accessed March 8, 2012).

21. Cotton Council Incorporated, press release, October 5, 2005.

22. Hunter Miller Group, http://www.huntermillergroup.com (accessed March 8, 2012).

23. Assets Market Profile, http://www.magazine.org/content/files/market_profile_black.pdf (accessed March 8, 2012).

24. Ethnic USA, http://www.ethnicusa.com/common/img/uploaded/Retail_traffic_article.pdf (accessed March 11, 2009).

25. Bridget Brenna, *Why She Buys* (New York: Crown Business Books, 2009), pp. 136, 137.

26. Op cit., p. 140.

27. Op cit., p. 90.

28. Ibid., p. 83.

29. Ibid., p. 113.

30. Ibid., p. 136.

31. Ibid., p. 138.

32. Joel Griffin, "Retail Theft Study: Shrink on the Rise Globally," SecurityInfoWatch.com, October 18, 2011, http://www.securityinfowatch.com/article/10481889/retail-theft-study-shrink-on-the-rise-globally (accessed March 8, 2012).

Part II

BUILDING A FASHION MARKETING STRATEGY

TO BUILD A fashion marketing strategy, you need to know the purpose of the marketing planning process and be able to create a viable mission statement. With an ability to understand and use these essential tools, fashion marketers formulate a competitive analysis, develop a marketing strategy and a marketing mix, and measure the results. Fashion organizations need marketing information in order to create their strategies. They must have a working knowledge of their sources, the marketing research process, and the uses of research findings. Building a fashion marketing strategy also involves market segmentation, targeting, and positioning, and the resulting application of the marketing mix. Creating the right relationship with fashion customers is the key.

CHAPTER 4

Creating a Company Marketing Strategy

This chapter describes the purpose of the marketing planning process and the mission statement. It then explains how to formulate a competitive analysis, develop a marketing strategy, create a marketing mix, and measure the results.

WHAT DO I NEED TO KNOW ABOUT CREATING A COMPANY MARKETING STRATEGY?

- What the planning process involves and why it is essential for every successful marketing strategy
- How to create a mission statement
- What is needed to formulate a competitive analysis
- How to develop a marketing strategy
- How to measure results

FASHION MARKETING IN FOCUS:
Knowing Your Customer

Suppose you designed a necklace and wanted to sell it. You can't just stand on a street corner hoping the right customers will come along. You need to think about who your customers are, where they like to shop, how much they would be willing to spend, how they will find out about your product, and more. In other words, you need a plan that meets your customers' wants and needs as well as a strategy by which to achieve that plan. Crafting such a plan and strategy is something that all successful marketers do.

Why is it necessary to have a plan for developing a successful marketing campaign before the project begins? Why not just plan as you go? Two old sayings address these questions nicely: "She who fails to plan, plans to fail," and "It pays to plan ahead; it wasn't raining when Noah built the ark."

Planning for Success

Plans contain steps you can act on to reach your goals. Whatever endeavor you are undertaking, if you think about what you want to accomplish, why that is important, how it will impact and be impacted by what's around you, where you are now, where you want to be, and how you might get there—all while identifying possible obstacles and alternative solutions along the way—you maximize the potential for success. In short, you need to look at the large and small context to figure out where

you want to go before taking any steps or actions to get there. This planning process should save you money, time, energy, and resources, and help provide "GPS" tracking along your route.

That same concept applies to fashion marketers as they work toward their goals using a **marketing plan**, a written document that is the detailed roadmap by which a company assesses its marketing objectives, determines what marketing strategies will help customers understand its product's value, and establishes how it will go about reaching its marketing goal. In a November 2005 article titled, "Creating a Marketing Plan: An Overview," the *Harvard Business Review* noted that the marketing plan serves to define the opportunity, the strategy, the budget, and the expected results of sales. Michael R. Solomon, Professor of Consumer Behavior at Auburn University, adds to the definition, noting that a marketing plan also serves to "identify how these strategies will be implemented, monitored, and controlled."[1]

FIGURE 4.1 Which of these two people do you think had a plan before leaving the house?

Consider this analogy: Marketers who do not spend time planning are like students who do not spend time reviewing course materials before the exam; they're at a major disadvantage. Or imagine an Olympic athlete and her coach not considering in minute detail—from training regimen to diet—how to prepare for an upcoming competition. The athlete's chances of taking home a medal would not be very strong, would they?

TYPES OF MARKETING PLANS

There are four main types of marketing plans: *strategic*, *functional*, *operational*, and *contingency*.

- ▶ *Strategic.* Senior management makes decisions designed to achieve long-range (five years or longer) goals that impact multiple departments throughout the organization. For example, a strategic marketing plan might include a variety of activities designed to increase market share by 12 percent through domestic expansion within 5 years.
- ▶ *Functional.* Middle managers in key business areas within the organization develop and monitor short-term plans on which supervisors or front-line managers act. For example, a merchandise manager at a department store might develop a functional marketing plan for attracting more children's wear customers in order to increase sales in that department.
- ▶ *Operational.* Supervisors or front-line managers create short-range action plans and coordination to "make things happen" in the accomplishment of specific goals. For example, a warehouse supervisor might devise an operational marketing plan

that involves a new technique for streamlining packing and shipping, with the goal of saving costs.

- ▶ *Contingency.* Appropriate levels of management create backup plans in order to be prepared if unexpected problems should arise. For example, an apparel company might have a contingency plan to use alternate suppliers for a key fabric if its primary source is unable to provide enough material to meet demand.

WHaT DO YOU THINK?

Thinking of a place where you work or have worked, of the four types of plans just mentioned, what type of planning do you think your organization had done the best? Why do you say that?

THE PLANNING PROCESS

How does a company begin the process of developing a marketing plan? It starts by following these six steps:

1. Decide what is important to the company; that is, identify its goals. Naturally, goals should reflect the main purpose of the organization and ideally will be spelled out in a company mission statement (discussed below).
2. Figure out what the company does well. Laura Lake, author of *Consumer Behavior for Dummies*, suggests describing the company's unique selling proposition (USP), and then identifying the related buyer benefits that add customer value.
3. Segment, prioritize, and target customers for a focused approach. If a company can identify

FIGURE 4.2 In developing a marketing strategy, Tory Burch set out to design the most stylish clothes possible for the least amount of money, and established a niche in the contemporary market, targeting style-seeking, confident women with a consistent mix of everyday outfits.

its typical customer using demographics (statistical information) and **psychographics** (lifestyle preference descriptors, such as individuals' attitudes, values, and interests), its marketing campaigns will reach key targets and return positive results, as long as the product or service offers unique value.

4. Establish a market niche, a particular position that the product occupies relative to similar products, and decide whether the company is a leader, follower, challenger, or general member in that segment.

5. Learn about targeted customers through focused research and identify how they process and interpret information. If consumers perceive and interpret the marketing message the way it's intended, the strategy should work.

6. Use the marketing mix tools to communicate with customers and determine which media are relevant (both traditional and electronic/mobile channels) to position the product/service in the most compelling and competitive manner.

SPECIFYING THE COMPANY'S MISSION

In most cases, a marketing plan has at its foundation the elements that are integral to the company's mission or organizational purpose. That means that creating a mission statement should be task number one in developing a marketing plan. A **mission statement** is a declaration that concisely conveys, in a big-picture perspective, the overarching goals of a company. Communicating the company's identity to all stakeholders—internal (employees) and

LG MARKETS WITH LIFESTYLE APPROACH

In 2004, South Korean manufacturer Lucky Goldstar changed its brand identity in the United States to the more premium LG Electronics, as in "Life's Good." Three years later, the technology company hired Kwan Sup (K. S.) Lee as vice president of global brand marketing for home entertainment—and one of Lee's first tasks was to reply to non-marketers in the company who asked him how much new marketing ideas would cost. Instead of appeasing them with a price tag, he told them to think about the strategy behind the marketing before worrying about cost.

"I said, 'Before we talk about the money, let's talk about the concept and the idea and that this is the right thing to do for the long term,'" Lee stated.

Today, a lot more people at LG understand the need for investment in the brand and marketing, and Lee is leveraging that growing trust to refashion LG as a lifestyle brand. To compete against established players in the market like Sony and Samsung, LG is focusing first on product leadership, recognizing that it can't win without great products. And instead of focusing on picture quality or this or that function, it's addressing the market with a different strategy using an emotional approach to speak to target consumers.

With the LG brand covering products from household goods to TVs to microwaves, Lee's marketing concept is to have one brand strategy for everything from mobile phones to TVs to DVD players, and even vacuum cleaners. "Our strategy is to portray our product portfolio as a strength—not as hardware manufacturers, but as a lifestyle company, and we have many household devices and home electronics and personal communication devices that are lifestyle devices," he said. "LG is talking about 'Life's Good,' freedom, and infinite possibilities—all those kind of emotional attributes—for a broad range of products."

Adapted from: Beth Snyder Bulik, "Lee's Push to Refashion LG as a Lifestyle Brand," *Advertising Age*, July 12, 2010, http://adage.com/cmostrategy/article?article_id=144870 (accessed March 7, 2012).

external (customers and other publics)—is key. The statement identifies the consumer benefits the company intends to deliver along with reasons for its sustainable growth. It addresses the company's purpose and core values. If this clear vision of success is understood by all stakeholders, it will expedite the decision-making process for both employees and customers.

For example, Ben & Jerry's mission statement addresses three areas of accountability and development: product, economic sustainability, and societal give-back. Zara's mission is to develop actionable sustainability in creativity, quality design, and rapid turnaround in an ever-changing marketplace; Inditex, Zara's parent company, is committed to its stakeholders, society, and the environment. Susan G. Komen for the Cure is a nonprofit organization "working to save lives, empower people, ensure quality care for all, and energize science to find breast cancer cures."[2] The Fashion Group International (FGI)'s mission is "to be the pre-eminent authority on the business of fashion and design and to help its members become more effective in their careers."[3] When an organization establishes a mission that delivers value and exceeds expectations, the result should be increased market share and brand loyalty.

Marketing Analysis

Finding out what is going on in the marketplace or with competitors, customers, and vendors is important, but what should be done with this data? Facts and numbers in and of themselves are useless to marketers unless they are analyzed for their relevance to the company and its marketing planning.

The following quotes illustrate the importance of doing more than just collecting data:

"Good journalism is always gathered, researched, and analyzed ..."
—Teri Agins, special projects writer, *Wall Street Journal*[4]

"The ultimate authority must always rest with the individual's own reason and critical analysis."
—The Dalai Lama, Spiritual leader of the Gelugpa order of Tibetan Buddhists, 1989 Nobel Peace Prize recipient[5]

"Central banks don't have divine wisdom. They try to do the best analysis they can and must be prepared to stand or fall by the quality of that analysis."
—Mary Kay Ash, Founder, Mary Kay Cosmetics[6]

"I'm taking the time to slow down, to strategize, to figure out ..."
—Sean "Diddy" Combs, American record producer, rapper, actor, fashion designer, and Council of Fashion Designers of America award recipient[7]

TYPES OF ANALYSIS

Analysis is a detailed examination of a specified set of data that may yield key strategic insights and is generally done after the completion of careful research. Marketers must have a thorough understanding of both the current and potential marketplace in order to draw accurate conclusions for planning. Our discussion includes two types of analysis important to fashion marketers: situational analysis and competitive analysis.

Situational Analysis

There are two types of situational analysis: SWOT and G-PESTELC. The most commonly cited type of situational analysis is SWOT, an acronym for Strengths, Weaknesses, Opportunities, and Threats. A **SWOT analysis** is an examination of both the internal factors (strengths and weaknesses) and the external factors (opportunities and threats) that potentially impact a marketing situation.[8] This

TABLES 4.1A AND B Sample SWOT Analysis

A. INTERNAL MARKETPLACE FACTORS (MOST OF WHICH CAN BE CONTROLLED)

S: Strength	W: Weakness
■ Strong brand equity ■ Competitive pricing strategy ■ Integrated marketing system	■ Oversaturated distribution ■ Weak product ■ Minimal viral or guerilla marketing used

B. EXTERNAL MARKETPLACE FACTORS (NEARLY IMPOSSIBLE TO CONTROL)

O: Opportunities	T: Threats
■ Expansion into overseas marketplaces ■ Strategic alliance with "green" organization ■ New product development in partnership with charitable organization	■ Depressed economy ■ Ineffective publicity due to misspent funds ■ Government recall of all products containing "x" ingredient

data collection and analysis helps in understanding what might be going well within a marketing plan or adjustments that need to be made.

A SWOT analysis examines quantitative and qualitative areas related to organizational inputs and outputs like costs, skill sets, image development, financial and human resources, and traditional and e-technologies. Because marketers have a high degree of control over these internal factors, they can try to further develop key strengths and work to minimize or eliminate the weaknesses. On the other hand, external factors that represent opportunities and threats are less able to be controlled, as they refer to marketplace conditions and influences. Because marketers cannot control those factors, they must plan for and respond to them as effectively as possible. Using a SWOT analysis helps in developing a balanced marketing

approach, one that balances the "dream" or ideal situation with a practical point of view. The underlying assumption is that by periodically reviewing these factors, marketers can come up with new or revised strategies for success.

While a SWOT analysis can help businesses develop and implement strategies to adapt to the opportunities and threats uncovered in their microenvironment and macroenvironment, another type of situational analysis focuses more heavily on the wider macroenvironment in which the marketer operates. This analysis is called **G-PESTELC** (for Global-Politics, Environment, Sociocultural, Technology, Economics, Legal, Competition), a variation of the traditional PESTELC model. (See Figure 4.3.) In *Foundations of Economics*, Andrew Gillespie describes the PESTELC model as a macroenvironmental tool categorizing the external

G-'PESTELC' FACTORS

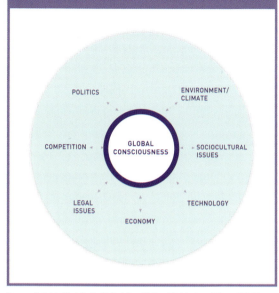

Source: Patricia Mink Rath, Stefani Bay, Richard Petrizzi, and Penny Gill, *The Why of the Buy: Consumer Behavior and Fashion Marketing* (New York: Fairchild Books, 2008), p. 301, figure 12.1.

FIGURE 4.3 The G-PESTELC model analyzes macroenvironmental factors within a global framework.
BY VANESSA HAN AND ALICIA FREILE

factors that impact the decisions made by managers: politics, environment/climate, sociocultural issues, technology, economy, legal issues, and competition.[9] In this textbook, we have added the "G" to the beginning of the acronym to emphasize the ever-present importance of thinking globally. Each category noted in Figure 4.3 carries additional weight when global implications are considered. An application for the "T," which represents technology, for example, was drawn from Thomas L. Friedman, author of *The World is Flat 3.0*. Friedman suggests that in the year 2000 a "Globalization 3.0" factor began; he describes this factor as "the newfound power for individuals to collaborate and compete globally."[10] This means that all of the global

factors can influence both industry segments and individual businesses. As such, identifying these forces, preplanning, adapting, and implementing appropriate action plans needed to succeed in today's shifting marketplace are mandatory steps for securing a competitive advantage and business growth. G-PESTELC forces exert their influence on organizations and marketplace expectations.

How might these drivers or factors apply? Review Case Study 4.1 "World Imports" at the end of this chapter, and answer its questions.

GLOBALIZATION AWARENESS DRIVERS: IED & G-'PESTELC'

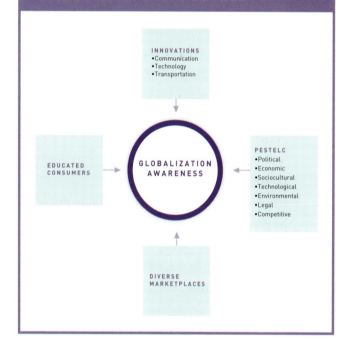

FIGURE 4.4 Along with the PESTELC factors, globalization awareness is driven by innovations, educated consumers, and diverse marketplaces.
BY VANESSA HAN AND ALICIA FREILE

TABLE 4.2 Sample Competitive Analysis

(1 = weak; 2 = average; 3 = above average)

Areas of Potential Competition*	Your Company	Competitor A	Competitor B	Competitor C
Product (assortment)	2	3	1	2
Price (range, strategy)	2	2	3	1
Promotion (advertising, PR, sales)	2	3	3	2
Distribution (methods, location, supply chain)	2	2	3	3

* Including the marketing mix tools

Competitive Analysis

While situational analysis looks at a wide range of internal and external influences on a marketer's business, competitive analysis focuses on products and companies that compete directly with the marketer. Using the marketing tools of product, price, distribution, and promotion, and/or other areas of potential competition, marketers analyze their situation in comparison to their competitors. The results of a competitive analysis, as illustrated in Table 4.2, allow marketers to recognize areas of weakness and develop appropriate strategies to improve their competitive standing.

WHAT DO YOU THINK?

Consider a new store that has opened in your neighborhood in the last 12 months when answering this question: If you were in charge of examining one of the "PESTELC" factors in a G-PESTELC analysis, how would you lead the discussion? Which factor would you discuss and what would you say?

Developing a Marketing Strategy

Having a plan is step one in any fashion marketing venture. The next step requires developing a strategy by which to carry out the plan. So what is a strategy? According to George Steiner, Professor Emeritus at UCLA Anderson School of Management, strategy is "what one does to counter a competitor's actual

TECHNOLOGY TAKES ANALYSIS TO WHOLE NEW LEVELS

Information is critical in developing a marketing plan, and everywhere throughout the marketing ecosystem, vast amounts of data are constantly being collected. Fortunately for marketers, there are powerful new software and hardware tools that can assemble, filter, compare, and model the huge wealth of data—which otherwise would be a truly daunting task.

For example, there is software that enables marketers to input data of all kinds on consumers, competitors, retailers, ad copy, and ad spending. From these inputs, the software will predict marketplace outcomes, and it even lets users rapidly change inputs to create multiple scenarios. A new "exception analytics" capability goes further, filtering through masses of data to identify anomalous events that might indicate an emerging or potential problem long before the human brain could become aware of the trend.

One practical application for advanced marketing analytics was illustrated by Mercedes, which wanted to sell a small number of its new "green" SUVs in the United States. A mass campaign for such a small number of available vehicles was out of the question, so the company used new data and analytics technologies to identify and persuade a target market perceived to be intensely attracted to and capable of affording this unique, expensive Mercedes. The company's agency cross-compared lists of individuals with a demonstrated interest in all things green, a history of purchasing green products, the economic capability to pay for a Mercedes, and known car-buying propensities. They combined dozens of databases covering a number of behaviors that suggested a propensity to buy a car like the new Mercedes, such as eco-friendly magazine subscriptions, cause-based organization memberships, Web site hits on green articles, TV viewing habits, and political contributions. Using the final list, the marketing team put together a creative strategy and a multi-component integrated campaign—and the result was that Mercedes quickly and profitably sold all the available SUVs.

Adapted from: Gordon Wade, "Marketers, Unlock the Possibilities within Data," *Advertising Age*, July 27, 2009, p. 12.

or predicted moves."[11] Harvard Business School Professor Michael Porter says "strategy is about competitive position, about differentiating yourself in the eyes of the customer, and about adding value through a mix of activities different from those used by competitors."[12] W. Chan Kim and Renée Mauborgne define strategy as "what a company offers to buyers and how they will benefit from that offering."[13]

In short, a strategy spells out the methods or tactics that will be used to achieve specific goals. Naturally, strategies are important for success in any arena. A recent segment on NBC's "Today Show" by Liz Vaccariello, editor-in-chief at *Prevention Magazine*, discussed "strategic splurging," that is, strategies for healthy eating. It's pretty clear that one who does not strategize for success may, in fact, be drawn to failure.

In essence, marketers try to figure out how to move from here to there on the road to their goals and do so in ways that are better than the competitors' methods. This chapter explores the need for planning, strategizing, building customer relationships, maximizing partnering opportunities, and measuring how well those marketing activities build value for a company's stakeholders at each level. Sustainable business success necessitates a planned investment in developing, adapting, and monitoring a thoughtful marketing strategy.

What will we do better than our competition to consistently add value to customers? That's really what **marketing strategy** involves: a plan of action designed to identify the target market and shape the marketing mix in order to satisfy target customers' needs and propel the marketer toward its goals.

Some companies design a marketing strategy that allows them to continuously adapt to the marketplace with appropriate products; to promote messages that are creatively fresh, business-driven, and socially responsible; and to utilize the marketing tools effectively. Companies that succeed in those areas will hold the competitive advantage. For example, 13 Canadian Tire stores—part of a 475-store Toronto-based retail chain that sells automotive, home, sports, and leisure products and employs more than 57,000 workers—recently received Marketing and Merchandising Awards for their best-in-class service and successful efforts to meet and exceed their customers' expectations. One store was recognized for its innovative displays and boutique areas, such as bike and pet boutiques, created to meet the needs of its customer demographic; another received the honor for its twice-yearly Ladies Night event, including a fashion show of clothing and products available in-store, demonstrations, entertainment, refreshments, and more.[14]

Companies that rely on the decision maker's intuition, rather than on a researched and directed path, may fall into marketplace "potholes" along the way to their marketing goals. Marketing is a process that includes the communication of all information that sellers want to share with consumers, from the time a product or service is just an idea on the drawing board through its purchase, use, evaluation, and disposal by the customer. Continuously collecting and analyzing consumer data for these key areas and distilling that information into an organized format and strategy provides a strong foundation for market success.

Think about it: Businesspeople make plans for the very same reasons that vacationers generally plan their itineraries in advance, event planners map out key details, brides spend countless hours on wedding plans, and students figure out how best to study or prepare for an exam or project presentation—that is, to save time, energy, and money, and help achieve positive end results. That makes developing the right strategy for carrying out the plan a critical piece of the marketing puzzle.

WHAT A MARKETING STRATEGY ACCOMPLISHES

A marketing plan identifies overall marketing objectives and specific marketing activities that

FIGURE 4.5 Canadian Tire Corporation continually reviews its stores' marketing strategy to ensure that customers' needs are being met.

should sustain a company's competitive advantages. The strategy for carrying out that plan pairs solutions with an evolving marketplace, one where opportunities are not always readily visible. If the coordinated marketing activities consistently deliver the defined strategic message and related buyer benefits in an innovative manner, the adopted marketing plan should drive quantifiable gains to the business. In other words, do it well and the business will grow.

The key elements of a marketing plan should map out how to:

▸ Attract customers.
▸ Build and expand customer relationships.
▸ Utilize appropriate communications.
▸ Adapt to the marketplace.
▸ Deliver value.

The marketing plan provides the goals, while the marketing strategy outlines the specific actions needed to achieve those goals within a certain time period.

TYPES OF STRATEGIES

Which marketing strategy is best for an organization? It depends on the specific circumstances and how well that strategy is coordinated and carried out in synch with the marketplace. We will examine five common types of marketing strategies used in fashion businesses: differentiation, exit, expansion, ocean (red vs. blue), and segmentation.

Differentiation Strategy

Differentiation is the marketing strategy in which a company clearly communicates to customers its distinct solutions to their wants and needs, that is, how its product is different from other products.

For example, what differentiates Tiffany from Cartier? Both offer costly fine jewelry made from precious gems and metals, and both have done so for over 150 years. But consumers familiar with these legendary companies perceive them differently. Tiffany, an American company, is known for its trademarked blue box, its exclusive distribution of several designer collections (Paloma Picasso, Elsa Peretti, Schlumberger), the movie that bears its name, and so on. Despite the company's upscale reputation, however, some Tiffany products are accessible to those who aren't necessarily super wealthy. The company targets teens, for instance, with its popular collection of sterling silver charms, key rings, necklaces, and bracelets. Tiffany also has another target market—upscale luxury buyers. It successfully merges its marketing mixes to reach both of these groups. On the other hand, Cartier, a French company, is known for having invented the wristwatch and continuing to make some of the world's most popular timepieces, for creating commissioned gem masterpieces for European, Russian, and Indian royalty, and for its distribution through stores other than its own. So you see, these two organizations are similar, but they clearly differentiate themselves in the eyes of their customers.

Exit Strategy

Exit is the marketing strategy in which a company no longer provides a product it has marketed in the past or sells it to another organization, so customers no longer get it from the original company.

There are currently a number of businesses that buy old or underperforming products from companies that no longer want to spend time, money, or effort to market them. The new owners then proceed to reposition these brands with new, updated strategies. For example, in 2007, Liz Claiborne, Inc. (now called Fifth & Pacific Companies) planned to sell or discontinue several unprofitable brands geared to older customers to reverse six straight quarters of lower profit. Its Dana Buchman brand was subsequently licensed to Kohl's, and its Ellen Tracy brand was sold to Fashionology Group LLC. [15]

Expansion Strategy

Expansion is the marketing strategy in which a company seeks ways to extend its business beyond its current status. Following are five methods of expansion:

1. Market development: Entering new markets with existing products. For example, if a product is doing well in one location, why not enlarge the market to include other areas? A successful Chicago company that produces and sells decorative pillows and window treatments might look into opening additional stores in nearby geographic locations like Springfield, Milwaukee, and Indianapolis. Or it might consider selling its products at wholesale prices to other retailers across the country, or eventually even around the world. The global expansion of retail corporations such as Macy's—which in 2010 opened a Bloomingdale's branch in the Dubai Mall in the United Arab Emirates—is an example of a company using the market development strategy.[16]

2. Penetration: Pursuing current markets more aggressively with existing products. When the Italian apparel company Benetton began to attract the attention of young people in the United States, it started opening multiple stores in many American cities. In Chicago, for example, the brand was so popular that Benetton had several stores within a few blocks of each other. Starbucks, the company that made coffee drinking oh-so-chic, is perhaps the best example of an organization that's made market penetration a primary strategy.

3. Product development: Conceptualizing and creating new products to add to a company's already existing assortment. In order to keep their offerings fresh, exciting, and in tune with current trends, or possibly to attract new groups of customers, companies frequently consider new product concepts. Those that appear viable go through a process that includes development, testing, and ultimately production and distribution. Louis Vuitton, for example, has

FIGURE 4.6 Louis Vuitton has used product development as an expansion strategy, creating new items such as pet carriers that are consistent with the company's signature style.

on mattresses, bedding, and assorted housewares. This expansion strategy is often done by licensing the brand name to a company already in the other field. (For more information on the brand extension strategy, see Chapter 7.)

5. Diversification: Expanding into other arenas of the marketplace, often by acquiring other organizations or products that are unrelated to the current mix. Perhaps a successful company, known for its delicious baked goods, purchases another company that makes something other than food, like underwear or handbags. That's what Sara Lee Corporation did when it acquired Hanesbrands Inc.,[17] and then Coach Inc. Sara Lee executives undoubtedly recognized that the time was right to expand their product mix, and consequently took advantage of two opportunities to diversify, both of which allowed them more options for growth and profitability. Later, when the marketing environment had shifted, Sara Lee revamped its marketing goals and plan, and employed an exit strategy in spinning off (selling) both those units.

added items ranging from pet carriers and dog collars to iPhone cases and hair clips to its signature collection of accessories.

4. Brand extension: Putting a brand name on other products/services, which usually relate to those that already exist. When marketers at Ralph Lauren realized how powerful that brand name had become, they decided to use it on fashion-related items other than clothing, like linens, furniture, and paint. Vera Wang's organization has also extended the variety of products under its brand name, which now appears

Ocean Strategies

Ocean strategies is the term used to describe marketplace competition that occurs in either a traditional head-to-head manner or in an uncontested, no boundaries framework. These two ocean strategies are known as Red Ocean Thinking and Blue Ocean Thinking, respectively.[18]

▶ Red Ocean Thinking: Marketers compete with other companies in a traditional manner, seeking to "do it" better than their competition; the ocean turns red with the "blood" of competitors. In Red Ocean Thinking, companies choose a pricing or other differentiation strategy to fight their competitive battles. This is also called a structuralist approach. When a company has the resources, time, and money to compete effectively on a head-to-head basis, this is a good strategy to use. Walmart is a perfect example of a marketer that uses Red Ocean Thinking, as it competes constantly with other retailers to offer its customers the lowest prices.[20]

▸ Blue Ocean Thinking: Marketers create new value for customers to stimulate demand, offering innovative benefits that the competition doesn't have. This strategy views the marketplace like an unexplored deep blue ocean filled with opportunity. In Blue Ocean Thinking, the competitive environment does not really impact the bottom line because direct competitors do not yet exist. This is considered a reconstructionist approach. In September 2009, *The Harvard Business Review* noted that "today's economic difficulties have heightened the need for a reconstructionist alternative." A company that has a new idea or breakthrough innovation would use Blue Ocean Thinking. For example, the film *Avatar* stood out from the raft of competing 3D films released around the same time because of its new and unique "e-motion capture" technology, which revolutionized the way live actors could be translated into digital characters for the film.[20]

Segmentation Strategy

Segmentation is the marketing strategy in which marketers identify potential customers who share similar preferences, behaviors, values, and so on, knowing that those who share lifestyle patterns may also share buying patterns. With segmentation, marketers pinpoint consumers they want to reach and how best to reach them, and thereby increase their opportunity for profitability. For example, Estée Lauder uses segmentation of

TABLE 4.3 Marketplace Segmentation Categories

Type of Segmentation	Examples
Demographic	Age, sex, marital status, income, education, occupation
Dominant benefit sought	Convenience, value, fashion, status
Geographic	Domestic: state, city, region; international: country, zone
Hybrid	Combination of any groups
Psychographic	Lifestyles
Sociocultural	Culture, religion, ethnicity, class, family
Usage	Purchase frequency, brand loyalty, purchase location

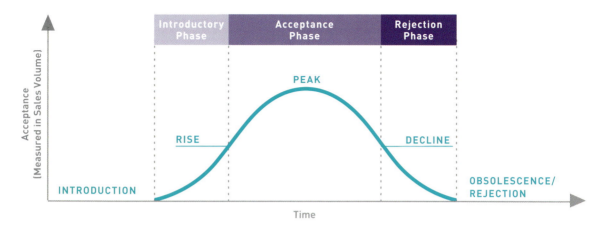

FASHION LIFE CYCLE

FIGURE 4.7 Stages of Fashion Life Cycle. BY VANESSA HAN AND ALICIA FREILE

the cosmetics marketplace to target the distinct groups of women, each sharing similar characteristics, who are most likely to purchase the company's products.[21]

WHAT DO YOU THINK?

Assume that you currently own a fashion business. Which of the five types of marketing strategies would you use and what marketplace factors would you consider when making your decision?

Strategy for Growth

In a fashion life cycle, products go through stages from introduction and rise, to peak, through obsolescence or rejection. (See Figure 4.7.) Once an organization has introduced a fashion item into the marketplace, it needs to develop a growth

strategy within its marketing plan, implementing tactics that will keep the product in the rise phase as long as possible by expanding brand awareness and increasing sales. Successful acceptance of a product by consumers means increased market share and brand loyalty for the company. Sustained growth in these areas will please stakeholders and make the company appealing to current and prospective employees.

SEGMENTING AND TARGETING MARKETS

Identifying exactly who their customers are is a critical first step for marketers before they are able to flesh out a marketing strategy. As you'll recall, **segmenting** the marketplace refers to dividing it into groups that share common or similar (homogeneous) interests or needs by clarifying the demographic and psychographic data. Businesses then study the various segments to identify which

MARKETER'S INSIGHT:
L'ORÉAL PLANS 'BIG GROWTH' STRATEGY

When L'Oréal USA tapped Marc Speichert as its first chief marketing officer (CMO) in 2010, the Paris-based beauty marketer had never had CMOs at the country level or globally. But Speichert, a former executive with Colgate-Palmolive Co., didn't hesitate in stepping up to the task, spending quite a bit of time on "preparing for the future and trying to align innovation to where the big growth bets will be."

Up to now, L'Oréal's divisions included consumer products, with the mass L'Oréal Paris and Maybelline-Garnier units; a luxury division anchored by Lancôme; an active-cosmetics division including La Roche-Posay; and a professional division with Matrix and Redken, in addition to such retailers as Kiehl's and The Body Shop. Speichert's mission is to find synergies among those divisions and help develop common strategies to realize L'Oréal's global chairman's vision of adding a billion new consumers by the end of the decade. While competitors such as Procter & Gamble have similar ambitions (in this case, a billion new consumers by 2015), one difference with L'Oréal is that it's counting on a lot more of those consumers to come from the United States, where the company still believes it can be much bigger. To work toward that goal, L'Oréal is already spending more on advertising, as well as trying to spend smarter, including spending more on digital media.

As Speichert described his role: "The vision is really twofold. One is to really push innovation to the next level. Having the brands set up within a channel of distribution is what made the company successful, and that is not going to change, but it's where do we create synergies that make sense? There's also the opportunity to think about it from a market-research perspective [to create a] view of our consumers and our shoppers in how they move from one department or one channel to the other."

Adapted from: Jack Neff, "Speichert Looks for 'Big Growth Bets' as First CMO of L'Oréal," *Advertising Age*, February 21, 2011, http://adage.com/article/cmo-interviews/q-a-l-oreal-s-cmo-marc-speichert/148915/ (accessed March 7, 2012).

contain customers most likely to buy their product, and therefore which segments to target with their marketing. See Chapter 6 for a more detailed explanation of these terms.

Once marketers understand who their consumers are, what they value, and what influences their purchasing decisions, solutions that address the needs and wants of the customer base can be developed and marketed. Those solutions are customer-segment specific. What makes one product or service stand out above the competitors' is really a customer's perception of which product offers the better value for the price. By understanding its target customer segment, a marketer can create marketing strategies designed to optimize that value perception.

CREATING VALUE-ADDED SOLUTIONS

Often, going above and beyond the basics—that is, conspicuously adding more value to the equation for consumers—is what makes the difference in the success of a fashion marketing strategy. One way retailers add value is by providing better-trained employees to help shoppers make smarter purchasing decisions. Other methods might be by offering easily accessible computer kiosks for impromptu comparison research, virtual fitting rooms that allow customers to try different outfit styles and color options. streaming video displaying the latest fashion trends, or lounge areas with 55-inch TVs for the non-shopping partners. If both stores pictured in Figure 4.8 are trying to compete for the same consumer segment, which do you think will experience more problems and challenges in maintaining customer loyalty and sustaining a profitable sales volume?

The rule for marketers: Research what the target customer values in the purchase of goods and delivery of services; then use both proven and innovative ways to deliver that value message along with the product.

Naturally, an organization must stay healthy and able to weather potential economic storms, while reading and adapting to market opportunities. A February 2009 article in the *Harvard Business Review* referred to this as "agile absorption."[22] In retrospect, the recessionary period that began in 2008 highlights the importance of organizing and utilizing financial and human resources more effectively than the competition. Our next section examines one way to make our stakeholders accountable and make the marketing plan more actionable.

FIGURE 4.8 A successful growth strategy requires adding value for customers, such as services, amenities, and ambiance. Based on what you can see in these photos, how are the two retailers adding value for their target customers?

IDENTIFYING SMART OBJECTIVES

Webster's Dictionary 5th Edition defines smart money as "money bet or invested by those in the best position to know what might be advantageous."[23] Likewise, marketers use the acronym **SMART objectives**, which stands for *specific, measurable, attainable and realistic, results-driven,* and *time-based,* to help them quantify and qualify goals and, therefore, turn strategies into direct, meaningful statements about how they will achieve intended results. This helps the marketers and others understand what they are trying to do, and what they must do if the organization is to accomplish its business goals.

Using the SMART process, marketers would develop and insert some ideas in each of the five SMART categories. They would then condense the best statements from each level, and finally combine the condensed statements into two to four concisely worded sentences. The result should be an actionable statement that clearly identifies an objective, while setting the accountability criteria for its success. For example:

▸ **S**pecific: Be as focused on the goal as possible, as opposed to making a general statement. *Example:* We aim to increase annual net profit (not "get general sales up").

▸ **M**easurable: Quantify wherever possible so you can gauge your progress. *Example:* Our goal is to increase profits by 12 percent (not "do better").

▸ **A**ttainable and realistic: Formulate/justify achievable goals and not mere "wishes," which could lead to failure. *Example:* Industry trends are very favorable for increasing sales by 15 percent (not "we want to sell more than all our competitors combined").

▸ **R**esults-driven (not merely activity-driven): Focus on describing the end result or goal, not just the means to get there; this should clarify what success looks like. *Example:* Improved sales will justify our new outlet expansion during second quarter of 2014 (not "we'll work on selling more product").

▸ **T**ime-based: Specify timeline checkpoints that lead to the achievement of your goal. *Example:* We want to achieve 70 percent of our goal during the first six months of fiscal year 2013 (not "we want to make progress soon").

TABLE 4.4 Using "SMART"

Acronym Letter	Meaning
S	Specific
M	Measurable
A	Attainable and realistic
R	Results-driven
T	Time-based

TABLE 4.5 Marketing Tools and their Actions in Positioning a Product

Tool	Action
Product	Innovate to make it better.
Place	Improve distribution channels; make it easier for customer to buy.
Promotion	Use relevant media and technology with targeted message.
Price	Stimulate customer activity with appropriate pricing strategies.
People	Train and motivate employees to exceed customer expectations.
Process/procedure	Make it efficient for customers and employees to succeed.

Following this process will result in an organized statement that identifies the marketing objective in a clear manner. It will also point out accountability factors for team members along the way. Here is a concisely worded goal statement from the example above: "To increase sales by 15 percent and annual net profit by 12 percent in order to justify a new outlet expansion during the second quarter of 2014."

POSITIONING THE PRODUCT

Let's look again at the movie *Avatar*. When James Cameron made the film, he had specific images in mind regarding how the consumer (moviegoer) would view his story. Producer Jon Landau said, "Instead of going with what people did in the past, [we instituted] e-motion capture, [an image-based capture in a frame-by-frame basis] instead of traditional reflective markers." Live actors were translated into digital characters, 10-foot tall blue beings called the Na'vi.[24] What the moviemakers were doing was improving their product by delivering a new dimension of entertainment to viewers, and at the same time, positioning their movie in relation to other films on the market.

Positioning refers to using the various marketing tools (product, price, place, and promotion, with people and process also part of the equation) to determine how a product fits within the marketplace and in relation to other products, and to influence how consumers in specific segments view the product. (See Figure 4.10 and Table 4.5.) In the *Avatar* example, the filmmakers positioned the movie (product) as an experience that incorporated the most groundbreaking and innovative use of technology to date, and promoted it with the goal of trying to wow both critics and moviegoers who appreciate spectacular effects. By using the marketing tools better than the competition, the filmmakers were able to capture tremendous market share at the box office and generate substantial revenue.

FIGURE 4.9 Marketers often reposition their brand to adapt to changes in the marketplace or to change the way customers view them, as Jamba Juice did when it added food items to its original smoothie offerings.

As previously noted, identifying the customer's "value" driver is very important to success in any marketing goal. Consider the following equation:

$$P \text{ (price)} / V \text{ (value)} = PC \text{ (perceived cost)}$$

This equation mathematically supports this discussion because as the denominator (V, or value) increases, the result (PC, or perceived cost to the customer) decreases.[25] In other words, as customers derive added value, they might more easily justify the price of a purchase because of the perceived savings/benefits. This explains why some stores might charge and receive more money for similar products; customers receive more valued-added benefit bundles. For example, a consumer might decide to buy a new Gucci bag directly from a Gucci boutique instead of from a store that carries Gucci and other products, because in the specialty stop she feels pampered, respected, and able to enjoy other benefits such as valet parking, recognition, and cross-purchasing opportunities within the brand.

How do marketers know what consumers are thinking? Marketing research (discussed in Chapter 5) can provide data that reflects consumers' perceptions. To illustrate consumers' view of the marketplace, marketers may use a **perceptual map**, a visual interpretation of data that depicts the relationships between competitive offerings and factors or perceptions used by customers in making buying decisions among those choices. Remember, customers buy items based upon perceived benefits. From Figure 4.10, it is clear why "a picture is worth a thousand words." On the sample perceptual map, you can see the following:

▶ How many movies per week are watched by each researched age group on the y (vertical) axis.

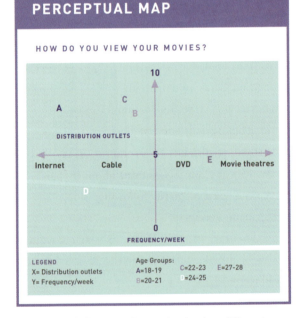

FIGURE 4.10 Perceptual map showing how different age cohorts view movies. BY VANESSA HAN AND ALICIA FREILE

- The various competitors for movie audiences on the x (horizontal) axis.
- The relationship among the groups in terms of their preferred movie distribution outlet and frequency of watching, with the youngest of the age groups, ("A"—18- to 19-year-olds), watching movies primarily on the Internet and at a higher frequency than the oldest age group ("E"—27- to 28-year-olds), who lean more toward DVDs and movie theaters.

After a marketer has collected and analyzed research about its customers, competitors, and the marketplace, positioning becomes the lifeblood of success or failure. Based on the perceptual map example, if you were marketing a new movie to young adults ages 18 to 28, how would you use the "place" element of the marketing mix to position your product?

In time, when the marketplace inevitably changes and a company finds that its current marketing strategies are not driving adequate sales growth, or are resulting in a decline in market share, modifications to the marketing strategy must be made once again. This is called repositioning.

Repositioning, revising a marketing strategy in order to adapt to marketplace changes and modify the way consumers think about (or perceive) the brand, could mean the following:

- Targeting a new age cohort segment (a fashion designer targeting the 18- to 35-year-old woman now also makes clothes for the 35- to 50-year-old woman).
- Adding an unrelated product or service to the product mix (a shoe store begins to carry purses, belts, and other leather goods).

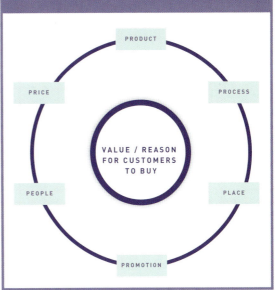

FIGURE 4.11 Fashion marketers use all their available marketing tools in positioning a product to offer value to target customers. BY VANESSA HAN AND ALICIA FREILE

- Integrating a lifestyle change (bringing upscale retail shopping to an area not currently serviced).

For example, apparel brands might add non-apparel items, such as handbags, eyewear, or cologne. This brand extension is a type of repositioning. Of course, repositioning must be realistic and achievable in order for it to work. In 2010, Target began to offer bulk buying at selected stores, in hopes of adding a warehouse club-like shopping experience and trendier product offerings. Likewise, Jamba Inc., owner of the Jamba Juice chain, began offering food items and more than cold beverages, in order to encourage customers to think of it as "not just a smoothie maker."[26] Jack Trout, author of *Repositioning*, notes that loyal customer relationships are developed through value-added experiences and the implementation of key differentiation strategies to deal with "competition, change, and crisis."[27]

CAPTURING AND MEASURING RESULTS

How does a marketer know if its marketplace strategies are actually working? It must capture data and measure results, meaning that systems must be in place to quantify (present the result in terms of numbers) the success of a strategy. In the final analysis, the number counters count because counting keeps us accountable. Quantitative results refer to hard, objective data that involves numerical measurement; that is, finding out how many, what kind, how often. In contrast, qualitative results seek to identify subjective, relevant descriptors or characteristics; that is, how does it look, how was the service, how does it feel, and why is that important. Table 4.6 provides several examples.

Imagine preparing for a 26-mile marathon but never tracking your distance and time as you train. Serious competitors record their times, then compare and analyze them. Similarly, marketers must track their results in order to gauge whether their marketing efforts are generating the desired results—in other words, they must calculate their return on investment. **Return on investment (ROI)** defines the value (sales and profits) a company realizes after accounting for its expenses.

TABLE 4.6 Qualitative vs. Quantitative Measurements

Product Example	Qualitative Viewpoint	Quantitative Perspective
Shoe store	Carries a variety of trendy shoe styles and offers personal assistance.	Inventory has minimum of 12 pairs in each of the most popular sizes.
Bed sheets	Very soft, comfortable feeling.	Thread count is 1,000.
Cell phone	Quick e-mail response time.	1-second response time.
Purse	Ample storage compartments, with zippers for added security.	12" L x 3" W x 4" H; three 2" x 3" zippered sections.
Automobile	Excellent fuel efficiency to save money on gas.	50 miles per gallon.
Barber services	Trim my hair, clean up my sideburns; make me presentable.	Cut 1/2" off the top; take 1/4" off my sideburns.

When marketers quantify the accomplishment of key goals and objectives, an analysis of the ROI helps them determine how effectively their strategies worked and, therefore, how they should invest future resources. Both quantitative and qualitative goals play a role in crafting marketing plan objectives. For example:

▶ Quantitative goal: To achieve a 12 percent increase in net profit during the first six months of fiscal year 2013.

▶ Qualitative goal: To increase brand awareness among target market consumers in order to improve customer response ratios.

Fashion marketers measure results, not just activities. If the numbers tell them that others perceive their product, performance, and brand image favorably, that suggests their strategies are effective. If not, strategy adjustments or repositioning should be undertaken.

summary

Marketers develop and sustain a competitive advantage through planning, implementing appropriate strategies, monitoring the results, and adapting to the marketplace. The process of developing a marketing plan begins with the establishment of a company's goals and the identification of what it does well. Thorough research and analyses (situational and competitive) then lead to decisions that address the best ways to satisfy targeted customers.

After a plan is created, marketing strategies identify the specific action steps (tactics) needed to get the job done—that is, to accomplish objectives such as expanding brand awareness and increasing sales. If the strategies consistently deliver the company message and related buyer benefits in ways that are better than those of competitors, the company should thrive.

Developing a marketing growth strategy helps a company navigate through the fashion product life cycle, and marketers measure both the quantitative and qualitative results from the implementation of the marketing mix tools, using this data to adjust (reposition) the future delivery of value-added solutions to the target market.

World Imports

World Imports is a wholesaler dedicated to the creation and sales of environmentally and socially responsible fashion accessories, gifts, and home products. The company designs its own products and works directly with local artisans and producers worldwide to assure quality, workmanship, and competitive prices. To produce its attractive and unique home and fashion goods, World Imports uses a combination of renewable natural resources and reclaimed, recycled, refurbished, and biodegradable materials, crafting the products through environmentally friendly technologies and traditional techniques. The company is also known for its contributions to various altruistic causes and charities. For instance, the company donates 3 percent of the proceeds from one of its products toward the purchase of medical and educational supplies for an orphanage.

As part of its marketing plan, World Imports set itself a financial goal of 10 percent annual growth. That objective, however, has been challenged by economic factors, changes in world trade policies, scientific developments and technological innovations, and increasing environmental and social concerns. These factors influence the demands and expectations of the company's customers, which include retailers, entertainment businesses, hotels, restaurants, and others. As a result, World Imports decided to launch various short- and long-term marketing strategies including discounts and promotions, even though the company had never before used those tactics.

For instance, to increase the frequency of repeat orders and average order amount, and to attract new customers, World Imports instituted monthly promotions that were valid for orders placed during that particular month. Initiatives such as 10 percent off on orders of set minimums and free gifts succeeded in bringing in new customers and increasing average order amounts. A free freight offer, on the other hand, resulted in excessive expense for the company when heavy furniture pieces had to be shipped to Alaska or Hawaii. At times, the cost to ship such an order was greater than the order itself.

To involve and excite customers even more, World Imports' management initiated a year-long merchandising contest. Retailer customers were asked to submit images of World Imports merchandise displays in their stores, and winners received shopping sprees at World Imports and exposure on the company's Web site.

To motivate its sales staff, World Imports established weekly sales spiffs—cash prizes for reaching individual sales goals. This initiative was well received and created the desired results: increased sales. Sales agents who had previously struggled with achieving goals reached them every month in anticipation of winning cash. One pitfall: Some sales staff started holding orders until the following week if the prior week's goals were already achieved, in order to earn their bonus.

Facing increased competition and an economic downturn that diminished the disposable income of potential consumers for its products, World Imports took the additional strategic marketing step of designing informational tags for each of its products. The tags identified the product's environmentally friendly material and described the unique origin of its design. They also explained how the purchase of the product would benefit society, as a percentage of the proceeds would be donated to a charitable cause.

At the end of the year, World Imports exceeded 10 percent financial growth despite the cost of unanticipated shipping expenses and adding tags to each product. In addition, the company's market share increased by 5 percent in United States, and the company received great feedback from its customers and sales staff regarding its various promotions throughout the year.

Source: Inese Apale, Marketing Director, World Imports.

QUESTIONS

1. Define the business of World Imports and identify the company's values.
2. In your opinion, is World Imports a socially and environmentally responsible company? Please explain your answer.
3. If you were in charge of marketing strategy, what additional short-term sales promotions and long-term initiatives would you offer to World Imports customers?
4. What additional strategies would you suggest to motivate World Imports' sales staff?
5. Did World Imports compromise its values to reach the company's financial goal?

KEY TERMS

analysis

G-PESTELC

marketing plan

marketing strategy

mission statement

perceptual map

plan

positioning

psychographics

repositioning

return on investment (ROI)

segmenting

SMART objectives (specific, measurable, attainable and realistic, results-driven, and time-based)

SWOT analysis (strengths, weaknesses, opportunities, and threats) analysis

REVIEW QUESTIONS

1. Define marketing plan, and explain why its careful development is critical to the success of every product or service, especially in the twenty-first century.
2. List and discuss the four main types of marketing plans.
3. Explain the six steps used to develop a marketing strategy.
4. After defining the term *analysis*, describe the two types and explain the importance of both.
5. What does marketing strategy involve, and why is continuous marketplace adaptation important?
6. Identify five objectives of a marketing plan, and explain the main difference between a marketing plan and marketing strategies.

DISCUSSION ACTIVITIES AND PROJECTS

1. Search online for the mission statements of two fashion companies and evaluate how each provides an overview of the organization's goals.
2. Individually or with a partner, prepare to lead a class discussion on SWOT or G-PESTELC analysis. Key points should include definition of the term, and uses, benefits, and applications of the type of analysis chosen.
3. Conduct research to identify a company using one of the five types of marketing strategy discussed in the chapter and prepare a four- to six-minute oral presentation for the class on how the strategy is implemented.
4. Using SMART objectives, create an example of a concisely worded marketing objective for a real or imagined fashion company.
5. Create a chart illustrating the measurement of both quantitative and qualitative results for three fashion products. Present this information to the class, and discuss the benefits of such measurement tracking.

DEVELOPING YOUR MARKETING PLAN

Now you're ready to lay the foundation for your marketing plan using the tools described in this chapter. Looking at your chosen company or product, perform each of the following tasks:

1. Complete SWOT and competitive analyses.
2. Select one of the five types of marketing strategies that you think works best for your plan, and explain why you decided to use it.
3. Develop a growth strategy, making sure to utilize SMART objectives and a value-driven mix of marketing tools.
4. Finally, identify two methods to measure results.

Refer to the Marketing Plan Outline, Table 1.2, provided at the end of Chapter 1, as well as Appendix A: Sample Marketing Plan.

REFERENCES

1. Michael R. Solomon, *Marketing,* 4th ed. (New York: Pearson Prentice Hall, 2006).
2. Susan G. Komen for the Cure, "About Us," http://www.komen.org/AboutUs/AboutUs.html (accessed August 25, 2011).
3. The Fashion Group International, http://www.fgi.org/index.php?news=645 (accessed August 25, 2011).
4. New York Social Diary, "Teri Agins," http://www.newyorksocialdiary.com/node/2282 (accessed August 25, 2011).
5. Thinkexist.com, "Dalai Lama," http://thinkexist.com/quotes/dalai_lama (accessed August 25, 2011).
6. Thinkexist.com, "Mary Kay Ask," http://thinkexist.com/quotes/with/keyword/analysis/4.html (accessed August 25, 2011).
7. Sean "Diddy" Combs, http://www.evancarmichael.com/Famous-Entrepreneurs/622/Sean-Combs-Quotes.html (accessed August 25, 2011).
8. Making a SWOT Analysis, http://www.1000ventures.com/business_guide/crosscuttings/swot_analysis.html (accessed August 15, 2011).
9. Andrew Gillespie, *Foundations of Economics Pestel Model* (New York: Oxford University Press, 2007), http://www.oup.com/uk/orc/bin/9780199296378/01student/additional/page_12.htm (accessed August 28, 2011).
10. Thomas L. Friedman, *The World is Flat Release 3.0: A Brief History of The Twenty-First Century* (New York: Picador, 2007).
11. George Steiner, *Strategic Planning* (New York: Simon and Schuster, 1979).
12. Michael Porter, "What Is Strategy," *Harvard Business Review*, Nov.–Dec. 1996.
13. W. Chan Kim and Renée Mauborgne, "How Strategy Shapes Structure," *Harvard Business Review*, 2009.
14. *Canadian Tire Stores among Best in Class in Retailing*, October 1, 2009, http://micro.newswire.ca/release.cgi?rkey=1710012795&view=80460-4&Start=20&htm=0 (accessed October 1, 2009).

15. Doris Hajewski, "Kohl's to Sell Liz Claiborne's Dana Buchman Brand," *Journal Sentinel Post*, January 18, 2008; Just-style.com, "US: Liz Claiborne Completes Sale of Ellen Tracy," April 11, 2008 http://www.just-style.com/article.aspx?id=100447&lk=fs (accessed November 29, 2011).

16. Macy's, "Bloomingdale's to Open in Dubai in 2011," press release, September 22, 2008 http://phx.corporate-ir.net/phoenix.zhtml?c=84477&p=irol-newsArticle&ID=1199248&highlight= (accessed November 18, 2011).

17. Schwab Performance Technologies, "Sara Lee/Hanes Brands Split Off," press release, https://schwabpt.com/downloads/docs/resources/actions/library/SLE_HBI_06Sep06.pdf (accessed March 18, 2010).

18. W. Chan Kim and Renée Mauborgne, *Blue Ocean Strategy* (Boston: Harvard Business Press, 2005).

19. Walmart Corporate Web site, "About Us," http://walmartstores.com/AboutUs, (accessed November 29, 2011).

20. Scott Essman, *The Making of Avatar,* December 13, 2009, http://filmtvindustry.suite101.com/article.cfm/the_making_of_avatar (accessed March 8, 2012).

21. Eds., "Estée Lauder Targets a Wide Variety of Consumers," *Prospere Magazine*, 2009, http://prospere-magazine.com/2009/04/08/estee-lauder-targets-a-wide-variety-of-consumers (accessed March 19, 2010).

22. Donald Sull, "How to Thrive in Turbulent Markets," *Harvard Business Review Magazine*, February 2009, http://hbr.org/2009/02/how-to-thrive-in-turbulent-markets/ar/1 (accessed November 18, 2011).

23. *The Merriam-Webster Dictionary*, 5th ed.

24. Op cit.

25. Patricia Mink Rath, Stefani Bay, Richard Petrizzi, and Penny Gill, *The Why of The Buy* (New York: Fairchild Books, 2008).

26. Eds., "Jamba Juice Continues Repositioning Strategy and Enters Hot Drinks," *Flex News*, March 11, 2010, http://www.flex-news-food.com/pages/28018/Beverages/USA/jamba-juice-continues-repositioning-strategy-enters-hot-drinks.html (accessed October 7, 2011).

27. Jack Trout, *Repositioning: Marketing in an Era of Competition, Change and Crisis* (New York: McGraw-Hill, 2010).

CHAPTER 5

Obtaining and Using Fashion Marketing Information

This chapter examines marketing research as a crucial tool for fashion marketers and outlines the various sources for information as well as the elements of the marketing research process.

WHAT DO I NEED TO KNOW ABOUT FASHION MARKETING INFORMATION?

- Why fashion marketers need information and the types of information they require
- The various sources that marketers use for gathering information
- The steps in the marketing research process
- The different types of research and research methods
- How fashion marketers apply research results to their marketing plan

Where Does Fashion Come From?

"Fashion is born by small facts, trends, or even politics, never by trying to make little pleats and furbelows, by trinkets, by clothes easy to copy, or by the shortening or lengthening of a skirt."

That bit of wisdom from Elsa Schiaparelli, the Italian-born French fashion designer whose innovative styles, unique use of accessories, and dramatic colors enlivened the fashion scene from the 1920s to 1950s, tells an important truth that is perhaps even more true today: Fashion is not created in a vacuum.

Whether you are talking about the latest jacket style, a new sofa silhouette, the season's hottest shade of lipstick, or a cool new iPad, fashion is based on much more than just a random sketch on a designer's pad. Every idea and every resulting design is influenced and shaped by a myriad of small experiences and large events, by prominent figures and everyday people—in short, by the vast reams of information the world throws at all of us on a daily basis. And if fashion itself cannot be created in a vacuum, it follows that fashion marketing strategies cannot be developed in isolation either.

As you learned in the previous chapters, fashion marketers must constantly be aware of everything happening that affects consumer behavior and the marketplace, and must seek out information that will give them the tools to develop a marketing plan that makes sense for their product and their target audience. It is often said that "knowledge is power"—and that could not be truer than it is for marketers of fashion products.

Fashion Marketers' Need for Information

Fashion is all about change, so at every point in a product's development and life cycle, marketers must have current information that tells them whether they are meeting the needs and wants of their target customers. They need data that lets them know whether they have properly positioned (or repositioned) their products in the marketplace,

FIGURE 5.1 Information that may be important to a fashion marketing decision can come from virtually any source—people, places, events, and ideas.

and whether they are supporting the products with marketing messages that will help them achieve the strongest possible sales.

Some of that information may be readily available from the company's normal day-to-day operations. For instance, if Macy's runs a newspaper ad with a coupon good for 15 percent off any women's outerwear purchase, and sales of coats and jackets increase 30 percent during the time the coupon is valid, the marketing department knows instantly that the coupon promotion was successful in drawing customers to the store and persuading them to buy.

Not all information that a marketer might need is quite so obvious or easy to come by, however. That is why companies must turn to multiple sources to obtain more targeted or in-depth information or to solve a specific marketing problem.

WHERE MARKETERS OBTAIN INFORMATION

In general, companies begin with marketing information they can gather internally within their own organization, since that data can be obtained quickly and at the least expense. When internal data is not sufficient to answer a question or solve a problem, marketers then look beyond their own company and seek out data from a variety of external sources. Let's take a look at both of these avenues for obtaining marketing information.

Internal Sources

The most useful source of internal marketing data is undoubtedly a company's sales department, which can provide overall sales results as well as detailed information on how well individual products are selling and where they're selling best. A marketing manager for a company making computer carrying cases, for instance, might learn from the sales manager that the two-tone pink polka-dotted laptop sleeve is outselling the lime green version with female consumers across the country—or maybe that pink is selling better on the coasts but green is more popular in the Midwest. Other departments within an organization can also offer useful marketing information. The accounting department can share numbers that help marketers with price structures and advertising budgets, for example; and the production department can offer data regarding inventory and scheduling of shipments timed to a promotion, among other things.

Customer service departments and, in the case of retail marketers, sales associates and other store personnel can be an invaluable source of information gathered on the sales floor and in direct interactions with customers. That information "from the trenches" can sometimes reflect consumer attitudes better than data from the company's marketing experts. Best Buy, for example, has tapped into its employees' knowledge base with a "prediction market" program called TagTrade, in which questions about a product or service are presented as imaginary stocks, and all the retailer's U.S. employees are invited to "buy" or "sell" based on how they think the product or service will perform. In one case, the TagTrade prediction for sales of a new laptop computer service package was 33 percent lower than the management team's official forecast right from the start, and sank even further before the service was launched. Initial low sales figures soon confirmed that the employees' prediction

FIGURE 5.2 Retail sales associates can provide a wealth of information to their marketing departments based on their direct knowledge of what customers like and don't like, and how they shop.

was the correct one, and the company pulled the package in order to redesign it.[1]

In addition, virtually all companies today maintain extensive databases of customer information that is a goldmine of marketing data. Every time a customer makes a purchase, information about the purchase—including what was bought, sizes and colors, price paid, and so on—is captured at the point-of-sale, whether it's at the cash register in a store or in a shopping cart online. Companies gather more information when customers join loyalty programs or sign up to receive catalogues or marketing e-mails, when they register a new product purchase or send a query or complaint, and when they visit a company's Web site or "like" the company on Facebook.

Of course, not every piece of data stored in a company's customer database is equally useful to marketers. For instance, simply knowing that Jill Smith bought a brown cashmere sweater doesn't necessarily offer marketing insight, since the sweater could have been a gift for her sister, and Jill herself could be allergic to wool. On the other hand, if Jill took advantage of a Web site's personal shopping features and entered information on her size and body type, and then bought the sweater along with a pair of beige slacks after viewing several different outfit combinations on her avatar in a virtual dressing room, that purchase could indeed reveal useful information regarding her preferences.

There is one caveat to marketers' collection of customer data, and that relates to privacy issues. Some individuals are concerned that companies request too much personal information, which they view as an intrusion. More troubling is the concern that collected data may be misused, sold to a third party for unknown purposes, or not properly secured, leading to the potential for unethical activities or identity theft. Government regulations provide some safeguards, but it is up to consumers to use good judgment and a dose of caution regarding how much personal information they share, and with whom—and up to marketers to recognize their responsibility to ethically use and properly protect any consumer information they possess.

Marketing Intelligence

Going beyond the company's own internally generated information, marketers also rely on **marketing intelligence**, which is a systematic collection and analysis of publicly available information about competitors and developments in the marketplace.[2] The purpose of marketing intelligence is to reveal market opportunities, monitor

WEB COUPONS: 'WE KNOW WHO YOU ARE'

Whereas marketers once had only a slim dossier on each of their customers, now they have databases packed with information. What's more, every time a person goes shopping, visits a Web site, or buys something, the database gets another entry. But who would imagine that a coupon printed from the Internet or sent to a mobile phone could be loaded with information for marketers, including the consumer's identification, Internet address, Facebook page data—even the search terms the consumer used to find the coupon in the first place?

That is indeed the case with a new breed of online coupons whose barcode, in some cases, might provide a retailer with details as specific as that Amy Smith printed a 15 percent off coupon after searching for appliance discounts at Ebates.com on Friday at 1:30 p.m. and redeemed it later that afternoon at the store.

Using coupons to link Internet behavior with in-store shopping lets retailers figure out which ad slogans or online product promotions work best, how long someone waits between searching and shopping, and even what offers a shopper will respond to or ignore. None of the tracking is visible to consumers, but the third-party company, RevTrax, that handles the coupons for retailers—including Lord & Taylor—can identify online shoppers when they are signed in to a coupon site like Ebates or FatWallet or the retailer's own site.

RevTrax says that to steer clear of privacy issues, it avoids connecting online shoppers with real people, although its clients can make that match if they want to. So a retailer might later connect a coupon with the actual person, perhaps to send a follow-up offer or a thank-you note.

WHAT'S YOUR POINT OF VIEW?

Is it ethical for marketers to identify you based on your browsing at a particular Web site?

Adapted from: Stephanie Clifford, "Web Coupons Know Lots About You, and They Tell," *New York Times*, April 16, 2010, www.nytimes.com/2010/04/17/business/media/17coupon.html (accessed March 8, 2012).

the competition, improve strategies, and enable more informed decision making.

Marketing intelligence can be gleaned from many sources, and today, thanks to the Internet, it is easier for companies to gather than ever before. Online or off, news reports and feature articles can illuminate trends or events that impact a company's products or target customers, and can provide details about a competitor's products and marketing plans. Tracking topics related to a marketer's business on social media sites and blogs can offer insight into what consumers are interested in or how they feel about a product or service. The Web sites of competitors also provide a wealth of marketing intelligence,

FIGURE 5.3 The Internet is a goldmine for marketing intelligence, including the Web sites of a company's competitors. What might a competitor learn at Apple's Web site (apple.com)?

from annual reports to announcements of new products or promotional activity. In some cases, a company will purchase a competitor's products to evaluate their strengths and weaknesses—such as the weight of the cotton in an embellished towel or the quality of construction of a digital camera bag—and then use the differences as a marketing tool for their own products.

WHAT DO YOU THINK?

What additional ways can you think of to gather marketing intelligence?

Forecasting Services

Having information on past and present trends and the current marketplace is central to any marketing strategy, but in fashion industries, looking ahead also plays a role. While no one can fully predict the future, some astute firms and individuals are able to offer marketers a glimpse of likely trends through the field of forecasting. **Forecasting** is a process in which professional observers of culture and cultural shifts provide calculated predictions about the likely direction in which design and other consumer preferences are moving.

Some fashion producers and retailers employ their own forecasters, but others rely on outside firms that offer various forecasting services. One of the leading fashion consulting companies, The Doneger Group, maintains a trend and color forecasting division, Doneger Creative Services, devoted to the apparel, accessories, beauty, and lifestyle markets. Have you noticed an increasing array of apparel and home textiles made from eco-friendly bamboo fiber? Doneger's creative director forecast in early 2005 that bamboo apparel would be hitting the market by spring 2006.[3] Among other firms offering trend, fashion, and color forecasting services are Promostyl, SnapFashun, Trendstop.com, Peclers Paris, Cotton Inc., Color Association of the United States, and Pantone.

Market and Marketing Research

Gathering information from internal sources and as part of marketing intelligence is generally an ongoing activity. But there are times when companies need more structured or focused information for a specific purpose. In those situations, they turn to formal market or marketing research.

While the two types of research are closely related, they serve different goals. **Market research**, as defined by the Marketing Research Association, is a process used to define the size, location, and/or makeup of the market for a product or service.[4] In other words, it provides an overview of the customer base (or potential customer base) for a product, including demographic data, competitive data, and other key information.

One situation in which market research is useful is when a company is considering launching a new product line or diversifying from its core business. For example, a footwear company might decide to design a collection of handbags to coordinate with its shoes but would first need to gain knowledge about the total handbag market, the competition from other manufacturers, pricing trends, and other data that will help in both the product design and the development of a marketing plan. Another scenario calling for market research might involve a company looking to expand into a new region. Perhaps a U.S. home textiles manufacturer is interested in selling its sheets and comforters in England. The company would first need to research fundamental aspects of the British market for bed linens—how much consumers spend on the products, how many other companies already sell them, which stores consumers prefer, and so on—to ensure that its products would be successful there.

A more focused type of research is **marketing research**, a process by which businesses collect and analyze information specifically related to a marketing question, problem, or opportunity. As the American Marketing Association defines it, "Marketing research is the function that links the consumer, customer, and public to the marketer through information—information used to identify and define marketing opportunities and problems; generate, refine, and evaluate marketing actions; monitor marketing performance; and improve understanding of marketing as a process."[5]

One example of how marketing research can be used to solve a problem comes from Lee Jeans, which has been making denim apparel since 1889. Once counted among the top jeans brands, Lee found itself struggling in recent years as designer jeans and luxury denim took off in popularity. After its parent company, VF Corp., acquired 7 For All Mankind—one of Lee's nemeses—the

TREND FORECASTING AT YOUR FINGERTIPS

It used to be that design houses sent fashion scouts around the globe to attend fashion shows, shop in boutiques, and photograph people on the streets in order to identify emerging trends. Today, the world comes to them, via the Internet and a growing roster of online trend forecasting services.

After dragging their stilettos for years, fashion designers are now embracing online tools. Trend forecasting publications, which designers have relied on for decades, are increasingly offering Web sites with real-time video and photos, downloadable sketches and prints, and collaboration and design tools; and other online forecasting services are adding their voices to the mix. One of them, London-based Trendstop, has even added a free TrendTracker application that anyone with a passion for fashion can download to a mobile phone in order to monitor the latest runway looks and trends.

Another online forecaster is Stylesight, whose 1,000 clients—including Macy's, Target, Victoria's Secret, and Liz Claiborne—have access to a library of 3 million images, including everything from clothes in fashion shows or on the street, to inspiration shots like graffiti or scenery. Said Frank Bober, Stylesight's chief executive who worked for 30 years as an apparel manufacturer, "All of these activities I used to have to perform in a disparate way are now being performed on the Web site."

Adapted from: Claire Cain Miller, "Fashion Designers Go Online for Latest Trends," *International Herald Tribune*, September 8, 2008, www.iht.com/articles/2008/09/08/technology/trend.php (accessed March 8, 2012); and "Expert Fashion Forecasts for the Masses," Springwise.com, March 17, 2010, http://springwise.com/weekly/2010-03-17.htm#trendstop (accessed March 8, 2012).

company recognized that it had to take action to regain its profitability. It undertook extensive marketing research to better understand its customers, including asking consumers about their purchasing intent before and after trying on its jeans. The research told the company that its customers wanted reliable jeans with a bit of style; but most important, they wanted jeans that resolved various issues of fit. In fact, the company learned that fit mattered more to women than style and price, and that figure flattery was the number one thing that 59 percent of women look for in a pair of jeans. As a result of its research, Lee redirected its product and marketing efforts to refocus on its core customers, and developed new styles of jeans with elements designed for better fit, such as a no-gap waistband and tummy-flattening interior panel. Lee gave its new jeans descriptive names like "Slender Secret," "Custom Fit," and "Instantly Slims You." It also created a new advertising tag line ("Get What Fits") and marketing slogan ("More styles. More fits that actually fit.") to convey its updated marketing message to customers.[6, 7]

HOW MARKETERS MANAGE INFORMATION

In today's information age, marketers have a virtually unlimited supply of facts, data, and opinions available to influence and inform their marketing decisions—and with instant and mobile communications, the data is more easily accessible than ever before. The challenge becomes how companies manage the vast amounts of information so that the right data is available to the right people at the right time.

That is the purpose of a **marketing information system (MIS)**, or a set of procedures and practices a company puts in place in order to analyze, assess, and distribute the marketing information being gathered continuously from sources inside and outside of the firm. The ultimate goal of the MIS, which comprises both people and technology, is to provide accurate and timely information to managers to assist them in making marketing decisions.

The development of ever-faster computers and increasingly sophisticated analytic software is helping make marketing information systems more powerful and effective every year. Not only is there continual growth in the amount and types of digital data that marketers can tap, but improved computing tools help them make more sense of it. Today's technology is able to add science to the art of many marketing decisions, such as fine-tuning pricing or adjusting retail product assortments. For Elie Tahari, a private manufacturer of designer clothes for women and men, analytics technology enables the company to constantly mine its huge data warehouse for sales trends and to orchestrate supplies and shipping. As a senior technology manager for the company noted, "It takes all this data and makes it visible and meaningful, so you can make sense of it and act on it." "But," he added, "you're not creating something that wasn't there. Designers and merchandisers have to go with their gut if they're making something new. No computer can mimic human intuition."[8]

The Marketing Research Process

As discussed above, when a company recognizes that it does not have sufficient information at hand to answer a marketing question or solve a marketing problem, it turns to formal research. Very large companies may have the financial resources to maintain their own marketing research department, but most companies rely on outside firms with an expertise in the type of research they require. In some cases, marketers will commission a research firm to conduct a study exclusively for them and directly tailored to their needs. In other cases, research firms identify a topic to be examined and conduct studies of their own design, providing a full report and detailed findings of the research to interested companies for a fee.

In addition, some research firms perform ongoing research, usually related to a particular industry or product category, and marketers can pay a subscription to receive regular updates and the latest results as new studies are completed. The NPD Group, for example, is one of the leading global providers of consumer and retail market research information, and offers a range of research options including consumer panel research, retail sales tracking services, special reports, and custom research. One well-known NPD offering is its Consumer Tracking Service, which provides

FIGURE 5.4 Lee's marketing research led to new product designs and new marketing messages to its customers that repositioned the company's jeans around the issue of fit.

FIGURE 5.5 The NPD Group's ongoing Consumer Tracking research allows the company to provide fresh insights into consumer buying behavior on a regular basis.

comprehensive market research on consumer behavior and attitudes in a variety of industry sectors including fashion, toys, home, and consumer technology. In the Consumer Tracking program, NPD gathers data from more than 1.8 million individuals who are registered participants in the firm's online consumer panel and who have agreed to provide information on what, where, and why they are buying. For NPD's manufacturer, retailer, and service company clients in the fashion industry, the ongoing research helps them understand who is buying apparel, footwear, and accessories, and how, why, and where they are shopping.[9]

DEFINING RESEARCH OBJECTIVES

Before undertaking any research project, marketers must first define the **objectives** of the study—that is, the specific information that they want to learn. Knowing the destination they want to reach with the research will help determine what route they

need to take to get there. For instance, if a computer company's objective is to discover what age group is most likely to purchase a new netbook featuring a pop-art design on the shell, its research approach will be different from a study in which the objective is to understand how its customers are using netbooks in order for the company to incorporate appealing new functions.

Types of Information to Be Gathered

Depending on the objectives of a company's research, the type of information being sought will fall into one of two categories: quantitative data or qualitative data. **Quantitative data** is objective information, and focuses on numbers and facts that can be interpreted statistically. Quantitative data will tell a jewelry retailer how many customers shopped at its mall location last month versus the month before, and how that compares to the number of customers shopping at its downtown store. Or a different quantitative study might look at what percentage of the store's sales involved customers purchasing jewelry for themselves as opposed to purchasing a gift for someone else—and what price was most popular for each category of purchase.

Qualitative data, on the other hand, is subjective information and focuses on people's attitudes, opinions, and feelings about a product or service. Sometimes research objectives will call for a combination of qualitative and quantitative data, or a qualitative study will be done to obtain more information about the results of a quantitative study. For example, the same jewelry retailer might conduct a qualitative study to find out *why* its customers prefer the mall store or downtown location.

Do they have a favorite restaurant nearby where they like to eat during the same shopping trip? Do they find parking easier at one or the other? Do they find the ambience of the downtown store more appealing? Or the store might want to discover its customers' motivations when buying jewelry for themselves. Do they plan the purchase or make it on impulse when they see something they like in the display? Do they stick to less expensive costume jewelry when it's for themselves, or do they prefer to make the investment in higher-priced fine jewelry? Answers to those questions can help the retailer adjust its marketing strategy to better attract customers, such as offering free parking coupons one day a week or creating more eye-catching displays for fine jewelry.

Type of Study to Be Conducted

A marketer's research objectives also determine the type of study that is required. A **cross-sectional study** is research in which data is collected once from a random sampling of people. It provides a "snapshot" of statistics or opinions at a particular point in time. An example of a cross-sectional study is one that the marketing department for a mall might undertake, by positioning one or more survey takers at high-traffic spots and asking random customers about their shopping activities that day, or whether they are satisfied with the mix of stores located in the mall.

By contrast, a **longitudinal study** is research in which data is collected over time or at a series of specific points in time. It provides marketers

FIGURE 5.6 Longitudinal research often studies a specific cohort, or population segment that shares key characteristics important to the marketer. What information do you think a marketer might want to gather from these two different cohorts?

with information on trends in the marketplace and changes in consumer behavior and attitudes. The NPD Group's Consumer Tracking Service mentioned above is an example of longitudinal research, since it gathers information over stretches of time.

There are three types of longitudinal research, as identified by Flynn and Foster in *Research Methods for the Fashion Industry*.[10] A *trend study* gathers information from random samples of the population at specified and usually recurring points in time. The National Retail Federation, for example, conducts a survey of consumers each fall to find out how much money they plan to spend on holiday shopping that year. Even though the actual respondents are different each year, the survey can identify the general trend in consumer spending as compared to previous years.

Another type of longitudinal research is a *cohort study*, which surveys a specific segment of the population at repeated intervals. A company marketing to college students might conduct this type of study each summer among a group of high school graduates to ask what furnishings and accessories they plan to buy for their college dorm room, tracking trends among various products from year to year. Other examples of cohorts that might be studied are teenage girls (to determine trends in back-to-school clothes shopping, for example), parents of new babies (so as to track trends in favored styles of nursery décor), or retirees (for example, to follow trends in how they shop for consumer electronics).

The third type of longitudinal research is a *panel study*, which enlists a group of subjects who are willing to share data repeatedly over time about their purchasing habits and attitudes. The Nielsen Company, which pioneered the field of market research nearly 100 years ago, is renowned for the breadth of its consumer panels, one being Homescan, which measures the purchasing behavior of more than 250,000 households in 27 countries. Through a variety of data collection methods, these households provide information on the specific products they purchase, the retailer where each purchase occurs, and the price paid—information that Nielsen makes available to companies in its client base.[11]

CREATING A RESEARCH PLAN

Once a company has defined the objectives of its research and identified the type of study that works best for those objectives, it then develops a research plan. Among the key aspects that go into the plan are identifying what sources will be used to obtain data, pinpointing what segment of the population is to be surveyed, and deciding what methods of research will be employed.

Determining Research Sources

With the vast amount of information that flows across all channels in today's world, there is a possibility that answers to some of a marketer's research questions already exist; the marketer just needs to look for the information among a variety of potential sources. That process of exploring existing sources to find desired information is called **secondary research**, and the information that is collected is called **secondary data**. When the information cannot be found in existing sources, marketers must conduct their own original research, called **primary research**, to develop new information, or **primary data**.

Secondary Research Among the biggest advantages of secondary research is that it can save marketers the time and money required to conduct their own original research, whether in-house or by hiring an outside firm. What's more, the sources for secondary data are plentiful and much of the available data is free. In some cases, secondary research can answer initial questions or help clarify the parameters of a problem, laying the foundation for further primary research.

One of the largest sources of secondary data is the federal government. Many government agencies develop and maintain massive databases of information that is free and easily accessible to the general public. For example, information on the number, geographic distribution, and social and economic characteristics of Americans is available from the U.S. Census Bureau, while details on product safety standards and recalls of defective or dangerous products can be obtained from the Consumer Product Safety Commission.

To assist in the search for data, the government maintains a Web site at www.fedstats.gov, where anyone can link to statistics from more than 100 federal agencies, organized by agency and by subject. For instance, if you click on the topic "Consumer Spending," the site takes you to the Bureau of Labor Statistics and its Consumer Expenditure Survey program, which provides "information on the buying habits of American consumers, including data on their expenditures, income, and consumer unit (families and single consumers) characteristics." Drill down further and you can learn, among other things, that in two-income households, the average annual spending on women's apparel grew from $620 in 1998 to $806 in 2007—but dropped to $792 in 2008, perhaps due to effects of the global economic crisis that year.[12]

Books can be another source of secondary data, along with newspapers and magazines, both in print and online. Trade publications, in particular, provide focused information and trends for their respective industries, and many also conduct surveys or other research that is published within their editions. In the fashion industries, dominant trade publications—such as *Women's Wear Daily* (*WWD*) and *TWICE* (*This Week in Consumer Electronics*)—often conduct and publish results of their own market research, as well as reporting on the results of research by other organizations.

In addition, research findings and other useful information are sometimes available from groups such as trade associations and advertising agencies, as well as from dedicated market research firms. Even when access to full details of a study might be restricted to members or clients, an executive summary or press release outlining key findings is often available to the general public. For instance, a press release from the market research company Packaged Facts provides a broad overview of results from its study on "Ethnic Hair, Beauty and Cosmetics Products in the U.S.," but the full report on the study has a price tag of several thousand dollars.[13]

While secondary research can save time and money, there are some potential issues that require marketers' careful attention. Beyond the initial challenge of finding information that is relevant to their research objectives, companies must also ensure that the data they find is accurate and current. If some of the secondary research is conducted on the Internet, the concern is even greater, since much of the information posted online—unless

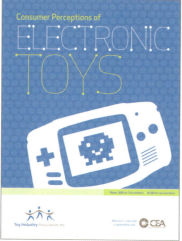

FIGURE 5.7 Secondary data may come from government agencies, news publications, trade magazines, associations, and other sources.

it's found on an established, reputable Web site—is not necessarily verified independently for truth and accuracy. Therefore, if there is any doubt, it's a smart idea for marketers to add a level of research about the source of data itself to their secondary research plan, to ensure that the information they collect is legitimately useful.

WHAT DO YOU THINK?

What are some other statistics or types of information you think might be available from federal government sources?

Primary Research When secondary research does not provide current information or sufficient information for a marketer's needs, primary research becomes the next option. Although conducting primary research can be very costly, the expense can often be justified, since it is designed to address a marketer's specific problem or question.

Working from defined objectives, primary research studies enable marketers to pinpoint the exact information they would like to obtain, and decide by what method or methods they will collect the data. They can also select what types of people are the main research targets. Depending on the study, subjects for marketing research might be existing customers, potential customers, employees, suppliers, one or more specific cohorts within a customer base, or a combination of audiences.

Determining the Research Sample

The overall group from which a marketer wants to collect data is referred to as the study's population or universe—perhaps it is women ages 25 to 44 who shop at department stores, or households that have pets. Because it is almost always impossible to contact everyone in a target population, researchers must select a **sample**, which is a subset of the group that will represent the larger population as a whole.

Three key decisions enter into designing a sample.[14] One decision is the size of the sample, since it is important to find a balance between surveying enough people to get reliable results and keeping the cost and time of the research manageable. Another decision involves who specifically is to be surveyed. A study regarding how decisions are made in the purchase of living room furniture, for example, could involve the primary income earner of the household, one or more other family members, and/or sales staff at furniture stores.

The third key decision is what sampling procedures will be used—that is, how the people in the sample are chosen. With a **probability sample**, each member of the survey population has a known and equal chance of being selected, and sampling is random within the defined population. In a **nonprobability sample**, members are selected with little or no attempt to get a representative cross section of the population. The advantage of probability sampling is that sampling error—or the degree to which a sample might differ from the total population—can be calculated. (You've probably heard people mention a survey or poll having a "margin for error of plus or minus three percent," for example.) In nonprobability sampling, sampling error cannot be measured, meaning that results may be skewed from the population as a whole. Nonprobability sampling is generally easier

TABLES 5.1A AND B Probability and Nonprobability Samples

A. TYPES OF PROBABILITY SAMPLES

Sample Type	Description of Sample
Simple random sample	Every member of the population has a known and equal chance of selection.
Stratified random sample	The population is divided into mutually exclusive groups (such as by age or gender), and random samples are drawn from each group.
Cluster (area) sample	The population is divided into mutually exclusive groups (such as blocks or defined neighborhoods), and a random sample of clusters is selected. The researcher may collect data from all the elements in the selected clusters or from a probability sample of elements within each selected cluster.

B. TYPES OF NONPROBABILITY SAMPLES

Sample Type	Description of Sample
Convenience sample	The researcher selects the easiest population members from which to obtain information.
Judgment sample	The researcher's selection criteria are based on personal judgment regarding which elements from the population are the best prospects to give accurate information.
Quota sample	The researcher finds and interviews a prescribed number of people in each of several categories, such as users of cell phones versus users of smart phones.

Adapted from: Armstrong & Kotler, *Marketing: An Introduction*, 8th edition, p. 111.

and less expensive, however, and the results may still be valid for the purposes of a given research project. Tables 5.1a and b show different types of samples in each of these sampling procedures.

CHOOSING THE RESEARCH APPROACH

There are several different methods by which research data may be collected. These include surveys, observation, focus groups, and experiments.

Survey Research

The most common technique for gathering data is the **survey**, a quantitative research method in which researchers ask people questions in order to obtain facts and information on attitudes, preferences, and buying behavior. Surveys are a very flexible tool because they can be done in person, in written form by mail or e-mail, by telephone, or online at a Web site.

Surveys are conducted with questionnaires, which feature a series of questions that reflect the research objectives and that are identical for all respondents. In addition, a few demographic questions are included in order to verify that a respondent is part of the survey's target sample—for instance, to weed out college kids from a survey targeting high school students. The demographic questions can also serve to identify respondents' subgroups within the total sample, such as identifying their year in high school if the survey objectives call for tracking differences among students by grade.

Some surveys include open-ended questions, which require respondents to answer in their own words, such as "What celebrity's look would you most like to emulate?" or "What design features do you like best on your cell phone?" More often, survey questions are closed-ended, meaning they can be answered with a simple response such as a number, a "yes" or "no," or by selecting from a multiple-choice list. This allows researchers to easily develop percentage breakdowns of responses for each question and create statistical reports. From a closed-ended question, a car company might learn, hypothetically, that 58 percent of all new car buyers prefer leather upholstery while 42 percent prefer fabric, or that among women buyers, 76 percent care about the upholstery's color more than its fabric.

Another type of survey question is an **attitude scale**, which is designed to capture the level or degree of a respondent's feelings about something. One type of attitude scale might ask respondents to rank several trendy restaurants in order of where they'd most like to have dinner. Another type might present opposite characteristics—such as "fashion innovator" and "fashion follower" or "extravagant" and "frugal"—at each end of a five- or seven-point scale and ask respondents to mark where they consider themselves to fall within the spectrum.

The most popular attitude scale is the **Likert scale**, which presents a statement and asks respondents to indicate how much they agree or disagree. For example, a survey might include the statement "Color is the most important factor when I'm choosing a new iPod," with possible responses ranging from 1 for "strongly agree" to 5 for "strongly disagree." Or another survey might include "I'm willing to spend more money to buy apparel with a designer name," and respondents could choose a response ranging from 1 for "always" to 5 for "never." See Figure 5.8 for examples of Likert scales.

TYPICAL USES OF THE LIKERT SCALE

Measure of Agreement

For each of the following statements, please check the response that best describes the extent to which you agree or disagree with each statement:

I enjoy shopping online.	Strongly Agree	Somewhat Agree	Neither Agree nor Disagree	Somewhat Disagree	Strongly Disagree
I worry about identity theft when shopping online.	Strongly Agree	Somewhat Agree	Neither Agree nor Disagree	Somewhat Disagree	Strongly Disagree

Measure of Satisfaction

How satisfied are you with the variety of nail polish colors at retailer X? Please check one:

☐ Very Satisfied　　☐ Somewhat Satisfied　　☐ Neither Satisfied nor Dissatisfied　　☐ Somewhat Dissatisfied　　☐ Very Dissatisfied

Measure of Importance

For each of the following features relating to cell phones, please check the response that best expresses how important or unimportant that feature is to you:

Texting keyboard	Extremely Important	Somewhat Important	Neither Important nor Unimportant	Somewhat Unimportant	Extremely Unimportant
Touchscreen	Extremely Important	Somewhat Important	Neither Important nor Unimportant	Somewhat Unimportant	Extremely Unimportant
Color	Extremely Important	Somewhat Important	Neither Important nor Unimportant	Somewhat Unimportant	Extremely Unimportant

FIGURE 5.8

Observational Research

Just as it sounds, **observational research** is based on watching people to determine their actions or to gain other knowledge based on visible cues or behavior. One advantage of observational research is that it does not require the active participation of those being studied, and it can even be conducted without their knowledge.

Observational research may be done on an informal basis or as a more structured study. A boutique owner, for instance, might discreetly watch customers browsing the store to see whether or not a new display of patterned legwear draws them over for a closer look. A fashion reporter might attend a celebrity gala and make observations about how many celebrities are wearing the season's hot new shade of red, or whether beaded clutch bags are more prevalent than metallics. If more statistically based information is needed, researchers might conduct a *count*, during which they keep a written tally of what they observe. A researcher positioned at a downtown intersection, for example, might conduct a count of how many silver hybrid cars drive by, versus the number of red, green, or blue models.

A form of observational research that is gaining wider use with marketers is **ethnographic research**, or the study of consumers in the natural context of their activities. Adapted from the field of anthropology, an ethnographic study lets researchers get "up close and personal" with their subjects, helping them obtain information that would not be revealed in more distant types of observation. In an ethnographic study by Diamond Cabinets, for example, researchers spent a full day in a variety of consumers' homes to observe the families' "interaction" with their kitchen cabinets, in order to develop and market better organizational features and cabinet designs.[15] While not a marketing research study, a professor and team of student researchers at Cornell University conducted a three-year ethnographic study of youth subcultures in Ithaca, New York, with the goal of gaining "a richer understanding of where youth subcultures exist in the fashion system, the social forces behind their fashion expression, and how their fashions are created, presented, manipulated, updated, and ultimately expressed both within and across social groups."[16]

Observational research can also be conducted by mechanical or electronic means. A retailer might install a sensor at the store entrance that counts how many customers come in at different times of day. Store cash registers can capture observational information such as how many items are in

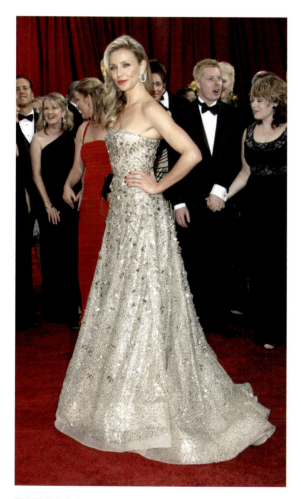

FIGURE 5.9 Celebrity gatherings, such as the red carpet on Academy Awards night, are an ideal spot for observational research on fashion trends.

customers' average purchase. On the Internet, invisible "cookies," or electronic markers placed by Web sites, can allow a company to "observe" consumers when they open a marketing e-mail or visit the company's Web site—and sometimes, in the case of tracking cookies, can actually follow consumers to see where they browse after leaving the site. While much of the information gleaned by cookies is harmless to consumers and helpful to marketers in tailoring their approach to consumers' needs, some people believe them to be an invasion of privacy. To help address customer concerns, Web sites generally provide a "privacy statement" to clarify their use of cookies and any information gathered through them, and all Web browsers incorporate privacy settings that enable consumers to control who may and may not set cookies on their computer, and to delete cookies after a browsing session.

WHAT DO YOU THINK?

Do you feel that online cookies are an invasion of your privacy? Would you feel the same if you found out a researcher was observing you as you browsed in a store? How about if they followed you to see where you shopped next?

Focus Group Research

When a marketer's objective is to obtain qualitative research, the data most often comes from focus groups. A **focus group** is a gathering in which approximately 8 to 12 consumers share their opinions of a product, service, or other marketing-related topic, guided in their discussion by a moderator. While the moderator has a specific

agenda and controls the overall direction of the discussion, focus group members are encouraged to speak freely and respond to each other's comments, often leading to greater insights for the marketer.

Very similar to a focus group is a **depth interview**. Depth interviews follow much the same format as a focus group but involve only one person sharing thoughts and opinions with a researcher. Both types of sessions involve a greater commitment of time than some other research methods, so participants are usually offered cash or other incentive to take part. At the same time, participants are chosen according to very precise criteria to ensure they match the target audience the marketer is trying to research. A focus group designed to obtain opinions about a new spray-on self-tanning lotion, for instance, might require participants to have used some other tanning product in the past, or it might be restricted to women, or even just to women ages 18 to 34 who frequent tanning salons.

In either a focus group or a depth interview, participants may be shown product prototypes, samples of packaging, television commercials, or other information, or may simply be told about ideas and concepts on which to give their opinions. By getting consumer feedback before a new product, advertising campaign, or other marketing strategy is finalized, marketers can often discover ways to tweak their plan that will better match customers' preferences and expectations.

Traditionally, focus groups have taken place in special conference rooms equipped with one-way mirrors, so that other researchers, or perhaps representatives from the company sponsoring the research, could observe unseen. Audio/video equipment is also concealed behind the glass to record the session

Consumers are more frugal as a result of the recession — greater focus on value is likely to stick for the next few years

Key Findings	Implications

Key Findings

- Per capita consumption expenditure has declined for 2 straight years – the first time since the Great Depression

- Reductions in spending are most pronounced for lower-income women, but all demographic groups cut back

- Consumers' outlook is modestly conservative – only 32% of households expect to be better off this year

- Frugal behavior is now the norm: two-thirds of consumers frequently use coupons, value price over convenience, and believe saving is more important than spending

- Product categories whose purchase can be postponed or substituted (e.g., durables, entertainment) were hit the hardest, but small indulgences (e.g., health & beauty) continue to be bought

- Switching to lower-priced brands is common among everyday categories (food items, household products) but less common for alcohol, tobacco, consumer electronics

- Share shift to private-label products has accelerated

Implications

- As the economy emerges from a very deep and prolonged recession, high unemployment and income anxiety are likely to cause frugal behaviors to remain persistent

- Given greater focus on value, marketers and retailers need to better align their product assortment:
  - Reassess the number of price points and optimal gap between them by category
  - Review the planned innovation pipeline to ensure that new product launches deliver clear value (not necessarily lowest price) to attractive and growing target segments

- As price-based competition remains fierce, developing deeper insights into shopping behaviors is critical before responding to lower price competitors …

- … while ensuring that the operating model is well aligned to the value proposition and pricing strategy – there is a price floor at which you are not profitable for certain segments

Consumers differ in terms of how much they emphasize getting the best price, brand loyalty, and convenience

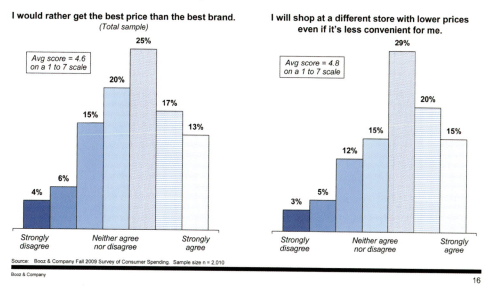

I would rather get the best price than the best brand.
(Total sample)

Avg score = 4.6 on a 1 to 7 scale

4% | 6% | 15% | 20% | 25% | 17% | 13%

Strongly disagree ... Neither agree nor disagree ... Strongly agree

I will shop at a different store with lower prices even if it's less convenient for me.

Avg score = 4.8 on a 1 to 7 scale

3% | 5% | 12% | 15% | 29% | 20% | 15%

Strongly disagree ... Neither agree nor disagree ... Strongly agree

Source: Booz & Company Fall 2009 Survey of Consumer Spending. Sample size n = 2,010

FIGURE 5.11 Researchers present detailed statistics and analysis of their findings, as illustrated by these excerpts from a 28-page report by Booz & Company on its study entitled, "New Marketing Imperatives: U.S. Consumer Spending & Shopping Behavior Emerging from the Recession."

ads, for instance, and 95 percent strongly disliked one particular ad, that overwhelming response would stand out and receive special note.

Besides creating a statistical analysis of the survey data, researchers are trained to interpret the information and draw conclusions based on the results they have gathered. Both the tabulated data and the researcher's interpretation of it are compiled into a report for the marketer. That report generally begins with an executive summary, which restates the research objectives, provides a concise overview of results, calling out the most salient findings, and includes a general conclusion of what the results mean. The report then goes on to detail each element of the study, including charts and graphs of statistical data, relevant quotes from survey respondents or focus group members, copies of the research materials, and analysis of each segment as it relates to the research objectives. Researchers will also offer recommendations for action based on their interpretation of the results.

APPLYING THE RESULTS

When marketers receive a research report, it does not turn immediately into action. In many cases, data can be interpreted in more than one way—and an interpretation from the researchers' perspective may not jibe with the marketers' interpretation, based on their own realm of expertise. So discussions between the researchers and marketers can often point to a conclusion that blends both points of view while still being supported by the data.

Even then, research analysis rarely offers a single, clear-cut answer that points to a single avenue for action. To help make the best decisions based on research results, marketers might have information analysts create a series of analytical models, each representing an actual scenario based on the newly acquired data blended with existing data. These models can often help marketers answer questions such as "what if" and "which is best" to determine the best path to take.[17]

summary

Fashion marketers have an ongoing need for information that tells them whether they are meeting the needs and wants of their target customers. Some of that information is available from internal sources within the organization, particularly from the sales department, which can provide data on how well different products are selling and where they're selling best, and from customer service or retail store personnel, who have insight from direct interactions with customers. Marketers can also access the extensive information stored in their company's customer databases.

Additional sources of information include marketing intelligence, forecasting services, and market or marketing research. Market research provides a broad definition of the size, location, and makeup of the market for a product service. Marketing research is designed to offer information that relates to a specific marketing question, problem, or opportunity. Companies use a marketing information system, consisting of both people and technology, to manage, organize, analyze, and distribute the vast amounts of marketing data gathered from all sources.

When marketers turn to research to gather needed information, they begin by defining the objectives of the study. They may seek quantitative (objective) data or qualitative (subjective) data, or a combination of the two. The study may be cross-sectional, providing statistics or opinions at a particular point in time, or longitudinal, collecting data over time or at a series of specific points in time.

A research plan may include gathering of secondary data that is available from existing sources, or conducting primary research to develop new information. Secondary research is less expensive and sources may be plentiful, whereas primary research costs more but is designed to address a marketer's specific question or problem. Conducting primary research requires selecting a sample from the study's target population.

Research approaches include surveys, observation, focus groups, and experiments. At the conclusion of any study, researchers analyze the data, prepare a report including statistical and descriptive details, and provide recommendations for action based on their conclusions. Marketers review and discuss the data, often creating a collection of analytical models that help determine the best course of action that combines the new data with their existing information.

Web-Tracking Research Lets Marketers Listen to Consumers

Replacing "asking" with "listening" has been a hot topic at market-research conferences in recent years. But now, some researchers are doing more than talking—they're taking steps toward replacing surveys with Web tracking, hoping to monitor brand health by observing and analyzing people's spontaneous comments in social media and other Web venues. Some advocates are even suggesting Web tracking could be a dominant form of research.

"The way a lot of people are using social media right now is to help explain survey results," said Larry Friedman, chief research officer of TNS, a world leader in market research, global market information, and business analysis. "What we're arguing is that you need to think about it the other way around" by using surveys instead as the supplement to expand on trends identified in various forms of Web tracking.

It's not just about observing conversations in social media, Friedman said, but tracking people's online behavior in other ways, such as visits to Web sites and search queries. To that end, he put together a study comprising Web traffic, Google-search volume, sentiment of online buzz, and tracking surveys from TNS and other sources to show how Tiger Woods' infidelity scandal affected his popularity and the brands he endorsed.

One problem with tracking surveys is that respondents often don't care about the questions beyond any compensation they're getting. So the passion, or even lower-level caring, that survey research tends to miss is one thing online buzz may be able to capture, in some ways better even than ordinary word of mouth.

David Wiesenfeld, a long-time researcher who for years relied on tracking surveys both on the client and vendor side, has come to believe that tracking surveys miss too much of consumers' passion and complexity. "Things that are more emotional, things that are more complex ideas than it tastes good or doesn't, surveys don't easily express that," said Wiesenfeld, who is now vice president of marketing solutions for Nielsen Online.

But while Web tracking is cheaper, faster, and according to Wiesenfeld, better than survey tracking, what has been missing is statistical validation of its quality and results. That is starting to appear, however, as in a study commissioned by Toronto-based OnResearch. The parallel study of 75 brands used a survey of 524 consumers side by side with tracking 200,000 blog comments about the same brands. What it found was that the "net promoter score"—essentially the number of survey respondents with positive outlooks on the brand minus those with negative outlooks—correlated closely with the "net blog score" that OnResearch created, subtracting the number of negative blog comments from the number of positive ones.

Still, there's considerable need for analysis, and plenty of evidence that online comments, particularly the occasional Tweet-storms of outrage over a marketing campaign or mishap, don't always reflect sentiments of the broader population.

Adapted from: Jack Neff, "Web-Tracking Research Emerging from Surveys' Shadow," *Advertising Age*, April 5, 2010, http://adage.com/article/digital/web-tracking-research-emerging-surveys-shadow/143104/ (accessed March 8, 2012).

QUESTIONS

1. What would you say are some of the advantages of Web tracking over traditional survey-style marketing research? What are some of the disadvantages?
2. Do you think Web tracking could be considered an invasion of consumers' privacy and an ethical issue for marketers? Explain your view.

KEY TERMS

attitude scale

cross-sectional study

depth interview

ethnographic research

experimental research

focus group

forecasting

Likert scale

longitudinal study

market research

marketing information system (MIS)

marketing intelligence

marketing research

nonprobability sample

objectives (research)

observational research

primary data

primary research

probability sample

qualitative data

quantitative data

sample (in research)

secondary data

secondary research

survey

REVIEW QUESTIONS

1. Why is it important for marketers to constantly have current information?

2. What are four or five different sources that companies use to obtain marketing information?

3. Explain the difference between market research and marketing research, and give an example of a situation where each might be used.

4. What is the difference between quantitative data and qualitative data? Name a research approach that would gather each type.

5. What are three possible sources of secondary data? In what situation would a marketer need to conduct primary research instead of or in addition to secondary research?

6. Name the four different methods by which marketing research can be conducted, and give a brief description of each.

DISCUSSION ACTIVITIES AND PROJECTS

1. Choose a product category (men's shirts, baby cribs, smartphones, etc.), and imagine you work for a company in that field and need to gather fresh marketing intelligence. Describe how you would go about collecting data, some of the internal and external sources you would use, and some of the types of marketing intelligence information you would expect to find.

2. Go online and search for recent research related to a fashion category or trend. Pick one study and write a report detailing what you are able to learn about the study, including who conducted or commissioned the research, who was included in the research sample, whether it was cross-sectional or longitudinal, what research method was used (survey, focus group, etc.), and results of the study. Were you able to view a full report, or only a press release or other public summary?

3. Imagine you are thinking of launching a line of children's footwear and need additional data on the growth of that market, as well as on colors and style features (laces, Velcro fasteners, fabric, etc.) that will be most attractive to customers. First, conduct secondary research to find statistics on sales of children's shoes over a 5-year period. Next, create a questionnaire with 8 to 10 questions, including closed-ended questions, attitude scales, and one open-ended question that will help in your primary research about shoe styling. Include in your write-up who your target sample for the survey would be.

4. With a partner, select a fashion item or style trend and create a marketing research plan using observational research. Define the objectives of your research, whether or not it will include a count, and where the study will take place; then spend at least a half hour, each at a different spot at the site, collecting data. Prepare an executive summary for the class, including overall results, differences in data between the two observers, and your interpretation of what the results mean.

DEVELOPING YOUR MARKETING PLAN

In this chapter, you learned the importance of information gleaned from marketing research. Based on the growth strategy you developed in the previous chapter's assignment, identify a key area to research that would help you implement that strategy (population trends in your target age group, pricing of similar products on the market,

etc.), and write a plan for your research. Be sure to include the following:

1. The information you want to obtain
2. The type (secondary or primary) of sources and the specific sources you might use to gather it
3. What types of research methods would be most suitable to gathering the information
4. How you would apply the research results to your marketing plan

Explain your choices and decisions.

Refer to the Marketing Plan Outline, Table 1.2, provided at the end of Chapter 1, as well as Appendix A: Sample Marketing Plan.

REFERENCES

1. Phred Dvorak, "Best Buy Taps 'Prediction Market,'" *Wall Street Journal*, September 16, 2008, http://online.wsj.com/article_email/SB122152452811139909-lMyQjAxMDI4MjExNjUxMjY0Wj.html (accessed March 8, 2012).

2. Gary Armstrong and Philip Kotler, *Marketing: An Introduction*, 8th ed. (Upper Saddle River, NJ: Pearson Prentice Hall, 2011), p. 99.

3. Jeanne Sahadi, "Fashion's Future Is a 6-Figure Job," CNNMoney.com, January 7, 2005, http://money.cnn.com/2004/09/28/pf/sixfigs_eight/index.htm (accessed March 8, 2012).

4. Marketing Research Association, "Glossary of Terms," www.mra-net.org/resources/glossary_terms.cfm?ID=K (accessed November 28, 2011).

5. American Marketing Association, "Dictionary," www.marketingpower.com/_layouts/

Dictionary.aspx?dLetter=M (accessed November 28, 2011).

6. Jennifer Mann, "Jeans Maker's Sales Plan a Perfect Fit," *Journal News* (McClatchy Newspapers), January 27, 2008, D1.

7. Lee Jeans, "Our Company/," www.lee.com/wps/wcm/connect/lee-en_us/our_company/press/ and www.lee.com/store/LEE_STORE_US/en_US/category/women/jeans.html (accessed November 28, 2011).

8. Steve Lohr, "A Data Explosion Remakes Retailing," *New York Times*, January 3, 2010, www.nytimes.com/2010/01/03/business/03unboxed.html (accessed March 8, 2012).

9. The NPD Group Web site, www.npdgroup.com (accessed November 29, 2011).

10. Judy Zaccagnini Flynn and Irene M. Foster, *Research Methods for the Fashion Industry* (New York: Fairchild Books 2009), pp. 146–148.

11. The Nielsen Company, http://www.nielsen.com/us/en.html (accessed March 8, 2012).

12. Consumer Expenditure Survey, United States Department of Labor, Bureau of Labor Statistics, www.bls.gov/cex/home.htm (accessed November 29, 2011).

13. Personal Care Market Reports, "Packaged Facts," www.packagedfacts.com/personal-care-market-c113/ (accessed November 29, 2011).

14. Op cit., p. 110.

15. "New Research Study Reveals What's 'Hiding' Inside Cabinets," *Kitchen & Bath Design News*, August 2006, www.kitchenbathdesign.com/publication/article.jsp?pubId=2&id=3311 (accessed November 29, 2011).

16. "Street Style: An Ethnographic Study of Fashion Subcultures in Ithaca, New York: Research and the Costume Collection," Cornell University, http://char.txa.cornell.edu/treasures/streetstyle.htm (accessed November 29, 2011).

17. Op cit., p. 113.

CHAPTER 6

Creating the Right Relationships with Fashion Customers

This chapter examines how to organize and apply marketing research in order to segment the market, target appropriate consumers, and position a product to meet marketing goals. It also discusses the importance of managing customer relationships to build and maintain loyalty.

WHAT DO I NEED TO KNOW ABOUT RELATIONSHIPS WITH FASHION CUSTOMERS?

* How marketers create segmentation models to identify the right fashion customers
* The importance of prioritizing segments for business opportunities
* How marketers identify an effective targeting strategy
* How positioning tools are used to gain a competitive advantage
* What measuring tools are used to quantify success
* How the CRM, CEM, and PRM processes optimize the value chain
* The importance of building competitive and ethical value into customer solutions

Selecting the Right Customers

One day at lunch, Yesenia Marcos, a fashion design student, told her girlfriend Lydia, a fashion marketing major, that she dreamed of owning her own boutique. She would design, manufacture, and sell casual clothes and accessories to women. Lydia smiled, then asked Yesenia to identify the key demographic and psychographic characteristics of her typical client, the best ways of delivering value to them, and the logical or psychological product and service expectations of Yesenia's potential customers. Yesenia said she wasn't sure, so Lydia continued, "If you want to stack the dice in your favor, you should first figure out who your realistic potential customers are, then use all the marketing tools to give those customers specific reasons why they should choose, and continue to choose, your store and fashion designs, not your competitors." When Yesenia asked her friend to go into more detail, Lydia commented, "You should read Chapter 6 in my fashion marketing textbook. I'll bring it tomorrow."

Yesenia Marcos' boutique and fashion design interest story in "Selecting the Right Customers" and the statements in the Marketer's Insight "Customer Diversity" feature demonstrate that focusing your marketing efforts on specific, not general, answers as they relate to your customers is a key ingredient for success.

This chapter illustrates the steps that fashion marketers should take to segment the overall market, target the appropriate market segments that contain the customers they want to reach, and position their products or services in ways that appeal to and work best for that target market. In short, if you know how to use the marketing tools discussed in this chapter, you should be able to guide Yesenia, the fashion design student mentioned above, in answering the questions that her girlfriend Lydia asked.

Why Selecting Customers Is Vital

As you've read in earlier chapters, the marketplace is composed of a diverse group of buyers, many having different wants and needs. Marketers that want to be effective addressing those needs strive to determine who their customers are, group them according to shared similarities, and then deliver

FIGURE 6.1 When Yesenia asked her friend Lydia, "Do you think I should buy this specific fabric for our new designs?" Lydia replied, "I don't know. Let's first figure out who's going to buy the dresses you make."

products that meet and exceed those customers' expectations. This is called **target marketing**, a concept that was introduced in Chapter 1. Building relationships with the right customers, not just any customers, consistently delivering better value than the competition, and adapting to the marketplace as needed results in sustainable business growth. The following pages explain the STP (*segmenting*, *targeting*, and *positioning*) model. Step 1 is "S," the segmentation process.

What Is Market Segmentation?

Market segmentation, as you'll recall from Chapter 1, divides total markets into smaller clusters of possible customers who display similar characteristics, wants, and needs. Dividing a larger market into smaller units that share some specific commonalities increases the odds for a fashion marketer to focus on the right group of prospects. Making the distinction between targeting prospects in a broad audience who can *potentially* use your product and those who are *likely* to use your product is very important, according to Bob Leduc, a sales consultant and business publications author.[1] Identifying those key segments of likely customers within the larger market is the first step in a successful marketing plan.

Creating Market Segmentation Categories

Market segmentation is a critical factor whether a fashion company wants to sell to consumer markets, business markets, or global markets, each of which has a different set of criteria for segmentation. Let's look more closely at some of the **segmentation categories** marketers might use, that is, the demographic, psychographic, or other characteristics by which a large market can be subdivided into similar (*homogeneous*) parts—as opposed to a *heterogeneous* group whose members have varied or widely dissimilar traits. (You might find it helpful to refer back to Table 4.3.)

MARKETER'S INSIGHT: CUSTOMER DIVERSITY

The response to each of these statements is "not necessarily."

▶ All customers are the same.

▶ We know for sure what will happen tomorrow.

▶ Straight-leg jeans work for most people.

▶ A hamburger is a hamburger.

▶ Never mix and match contemporary and classic looks.

TYPES OF FABRIC

TYPES OF SILK

SILK · CASHMERE · COTTON · LEATHER · WOOL

CHARMEUSE · CHIFFON · SATIN · TAFFETA · BROCADE

FIGURE 6.2 In addition to segmenting target markets, fashion businesses also segment merchandise characteristics.
BY VANESSA HAN AND ALICIA FREILE

CONSUMER MARKETS

For consumer markets, most experts agree on four major segmentation categories: *demographics* (statistical data points), *geographics* (location), *psychographics* (lifestyle and attitude preferences), and *usage* (how frequently and why consumers buy).

1. *Demographics*. This segmentation category measures statistical characteristics of a population, traits that can be observed or objectively identified about the group, including age, sex, household income, education level, occupation, ethnicity, religion, birth and death rates, gender orientation, marital status, and family size. Demographic information helps marketers understand the "who" and "what" factors of their customer base.

2. *Geographics*. This term includes the physical environment, climate, and natural resources inherent to a particular market. The geographical location where consumers live or spend time, whether a coastal region, rural farm belt, big city, or suburban area, can provide marketers with key information on customers' needs and likely purchase habits.

3. *Psychographics*. This element of segmentation involves consumers' lifestyle, leisure activities, or other personal preferences to provide information that marketers use to uncover the

"why," or the motivations of consumer decision making. By researching the activities, interests, and opinions (AIOs), attitudes, and values important to customers, marketers try to better understand how consumers integrate and process their social, cultural, political, economic, or spiritual beliefs, and how that may affect their product choices.

4. *Usage.* This segmentation category specifies the quantity and rate at which consumers make brand purchases, as well as their level of loyalty to a particular brand, purchase location preferences,

and other helpful information that provides marketers with key insights into how their products are perceived, purchased, and consumed.

Remember: The purpose of identifying and organizing these various segments is to group consumers together who share some similarities in wants, needs, and living or purchasing habits.

FIGURE 6.3 Segmenting the market for high-end patio furniture can involve all four consumer segmentation areas, including demographics (income level), geographics (appropriate climate), psychographics (leisure activities), and usage (likelihood of purchasing the brand).

WHAT DO YOU THINK?

Imagine that an entrepreneur opened a fashion boutique in your neighborhood but did not first segment the marketplace to create a demographic and/or psychographic profile for her typical customer. What are some of the potential problems she might experience with buying products for the store and satisfying customers' purchase expectations?

BUSINESS MARKETS

For fashion marketers selling to other businesses, it is equally important to identify specific customer segments in order to deliver solutions that are meaningful to those customers, instead of trying to satisfy everyone with the same products. For instance, an apparel manufacturer might segment the industrial market and design clothes to meet the needs of construction workers in oil, chemical, or mining companies. An architect might segment the commercial market and specialize in designing distinctive dining room layouts for upscale restaurants. A watch repair professional might segment the retail market and offer his services specifically to high-end jewelry stores.

TABLE 6.1 Segmentation of Business Markets

Category of Segmentation	Examples
Primary business activity	Business sector as identified by North American Industry Classification System (NAICS)
Business type	OEM End user Aftermarket
Usage requirements	Product performance Price Quality Service level

There are several different ways by which to segment business markets. The major categories include business classification (the type of products or services that companies provide); usage requirements (what is needed in terms of product, level of performance, price, quality, service); and business type (OEM–original equipment manufacturers, end users, aftermarket). To segment by classification, marketers can turn to the NAICS—North American Industry Classification System—developed jointly among the United States, Canada, and Mexico. NAICS (pronounced "nakes") was created to classify establishments according to the primary type of business activity in which they engage. The system includes 20 broad sectors, ranging from manufacturing, wholesale trade, and retail trade, to information, finance and insurance, and transportation and warehousing. Each sector is further narrowed down by industry sub-sector, industry group, and industry, summarized in a five- or six-digit code.[2]

Consider this example of business market segmentation: Stefani B, a jewelry design company, begins by segmenting according to classification, selecting upper-end department stores and other fine jewelry retailers that attract the right customer for the company's distinctive pieces made from gold, silver, and precious and semiprecious stones. Additional segmentation of its business customer base is then based on the usage requirements of specific stores, since some focus on diamonds, others have a loyal clientele who prefer pearls or silver, and so on. The point to remember is that zeroing in on the correct market segment will result in greater sales and marketing success.

GLOBAL MARKETS

Segmenting global markets involves the same criteria used to segment domestic markets, including demographics, geographics, psychographics, and

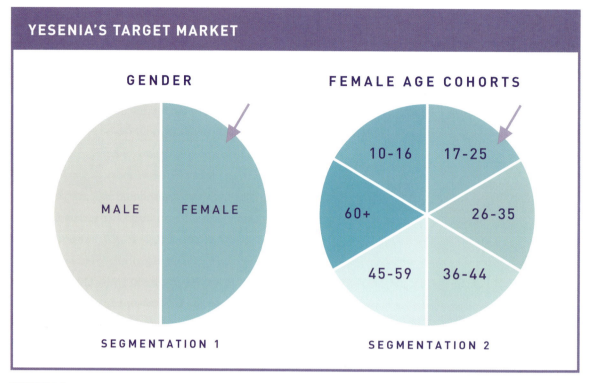

FIGURE 6.4 BY VANESSA HAN AND ALICIA FREILE

usage. But there is often more to it than that. When organizations compete in the global marketplace, there are inherent challenges, as you'll recall from the discussion of G-PESTELC factors (Global-Politics, Environment/Climate, Sociocultural issues, Technology, Economics, Legal issues, Competition) in Chapter 4. While different countries can be segmented using these factors, these divisions may not be consistent in each market and, therefore, could lead to market share reduction.

Another approach used for global markets is *intermarket segmentation*, which addresses groups of customers in different countries whose buying behavior, needs, or special interests are similar. [3] For example, during the summer of 2010, South Africa hosted the FIFA World Cup for 32 worldwide

qualifying soccer teams. Pepsi targeted soccer fans in its advertising and showed enthusiasts from a variety of global locations playing soccer while enjoying a cool Pepsi drink. The benefit: Pepsi zeroed in on this specific segment and reached people from multiple cultures with a single ad campaign. [4]

Here is a segmenting example of Step 1 in the STP process as it relates to Yesenia's situation mentioned at the beginning of the chapter. She decides to focus on women, not men, for her fashion designs; see Segmentation 1 in Figure 6.4. Next, she subdivides the category—women—by *age cohorts* (defined in Chapter 5), groups of women within the same age range; see Segmentation 2 in Figure 6.4.

Each segmentation illustrates how the total category is subdivided. Segmentations derived from reliable research, which also meet a marketer's key criteria, create the foundation blocks for effective marketing strategies. What makes one segment more attractive than another, and how do you decide which segment to address? The next section addresses useful segmentation prerequisites and targeting strategies.

Targeting Market Segments

Once fashion marketers have segmented the potential customer universe into smaller units with demographic or psychographic similarities, they analyze the segments to decide which ones to pursue. Identifying the segments most appropriate for the marketer's product is Step 2: targeting, or the "T" in the STP model. In our chapter example, Yesenia reviews the various age groups of women to determine which will be the best fit for her products; the group she ultimately chooses is the target market. Rather than spending time and money trying to sell their fashion products to everyone, successful marketers make a point of knowing who their ideal prospects are, where they are, what they enjoy doing, and where they enjoy doing it—making it easier and more efficient to reach those target customers and communicate the benefits of the product. A good analogy is that of using a narrow funnel, instead of free-hand pouring, to transfer an expensive, imported, extra virgin garlic olive oil into a slim-mouthed, designer crystal cruet. Naturally, one process will be more effective than the other.

How should this decision process begin? How does a company evaluate and decide which segments to target?

ESSENTIAL SEGMENTATION FACTORS

To utilize the segmentation process in making targeting decisions, certain factors should be considered or this effort may not be a very effective foundation for subsequent strategic actions. In deciding whether or not to use a particular segment, fashion marketers evaluate potential target segments based on a number of criteria:[5]

1. *Substantiality.* Does the segment encompass a large enough customer base to generate sufficient sales and profit, and what is the potential for future growth? A fashion designer who has created a solid-gold handbag that appeals to an extremely limited group of potential buyers may not be in business too long.

2. *Measurability.* Can the segment be quantified in terms of its size and buying power? How much discretionary income do members of the segment have available? Research can help verify measurable criteria, such as information that might be sought by a sportswear company thinking of expanding its line to include prom and party attire. For example:

   ▸ How many high school seniors are there in a specific geographic region?

   ▸ How many high schools in that region are having senior proms?

   ▸ What is the average income of families with high-school-age children in the region?

3. *Accessibility.* How easy will it be to reach customers in the segment? What media do they prefer? If the segment is too difficult or costly to reach, it may not be a viable segment to target. For example, a growing number of

FIGURE 6.5 Do you think the marketer of this shoe used substantiality as a key element in evaluating its target market segment?

consumers are easy to reach through social media such as Facebook or YouTube, but that might not be an effective way to communicate with an over-65 segment. During the summer of 2010, Ford Motor Company decided to launch an all-new Ford Explorer on Facebook, instead of at an auto show.[6] What does that tell you about the segment the company was targeting?

4. *Serviceability*. How well can customers' needs in the segment be met in terms of delivering what they want, when they want it, and how can a company do this better than the competition while making a profit? For example, it's not very sensible and realistic for a single milliner (hat designer) to target a multi-store hat boutique that will need 30 to 40 units per week if she can only produce 12 to 20 units per week.

If a marketer's analysis finds that particular segments meet or exceed the above criteria in ways that will be profitable for the organization, a decision to move forward can be made. If the data show that the segments just do not have the capacity to support sustainable business profit or growth, new segments will be researched.

Let's return to the conversation between Yesenia and her girlfriend, Lydia, from the beginning of this chapter. After completing the necessary research and weighing that essential segmentation data in light of her personal interests and goals, Yesenia decides to target women in the 17 to 25 age cohort, believing that this segment is sufficiently substantial, measurable, accessible, and serviceable.

SEGMENTATION PROFILE

The next question for Yesenia is this: How much information does she need to know about her chosen target segment? Ideally, she will create a **segment profile**, a clear description of the specific customer characteristics within the targeted segment that reflect distinctive patterns.[7] A segment profile is like viewing a high-definition photo with a detailed demographic or psychographic description of a typical customer. Why is this important? Building profitable relationships with the right customers is good for a marketer's stakeholders at every level. Conversely, investing resources to build relationships with the wrong customers turns into a wasted, nonproductive chore.

It comes down to defining how precise or narrow the market is that the company is targeting. Think of a homeowner who has decided to water her beautifully landscaped and celebrity-designed yard. Does she adjust the rotating water sprinkler system so the spray distributes water in fine, crisp, directional lines on specific areas, or should she try to reach every part of the lawn in a random, rainstorm manner? With additional research and analysis, Yesenia will create a plan and a targeting strategy to reach her ideal customers, and create interest in her store and fashion designs.

Identifying a Targeting Strategy

Selecting a targeting strategy means figuring out whether to go after the whole market, part of it, or a smaller part of it. Completing this process fits in with the saying, "Work smarter, not harder," and further supports the "T" leg in the STP triangle shown in Figure 6.6.

Let's look at four types of targeting strategies: *concentrated*, *customized*, *differentiated*, and *undifferentiated*.

CONCENTRATED

In a concentrated targeting strategy, fashion marketers focus on a narrow customer segment with an appropriate product—a strategy that provides opportunities for smaller businesses that don't want to or financially can't take on multiple segments. This approach is also known as **niche marketing**, or targeting specialized market sub-segments within a larger group. For example, a carpenter may restrict his business only to clients who install fashion-designed, high-end residential doors. Or a medical doctor who is a board-certified cosmetic surgeon may limit her practice to performing only face-lifts. In both cases, their specialty products and marketing address a very select group.

CUSTOMIZED

In a customized targeting strategy, sometimes called micro marketing, fashion companies fine-tune their marketing communications and products to address very specific and individualized customer needs and wants. Just as a microscope is used to magnify objects, this finely tailored strategy zooms in on the unique needs of each target customer and delivers appropriate customized products. A maker of couture bridal apparel would use this targeting approach, designing one-of-a-kind gowns for clients.

DIFFERENTIATED

Billy Wilder, renowned film producer, director, writer, and Academy Award winner, once said, "Give people what they want, and they'll come out for it."[8] In a differentiated targeting strategy, marketers provide products for multiple market segments and satisfy the customer needs of each by creating a distinct marketing mix for each segment. A company using this strategy develops products

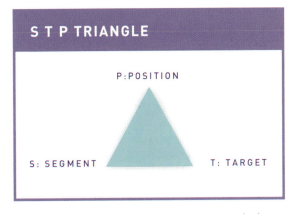

FIGURE 6.6 Each leg contributes to a strong marketing plan BY VANESSA HAN AND ALICIA FREILE

TABLE 6.2 Targeting Strategies

Type	Target Customers	Marketer Benefits	Potential Problems	Examples
Undifferentiated (mass marketing)	All segments	Can save money by producing the same product for all	Competition from niche competitors; same product does not satisfy all customers	Cereal company offering plain corn flakes; underwear manufacturer making basic white briefs
Differentiated	Several segments	Can reach different groups of customers by creating separate products for each segment	Higher costs for production, distribution, and promotion	Guitar manufacturer creating multiple product lines for different types of music (jazz, rock, folk)
Concentrated (niche marketing)	One specialized sub-segment	Can focus effort efficiently on likely purchasers	Fluctuating market demand; competitor entering market with more resources	Cosmetic surgeon performing only face-lifts; interior designer focusing on high-end residential kitchens
Customized (micro marketing)	Very small and specific segment	Can create unique solutions and personalized market messages	High cost per customer; logistics challenges; brand dilution	Dealer selling only classic cars to client base of collectors; fashion designer specializing in unique bridal gowns

catering to particular groups or levels of customers. For example, Neiman Marcus Group opened CUSP stores and boutiques, offering clothes and accessories to younger women than the traditional Neiman Marcus customer, and Fruit of the Loom expanded its underwear selection from only men to include women and children.

UNDIFFERENTIATED

Undifferentiated targeting is a "one size fits all" strategy that does not take into account differing customer wants and needs. It may reduce expenses—development, production, distribution, and promotion—in the creation of one product, but

FIGURES 6.7A–D These fashion looks illustrate the targeting strategies of (a) undifferentiated (mass) targeting, (b) differentiated targeting, (c) concentrated (niche) targeting, and (d) custom (micro) targeting.

it only fits some of the people all of the time. This can translate to wasted resources, because reaching everyone, even those people who are not at all interested, may be very costly.

An undifferentiated targeting strategy focusing on an entire market universe is also called **mass marketing**. In the summertime, people of all ages want cool, comfortable footwear. That's why you see virtually identical rubber or plastic flip-flops in discount and convenience stores and pharmacies, as well as specialty shops. If customers all want the same thing, this is a good strategy.

Once segmentation and targeting tools are used to organize the efforts, fashion marketers then focus on ways to get customers to understand how their particular product is better than the competitor's offering—as we'll now examine.

Positioning the Product

To position means to arrange or place something in a particular way or order. In marketing, as you'll recall from Chapter 4, positioning is using the marketing mix to determine how a product fits within the marketplace and in relation to other products, and to influence how consumers in specific segments view the product—or "creating a certain perception or image about the product in the minds of consumers that differentiates it from the competition."[9] The marketer's job is to convey information about a product in such a way that customers view it as one that occupies a better, more attractive position than that of a competing product. This is Step 3—the "P" of the STP process.

ARRANGING INFORMATION

Jack Trout, generally recognized as one of the world's foremost marketing strategists, actually developed the concept of positioning. Many feel that this is the most important element of modern marketing, today more than ever. Why is positioning viewed as even more important today than it was 20-some years ago when Trout first introduced the idea? Perhaps it's because modern marketing's biggest challenge is how best to communicate a message to members of a society who are already experiencing message overload. Just think about how many marketing messages the average American receives in a day—the number of promotions/ads we see and hear in magazines or on TV, the number of pop-ups we get on our computer screens, the number of enticing images we see when we walk through a mall or even just down the street … it's not surprising that estimates are between 2,000 and 5,000. That's a lot of messages!

So how do the receivers of all these marketing messages determine which ones are meaningful, beneficial, or even interesting to them? Effective positioning is the key. Create the perception in the mind of the customer that your product/service/client is superior to competing ones, and success will likely be the result. How do you accomplish this? There are many methods. You might position a product as "the best," "the biggest," "the original," "the most prestigious," "one of a kind," "the easiest to use," "the one that's adored by [fill in the name of the hottest new singer]"—it all depends on the makeup of your target market and what its members are likely to find most appealing.

For example, if a cosmetic company's target market is young girls between the ages of 10 and 14, it might introduce a fragrance that has a light, sweet, lemony essence. But other cosmetic companies might also be targeting the same age group with similar fragrances. So, how can the new fragrance be positioned to be perceived as the best of all similar fragrances vying for girls' attention? If you are responsible for marketing this product, you should be asking yourself what is most important to prospective customers. Then you need to look at how competitors are positioning their citrus scents and determine how well their strategies are working. Once you zero in on what your customers value and carefully analyze what the competition is claiming, you can work on convincing customers that your fragrance offers something superior to the others—that is, a **competitive advantage**. In this case it might be an eco-friendly and refillable dispenser or an endorsement by Taylor Swift. Whatever your positioning strategy is, it has to convey a unique advantage that the competition does not have.

Let's look at some real-life examples. Southwest Airlines positions itself as an airline with a sense of warmth, friendliness, individual pride, and company spirit. Gucci touts that its timepieces reflect superior quality and a distinctive Italian style with Swiss watch-making craftsmanship. Other companies use differentiation to position themselves: Tod's shoes notes the impeccable quality, craftsmanship, and functionality of its footwear; Cold Stone Creamery flaunts its customized ice cream; Red Bull promotes the energy users receive from its drink; Starbucks describes itself as a European-style coffee house; BMW distinguishes itself with classy, high-performance cars for the driving enthusiast. If marketers did not position their products, consumers might do it themselves—and not necessarily in a way the marketer intended.

WHAT DO YOU THINK?

Identify two established businesses in your neighborhood that compete with each other in providing the same fashion goods or services. From what you can tell, do they target the same or different market segments? Do they position themselves differently in the marketplace? Why do you think one business does better (competitive advantages) than the other in satisfying customers' needs and wants?

COMPLETING THE POSITIONING PROCESS

Once a positioning decision is made, the next step for a marketer is to ensure that customers see, hear, and experience the full range of value-added benefits available to them. Having a solid understanding of what's going on in the marketplace as it relates to your product is a great place to start.

1. *Researching the marketplace* provides answers to key positioning questions such as who is the competition, how does the public respond to them, what are the buying preferences and trends, what is the impact of technology, and what substitute products are available to consumers, currently and in the future. Once this research is collected, the data can be displayed on a perceptual map, a visual tool you'll recall from Chapter 4. This graphical representation can make it easier to analyze the data and spot trending opportunities and pitfalls, as well as providing a foundation for appropriate decision making. (See Figure 6.8.) Companies that do not research the competition, analyze marketplace trends, and study consumers for purchasing habits run a big risk of failing.

2. *Doing it better than others* or providing a more viable solution than the competition gives marketers an instant leg up in positioning themselves favorably against competitors. A successful fashion marketer will make it easy for consumers to understand how its product uniquely benefits them. It may save customers money or time, provide distinct networking or image-enhancing opportunities, include better service and follow-up, provide a more satisfying experience, improve delivery time, increase employment chances, reduce exposure to pain, or maximize personal security. Would you say the cell phone companies are doing exactly this? Whatever a company identifies as its competitive advantage, it needs to communicate clearly to customers why its benefits exceed those of its competitors.

3. *Using the marketing mix tools* effectively will cement the positioning in customers' minds and underscore the product's competitive advantage. With an integrated and coordinated strategy for product, price, place, and promotion, marketers can maximize customers' experiences and complete their process of positioning by exceeding customers' expectations in each area that is important to them.

MARKETER'S INSIGHT:
HOW TO CREATE A PERCEPTUAL MAP

The purpose of a perceptual map is to visually display data that can be used to analyze market opportunities in the positioning of new products or repositioning of existing ones. Here's a step-by-step guide to creating your own perceptual map:

▸ Select a product and identify three or four different marketplace or consumer-driven variables that could influence the product's positioning. (Ask yourself: What demographic, geographic, psychographic, or usage factors are important for understanding the different consumer or marketplace preferences?)

▸ Conduct appropriate primary (original research such as a survey, interview, focus group) or secondary (previously reported facts, statistics, customer preferences) research, and collect data on the variables you've identified.

▸ Decide how to set up and title the perceptual map:

  ▸ Use one of the demographic or psychographic variables to make up the x axis and use another for the y axis.

  ▸ Use the third variable to be plotted on the perceptual map.

▸ Sketch your map:

  ▸ Draw the x axis and y axis, label them with the correct variables, and put regular intervals on the axes to reflect your quantifiable results.

  ▸ Create a legend that concisely describes the x and y axes and the third variable (specific points) being plotted; color-code or alphabetically label them.

  ▸ Based on your research findings, plot the third variable on the map.

▸ Analyze the information as plotted on the map. What trends does it show? Can you identify opportunities, challenges, customer preferences?

▸ Use the map to make recommendations for the positioning of new products or repositioning of existing ones.

Of course, it would be easy for marketers if customers always wanted the same products and bought them forever. But consumers, and fashion consumers in particular, want change and seek out what's new. Think of fast-fashion retailers such as Topshop, Uniqlo, or Zara that change out the looks in their stores as frequently as twice a week. A fashion doesn't remain popular forever, and marketers need to anticipate and prepare for changes in consumer tastes. Naturally, in order to adapt to changes in consumer demand, marketers need to change, too.

Repositioning, or revising the marketing strategy to change consumers' perception of a product or brand in order to increase sales, is very important for sustained business growth. Remember the five stages of the fashion life cycle: introduction, rise, peak, decline, and rejection? (You can review the fashion life cycle curve in Chapter 4, Figure 4.7.) Fashion marketers closely track the progress of their products through those stages, and when a product appears to have hit its peak, the company may decide to reposition it in an effort to extend its life span. Or a fashion organization may adjust the positioning of its brand as a whole. For example, Coach identified a market opportunity and emphasized its lower-priced ($300 to $500) line of handbags for the European market to fill a gap there. Think of your favorite TV programs, musical groups, individual entertainers, Broadway

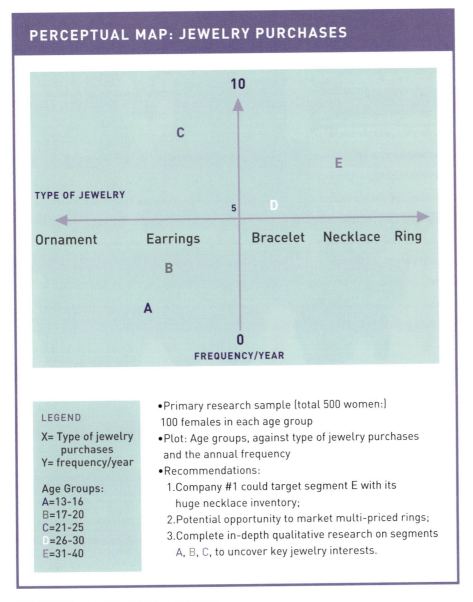

PERCEPTUAL MAP: JEWELRY PURCHASES

TYPE OF JEWELRY

Ornament   Earrings   Bracelet   Necklace   Ring

FREQUENCY/YEAR

LEGEND

X= Type of jewelry purchases
Y= frequency/year

Age Groups:
A=13-16
B=17-20
C=21-25
D=26-30
E=31-40

- Primary research sample (total 500 women:) 100 females in each age group
- Plot: Age groups, against type of jewelry purchases and the annual frequency
- Recommendations:
  1. Company #1 could target segment E with its huge necklace inventory;
  2. Potential opportunity to market multi-priced rings;
  3. Complete in-depth qualitative research on segments A, B, C, to uncover key jewelry interests.

FIGURE 6.8 BY VANESSA HAN AND ALICIA FREILE

musicals—these are sometimes "retired" and then brought back to the marketplace to experience renewed success.

We end this section on positioning with a quote from Trout: "[P]ositioning is actually a battle for your mind."[10] And, may the best marketer win. If marketers tie all the loose ends together and deliver solutions that exceed customers' expectations, then the right relationships have been established. But the marketing "secret" is this: How do organizations now make these relationships last? We'll look at that challenge next.

Managing Relationships

People tend to buy and then rebuy from marketers that add value to the process, the end product, or the experience. Once companies identify their key customers, they try to keep them because it takes more resources (money, time, and people) to find and capture new customers.

Just as gold prospectors set about seeking riches by asking questions, collecting and studying data, and maintaining key relationships, marketers complete a similar cycle to keep their customers happy and loyal.

FIGURE 6.9 When Nintendo introduced the Wii video game console in 2006, it had a unique position in the marketplace with its motion-activated controllers and Internet connectivity. What has changed in the market since then that might call for Nintendo to reposition the product?

MARTHA STEWART REPOSITIONS HER BRAND

It wasn't too many years ago that Martha Stewart's name was associated with tasteful but bargain-priced housewares and garden items sold exclusively through Kmart. But today, the Martha Stewart merchandise has been reborn and repositioned--with a new range of branded products targeting customers to whom the name is synonymous with affordable quality and style.

Among the products now sporting the Martha Stewart brand name are a line of beds, collars, leashes, and doggie dishes sold exclusively at PetSmart; a collection of craft items sold at Michael's and Jo-Ann Fabrics; build-it-yourself furniture marketed by Home Depot; and stylish desktop organizers offered exclusively by Staples. A Martha Stewart Collection launched at Macy's in 2007 featured home goods from furniture and bedding to cookware and tabletop; and a later negotiation with JCPenney was calling

for the opening of mini-boutiques in its stores starting in 2013. The 70-year-old former model is even considering adding a Martha Stewart skin care line to her merchandise empire. It's all part of understanding the brand and its target customers.

"We search for the areas where we know we have powerful brand equity, where our consumer base tells us they want us to be and we believe we can make a unique difference," said Robin Marino, CEO of merchandising for Martha Stewart Living Omnimedia. The shift from Kmart to Macy's and Home Depot, for instance, was based on extensive research showing that consumers wanted to see the brand in more places. "Those who weren't engaged with us said the brand wasn't available where they shopped," Marino said. "Looking at that research, we said we need to branch out and be everywhere they are."

Adapted from: Jack Neff, "The Martha Stewart Brand Is Transcending the Person," *Advertising Age*, August 2, 2010, http://adage.com/mediaworks/article?article_id=145192 (accessed March 6, 2012); Tom Ryan, "Is Martha Stewart Overextended at Retail?," RetailWire, March 5, 2012, www.retailwire.com/news-article/15857/is-martha-stewart-overextended-at-retail (accessed March 5, 2012).

CUSTOMER RELATIONSHIP MANAGEMENT (CRM)

Chapter 1 laid the foundation for twenty-first century marketing: the importance of identifying what consumers value and providing solutions that address their wants and needs in a fiscally, socially, and environmentally positive manner. That chapter also introduced the concept of **customer relationship management (CRM)**, the process of building and maintaining profitable customer relationships by providing superior customer value and satisfaction. CRM is a multifaceted process that results in win-win relationships for marketers and consumers. By using the tools of CRM, a company can collect and organize information on consumer preferences, track consumer behaviors, prioritize and synchronize marketing messages, and communicate effectively with consumers and stakeholders at every level.

Each point along the direct line of communication provides opportunities for this data collection. Touch points include contact via phone, Internet, mail, fax, video conference, credit (smart) card usage, or any other communication method.[11] For example, if you go online and buy a coat, the marketer most likely stores a digital record of your information and preferences using cookies. The company can use this data later to solidify its relationship with you, perhaps through a pop-up window the next time you visit the site that welcomes you back and shows a scarf that coordinates with your new coat, or maybe via a follow-up e-mail offering a discount on your next purchase.

Fashion marketers adapt and incorporate appropriate solutions into their CRM efforts as they learn what is important to and valued by their customers. Remember the price/value equation from Chapter 4? It's worth repeating here because it underscores the importance of identifying and satisfying the value component in the CRM process:

$$P/V = PC$$

where P = price, V = value, and PC = perceived cost to consumer

As the denominator V (value) increases, the customer accepts or rationalizes the perceived cost more readily and is more likely to maintain a loyal relationship with the marketer.

Consider this scenario: A boutique raises its price on selected items in a designer collection, and a previously loyal customer now finds the price too high for the value received. Say, however, that at the same time, the boutique adds new amenities for loyal customers, such as parking vouchers, free alterations, or an invitation-only trunk show. If the amenities offer value to the customer, such offers can lower the total perceived cost back to an acceptable level, allowing the consumer to justify the higher price on the goods. The boutique will have done its job in meeting the customer's expected value for shopping there—and will have succeeded in one aspect of CRM.

Refer to Table 6.3 for this example. The amounts noted in the value section range from one to three units, while the $300 price stays constant. The perceived cost to the consumer decreases as the value units increase. In short, as the customer receives more value with the total shopping experience, the "Should I buy" question progressively makes more sense.

These samples illustrate an **inverse relationship** (one factor moves in the opposite direction of the other factor) between the customer value (going up) and perceived cost (going down) components. On the other hand, a **direct relationship** exists when both factors move in the same direction, either both up or both down. For example, as the number of employees increases, so will the employer's payroll expenses, or as more people walk into a store to shop, the likelihood of selling more goods goes up.

Ideally, a marketer wants to see increases in three key areas: market share, share of customer (customer buys more from the same company), and brand loyalty. This leads us to the question: How does an organization know when its marketing efforts are working?

TABLE 6.3 Value vs. Perceived Cost

Value (in units)	Price	Consumer's Perceived Cost	Should I Buy?
1	$300	$300	I'm not sure.
2	$300	$150	Maybe.
3	$300	$100	It's really worth it.

CUSTOMER EXPERIENCE MANAGEMENT (CEM)

Marketers use CRM tools to harvest data to monitor and further develop customer relationships. These activities lead to mutual benefits because customers are able to satisfy their needs and wants in more efficient ways, while organizations proactively sustain business profitability. When these tools are used effectively, and analyzed and customized as needed, the end result raises the overall shopping encounter to a higher level. The function of managing the overall experience that the customer has with the supplier is called **customer experience management (CEM)**. Linda McIntosh, a marketing and sales professional, describes it as "a business strategy that focuses and redefines the business from the customer's view point."[12] If this big-picture involvement synchronizes all stakeholders, systems, and strategies, while providing a unique experience and engaging customers in their preferred manner, a competitive advantage surfaces for the host company. Dr. Fred Van Bennekom, consultant and Executive MBA faculty member at Boston's Babson College and Northeastern University, identifies two elements for optimizing a customer's total experience: (1) Constantly improve the key value factors that distinguish the customer experience, and (2) implement a plan that routinely addresses and resolves negative experiences.[13] For example, if your landlord or its management company quickly completes your repair requests and also keeps improving things in your apartment building (faster Internet connectivity, cleaner hallways, improved security), your experience may be so positive that you renew your annual lease without checking out alternatives in other apartment buildings.

By contrast, if an organization has a system in place that does not consistently pay attention to its customers' value propositions or downgrades the customer experience, there is a high probability that customers will not stay loyal. Suppose that during your last two shopping trips to your favorite store, the merchandise was so overcrowded on racks that it was difficult to browse through it, you noticed obvious clutter or dirt in the dressing rooms, and it took a lot of extra time to find a salesperson. You just might find some other store to visit for your next shopping trip.

Incorporating innovation and adapting to the marketplace as needed will build and nurture the right relationships with fashion consumers, and

WIN-WIN SOLUTIONS

PRODUCT

CRM

WIN-WIN

CEM

FIGURE 6.10 BY VANESSA HAN AND ALICIA FREILE

result in win-win solutions for the customer and the marketer, as illustrated in Figure 6.10. Customers will have enriched and memorable experiences with a company when technology, business processes, and organizational channels are in sync. They will feel connected and committed and, in turn, will probably come back to make repeat purchases. Imagine this: You've finished shopping in the small leather goods section of a department store and the salesperson mentions that there is a 50 percent sale going on in the jewelry department. He shows you some of the sale pieces on the store monitor, walks you over to that section, bypasses the line and goes behind the counter to get a couple of your requested pieces, scans the items for more information that you want, inputs your preferred customer code, quickly processes your credit card, and then gift

MARKETER'S INSIGHT:
NEVER UNDERESTIMATE THE VALUE OF A GOOD CRM SYSTEM

In his article titled, "The Greatest Customer Service Story Ever Told, Starring Morton's Steakhouse," Peter Shankman, an author and entrepreneur, discussed an experience he had at Morton's Steakhouse. He said: "I'm a frequent diner, and Morton's knows it. They have a spectacular Customer Relations Management system in place, as well as a spectacular social media team, and they know when I call from my mobile number who I am, and that I eat at their restaurants regularly."

Peter was travelling by plane from Tampa, Florida, to Newark, New Jersey. He jokingly tweeted at Morton's to meet him with a steak at the Newark airport when his plane landed because he knew he'd be hungry, after having a very busy day. When Shankman's plane landed a Morton's employee—in tuxedo and all—met him there, all the way from Hackensack, with a Morton's bag full of food.

Source: Peter Shankman, "The Greatest Customer Service Story Ever Told, Starring Morton's Steakhouse," August 17, 2011, http://shankman.com/the-best-customer-service-story-ever-told-starring-mortons-steakhouse/ (accessed October 8, 2011).

wraps your purchases. You leave the store witnessing how technology, departmental communication, and organized business processes made your shopping experience very positive.

The term **customer retention management** refers to consistently coordinating these important areas of the customer experience when delivering products or services in order to improve customer retention—keeping loyal customers loyal—and lead to business growth.[14] Businesses that provide value to their customers, along with growth and security to their employees, while effectively managing these key relationships, position themselves for success.

Adding accountability to this mix by using tracking and measuring tools keeps an organization's line of sight realistic when comparing results among competitors. Merely collecting data and hoping things go well is insufficient for achieving these goals and objectives.

WHAT DO YOU THINK?

What do you think about Peter Shankman's experience in "Never Underestimate the Value of a Good CRM System?" How can you relate this story to the equation (P/V = PC)?

MEASUREMENT TOOLS

Some marketers have described the term "data" as hard facts and "information" as the end-result

FIGURE 6.11 Customer experience management and customer retention management are enhanced by a high level of personal service.

analysis of those facts. What that means is that once facts are collected using the various CRM tools, fashion marketers must quantify them and complete measurement analyses to understand where they are and where they need to go with their efforts.

Measurements are about finding out how much or how many. If marketers are going to create and manage the right customer relationships and provide win-win solutions for themselves and their customers, they need answers to these "how much" and "how many" questions in order to target customers appropriately.

Four areas that fashion marketers might use to measure their success in CRM are *market share*, *customer purchases*, *lifetime value of a customer*, and *customer categories by profitability*. The first, **market share**, refers to a company's proportion of total sales within a given business sector—that is, what percentage of the total sales were generated by a specific company. For example, if 100,000 pairs of straight-leg jeans were sold in the Midwest last year and your organization sold 25,000 of them, your market share was 25 percent (25,000/100,000 × 100). Market share can often be improved by making a better product, lowering prices, running more sales promotions, or increasing advertising efforts to increase consumer awareness.

The next measurement, *customer purchases*, quantifies how much or how many items a customer is buying from the same company. It is more cost-effective to encourage existing customers to purchase additional goods and services than it is to develop new customers. Solomon, Marshall, and Stuart liken it to share of market when they refer to this as "Share of Customer."[15] Ian MacMillan and

Larry Selden, business professors at the University of Pennsylvania's Wharton School, suggest tapping into a company's existing customer information for invigorating growth; they call it the "incumbent's advantage."[16]

Next, calculating the *lifetime value of a customer* (*LTV*) quantifies the expected profits that will be derived from the repeat purchases a customer makes over time. This guesstimating takes into account how much the customer might spend versus how much it costs to acquire and keep that customer. Finally, *prioritizing categories of customers by their profitability* provides the framework for identifying which customers are spending and how much; this can improve the efficiency of a company's database marketing efforts (using customer information already collected and digitally stored for personalized communication follow-ups). Let's say that a retailer decides to hold a trunk show of pricey jewelry items. Rather than contacting everyone in the store's database, wouldn't it prove much more successful to contact only those clients who previously purchased other high-end fashion products, and inform them of an exciting, value-driven sales event catering specifically to their wants and needs?

Once marketers collect and prioritize the data from the various measurements, they may create a perceptual map, the graphic marketing tool discussed earlier, to display that data in a visual format. The viewer compares and analyzes the relationships among marketplace competitors and the factors used by customers in making buying decisions. Refer back to the perceptual map shown in Figure 6.8 and see how it reveals marketplace patterns gleaned from CRM measurements. Graphically illustrating data can help in the identification of trends or lack thereof, and help to frame the analysis and corresponding recommendations for marketing actions.

PARTNER RELATIONSHIP MANAGEMENT (PRM)

How important is it that companies work hand in hand with other people and businesses that are involved in getting products to the customer? Every fashion organization relies on other companies for support in developing its product or service offerings. For example, your favorite restaurant or boutique provides a very positive experience only with the help of many suppliers; these suppliers provide services or products to their channel partners so that the restaurant or boutique can deliver what you, the customer, wants. (See Chapter 10 for more on marketing channels.) The boutique, for instance, gets deliveries of fashion goods and accessories; fashion designers and manufacturers create these. There are also utility companies providing energy services, telephone and data companies securing communication networks, display companies supplying racks and shelving, packaging firms crafting the boutique's distinctive shopping bags, and a variety of other service providers. Each of these channel partners (suppliers) form a large value chain where interconnected activities result in getting the job done; that is, the conversion of raw materials or services into value-added end products that ultimately reach the consumer.

The supply chain includes the companies and all the activities associated with the production and delivery of the product; see Table 6.4. When there are conflicts among supply chain members, both

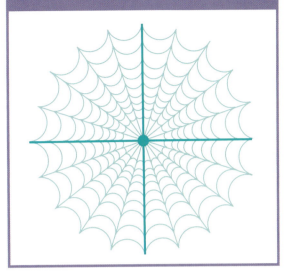

PRM WEB OF COMMUNICATIONS

FIGURE 6.12 The organization is in the middle: all channel partners are connected and communicate.
BY VANESSA HAN AND ALICIA FREILE

consumers and producers suffer. For example, during summer 2010, Walgreen Co. threatened to stop filling prescriptions for millions of CVS Caremark Corp. drug plan members; this meant the potential loss of billions of dollars for these companies and hardships for customers. Within 11 days, this dispute was settled, but it shows the importance of nurturing interrelationships within a value chain.[17]

The coordination of supply sources with market demands is called **supply chain management**; its objective is to get customers what they want, when they want it, in the most efficient and cost-effective manner possible. **Partner relationship management (PRM)** describes the methods used in dealing with these partner organizations in the supply chain. An end result of effectively managing these relationships is that the primary company satisfies its internal (employees) and external

TABLE 6.4 Supply Chain Partners

Product Being Sold	Example of Marketer	Some Key Supply Chain Partners
Goods and services	Restaurant	Farmer, dairy company, bulk foods wholesaler, truck driver, linen supplier, laundry service, menu printer, and others
Goods	Handbag manufacturer	Fabric/leather supplier, fasteners manufacturer, trim company, trucking firm, tag/label printer, packaging supplier, wholesaler, retail buyer, and others

Adapted from: Patricia Mink Rath, Stefani Bay, Richard Petrizzi, and Penny Gill, *The Why of the Buy: Consumer Behavior and Fashion Marketing* (New York: Fairchild Books, 2008), p. 45

(customers) stakeholders' wants and needs in an efficient, professional, and fiscally responsible manner. Organizations that use PRM computer software programs to track, monitor, and communicate with customers find it even easier and more effective. Additionally, many companies create *intranet* (a restricted, internal, organizational connection) or *extranet* (a dedicated, secure, private Internet connection) electronic links to make these data transfers more efficient. For example, a company that allows two of its departments, located in different buildings or states, to share files internally uses an intranet connection. An external supplier that has access to data specifically related to the products it supplies an organization uses an extranet link. If supply chain partners do not work together well in the delivery of products to the fashion consumer, these customer relationships once thought to be "right" will now be wrong and unprofitable. Although technology can make the communication process flow more smoothly, there are times when some companies and individuals just don't treat

others the way they should; their behavior may not be illegal, but it is not appropriate.

Ethics and Globalization in Customer Relationships

As stated in previous chapters, ethics is about doing the right thing. It includes respecting others, acting fairly and compassionately, doing things we should do to make life more palatable for others, and not just looking out for ourselves. Perhaps you know people who make Internet purchases or surf the Web on company time when they should be working, or they intentionally say or do things that will emotionally hurt others.

Doing the right thing with customers, fellow employees, and managers might seem simple, but there may be times it seems too difficult or not even worth doing. Shortchanging or overcharging someone may be done accidentally, but shouldn't it be made right? If a supplier makes a mistake by sending too many items in an order, an employee should note that error in the inventory count or expense report; if an employee makes a mistake with price tags, equity and balance should be restored. Making the right choices strengthens relationships.

Rationalizing the how and why of breaking rules, pressing others to act in unethical (perhaps financially profitable) ways, lying, cheating, or misleading others may bring short-term rewards, but these actions foster mistrust and, eventually, ruin business relationships. In August 2010, Whole Foods Market held suppliers of organic-labeled, non-food (personal care) products accountable to make sure that organic ingredients were actually used in the manufacturing process or that labels were changed to reflect the product derivatives; making sure its shoppers get what they believe they are getting is very important to the retailer.[18] Relationship building demands trust. And this trust results in repeat purchases.

However, some organizations sanction actions that are not necessarily illegal, even though they might be unethical. Here are two examples: A tailor performs unnecessary alterations on a suit, when all that was needed was a length adjustment to sleeves and slacks, in order to charge more money, and a woman buys a dress intending to return it after wearing it once or twice. Doing the wrong thing or breaking a promise does not nurture relationships. According to management guru Stephen Covey, "All broken relationships can be traced back to broken agreements."[19] When we lie to ourselves or others, our actions begin to erode those very relationships that marketers have worked so hard to identify and establish. Today, maintaining the right relationships with consumers also means demonstrating an awareness and respect for societal issues. Whether it is a commitment to one's community (using local, fresh produce at your restaurant), a national campaign (Avon's walk for breast cancer), an international environmental interest (climate change), donating time or money to aid the homeless, or an eco-friendly clothing line (using fabrics from sustainable sources), organizations should herald social causes to showcase their readiness to help humankind. In doing so, they may well bolster their customer relationships as well.

SOCIAL RESPONSIBILITY

More and more, consumers are shopping at or using the services of companies that share their interests regarding particular social issues. Some marketers research the social interests of their customers in order to be in tune with their concerns; others take the lead in supporting specific causes important to their employees or owners. These common interests strengthen relationship bonds between companies and consumers, and can potentially lead to a positive difference in generating revenues. During "The Green Shows," Fall/Winter 2010 in New York, the spotlight was turned on environmentally responsible products and venues; the event also presented items created from recycled clothes and old newspapers, and even incorporated eco-conscious makeup.[20] The message is that companies that align themselves with socially relevant issues, important to their customer base, create more business opportunities. That goodwill and opportunity can extend to global markets as well, thanks to today's possibility for instant communications with anyone anywhere in the world.

GLOBALIZING IDEAS

Combining relationship management efforts with forward-moving technology results in what Thomas Friedman says is "the flattening of the world—equalizing opportunities for all to connect, compete, and collaborate."[21] His three-book series *The World Is Flat* addresses this "flattening" between countries, companies, and individuals, and sends clear signals to everyone in the marketplace.

One interpretation relating to global messages is clear: Companies, small or large, that develop, monitor, and nurture relationships through both traditional and nontraditional channels will earn sustainable business growth.

FIGURE 6.13 Adopting a cause that is meaningful to its target base is an important way in which marketers strengthen their customer relationships. New Balance developed an entire "Lace Up for the Cure" product line in support of Susan G. Komen for the Cure and its efforts to eradicate breast cancer.

TABLE 6.5 Social Responsibility in Practice

Socially Responsible	Not Socially Responsible
Environmentally friendly cold storage freezers	Hydrofluorocarbon refrigerant gases
Eco-friendly or recycled fabrics	Use of animal-derived fabrics
Electric vehicles	Gas-driven vehicles
Recycled goods	Nonbiodegradable products
Products made using highly renewable bamboo	Products made from petroleum-based PVC
Electronic business invoices	Paper copies of business invoices
Faux fur	Real animal fur inhumanely taken
Clean, renewable energy from wind or solar sources	Polluting, nonrenewable energy from fossil fuels (coal and oil)

summary

Fashion marketers use the STP model to segment the marketplace, target the appropriate customers for their product, and position the product to address customer needs. Market segmentation for consumer markets generally is accomplished by focusing on demographics, geographics, psychographics, and usage. Business markets can be segmented by business classification (type of products a company provides), usage requirements (what's needed in terms of product as well as level of performance, price, quality, and service), and business type (OEM, end users, aftermarket). Global markets may be segmented in a similar manner or by intermarket segmentation, which addresses groups of customers by buying behavior or special interests, regardless of their home country.

Targeting involves evaluating potential customer segments based on criteria including their substantiality, measurability, accessibility, and serviceability. A segment profile provides the marketer with a clear description of customer characteristics within a chosen segment. A targeting strategy identifies how much of the total market a company will go after. Targeting strategies may be concentrated, customized, differentiated, or undifferentiated.

In positioning their product, marketers convey a message to customers about how the product fits their needs and why it is preferable to competitive products. This involves researching the marketplace, providing a more viable solution than the competition, and using the marketing mix tools effectively. Once the STP process is complete, marketers use customer relationship management (CRM), customer experience management (CEM), and customer retention management tools to measure and maintain market share and customer loyalty.

Stefani B

Stefani B is a design firm specializing in the creation of artistic, limited-edition, well-made, and lasting jewelry items that can be worn for both casual and special occasions. The owner started the company in 1992, when a new category in jewelry was quickly becoming popular. It was referred to as "bridge" jewelry, which served to bridge the gap between inexpensive, obviously fake pieces and costly high-end jewelry. Items in this new category were not *costume*—that is, made of base metals and fake stones, nor were they considered *fine*—in other words, made with precious metals (gold and platinum) or precious gems (diamonds, rubies, emeralds, sapphires). Rather, *bridge* pieces were primarily rendered in sterling silver with semiprecious gems, such as freshwater pearls, citrine, topaz, amethyst, garnet, and so on. This appealed to customers, not only because the prices were affordable to a vastly larger group, but because the pieces were all "real."

Immediately the collection was successful and offered by several upscale retailers such as Neiman Marcus, Saks Fifth Avenue, and Henri Bendel, as well as popular high-fashion boutiques. With the nation's economy then in high gear and the wearing of jewelry a prominent part of a woman's total look, bridge lines—referred to as *fashion jewelry* by retailers seeking to brand the category—took off. Many well-known jewelry designers, from David Yurman to Janis Savitt, started their careers as creators of bridge pieces around that time.

The tempo began to change in 2001 with the political climate uncertain, and the economy took another catastrophic dip in 2008 when the financial crisis drastically diminished consumer spending across the board. Retailers reduced their budgets and their inventories; many high-end boutiques closed. Small design companies, like Stefani B, were among those whose orders decreased significantly—many were unable or unwilling to supply inventory on consignment, the cause of the risk and expense. Some began to make less expensive, less intricate pieces, but Stefani B chose not to compromise the quality. The company tried several different sales approaches in order to remain in business. Private clients were invited to come to the studio where one-of-a-kind pieces were created for them. Stefani B encouraged clients to bring in their old pieces and used the gems and metals to create new items. Additionally, jewelry showings were scheduled in private homes and clubs or in conjunction with various charities, which would then get portions of the proceeds.

As of this writing, there are indications that consumers are once again beginning to think about shopping for products they've denied themselves during the past few years. Also, the prices of gold and platinum are currently at an all-time high, making the availability of beautiful, yet affordable, bridge jewelry as appealing as ever. Finally, one of Stefani B's former accounts, a chic specialty store with several locations, recently agreed to view the newest collection and, having done so, placed a significant order. With these signs of encouragement, Stefani B was preparing to have a plan in place for a "relaunch" of the company and its offerings.

Source: Stefani Bay, owner, Stefani B

QUESTIONS

1. In preparation for the reintroduction and marketing of the Stefani B collection, what, in your opinion, is the first thing the owner should do?
2. What positioning strategy do you think would be advantageous? Support your answer.
3. Segment the marketplace and describe the demographic or psychographic profile of Stefani B's primary target customers. Why do you say that?
4. What steps concerning CRM (customer relationship management) would you suggest?
5. What CRM measurement areas should Stefani B consider and why?

KEY TERMS

competitive advantage

customer experience management (CEM)

customer relationship management (CRM)

customer retention management

direct relationship

inverse relationship

market share

mass marketing

niche marketing

partner relationship management (PRM)

perceptual maps

segment profile

segmentation categories

supply chain management

target marketing

REVIEW QUESTIONS

1. Define target marketing and explain three things that marketers should do to sustain business growth.

2. Explain the market segmentation process, and discuss what is meant by the demographic and psychographic segmentation categories.

3. List four essential segmentation factors and state why they are important for business success.

4. Describe four targeting strategies and discuss how they relate to the phrase, "work smarter, not harder."

5. How does the positioning process work, and what do the marketing mix tools have to do with this process?

6. Explain the importance of maintaining good relationships with customers.

DISCUSSION ACTIVITIES AND PROJECTS

1. Develop a two-step segmentation model (two separate circles with targeting arrows) that funnels potential customers into a viable target market; use any product of your choice.

2. Create a perceptual map that visually displays four to five reasons for selecting a particular location for enjoying a pizza, as they relate to the diversity in customer age groups and their preferences for pizza styles. Quantify and/or specifically label key points wherever possible on the x and y axes. Finally, make two recommendations based on your visual findings. (Refer to the perceptual map guidelines noted on the "Perceptual Map" in this chapter.)

3. Your recently hired boss, the fashion jewelry department manager, wants you to make two recommendations on how to get one of the supply chain partners to perform or communicate more effectively. What are your suggestions?

4. One day your assistant, a five-year company employee, confesses to you that she double-billed multiple clients with disorganized bookkeeping systems during the last 24 months for a total of $84,000. Each client has fully paid the invoiced amounts with no questions or hesitations. Seven months ago this amount placed your department in first place for internal recognition awards, in addition to special regional prizes that you personally received. What do

you do? Who, if anyone, do you tell? How do you resolve this situation? Involve the class in this discussion.

5. Working with one partner, lead a 10- to 12-minute class discussion on social responsibility and its importance to CRM. During the first five minutes, define what social responsibility is and how and why companies develop it, and explain how marketers position it.

DEVELOPING YOUR MARKETING PLAN

At this point in your marketing plan, you're ready to start targeting your market and strategizing how to build relationships with your customers. Look closely at your selected company or product, and create a document describing how you will accomplish each of these tasks:

1. Segmenting: Use the segmentation categories to divide the total marketplace into homogeneous units of current and potential customer groups.
2. Targeting: Examine the characteristics of those market segments to determine which are your most likely customers. Prioritize your target markets; then select and justify an appropriate targeting strategy.
3. Positioning: Explain how you will use each marketing mix tool to position your product or company in the market in a way that communicates your competitive advantage.
4. Managing relationships: Organize a plan to address and measure either a CRM, CEM, or PRM initiative.

5. Draft company guidelines for CRM as related to ethics and socially responsible interests.

REFERENCES

1. Bob Leduc, "Target Marketing Strategy: Find Your Own Niche Market," SOHO America (Small Office Home Office) Web site http://www.soho.org/Marketing_Articles/target_marketing_strategy.htm (accessed May 16, 2010).
2. NAICS Association, "The History of NAICS," http://www.naics.com/info.htm (accessed November 20, 2011).
3. Gary Armstrong and Philip Kotler, *Marketing: An Introduction*, 8th ed. (New York: Pearson Prentice Hall, 2007), p. 176.
4. Erin Hoff, "Intermarket Segmentation—Pepsi Ad," January 27, 2010, http://uwmktg301.blogspot.com/2010/01/intermarket-segmentation.html (accessed November 20, 2011).
5. Michael Solomon, Greg Marshall, and Elnora Stuart, *Marketing: Real People, Real Choices*, 6th ed. (New York: Pearson Education Inc., 2009).
6. Sharon Silke Carty, "New Ford Explorer to Make Debut on Facebook," *USA Today*, June 30, 2009.
7. *Webster's New College Dictionary* (Hoboken, NJ: John Wiley & Sons, 2009).
8. Urban Legends Reference Pages, quote from Billy Wilder–Louis B. Mayer–Red Skelton, Snopes.com, http://msgboard.snopes.com/cgi-bin/ultimatebb.cgi?ubb=get_topic;f=32;t=000457;p=0 (accessed November 20, 2011).

9. Al Reis and Jack Trout, *The 22 Immutable Laws of Marketing* (New York: HarperCollins, 1994).

10. Ibid., p. 25.

11. Solomon, Marshall, and Stuart, *Marketing: Real People, Real Choices*.

12. Linda McIntosh, "The Customer's Point of View," http://www.focus.com/briefs/customer-service/customers-point-view-where-crm-meets-customer-experience (accessed May 19, 2010).

13. GreatBrook, "Customer Experience Management by Design," http://www.greatbrook.com/customer_experience_management.htm (accessed May 31, 2010).

14. Francis Buttle, *Customer Retention Management: Concepts and Technology* 2nd ed., (Burlington, MA: Butterworth-Heinemann, 2009).

15. Op cit.

16. Ian C. MacMillan and Larry Selden, "The Incumbent's Advantage," *Harvard Business Review*, October 2008.

17. "RPT-Update 4-Walgreen, VCVS Settle Drug Plan Fight; Shares Rise," *Reuters,* June 18, 2010.

18. Sarah Mahoney, "Marketing Daily," *MediaPost News*, June 17, 2010, http://www.mediapost.com/publications/?fa=Articles.showArticle&art_aid=130397 (accessed June 25, 2010).

19. About-Personal-Growth.com, quote by Stephen Covey, www.about-personal-growth.com/relationship-quotes.html (accessed June 8, 2010).

20. Yuka Yoneda, "New York Fashion Week: Eco-Fashion Highlights from The Green Shows," *Inhabitat.com*, February 21, 2010, http://inhabitat.com/new-york-fashion-week-eco-fashion-highlights-from-the-green-shows/: (accessed March 6, 2012).

21. Thomas L. Friedman, *The World Is Flat Release 3.0: A Brief History of the Twenty-First Century* (New York: Picador, 2007).

Part III

FOCUSING MARKETING MIX ELEMENTS ON THE FASHION CONSUMER

FASHION CONSUMERS are constantly on the lookout for something new, requiring fashion marketers to continually develop new goods and services. This involves a basic knowledge of the various types of product branding, levels of consumer brand loyalty, and branding strategies. It also involves the product development process and the many considerations fashion marketers must make in establishing prices. Fashion marketers must also stay alert to marketing channel activities and supply chain management practices in marketing fashion goods. This includes channel organization, distribution intensity, and international marketing strategies. Finally, to effectively implement the marketing mix, fashion marketers must develop a keen understanding of the practices of fashion wholesalers, the organizational characteristics of global fashion retailers, and the activities of Internet fashion businesses.

CHAPTER 7

Branding Strategies for Fashion Goods and Services

This chapter looks at the importance of branding in fashion, describing the decisions that go into developing a brand identity, ways in which brands are positioned and expanded in the marketplace, and how branding carries through the entire marketing mix.

WHAT DO I NEED TO KNOW ABOUT BRANDING FOR FASHION GOODS AND SERVICES?

* How to identify four types of consumer goods

* Why marketers brand products and the major decisions fashion marketers need to make about products

* The advantages of branding both to consumers and to marketers

* The importance of packaging and labeling in marketing fashion brands

* Four branding strategies for marketing fashion services

* The importance of ethics and social responsibility to fashion branding

FASHION MARKETING IN FOCUS:
Speaking of Brands

At her college, shortly after the morning's business class, sophomore fashion student Kathy turns on her iPhone to touch base with her friend Tara.

"Did you get those Uggs at Bloomingdale's?"

"Yes. They're perfect for this weather. And I stopped at MAC to see the new colors."

"Dana and I are having cappuccinos at Starbucks; then we're checking out Marigold."

"Great. It's supposed to be as fabulous as Zara. By the way, I'd like to check out the new Sony e-reader. My parents want to get one for my brother's birthday. Wanna take a look with me?"

"Sure. But first I need to stop at Target, since I'm out of Tide and Dove body wash, and I need my Ghirardelli chocolate fix. Oh, and I want to look at a Mossimo shirt I saw in the circular this week. I'll meet you at Best Buy in an hour."

"Deal. See you there."

n a few locations, the cell phone exchange between the two friends in "Speaking of Brands" might sound as though it is taking place in a foreign language. However, in the many parts of the world with access to popular fashions, the messages are abundantly clear, since they concern well-known products and companies, each identified by name. Giving a unique name to a product translates to a win-win situation for consumers and marketers alike. Consumers have a way to remember the product, and marketers are able to distinguish it from other products throughout their marketing mix.

Why Marketers Brand Products

Most likely, you're familiar with the quote from Shakespeare, "What's in a name?" For fashion marketers, the answer to that question is "everything!" In order to name a product, marketers first spend a great deal of time identifying what customers want and developing an identity for the product that appeals to specific customers, a process known as branding (defined in Chapter 3). In this chapter, we'll look at the purposes and uses of branding in fashion.

FIGURE 7.1 Products identified by their brand names help market the item and the image.

FIGURES 7.2A–C Products range from pure goods such as (a) travel gear, to goods and services such as (b) an in-flight meal, to pure services such as (c) a guided sightseeing tour of Paris.

WHAT MAKES UP A PRODUCT?

After identifying its target market, that is, those customers it can best serve at a profit, a company creates its marketing mix starting with the products it will offer to satisfy consumer needs. You'll recall from Chapter 1 that a *product* can be anything that is provided in an exchange—whether that means goods, such as a coat or a cell phone; services, such as a haircut or an attorney's advice; ideas, such as a belief or philosophy; people, such as a celebrity or political candidate; places, such as New York City or Yellowstone Park; or experiences, such as a trip to an aquarium or vacation in Las Vegas or London.

A product itself contains three elements: the item, its attributes, and its symbolic meaning. This is illustrated in Figure 7.3, where the item is the suit jacket; the attributes—not always immediately visible—include the fit and the styling; and the symbolic meaning is the way the wearer feels about the garment, its style, tailoring, and appearance. Therefore, when customers buy a product, particularly a fashion item, they are actually purchasing the positive feelings they gain from wearing, using, or experiencing its benefits. Making product benefits recognizable and memorable by creating a brand name and identity makes the product more marketable, as we will discover in this chapter.

There are two classifications of products: those consumers use, such as food, clothing, household products, and entertainment, called *consumer products*; and those businesses use or resell, such as office computers, industrial sewing machines, and heavy construction equipment, known as *business products*. The focus of this text is on consumer products, particularly fashion goods and services, that is, currently popular designed products.

TYPES OF CONSUMER PRODUCTS

Consumer products fall into four categories, almost all of which are branded: convenience items, shopping goods, specialty goods, and unsought items. Consumers buy these products in different ways, which influence the methods marketers use to offer them.

Convenience products are goods and services consumers buy often; they are usually inexpensive, frequently purchased out of habit (with limited thought to product comparisons), and available in many places. They include items found in supermarkets and pharmacies such as toothpaste, shampoo, detergent, chewing gum, and disposable pens. To make shopping easier, many convenience items have well-established brand names such as Crest, Pantene, Tide, Juicy Fruit, and Bic. Manufacturers do most of

the advertising and packaging for convenience items, and make sure that customers can obtain them in as many locations as suitable. This category can be further segmented into staples, impulse items, and emergency products. Products that we need and buy regularly to keep on hand, such as milk, cereal, nail polish remover, and soap, are called *staples*. *Impulse items* are unplanned, spur-of-the-moment purchases, such as candy, gum, magazines, batteries, and gadgets, that we decide are must-haves at that

FIGURE 7.3 When buying a fashion item, customers are actually purchasing the positive feelings they experience in wearing or having the item, as well as the product itself. A well-fitting garment, producing a pleasing appearance to the customer, results in that customer's satisfaction.

FIGURE 7.4 For most people, convenience goods are products such as soap and toothpaste; shopping items include clothing and appliances; specialty goods include fine jewelry, art objects, and classic automobiles; and unsought items are products such as insurance policies, automobile tires, and tombstones.

split second. These items are frequently positioned near the checkout to catch consumers' eye as they're finishing their other shopping. Finally, there are *emergency products*, items that we need immediately; these include first-aid goods (bandages, sunburn ointments, nonprescription medications), or household items (wasp spray, drain clog remover).

Shopping products are generally more expensive than convenience goods and are items that consumers want to be able to compare in stores, catalogues, and on the Internet; they include apparel and accessories, cell phones, furniture, and appliances, among other products. Transacting business online in the virtual marketplace includes the use of *cyberintermediaries* (online intermediaries that bring buyers and sellers together such as Amazon Marketplace or eBay) and *shopbots* (special Web sites for finding price and product quality information). Consumers purchase shopping products less often than convenience items and want to determine the features and benefits of various choices offered by retailers such as Nordstrom, Dillard's, Bed Bath & Beyond, and Lowe's. Marketing organizations advertise their brands to give customers a product name to remember, choose fewer retailers to offer their shopping products than for convenience goods, and expect retailer participation in promoting and selling their goods. For example, retailers like Neiman Marcus and Bloomingdale's will sponsor events such as designer and celebrity appearances at their stores to draw out local customers, as when Beyoncé, Jennifer Lopez, or Michael Kors visit to promote their new fragrances.

Specialty products are unique and expensive, and are found in limited locations. With these products, customers hesitate in accepting alternatives. Omega watches, Stella McCartney apparel, Lamborghini automobiles, and National Geographic tours are examples of specialty products. Marketers offer these products in exclusive environments and provide highly trained sales personnel and services such as appliance installations, or alterations and delivery for clothing purchases.

Unsought products are those that consumers either don't realize they need, purchase only when a specific problem arises, or don't think regularly about buying, such as insurance, home protection alarm systems, or automobile repairs. Unsought products may often solve a problem, as when a family member has an accident and needs ambulance service and emergency room treatment. Swift response can be important in marketing unsought services, so these companies promote their reliability through making their names known. Rescue services for homeowners or motorists such as OnStar promote their quick response time. Pharmacies such as CVS and Walgreen's 24-hour stores advertise their locations and accessibility in prominent places. When goods are unsought, marketers develop awareness campaigns, create strong promotional and persuasive messages, or use primary channels such as salespeople or direct marketing to stimulate consumer interest.

The decision as to whether a consumer product belongs in one category or another is based strictly on the way the consumer views it. For example, some customers consider a Burberry plaid signature scarf an exclusive specialty item, while others may see it as a shopping good to be compared with similar patterned scarves. Or, conceivably, someone quite affluent caught in a snowstorm and popping into the store for a neck warmer might consider the scarf a convenience product!

WHaT DO YOU THINK?

What did you buy recently in one of the consumer goods categories described above? To which category does the item belong and why? What ways did the marketer use to encourage the purchase?

Product Decisions

In preparation for putting fashion goods on the market, fashion marketers must make decisions concerning not only their individual products but also their product lines and product mix,[1] making an effort to give each product a unique identity, whatever the price level. Let's look at each of these decisions in turn.

DECISIONS ABOUT INDIVIDUAL PRODUCTS

For each individual fashion product they develop, marketers need to make decisions concerning the product's quality level, style, and design.[2]

Quality Level

Marketers use quality to position a product in consumers' minds. When a consumer has had a successful experience with a product and later recalls the product's name, the marketer has achieved a distinct advantage. Many marketers build a quality image on their names. Disney, for example, has its full-length films and cartoons, resorts, television channels, merchandise, and stores, all featuring the company name and identity and signifying a consistent level of quality that consumers have come to expect from the brand. Many fashion designers build on their reputation for quality to widen their target market. For instance, along with their highest-priced merchandise, some designers have created *diffusion lines*, different quality merchandise offered at lower price levels than their top lines but often including the designer's name for consumer recognition. Some of these lower-priced

lines include ck Calvin Klein, DKNY (Donna Karan), and American Living by Ralph Lauren for JCPenney. While designers' top-line merchandise is sold in exclusive stores, their more moderate price merchandise is available in more popularly priced stores, catalogues, and on the Internet. Nevertheless, goods at various price levels that bear a designer image possess a strong influence among many consumers.

Product Design and Style

Many customers want to own certain fashion goods because of their particular design or style. While the term *style* describes the look of an item such as the style of a cardigan sweater, a pair of athletic shoes, an Eames chair, or a Renaissance chateau, the term *design* is more encompassing, namely, a process of creating things that satisfy people's needs ... "a process for making things right."[3] Designers such as Carolina Herrera, Ralph Rucci, Marc Jacobs, and others select the finest-quality fabric and create distinctive silhouettes and detailing for their top or signature lines; customers know that the garments they select in these highest price ranges reflect excellence in fabric and workmanship. Garments hand-made in the workrooms of French and Italian couturiers such as Karl Lagerfeld and Giorgio Armani are in the $15,000 range and more. Customers for these goods recognize, appreciate, and gladly pay for the design expertise and attention to detail that go into creating the garments. Nevertheless, good design need not be expensive. A teapot or toaster designed by Michael Graves for Target, or apparel that Isaac Mizrahi does for Liz Claiborne and QVC, are examples of moderately priced design.

DECISIONS CONCERNING PRODUCT LINES

Another product decision that marketers must make concerns the assortment of merchandise their company will offer. In order to survive, a company needs a variety of goods for its customers. A group of closely related products selected to appeal to the same customers, marketed through the same channels, and offered within the same price range is known as a **product line**. For example, as you can see in Figure 7.5, Banana Republic's Big and Tall product line consists of long- and short-sleeved shirts, sweaters, pants, jeans and chinos, suits, blazers, and outerwear all designed for men requiring sizes outside the "average" range.

The number of unique products in a product line is referred to as the *product line length*. Companies may decide to lengthen a product line in order to adequately serve their customers, or may shorten a line to eliminate less profitable items. On the other hand, *product line depth* refers to the number of different versions a company offers of each item in its line. For instance, Banana Republic offers both dress and knit shirts as well as long- and short-sleeved shirts in its Big and Tall product line, expanding the line's depth.

DECISIONS CONCERNING PRODUCT MIX

Usually companies have a number of product lines. All of a company's product lines together make up its **product mix**. For example, in addition to the Banana Republic lines, the parent company Gap, Inc., counts its namesake Gap, Old Navy, Piperlime shoes, and Athleta women's yoga lines in its product mix.

The number of a company's product lines in its product mix is referred to as the *product mix width*. A large cosmetics company such as Estée Lauder would have a much wider product mix than a smaller company such as Elizabeth Arden.

The framework of the product mix provides a basis for marketers in creating a marketing strategy to grow their business. A company can widen its product mix by adding new lines, as Shiseido did when it purchased the mineral-based cosmetics firm Bare Escentuals. It can create longer product lines, as Gap did when it added intimate apparel to its women's merchandise assortment. Or, it can build greater depth in its individual products, as a sportswear retailer might do in midseason by reordering its best-selling styles in a wider choice of colors. Finally, a company can be on the lookout for additional products and product lines that

FIGURE 7.5 Banana Republic has a product line devoted to big and tall customers.

reinforce its present image, as McDonald's did in promoting specialized coffees and soft drinks—or look to diversify by finding different products and product lines for its product mix, as Procter & Gamble did in adding fragrances to its lines of household detergents and cleansers.[4]

WHAT DO YOU THINK?

If a company has a good idea for marketing a fashion product, what would be the advantages of putting just that one product on the market? Are there disadvantages in offering only one product? What might they be?

The Importance and Value of Branding

Another major decision for marketers is how to name their products. Customers tend to remember marketers' products when they can recall them by name; a successful name gives the product an identity and even a personality designed to appeal to a specific target market. Naming identifies a product and creates a winning situation for both customers and marketers. Customers have a product name to recall when buying, and marketers can promote their products more effectively.

WHAT IS A BRAND?

The name, term, design, or symbol identifying a product is called a **brand**. Apple, Forever 21, REI, and Cherokee are all brands. Brands are important to consumers because of the image they present. A jacket by Sean John has more appeal to many customers than one with an unknown label. A Martha Stewart table setting has more glamour than one without that brand. The part of a brand that can be spoken is known as the **brand name**. Camaro, Baby Phat, Calvin Klein, and Microsoft are examples of brand names. The part of a brand that is a symbol or figure is called the **brand mark**. Ralph Lauren's polo pony, the Mercedes three-pointed star in a circle, the GEICO green gecko, and the Target bull's-eye are all brand marks. The legal designation of brand ownership is the **trademark**, often designated by a "TM" in superscript after a name, to indicate that it is registered with the U.S. Patent and Trademark office of the federal government.[5] Lands' End, Timex, HBO, Nordstrom, Coca-Cola, and PayPal are all examples of trademarks.

FASHION BRANDS AND THE MARKETING MIX

In creating a brand, marketers work to build a brand identity that engenders customer loyalty because of its consistently trustworthy and respected message and promise.[6] That means that branding has an effect on every aspect of the marketing mix.

Product

A successful brand reflects the image of the product and becomes a **brand personality** with human characteristics that coordinate with the target consumer's self-image.[7] Brands have individual personalities in consumers' minds, and searching for a match is an essential component of the consumer buying process. For example, Levi's appeal to men is

FIGURE 7.6 The various product lines of Gap, Inc. make up the company's product mix. (Clockwise from top: Gap, Old Navy, Piperlime, Athleta, and Banana Republic.)

MARKETER'S INSIGHT: BRAND PERSONALITIES: LANCÔME AND JULIA ROBERTS—TWO STARS SHINE MORE LIGHT

The well-known French cosmetics and fragrance company Lancôme offers its products in specialty and department stores throughout the world. Recognized for its leadership in skin care products, when it came to finding someone to stand as worldwide ambassador for the brand, whose customers range in age from their early twenties on up—clients in the market for skin care products—the company looked for a person customers already knew about, someone they could relate to, and whom many would like to emulate. Lancôme found just the person: attractive, in her forties, wife and mother of three, famous for her work, and in fact a brand in her own right—Julia Roberts.

Known for her film roles in *Pretty Woman*, *Erin Brockovich*, and *Eat, Pray, Love*, among others, Julia Roberts' name in a film is a drawing card for audiences everywhere. In representing Lancôme in advertising and events, the Julia Roberts "brand" and personality attract customers who identify with her age and lifestyle, and seek to be like her. "If Lancôme makes her look great, maybe the brand will do something for me," many consumers think as they view the ads for color cosmetics and age-prevention skin care. Designed to increase sales for the company and also heighten the visibility of the star, each brand complements and enhances the other. Why does this work? Since so many consumers today are attracted to celebrities and want to copy their favorites whenever possible, buying the celebrity-endorsed brands is one way to be closer to their favorites. For marketers, the hoped-for results of brand association, of course, are increased sales.

WHAT'S YOUR POINT OF VIEW?

Celebrity and product brands are often associated in order to promote both the celebrity and the product. Name three or four celebrity and product brand associations that are currently popular. What factors account for the success of each?

Adapted from: Jennifer Weil, "The Lady of Lancôme," *Women's Wear Daily*, January 22, 2010, pp. 1, 6, 7.

its rugged, independent, outdoors personality; the brand reaches out to men of all ages who see themselves that way. Prada's young, hip, fashionable personality is directed to urban career women who believe that the brand reflects the way they want to appear. Android smartphones, efficient and expensive with many convenient apps, have an upscale personality aimed both to business executives and wannabes who want others to know they are tuned in to the times.

Place

Brands need to be where customers can buy them comfortably. Different brand categories of goods

FIGURE 7.7 The Clinique brand name is widely known and recognized. What are some of the images or traits that come to mind when you hear the name? Do they match up with what you know about the brand?

have different requirements. Wrigley gum needs to be available in drugstores, supermarkets, airports, bus and train stations, newsstands, movie theaters, sports arenas, and vending machines—wherever people require it.

Popular fashion looks, such as those of Tommy Hilfiger, J.Crew, and Juicy Couture, need to be in locations where customers may compare their characteristics to find the best fit with their own personalities. On the other hand, exclusive fashion items need an elegant ambiance backed by the expertise of a superior salesperson who helps integrate the designer's intention with the fashion consumer's personality.

Price

The image of a brand is reflected in its price. Customers expect to pay high prices for exclusive brands such as Jaguar, Hermès, and Rolex, for the price is an indication of the status and the quality of the brand. Many customers shopping for those brands are seeking a status to add to their own self-esteem. In shopping for popular-priced brands, consumers expect to find a certain uniqueness for the price and want to compare brands as they search; their goal is to choose from a selection of similarly priced items the brands that best match their views of themselves. The wide assortment of brands such as Jones Apparel, Nine West, Talbots, and Bebe gives them that selection.

When buying inexpensive merchandise, many customers seek value for the money; they feel a sense of accomplishment when purchasing brands from Home Depot, IKEA, Walmart, and Taco Bell, which had attracted them through a combination of approachability, expertise, and reasonable cost.

Promotion

The brand name gives a handle to the product, enabling customers to recall it in the marketplace and marketers to identify the product and persuade customers to buy it. For example, the name alone of "Juicy Couture" imparts to many in its target market an anticipation of new and exciting fashions. Brand names such as Disney, Marc Jacobs, Montblanc, Samsung, and Missoni impart distinct images that target consumers relate to and remember.

THE ADVANTAGES OF BRANDING FOR THE CONSUMER AND MARKETER

Branding is not one-sided. It contains advantages for both the consumer and the marketer, as we shall see.

Branding Advantages for Consumers

For the consumer, a brand makes it easy to identify a product. When a new shampoo is prominently advertised and displayed on the store shelf by brand name, it makes it easy for customers to find and buy it. In a specialty store's sportswear department, customers seeking a North Face or Columbia jacket can quickly locate either one by the brand name.

A brand also indicates a certain style or look. The name Ford Mustang distinguishes it from that company's Explorer model. In addition, a certain level of quality is associated with a brand. When consumers are shopping for a watch, they associate a different quality level with the Timex brand name than they do with that of Rolex. Finally, a brand name reduces the risk of a purchase in the consumer's mind. A customer who wants a rugged, dependable hiking boot has more confidence in a brand such as L.L.Bean than in an unknown brand.[8]

For some products including certain fashion goods, branding also has a cultural feature recognized by marketers. **Cultural branding** describes a brand that conveys a "powerful myth that consumers find useful in cementing their identities."[9] Perhaps the best-known fashion example of cultural branding is the lifestyle offered to consumers through Ralph Lauren products. Early on, the company, reflecting upper-class British country life, featured apparel for men and women such as tweed jackets, cashmere sweaters, jodhpurs, and other stylish riding attire. Customers then could immerse themselves in a world of their own creation through cultural branding: buying furniture for their homes, painting their walls, and carpeting their floors all with Ralph Lauren goods, thus fulfilling their fantasy.

Branding Advantages for Marketers

A product that carries a brand name encourages repeat sales. Customers who have successful experiences with a given product tend to buy the same brand again. A college student who enjoys his Apple iPod is likely to seriously consider buying an iPhone or an iPad when the time comes.

Because a brand name is already known among customers, introducing a new product makes a company's marketing task easier. This is particularly true in fashion when a brand name is hot. For example, periodically the Swedish retailer H&M contracts with designers such as Jimmy Choo or Stella McCartney to create fashion goods for its stores. The day the designer goods arrive, customers line up early in the morning to buy the brand names.[10]

A brand name makes a company's entire promotion program easier. For example, customers associate the name Chanel with the company's apparel, purses, shoes, sunglasses, and fragrances. When a new product is introduced, it too will enjoy the benefits of the brand's reputation. The image of the brand gives all of the products both identification and status.

One of the most important aspects of branding is that it promotes **brand loyalty**, the customer's favorable attitude toward a certain brand. An intimate apparel customer who consistently selects Hanes, Jockey, or Victoria's Secret is considered brand loyal. Marketers classify brand loyalty at three levels: recognition, preference, and insistence. When a customer knows the brand name of a product but does not make it a first choice, the level is that of *brand recognition*. For example, a customer may be aware of the name Keds on athletic shoes but not have any further familiarity with the brand. If a customer favors one brand over another but will accept a substitute, the loyalty level is that of *brand preference*. A consumer who found a previous pair of Nike athletic shoes to be extremely comfortable may go shopping with the intent of buying Nike again. The customer notices a pair of adidas on sale, tries them on, but decides to buy the Nike shoes after all. That customer is showing brand preference. If the customer will not consider a substitute, saying, for example, "It's Nike's or nothing" and may even go to another store to find the desired pair of shoes, that customer is exhibiting *brand insistence*.

Creating Strong Brands

What marketers are striving to accomplish for their products is to build strong brands by creating **brand equity**, the marketing and financial value associated with the brand's strength in the market.[11] Products with brand equity are widely known and accepted, and often demonstrated in the higher amounts consumers are willing to pay for the product. Brands such as Cadillac, Disney, Tiffany, Evian, Bose, and Gucci all have brand equity. Marketers carefully nurture brand equity by making sure customers are aware of the brand (think of the fashion industry's seasonal runway shows to introduce new merchandise and new designers), make certain that customers have a positive emotional reaction to the brand (create promotions, parties, and other events to point out the brand's uniqueness, quality, and suitability), and work toward attaining consumer loyalty based on brand preference.[12]

BRAND POSITIONING

In order to maximize their effectiveness, marketers need to focus on their target markets as they position their brands. Marketers have a choice of three levels at which to position their brands: by product attributes, benefits, or consumer beliefs

MARKETER'S INSIGHT:
THE RISE AND REBIRTH OF LIZ CLAIBORNE, INC.

In 1976, Liz Claiborne and her husband, Art Ortenberg, along with two other partners, began to leave their mark on the fashion retail industry. The company recognized an emerging consumer need for a new kind of wardrobe: career apparel. At that time, an increasing number of women were employed and moving into influential jobs, and they needed versatile yet fashionable merchandise to enhance their growing prestige. Their careers and busy lives called for fresh looks for daily wear, and at reasonable prices. Many women wore several hats—wife, mother, caregiver—which added another requirement, ease of shopping. The upstart company's great idea was to mix and match separates as part of a collection, and the elements, whether a jacket, dress, slacks, blouse, or sweater, would be part of the Claiborne collection, in one area of the store, on adjacent racks for consumers to build their own looks based on their particular needs. The idea would eventually dominate the women's sportswear and separates departments in 22,000 department stores, turning Liz Claiborne, Inc., into a multi-billion dollar corporation.

Over the more than three decades when Liz Claiborne, Inc., was at its zenith, it also began to see the advantages of outsourcing (having many of its brands manufactured overseas), including the Liz Claiborne brand and later its derivations, Kate Spade, Juicy Couture, Dana Buchman, Lucky Brand, and the licensed DKNY Jeans Group.

More recently, due to the ever-evolving changes in consumers' fashion tastes, retailers began to find that once-dominant brands revered by department store customers were experiencing a steady decline in revenue and profit. Customers, it seems, were becoming more demanding and less loyal to the brand and to the retailers carrying the brand. With the Internet, shoppers were now able to visit a number of retailers and consider a range of other brands in their search for useful style and value.

When Liz Claiborne, Inc., saw the once-fertile department stores lose their most-favored status with consumers, the result had a dramatic effect on the company's signature brands, which had suffered a double-digit decrease in revenue and profit over three years. So the company took another look at the product and place elements of its marketing mix. While increasing its focus on its high-end Kate Spade, Lucky Brand, and Juicy Couture brands in department and specialty stores, it began relocating other brands where new, and possibly larger, target markets would find them.

As a result, the company signed an agreement with QVC for exclusive rights to sell the Liz Claiborne New York brand, designed by Isaac Mizrahi. In addition, Liz Claiborne, Inc., entered into an exclusive long-term agreement with JCPenney to market all Liz Claiborne and Claiborne branded merchandise (apparel for women and men, accessories, shoes, and home goods)—and later sold the brands outright to the retailer. Going further, the company sold its Dana Buchman brand to Kohl's; its Ellen

Tracy brand to Fashionology Group LLC (and subsequently to RVC Enterprises); and some of its fragrance brands to Elizabeth Arden, although Liz Claiborne, Inc., continues to own the Lucky Brand and Juicy Couture fragrances and license them to Arden. In short, it appears that the company believes the best strategic plan is to improve its profit by licensing or divesting its iconic (but less profitable) brands in order to relieve itself of the

costs of sourcing, manufacturing, and inventory, while keeping and emphasizing its upscale and more profitable brands under its own auspices. In fact, as a reflection of that new brand strategy, in 2012 Liz Claiborne, Inc., changed the name of the company itself to Fifth & Pacific Companies, a moniker chosen to identify the company as the place where "California cool meets New York chic."

Source: www.lizclaiborne.com (accessed February 27, 2010); www.jcpenney.net/about/jcpmedia/corporate news (accessed March 10, 2010); Art Ortenberg, *Liz Claiborne, The Legend, The Woman,* Taylor Trade Publishers, 2010; Nathalie Tadena, "Liz Claiborne Amends Licensing Pact with Elizabeth Arden," Wall Street Journal (ital), August 11, 2011, http://online.wsj.com/article/SB10001424053111904006104576502121820883 138.html (accessed March 7, 2012); fifthandpacific.com (accessed March 7, 2012).

and values.[13] Considering attributes, Coach can promote the construction, styling, and colors of its handbags. The challenge is that Dooney & Bourke, Stone Mountain, and others can compete on the same level. Coach could also position itself on the benefits of the brand: the fashionable look, uniqueness, and versatility. But Coach also conveys a deeper, more emotional meaning to consumers: its design reputation, American origins, and suitability. When a brand can reach out to customers with an intangible appeal as an emotional experience, the message is hard for competitors to duplicate. Many fashion marketers accomplish this goal. Think of Yves Saint Laurent, Bergdorf Goodman, BMW, and Four Seasons. Their customers have deep feelings for these brands that have developed due to product positioning.

SELECTING A BRAND NAME

A well-thought-out brand name is an effective marketing tool. Marketers give considerable thought to a name, sometimes even calling in businesses that specialize in product name creation. According to experts, a successful brand name should meet several criteria. It should:

1. Describe the product's benefits (think Stride-Rite shoes, Burger King, Maidenform, Totes).
2. Be simple and easy to pronounce in English and in a foreign language (think Dell, Derek Lam, Dior, Zara).
3. Be distinctive and fit the product image (think Clinique, Burberry, Comcast, Kmart).
4. Be able to register for legal protection, meaning it cannot interfere with other brand names (think Nine West, Kenmore, McDonald's, Macy's).

TYPES OF BRAND CHOICES

Brands may be described in a number of ways. These include *manufacturer's* (or *national*), *store*, and *private brands*; *family*, *individual*, and *generic brands*; *brand extensions*; *co-branded*; and *licensed brands*.

Manufacturer's, Store, and Private Brands

A brand carrying the name of its manufacturer is called a **manufacturer's brand** (or sometimes corporate or *national brand*). Avon, Levi's, Amazon, Nike, and London Fog are all manufacturer's brands, as are Volkswagen, Cover Girl, and Sony. Products marketed under designers' names are also manufacturer's brands, such as Ralph Lauren, Donna Karan, Jimmy Choo, Joseph Abboud, and Tommy Hilfiger. Names such as these are among the many fashion brands marketed throughout the world. .

Some retail organizations carry goods labeled with their **store brand** name. These include Brooks Brothers, Forever 21, L.L.Bean, Williams-Sonoma, and others. Many retailers carry brands that are available only in their stores; these are known as **private labels**. Macy's private labels include Alfani, Charter Club, and others. Perhaps the best-known private-label brands belong to Sears, with names including Kenmore for appliances, Craftsman for tools, and DieHard for batteries. Another Sears private label, featuring sportswear for the family plus home goods, is the Lands' End brand and its more preppy Canvas line. While private labels typically are exclusive to company stores, Sears also markets selected products from its Kenmore, Craftsman, and DieHard labels through Kmart (also owned by parent Sears Holdings, Inc.), Ace Hardware, and other stores.

Family, Individual, and Generic Brands

A marketer creates a **family brand** when all of its products carry the same name. Gap, Tiffany, Totes, and Apple are all family brands. Products that are marketed under separate names are called **individual brands**. The Escalade is an individual brand of General Motors Cadillac division, just as Minute Maid is an individual brand of Coca-Cola, and 501 is an individual brand of Levi-Strauss.

Goods without a specific brand name or identity are termed *generic brands*. Usually, generic brands are positioned by retailers to be at the lowest price range in a particular product category. In the supermarket, when you see a box labeled simply "sugar" or "flour," you know that the brand is generic. By not branding a product, the marketer helps keep prices down and improve customer value.

Brand Extensions

When a company decides to place its brand name on a product in an entirely new category from its existing product mix, it is practicing **brand extension**. An example of brand extension would be when the Ralph Lauren organization placed its name on sheets, towels, and paints, categories quite different from the company's apparel and accessories. Brand extension is different from *line extension*, which occurs when a company adds the brand name to a new product in the same category, say, when a coat and jacket manufacturer decides to add vests to the product line.

Co-Branding

Sometimes marketers find it advantageous to place two brand names on the same product, known as **co-branding**. For example, the magazine *Real*

TABLE 7.1 Fashion Brand Selections Available by Retail Store Type*

Department Stores	Discount Stores	Specialty Stores
AK Anne Klein	Miley Cyrus	Gap
Ellen Tracy	House & Garden	Old Navy
Lauren by Ralph Lauren	Hanes Underwear	Banana Republic
Rachel Rachel Roy	Champion	Athleta
Tommy Hilfiger	L'Oréal	Piperlime
Alfani	Olay	Gucci
Raymond Weil Watches	Norma Kamali	Coach
INC International Concepts	Danskin	Prada
Charter Club	Levi's	Bottega Veneta
7 For All Mankind	Fruit of the Loom	Anthropologie
Calvin Klein	Just My Size	Hue
Ed Hardy	Playtex	Vera Wang
Timberland	White Stag	Zera
Dana Buchman	Faded Glory	Forever 21
Vera for Vera Wang	Timex	H&M
Hanes	BlackBerry	IKEA
ABS	iPhone	Apple
Worthington	Fieldcrest	iPod
Brass Plum	Dell	iPhone
Michael Kors	HP	Dolce & Gabbana
Tracey Reese	Acer	Christian Louboutin
Eileen Fisher	Mossimo	Cole Haan
Juicy Couture	Merona Converse	Diane von Furstenberg
Starbucks	Starbucks	Dior
Coach	Kitchen Essentials by Calphalon	Fendi
Prada	Giada De Laurentiis	Burberry
Gucci	Joe Boxer	Chloé
Hue	Nintendo	Donna Karan
Kate Spade		DKNY
DKNY		
Donna Karan		

*Brand availability varies by individual retailer.

Simple partnered with Bed Bath & Beyond to market closet organizers and storage bins, and designer Sonia Rykiel teamed with H&M to offer a line of sweaters with French-inspired lettering such as "Mon Pull Rykiel" (my Rykiel pullover).[14]

Co-branding has the advantage of reaching out to a wider range of consumers because each brand is already known to its own customers. For example, fashion followers know the name Sonia Rykiel, and fashion bargain hunters closely watch the offerings of H&M, giving the co-branding effort greater impact than either brand alone. Co-branding affords the opportunity for the new brand to expand at a lower risk than had each company entered the new market individually. On the negative side, co-branding requires complex legal agreements and coordinated promotion, and difficulties can arise if one side is not pleased with the agreement, such as when Martha Stewart withdrew from a co-branding agreement with Kmart for her Everyday Housewares brand and signed on instead with Macy's and Lowe's.[15]

Licensed Brands

One of the most popular ways for fashion organizations to grow is through **brand licensing**, an agreement between the owner of the brand and another organization, such as a manufacturer specializing in related goods, to provide items bearing the owner's brand name in exchange for

FIGURE 7.8 Co-branding brings added recognition to both participants, in this case, Liberty of London and Target.

FIGURE 7.9 Licensed brands enable fashion marketers to offer additional products under a recognized name.

a royalty fee. Companies such as Christian Dior, Tommy Hilfiger, Calvin Klein, and many others sign licensing agreements for apparel and accessory items such as neckwear, handbags, shoes, sunglasses, and household goods such as towels, sheets, and tableware. And the apparel industry is far from alone in licensing. Merchandise for children, such as lunch boxes, toys, and school supplies bearing cartoon characters such as Spider-Man, the Peanuts gang, and Scooby-Doo are all licensed.[16] The Walt Disney Company licenses many of its characters, ranging from Snow White and Mickey Mouse to WALL*E, for a wide range of products, including toys, games, and apparel. Other organizations that engage in brand licensing include colleges and universities as well professional athletic teams, which license the rights to use their brand on sweatshirts, jackets, caps, blankets, and pennants, among other items.

GLOBAL FASHION BRANDS

Fashion brands such as Apple, Chanel, Louis Vuitton, Sony, and Gucci are known around the world. When a brand achieves more sales overseas than at home, and is marketed with the same name and according to the same strategic principles in every part of the world, it becomes a **global brand**. Some of the better-known global brands include Coca-Cola, Disney, McDonald's, IKEA, and Levi's. Some companies, called *international firms*, use a similar marketing strategy at home and overseas.

MARKETER'S INSIGHT:
LICENSING TAKES LACROIX BRAND GLOBAL

In 1987, LVMH Moët Hennessy Louis Vuitton set up a separate couture house for its talented young designer Christian Lacroix. Each subsequent season at couture showings, Lacroix would bring out innovative garments reflecting his fanciful imagination and the sunny colors of his southern French origin. Fashion devotees and the media praised his fresh approach. Unfortunately though, acclaim alone does not translate into profits. As can happen too often in business, the organization's expenses habitually exceeded its income. In spite of the couturier's creative designs, Christian Lacroix SNC, the haute couture and ready-to-wear organization, was forced to file for bankruptcy in 2009.

Nevertheless, the Christian Lacroix name still exists and is working to expand through brand licensing agreements in four new product categories: frames for women's eyeglasses produced by Mondottica in Hong Kong; stationery featuring Lacroix designs, produced in New York by Libretto Holdings; home textiles produced with England's Designers Guild; and decorative wood panels made by the French company Marotte. The Lacroix company already licenses some other products including men's wear and bridal dresses, with an estimated $61 million dollars revenue at retail. In 2007, the organization entered a licensing agreement with Avon and introduced the fragrance Christian Lacroix Absynthe, with estimated revenues of $132 million wholesale. The company also has licensing agreements with retailers in Argentina and Chile.

And what about the designer himself? What is Christian Lacroix doing now? He left the company bearing his name and now he is concentrating on designing costumes, hotel interiors, and other projects through his own XLCX studio. Meanwhile, as celebrities such as Chloë Sevigné and Diane Kruger continue to wear vintage Lacroix at public awards ceremonies, and Lacroix product agreements grow, the brand is going global in a number of ways, not the least being through licensing.

Source: Milton Socha, "Lacroix Brand Signs String of Deals," *Women's Wear Daily*, March 1, 2010, p. 2.

For example, Gap carries much the same merchandise in its European stores as it does domestically. Other businesses, known as *multinational firms*, recognizing the effect of differences among cultures, vary their marketing strategies according to local needs. For example, when entering India, Estée Lauder set up freestanding shops for its customers. The company had discovered through research that, unlike American and European women who shop for cosmetics in department and specialty stores, Indian women prefer the ambience and service of a more intimate environment. In various countries

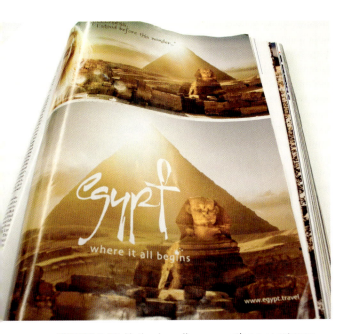

FIGURE 7.10 Nation branding, promoting a country as a brand, identifies it as an attractive place to visit and do business.

Packaging and Labeling

Packaging and labeling provide another way for marketers to promote their brands and for customers to enjoy them. Let's examine each of those topics individually.

BRAND PACKAGING

While not all fashion products are packaged, some, such as fragrances and cosmetics, are often elaborately dressed for consumer presentation. Think of the elegant crystal bottles containing perfume by design houses such as Dior, Hermès, Gaultier, Lanvin, and Chanel. The bottles are further packaged in boxes that match the companies' signature colors: gray and white for Dior, orange for Hermès, black and white for Chanel, and so on. Each of these wrappings signals the image of the design house to the customer. In marketing cosmetics, firms such as Estée Lauder, Lancôme, and others offer items individually and combined into distinctively packaged sets, plus fashionably conceived promotional gifts from time to time. At holiday times, jewelry, lingerie,

where it locates its restaurants, McDonald's adapts some of the food items and beverages to local tastes: Beer is served in its German outlets, wine in France, and fruit-based drinks in Asia.

Global brands are recognized throughout the world, targeting similar customers with a uniform product and promotional effort. To maintain their position in the market, companies monitor their brands carefully, managing the marketing mix to create constant contact with consumers. They do this not just through advertising but through all of the touch points available to them, including social media, word of mouth, and other methods, so that customers see a living entity in the *brand experience*.[17] We can identify the brand experience in some of the branding done by nations today, as in the advertisement promoting Egypt as a tourist destination, for instance, shown in Figure 7.11.

FIGURE 7.11 Tiffany uses its brand color in its packaging.

hosiery, and accessories such as small leather goods and neckwear appear festively packaged to promote gift sales. Beyond apparel, other fashion goods come in distinctive and informational packages. One example is cell phone accessories such as Bluetooth headsets, memory cards, and protective "skins."

Packaging has three major purposes: protection, identification, and promotion. Packaging protects the contents from physical damage en route from the manufacturer to the consumer and minimizes the likelihood of damage in the warehouse and in the store. The package of certain brands indicates the amount the package contains, such as 0.5 fluid ounces (15 milliliters) of cologne, or 4.25 ounces (120 grams) of soap. Notice that the weights are given both in ounces and in globally used metrics: milliliters (for liquids) and grams (for solids).

Packaging also identifies and promotes the brand. Not only is the brand name and/or brand mark generally featured prominently on the packaging, but brands that are packaged in signature colors and designs—such as Gap blue, Elizabeth Arden red, or with an apple or window pattern—are instantly recognizable to target consumers and create another touch point for customers to receive the marketer's message. Packaging also facilitates ordering in desired quantities and sizes and—due to its uniform size—makes transporting and storing easier. Packages often serve as containers for products while they're in use, such as stationery, laundry detergent, or bubble bath. When consumers are through with the product, sometimes the package can be used for other purposes (a metal cookie tin holds pencils or keys), given away later, or recycled, increasing its sustainability and deterring its ultimate destination in a landfill.[18]

THE MEANING OF LABELS

When part of a package, a label identifies the brand and may give information about its contents and directions for use and care. In addition to showing the brand colors and name, a label on a bottle of shampoo—sometimes in two or three languages—indicates its purpose (to hydrate and condition); describes the ingredients and gives directions; states where it's manufactured and by whom; and gives a Web site, mailing address, and/or toll-free phone number for questions. This information is geared to anticipate and alleviate customer concerns and provide manufacturer sources for additional answers.

The purpose of other fashion brand labels—on apparel and accessories in particular—is to identify, promote, and inform. These brands count heavily on

FIGURE 7.12 Labels identify a product's brand and, on apparel, provide information including fiber content, country of origin, and directions for care.

the recognition and emotional appeal of their labels. Picture the names Calvin Klein, Giorgio Armani, Guess, 7 For All Mankind, and Abercrombie & Fitch. These and similar brands carry a certain image and are placed prominently on their products, among them coats, jackets, handbags, sunglasses, and shoes. Some customers seek out and wear only a certain brand. The brand's emotional impact is impetus enough to buy. Other customers interpret their own fashion look by selecting from a variety of brand labels. In addition to labels that form part of the brand marketing, garments must, by law, feature labels that indicate the fiber content, country of origin, and their care.

Together packaging and labeling can offer a final touch point to create a living entity from a brand name.

FIGURE 7.13 Organizations forecasting fashion trends provide a valuable service to fashion marketers.

WHAT DO YOU THINK?

Brands are said to have personalities. In your opinion, what goes into the personality of a brand and why is creating a brand personality important to marketers? Name a fashion brand that possesses a personality and describe its characteristics.

Fashion Services

Unlike fashion goods that we can see, touch, and hold, services are intangible products such as activities, benefits, or satisfactions. In the fashion field, these include services offered to individuals, such as a haircut, college courses, automobile detailing, or plastic surgery; and business services, such as advertising and public relations, trend forecasting, or store design services. Service businesses in the United States occupy an important place in the economy, accounting for approximately 79 percent of the total gross national product (GNP, the sum of all domestic production).[19] There are three types of service organizations: government at all levels (think postal and military service and police), private nonprofit organizations (think universities, charities, and museums), and businesses (think consulting firms, financial institutions, lawyers, and doctors).

Services in the fashion field are of the last category, provided by businesses, and are meant for individual and business consumers. Some fashion services for individuals are beauty, spa, and fitness salons; fashion and image consultants; fashion and interior designers; and real estate and travel agents. Fashion services for businesses include trend forecasting; fashion and textile designing; advertising, media, and publishing; sales promotion and public relations; fashion show production; and visual merchandising. Further information on fashion services is available in Michelle Granger's *Fashion: The Industry and Its Careers* (New York: Fairchild Books, 2007).

In the next section we'll look at the characteristics and marketing strategies inherent in marketing fashion services.

CHARACTERISTICS OF SERVICES

As you can tell from Figure 7.14, four characteristics separate services from tangible goods. Services are:

CHARACTERISTICS OF SERVICES

INTANGIBLE
Services cannot be seen, tasted, felt, heard, or smelled before purchase.

HAIR SALON

INSEPARABLE
Services cannot be separated from their providers.

VARIABLE
Quality of services depends on who provides them and when, where, and how.

GOOD HAIRCUT   BAD HAIRCUT

PERISHABLE
Services cannot be stored for later sale or use.

CLOSED

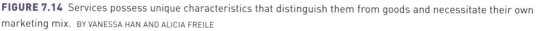

FIGURE 7.14 Services possess unique characteristics that distinguish them from goods and necessitate their own marketing mix. BY VANESSA HAN AND ALICIA FREILE

1. *Intangible.* You can't hold or touch services, but you are able to enjoy their benefits. Consumers appreciate the look of a freshly decorated room, the sound of a good concert, or the appearance of their smile after wearing braces.

2. *Inseparable from their provider.* You don't go to a dog groomer for advice on interior decorating. It was the interior designer who created the new room look; the band, the music; and the dentist, the application of braces resulting in a healthy smile.

3. *Variable or inconsistent.* Because they are performed each time by their provider, services are not precisely identical from one time to the next. An airline passenger might be totally satisfied with one flight on a particular airline but the next time feel annoyed if the flight is late or baggage lost. A hair color applied by one beautician may be totally unsatisfactory when compared with the results of another stylist. Meals at your favorite restaurant may be consistently delicious and expertly served in an inviting atmosphere, until a new chef is hired and the menu changes.

4. *Perishable.* Services last only a certain length of time. When a seat for a fashion show is empty, or customers don't purchase tickets for a cruise, or a dinner party is no-show at a restaurant, those experiences are gone. The service marketer has lost that specific income forever and must consider carefully how to make it up.

STRATEGIES FOR MARKETING SERVICES

Because of the unique characteristics of services, the marketing mix needs to compensate for their special challenges. Fortunately, each element of the mix is capable of contributing to the total strategy.

Product

One of the things that can be done to make a service more "real" is to give it a unique image or personality. Often this is done through a character or other specific image that becomes associated with the brand. For example, the Travelocity gnome appears somewhere in all of the company's ads and on its Web site. For the securities broker E*Trade, talking babies in television commercials and movie clips draw attention to the company's services. Some service companies such as banks, hotels, and airlines make their service more distinguishable by dressing their employees in a uniform look. For example, at the department store Takashimaya in Kyoto, Japan, on-duty elevator operators have been known to wear designer uniforms by Yves Saint Laurent.

Place

The marketing channels for services are short, providing abundant opportunities for service providers to interact with customers and strengthen relationships, the foundation for continuing brand success. The barber, cosmetologist, and manicurist all perform their services directly on their clients. The couture fashion designer creates a custom wedding dress for a client, such as the elegant gown designed by Sarah Burton of Alexander McQueen's fashion house for the royal wedding of Kate Middleton to Prince William. The trend forecaster works closely with manufacturer clients, who use the advice in developing their goods, and the visual merchandiser creates store windows and interiors that draw attention to the retailer's merchandise. Working frequently and directly with clients permits service marketers to respond swiftly and appropriately to client needs, thus establishing a framework for long-term customer relationships.

Promotion

Maximizing the brand name of a fashion service through advertising and personal selling is an effective promotional tool. Organizers of events such as the Las Vegas MAGIC fashion shows and wholesale apparel markets use a variety of promotional vehicles to attract the attention of retail buyers. Celebrity appearances and endorsements, such as Ellen DeGeneres for American Express, also help to promote fashion services. At fashion runway shows, many designers save front-row seats for celebrities who may buy and wear their lines and who are the subject of much word-of-mouth discussion. Some businesses such as tax accountants and repair services are able to offer guarantees of their work, alleviating consumer anxiety.

Price

The pricing of services is based on demand—that is, how eager prospective customers are to buy them and how much they value the brand. When demand is high, service pricing is also high. When demand falters, services think of creative ways to increase it. Many businesses offer *bundle pricing*, offering a bundle, or combination of features, at a lower price than each item would cost separately. For example, TGIF restaurants advertise an appetizer, entrée, and dessert at a price lower than the combined regular cost of each individual item. A travel organization creates a group tour of China at less than a couple would have to pay independently. A buying office offers store buyers sessions in trend analysis and fashion forecasting at a combined lower price for the two topics.

These strategies and others help service businesses manage customer relationship efforts that build and sustain their offerings. Such efforts also include inducements for loyalty such as airline miles, free meals or free nights in a hotel, and membership in fitness clubs and tennis courts, again, making the intangible service more valuable and the focus of customer relationship management. After all, what customers are seeking across the board are a certain dependable level of quality that meets their expectations, a service organization able to communicate those expectations to its employees, and employees capable of delivering what customers want.

Fashion Brands, Ethics, and Social Responsibility

Certainly companies offering brand names have a responsibility to their customers and themselves. A product bearing a brand name needs to represent a consistent quality and safety that consumers can rely on now and in future. In addition, fashion businesses have a responsibility to treat their employees and suppliers fairly, to invest shareholders' assets wisely, and to conserve and sustain the environment and its limited resources. And fashion marketers are in a position to do just this. Among the many organizations demonstrating this form of social responsibility in their brands are Gap, Ben & Jerry's, Walmart, Patagonia, Hewlett-Packard, Levi's, Timberland, and Martha Stewart. Organizations

FIGURE 7.15 The Woolmark trademark, owned by Australian Wool Innovation Limited (AWI), provides assurance to consumers that a textile product is made of 100 percent pure new wool.

such as Cotton Incorporated and the American Wool Council, whose major purpose is to promote the use of their respective fibers, make sure customers know that garments and other textile products made with those fibers meet certain quality levels.

Gap has joined with the World Economic Forum to promote (PRODUCT) RED, an effort to combat AIDS, tuberculosis, and malaria in developing countries. Customers buying Gap's (PRODUCT) RED garments—a recent line being artist-designed T-shirts—know the profits are going to help those less fortunate. Tying in with another color-designated brand cause, Green, Gap is promoting a denim clean-water program among its suppliers. Manufacturing denim calls for chemicals and dyes plus water. For factories creating denim wear for its stores (Banana Republic and Old Navy as well as Gap), the company requires that wastewater treatment procedures follow established guidelines. Gap is also looking for better environmental practices such as the creation of environmentally friendly dyes.[20] One of the ways the Martha

Stewart organization demonstrates social responsibility is through its foundation, which supports family shelters for women in need and assists women recovering from substance abuse to reenter the workforce.[21] One of Walmart's socially responsible activities is to work with its suppliers to achieve better packaging by reducing the amount of packaging for certain goods, using biodegradable materials, and incorporating recycling. Walmart is also working with clothing suppliers to attach garment care labels that indicate cold-water washing when feasible, lowering customer energy bills in laundering.[22] These organizations and others realize that to maximize sound customer relationships and their own profitability, they need to assume the responsibilities of good corporate citizenship voluntarily. Although the government has a number of laws and agencies to protect consumers—such as the Food and Drug Administration, which monitors the quality and branding of cosmetics, and the Consumer Product Safety Commission, which prevents the marketing of flammable fabrics, among other regulations—many marketers take steps to ensure the safety and quality of their brands before legislation is necessary.

Consumers, too, have a commitment to ethics and social responsibility, including avoiding purchasing counterfeit brands that have in all likelihood been produced in sweatshop conditions and marketed without paying necessary taxes, not to mention royalty fees to the owners of the brand. Other unethical and illegal acts that consumers have perpetrated include pirating copyrighted music and films. In addition to being illegal and unethical, these acts only raise the price of the brands that all consumers must pay.

summary

Brands are names and identities given to products, both tangible goods, such as a sweater, and intangible services, such as a haircut. There are two main types of products: those intended for consumers to use and those that businesses use in making other products or in conducting daily activities. Consumer products are classified as convenience products, shopping products, specialty goods, or unsought items. Each type has unique characteristics and distinct marketing strategies. Decisions that fashion marketers need to make about products are concerned with their quality level, style, and design. They also need to make decisions about the product lines and product mix they want to offer.

A brand is a name, term, design, or symbol that identifies a product. The brand reflects and reinforces the product's identity and becomes part of every aspect of the marketing mix. Branding has advantages for both consumers in identifying the product and marketers in promoting it. To create strong brands marketers position them with characteristics that relate to consumer wants, choosing an appropriate manufacturer, store, private brand name, or a generic brand. Successful brands often extend their brand identity into other product categories, as apparel brands such as Prada or DKNY appear on neckwear, sunglasses, shoes, and belts. Co-branding increases the visibility of two brand names together, while licensing provides for extensive brand extension through the licensee's agreement to pay royalties to the brand name owner for the use of the brand on certain items. Many fashion names are global brands because they are well known throughout the world. Packaging and labeling are important in marketing fashion goods because they help identify, maintain, and promote the image of the brand.

Certain organizations, such as travel agencies and interior design firms, offer fashion services to individual consumers. Other organizations offer services to businesses; these include fashion trend consulting, fashion show production, or visual merchandising services. Services have special characteristics that call for a unique marketing mix. For example, fashion services may create a recognizable character or image that makes them appear more tangible, such as the gnome in Travelocity's marketing vehicles.

Social responsibility is an important facet of many fashion organizations that want to give back to the community and contribute to the sustainability of the environment. Among the companies cited in this chapter, Gap is participating in (PRODUCT) RED, with sales of this brand donated to the alleviation of AIDS, tuberculosis, and malaria in developing countries. Fashion marketers are in a position to conserve and protect the world's limited resources, but consumers also have a responsibility to treat their marketing relationships honorably and to make choices that sustain the environment.

Football Players Build Their Personal Brand

The National Football League is known for bigger-than-life men who run up and down a field desperately trying to cross the goal line while holding on tightly to an odd-shaped leather ball before being tackled by the opposing team. The football player is a modern-day gladiator who, because of the extreme wear and tear on the body, will most likely have a short-lived career even though he may be the very best at the game.

To help prepare for a life after pro football, a group of NFL players took part several years ago in the first financial education workshop created strictly for them and held at Northwestern University's Kellogg School of Business. The discussion topic was "Developing Your Own Brand," a strategy that could be quite useful to them at the time and more so in the future. Tim Calkins, a marketing professor, pointed out to the players the fact that they each are a brand. He told them that in order to capitalize on their short football careers, upon leaving the NFL, they should each have built up the following: money in the bank or investments, memories, and a personal brand. The implication was that a well-constructed personal brand could perhaps lead to another career after the gridiron days. And this has happened in a number of instances. Some former players are now coaches, others sportscasters, and still others successful entrepreneurs. Terry Bradshaw, former Super Bowl MVP quarterback of the Pittsburgh Steelers, went on to become a football media commentator for CBS and Fox networks. The Football Hall of Fame player has also been a spokesperson for Radio Shack and Verizon Wireless.

When asked to name athletes with strong positive brand identity, all agreed that former basketball star Michael Jordan and Indianapolis Colts quarterback Peyton Manning are both strong examples. The audience also named several NFL players who have very negative personal brands; for them, career opportunities after football would be more limited.

Tim Calkins suggested that the players build their personal brands as a three-step process. First, develop a positive relationship with the media rather than an adversarial one. If the media are comfortable with the player,

"they're more likely to quote the player or say something nice about the player." Second, do something good for somebody else, become involved in a charitable effort, and actively play the role of a good community citizen. Some players have actually started non-profit foundations that benefit others. For example, Peyton Manning used his reputation as the highly respected team leader of a top performing football team to form The PeyBack Foundation, which promotes programs providing leadership and growth opportunities for disadvantaged youth. Acts of concern for others can improve lives and reflect well on the donor. And finally, control the brand in a positive way, for example, through a well-maintained Web site. Web pages have become a way for an athlete to keep fans informed and let them know where to find out more. The Peyton Manning site includes a newsletter, information about his foundation, news and media reports, and a fan forum section that allows fans to communicate with their favorite player 24 hours a day. Manning's is also the first NFL bilingual Web site.

The moral of this story is that "all jobs are temporary, whether 10 years or 10 days, and planning for the future is extremely important."

Adapted from: Susan Chandler, "Players Given Choice about How They Want To Be Branded for Life," *Chicago Tribune*, Business Section, April 16, 2006, p. 10; and www.peytonmanning.com, (accessed March 10, 2010).

QUESTIONS

1. Consider yourself as a brand. Name three or four of your positive attributes that contribute to your personality and brand identity.

2. How would you go about building your personal brand? Create a marketing mix with you as the product. Who are your target markets (people at home, college, work, your social life)? Where will you demonstrate the positive aspects of your personal brand? How will you promote it? What will be the price to you of carrying out your personal brand program?

KEY TERMS

brand

brand equity

brand extension

brand licensing

brand loyalty

brand mark

brand name

brand personality

co-branding

convenience products

cultural branding

family brand

global brand

individual brand

manufacturer's brand

private label

product line

product mix

shopping products

specialty products

store brand

trademark

unsought products

REVIEW QUESTIONS

1. Explain the difference between products and goods and describe four types of consumer goods, citing an example of each and stating the reasons for their individual classifications.

2. Explain why marketers brand products, and describe two decisions fashion marketers need to make about product branding.

3. Concerning branding, describe three advantages each to consumers and to marketers.

4. Citing an example of each, state the importance of packaging and labeling in marketing fashion brands.

5. Describe four branding strategies for marketing fashion services.

6. Explain the importance of ethics and social responsibility to fashion branding, with an example of one brand's current practices.

DISCUSSION ACTIVITIES AND PROJECTS

1. What is the effect on fashion marketing strategy when some consumers consider a brand to be a shopping good while others consider it a specialty item? Think of a brand that could be either, and devise a marketing strategy for it.

2. Go to the Web site of your favorite fashion brand, and determine the product line length and depth, and the width of the product mix. Create a chart indicating these elements, and present it to your class.

3. With a group of classmates or a single partner, select a brand that you believe has a well-defined personality. Define five characteristics of the brand, and then relate those characteristics to those of the brand's target market. Locate or create an ad that illustrates one or more of those characteristics, and report your findings to the class.

4. Think of a fashion service that you use (dry cleaner, shoe repair, beauty salon, barber shop, or other) and create a marketing strategy for it that you believe would improve the business. Write a brief report, stating your reasoning.

5. Go to the corporate Web site of a global fashion brand and locate the company's statements concerning its social responsibility practices. Report to the class on what the organization is doing in this area and its effect on the brand name.

DEVELOPING YOUR MARKETING PLAN

Up to this point, we have covered marketing and its environments, consumer buying behavior, creating a marketing strategy, using research, and developing positive customer relationships. Now we turn to the marketing mix, beginning with the product element and the importance and value of branding. To complete this segment, examine and explain the effect of one of the brands your company has developed on its marketing mix, answering the following questions:

1. What products are sold under the brand name?

2. How would you describe the brand's personality? Do you believe that it gels with the segment you've identified as your target market?

3. Consider where the brand is marketed, how it is priced, and ways in which it is promoted. How do those aspects of the brand strategy enhance the brand personality?

4. Is the brand licensed or co-branded? If so, what are the marketing advantages for the brand?

5. What type of brand loyalty does the brand nurture?

Refer to the Marketing Plan Outline, Table 1.2, provided at the end of Chapter 1, as well as Appendix A: Sample Marketing Plan.

REFERENCES

1. Gary Armstrong and Philip Kotler, *Marketing: An Introduction*, 9th ed. (Upper Saddle River, NJ: Pearson Prentice-Hall, 2009), p. 204.

2. Ibid., pp. 204–205.

3. Ralph Caplan, *By Design: Why There Are No Locks on the Bathroom Doors of the Hotel Louis XIV and Other Object Lessons*, 2nd ed. (New York: Fairchild Books, 2005). p. xx.

4. Op cit., p. 210.

5. William M. Pride and O. C. Ferrell, *Marketing*, 14th ed. (Boston: Houghton Mifflin, 2008), pp. 350–351.

6. Margot A. Wallace, *Museum Branding: How to Create and Maintain Loyalty and Support* (Lanham, MD: Alta Mira Press/Rowman & Littlefield, 2006).

7. Roger A. Kerin, Steven W. Hartley, and William Rudelius, *Marketing: The Core,* 2nd ed. (Boston: McGraw-Hill Irwin, 2007), p. 245.

8. Op cit., p. 351.

9. Douglas B. Holt, *How Brands Become Icons: The Principles of Cultural Branding* (Boston: Harvard Business School Press, 2004).

10. Charles Lamb, Joseph F. Hair, Jr., and Carl McDaniel, *MKTG4, 2010–2011 ed.* (Mason, OH: South-Western, 2011), p. 158.

11. Op cit., pp. 353–354.

12. Op cit., pp.246–247.

13. Op cit., p. 216.

14. Sharon Edelson, "Sonia Rykiel Launches Knit Line with H&M," *Women's Wear Daily,* February 9, 2010, p. 11.

15. "Martha Stewart, Upgrading from Kmart to Macy's," *Financial Wire,* April 26, 2006. p. 1.

16. Op cit., p. 216.

17. Ibid., p. 219.

18. Op cit., p. 162.

19. Op cit., p. 219.

20. Gap website, www.gap.com (accessed February 25, 2010).

21. Martha Stewart website (accessed March 13, 2012).

22. Stephanie Rosenblum, "Walmart Plans to Make Its Supply Chain Greener," *New York Times,* February 26, 2010, p. B3.

CHAPTER 8

Developing New Fashion Products and Monitoring Their Life Cycles

This chapter addresses the process and systems that are vital in developing, showcasing, and monitoring fashion product or service offerings. It examines the product elements that provide benefits to consumers, explores ways in which new products are conceived, and explains the fashion product life cycle.

WHAT DO I NEED TO KNOW ABOUT DEVELOPING NEW FASHION PRODUCTS AND MONITORING THEIR LIFE CYCLES?

* The components of value that the customer receives
* How companies differentiate their products while gaining a competitive advantage
* The product categories that companies use in developing winning marketing strategies
* The major steps in the new product development process
* How organizations monitor business progress and adapt accordingly
* The importance of ethical decision making in new product development

Coco Chanel once said: "Fashion is not something that exists in dresses only. Fashion is in the sky, in the street; fashion has to do with ideas, the way we live, what is happening." People use the term fashion for things that are *in the moment*. Those things could be related to clothes we wear, things we eat or drink, vehicles we drive, pens or pencils we use to write, e-readers such as the Kindle or Nook, sunglasses or eyeglasses, impact lipstick, our vacations, how we accessorize our homes or decorate our offices, and anything else. Therefore, a fashion product is a product that is popular at a given time. To see how companies stay ahead of competitors with these fashion products, let's start by understanding how marketers dissect the product concept.

A fashion marketer's job is to anticipate and identify what customers want. Only then can the marketer develop an appropriate value package (bundle of benefits) in its product, and communicate and persuade consumers to purchase them. A company succeeds by monitoring its product life cycles (the period from newness to old news) and adapting accordingly. Conversely, the marketplace will send negative messages to organizations that don't deliver the product benefits that consumers expect.

As discussed in prior chapters, we use the term "products" to describe either tangible goods or intangible services that meet customer needs. There are consumer products (individual or personal use) and business products (company use). Figure 8.1 illustrates how individuals and companies can use the same kinds of products. An individual consumer owns a laptop for Web browsing, e-mail, and other personal activities, whereas companies might use a laptop in the manufacture of other products (top right), to run their businesses (bottom left), or to resell to consumers or other businesses (bottom right).

A company may sell a product item (one single product such as a vacuum cleaner or a fashion service such as tailoring), a product line (think of all the available digital Apple products), or a product mix (multiple product lines and items—Procter & Gamble provides cosmetics, skin care, shaving, hair care, and cologne items, in addition to other product areas). The next section discusses products in detail.

FIGURE 8.1 Some fashion products, such as laptop computers, cross over between consumer use and different types of business use.

PRODUCT ESSENCE AND AN ENGAGEMENT RING

Precious jewelry has always been a status symbol, although as art and manners change, so do popular styles. But there's one highly symbolic piece of jewelry that has been coveted by women for centuries—the engagement ring. It is said that the idea of the engagement ring began with ancient Egypt's pharaohs, who were the first to proclaim it a symbol of love, without beginning or end. And so it is to this day, a circle of love, a reminder of vows, *and a product imbued with major meaning.*

The engagement ring is more than a beautiful piece of jewelry. It is an announcement to the world that one person has been chosen by another, selected from among all others as someone to be treasured and loved, and desired as a lifetime partner. It is also an item that can convey a certain level of income, taste, and accomplishment. If one receives a diamond engagement ring from Tiffany's, the implication is that it's the best quality, the most innovative cut, and not to mention that it comes in the famous blue box, along with all the prestige and respect those who make purchases at Tiffany's expect.

As you can see, there are many parts to the engagement ring, most of them having not as much to do with the *actual* product as with all that comes with it—the product essence.

What the Customer Gets

Customers want products that are made well, include quality materials, and address current wants and needs. The last time you were in the market to buy a computer, cell phone, makeup, shoes, home accessories, or salon services, didn't you want something that really worked, would not deteriorate too quickly, and took care of a current need?

Marketers that persuade consumers that their product offers the best bundle of benefits do well in the marketplace. This package that delivers superior customer value includes the **product essence**, basic benefits received from using the product; the **real product**, the actual components that make up the product; and the **expanded benefits**, the extra-value follow-up features.

PRODUCT ESSENCE

Product essence refers to the bottom-line basic benefits received from having and using a product or experiencing specific services. You buy something for what it will do for you, not necessarily for just the facts about it. People buy benefits, the end result of using the item, not just a combination of ingredients or components. If you have a digital camera, ask yourself if you bought it because of the metal and glass components or because the photo-taking process is convenient. When using sunblock, aren't you really interested in the protection it provides from UVA or UVB rays? The last time you bought a casual or business suit or pair of shoes, you considered the impact that particular look would have on your target audience or how the apparel would make you feel, correct? Marketers must ensure that the stated basic benefits are actually realized by their consumer.

REAL PRODUCT

The term "real product" identifies those key components that come together to deliver the benefits—that is, the product essence discussed above. Using the digital camera example, the real product includes the 3-inch LED screen, the 8GB memory stick, the 12X optical zoom, and other components that deliver the package of benefits you wanted when you bought it. When you get a haircut, a manicure, or salon services, the real product includes everything you experience (the ingredients in the shampoo or nail polish, the scissors or file wielded by the stylist) and the actual process as the attendant washes, trims, or colors your hair, or shapes and buffs your nails; this also includes the packaging. (See Table 8.1.)

TABLE 8.1 The Product Benefits Package

Benefit	Features	Examples	Example of a Related Descriptor
Product essence	■ Product outcome ■ Basic benefits received	■ Perfume ■ Health insurance ■ iPad	■ Compliment from a friend ■ Reduction in financial liability ■ Reading/listening convenience
Real product	■ Appearance ■ Actual components ■ Real experience ■ Distinctive features	■ Perfume ■ Health insurance ■ iPad	■ Specific chemical ingredients ■ Deductible amount, or coverage limits ■ Memory capacity or multi-touch screen
Expanded benefits	■ Follow-up incentives ■ Extra value	■ Perfume ■ Health Insurance ■ iPad	■ Company supports customer's special social cause ■ Company's educational Web site ■ Access to digital library

EXPANDED BENEFITS

Companies differentiate themselves from competitors by adding supportive and follow-up features to their product offerings. These factors result in the consumer receiving value-added benefits. The salesperson exceeds the customer's expectations, using a combination of exemplary service, warranty support, and targeted feature extras. Extending the digital camera example above would find a company providing virtual storage options for digital photos; the consumer realizes extra value by selecting this company. Neutrogena's skin cancer resource Web page provides sunblock educational information; one way the company demonstrates its social responsibility is by actively supporting the American Cancer Society.[1] Two expanded benefits from ABT Electronics, an award-winning retailer and largest single-store electronics and appliance dealer in the United States, are that it provides free technical support and shipping.[2] Best Buy started a Twitter-based method (@Twelpforce) for customers to pose technical questions and get answers from actual people in real time.

FIGURE 8.2 Consumers choose products such as digital cameras based on their bundle of benefits including product essence (ease of use), real product (zoom lens), and expanded benefits (free technical support).

Product Fundamentals

Now that we understand the various layers of value that consumers potentially get in their product or service of choice, let's explore the various product components that marketers consider.

TYPES OF PRODUCTS

If companies know how and where consumers purchase products, appropriate marketing strategies are created to make the buying process more attractive and efficient. There are two types of products: business and consumer.

Business products are goods and services used to make day-to-day operations work, incorporated in other manufacturing processes to create an end product, or resold to others. People buy **consumer products**, goods and services intended for consumption by individuals and families, because they fulfill their personal wants and needs. Naturally, some products fit both categories. It just depends on how the item or service is used. (See Table 8.2.)

For example, you might buy CD/DVD storage boxes, a new 50-inch HDTV with 3D, or HDMI audio/video cables, just as an electronic store would buy them to resell to you. Companies use desks,

TABLE 8.2 Product Usage

Category	Example	Personal Use	Business Use
Raw materials	■ Whole Foods organic dairy eggs ■ Designer bottled water ■ Propylene glycol ■ Faux fur	■ Homemade omelet ■ Health consumption ■ Hair shampoo in morning shower ■ Detachable coat collar	■ Ingredient in a cake for a catered wedding ■ Resale to consumers ■ Salon hair service ■ Component in manufacture of a coat
Equipment	■ Sewing machine ■ Designer treadmill	■ Hemming a new pair of pants ■ Staying in shape	■ Manufacturing a line of clothing ■ Equipping a health club for clients
Services	■ Spa treatment ■ Car insurance	■ Feel energized ■ Limit liability	■ Part of a hotel getaway package for travelers ■ Benefit for employees
Supplies	■ Hand cream	■ Gift for mother	■ Inventory item for health and beauty store

Think of a personal clothing purchase you made that cost $100 or more. You might buy one or maybe two of the same item, but many companies purchase in quantity. How do pricing strategies differ between a business owner and individual customer?

Customers are charged according to the bundle of benefits received, such as product item, demand, convenience, or customer service. On the other hand, business owner benefits may translate to full costs associated with the product. This means that the manufacturer used a pricing strategy with the business owner that was quite different than the one used with you.

The point? Figure out what your customer values and set your pricing strategy accordingly.

computers, or virtual keyboards, just as you would. Just as you buy your fresh fruit, vegetables, or fish for personal reasons, your favorite restaurant incorporates those items into a special recipe for you to enjoy. The point is that the marketing mix tools previously discussed are used in different ways depending on who is targeted. Marketers use different promotion, distribution, and pricing strategies to satisfy their particular target market. The next product fundamental addresses the question: How long will the items last?

USAGE TIME

When you go to the store to buy a box of cereal, a pen, hand cream, a pair of running shoes, shoe laces, an everyday blouse, food, batteries, or designer soap, you don't really expect it to last too long, do you? These items are examples of **nondurable goods**, products we use up relatively quickly. We don't necessarily spend too much time (low involvement) researching these items or making

the buying decision. Past usage and purchase experiences or habits, in addition to simple purchase rules (*heuristics*—a commonsense shortcut for making a quick decision), help to make the process move along nicely.

Because marketers know this, they develop appropriate pricing, distribution, and promotion strategies. The last time you went to the grocery store, what prompted you to buy the brand of milk that you did? How long did you think about this decision, or did you just stand in front of the dairy section at the last minute to compare prices?

Conversely, goods that we keep and use for a long time (years, even decades) that are not easily used up or don't wear out too quickly are called **durable goods**. Microwave ovens, washing machines, cuff links, and luggage are examples. We don't expect to dispose of any of these items too quickly. Because our decision making is more involved (*high involvement*), marketers need to educate, promote, instill a feeling of product confidence in us, and identify those key benefit drivers that meet and exceed our expectations. When you or your family bought your last major durable goods purchase, what was it that the company said, did, explained, showed, or guaranteed you that convinced you to buy that branded item? You might have decided upon another brand if the marketer didn't do a good job, right? Another product fundamental that marketers research relates to where and how the product is bought, and how much effort is used by the consumer to make that decision. Think of a product that you would buy using minimal thought and effort. Marketers planning their campaigns according to the product categories discussed below maximize their opportunities for success.

PRODUCT CATEGORIES

Understanding how consumers buy products and how they might categorize them provides the foundation for getting those items or services in customers' hands. Marketers vary their use of the marketing tools according to their target market and how consumers shop for products. You'll recall the Chapter 7 discussion on types of consumer products. *Convenience products* are purchased out of habit (with limited thoughts for product comparisons). With *shopping products*, consumers spend time sourcing purchase locations (traditional or Internet-based) and thinking about their buying decision. For *specialty products*, consumers are quite selective, willing to spend a good amount of money, search for unique benefits, and hesitate in accepting alternatives. Figure 8.3 illustrates the customer's mindset regarding product choices made.

On the other hand, in the B2B category, businesses sell products or might provide services to other businesses that will resell, redevelop, or customize them to fit the needs of that other businesses' clients. The items may include light or heavy equipment: A company builds an assembly line that processes its own end product, then sorts and delivers it; an accounting firm, a college, or a day health spa might require copy machines, desks, and digital audio-video equipment. Operational supplies, maintenance products, processed or raw materials, and custom parts all fit this category: fibers, fabrics, cleaning fluids, oils, staplers, light bulbs, metals, lumber, natural gas, electricity, memory cards, or tempered glass. Review Table 8.2 for examples of how some products overlap to satisfy the needs of both businesses and individuals. Additionally, a company could use purchased

FIGURE 8.3 BY VANESSA HAN AND ALICIA FREILE

products for itself. For example, a service station buys or leases shirts for mechanics, or employees at a for-profit business or nonprofit organization wear shirts and hats with the corporate logo.

FIGURE 8.4 Consumers seeking specialty goods, such as Prada apparel, are very selective and willing to pay high prices.

New Product Ideas

We begin our discussion of the last product fundamental, new product variations, with this quote from the late Steve Jobs, co-founder of Apple: "Our belief was that if we kept putting great products in front of customers, they would continue to open their wallets." **New products**, innovative product solutions developed to satisfy customer wants and needs, help to keep a business fresh, growing, and bring in new revenue. So, what do marketers mean when they say they have a new product? In an effort to better understand customer needs and then provide appropriate product solutions, marketers subdivide the term "new product."

NEW PRODUCT VARIATIONS

Six subgroups of new products to consider are *breakthrough*, *new*, *add-on*, *new-and-improved*, *repositioned*, and *cost reduction*.

Breakthrough Products

Breakthrough, or innovative, products bring an entirely new idea to the marketplace. Some marketers refer to them as new-to-the-world. Think of the various e-reader devices such as Amazon's Kindle, Sony's Reader, Barnes & Noble's Nook, Apple's iPad, Google's Tablet Talk, or RIM's PlayBook, all of which have dramatically changed the way many people acquire and read books and magazines.

New Products

New describes a product that the company did not previously provide, although there is an existing

NEW PRODUCTS AIM FOR MARKET APPEAL

On August 31, 2010, in 12 U.S. cities, Starbucks unveiled its new line of specialty coffees targeting the "coffee geek." This small-batch coffee brought a new product to customers in a limited-supply distribution manner.

In late 2010 Cono Italiano introduced its patented pizza cone, an inside-out slice of pizza that promises "drip-free, spill-free enjoyment" of a piece of pizza.

market that competitors occupy. The company enters this established market with a product offering that is new to them, but not new to the marketplace. Your local gym now offers mixed vitamin solutions or chiropractic consults. Nate Berkus, an interior designer and, until recently, host of his own national TV show, introduced a virtual design software package to his service repertoire in late 2010; the software also included point-of-purchase hotspots.

Add-On Products

Add-on products, as the name sounds, refer to additions to existing product lines. Think of how many flavor variations there are to your favorite soft drink. Walk into a food store for yogurt and you will find flavors such as watermelon, mango, and pomegranate in addition to the basic plain, strawberry, vanilla, and peach. Also, a Portland, Oregon, company that was started in 2004, Sock It To Me, now sells more than 200 original sock designs.

New-and-Improved Products

New-and-improved describes products that now have an extra feature or enhanced packaging that makes their use more convenient or efficient. For example, during fall 2010, Apple TV marketed its second-generation product, improving its streaming capability and energy efficiency and making it 80 percent smaller.[3]

Repositioned

When a product is repositioned, the term suggests that the original product may have additional uses that were not previously marketed, or that a new target market will be addressed. For example, Buick LaCrosse, a luxury sports sedan, and multiple Cadillac brand vehicles attract generations other than baby boomers or seniors. Under Armour began initially by making a performance T-shirt and has since repositioned itself from an apparel company to one that produces both apparel and footwear.

Cost Reduction

In the category of cost reduction, marketers lower the price on their products. In essence, a company has found a way to sell the "latest product version" less expensively than it previously did. Examples of goods for which marketers frequently use cost reduction include digital cameras, televisions, and computer printers.

SEGMENTING FASHION PRODUCTS

As we've discussed, fashion relates to those things that are "of the moment" and across all product or service lines. The term **fashion product** refers to anything that is designed and currently popular. Let's discuss three fashion categories: *fads*, *trends*, and *classics*. A fad is a short-lived craze that is followed for a limited period of time. Examples include the original hula hoop; jeggings; big, shiny plastic glasses; single-shoulder dresses; pet rocks; some health diets; twenties' flapper dresses; drawn-on eyelashes (as brandished by sixties supermodel Twiggy); and scented gummy bear animal bracelets. A trend is a longer-term marketplace influence, a direction in which things are moving. Examples include portable electronic devices, designer handbags, social media, anything denim, and hybrid vehicles. Classic fashions, such as a tuxedo or a little black dress, reveal a simple, not a flashily bold, idea; they incorporate minimal design changes through the years. Other examples are a white tailored shirt, a trench coat, French-cuff shirts, a string of pearls, a pair of loafers, or a navy blazer.

INFLUENCES

Fashion reflects the spirit of the times, or the *zeitgeist*. Because consumers are attracted to product options, the marketplace adapts by constantly developing new offerings. These products or services are "fashionable" because they mirror what customers believe they want at that moment. This means that it's a repetitive process where those items that become "unfashionable" are replaced accordingly.

FIGURE 8.5 Classic fashion products, such as the "little black dress," may be updated from time to time, but they maintain the same basic design concept over many years.

Influencers (blogs, people, events, world crises) have an impact on consumers and their decision-making processes. External influences include those macroenvironmental factors illustrated in the

TABLE 8.3 Examples of External Factors Influencing Fashion

Driver	Example	Fashion Influence
Global	Cheaper labor in Southeast Asia	Fewer fashion jobs in the United States
Environment	Hotter-than-normal spring weather	Customer selects more typical summer items
Technology	Virtual online dressing room	Customer uses a personalized visual body model to "try on" apparel items
Economy	Unemployment rate is high	More customers buy low-cost and volume-produced fashion alternatives
Government	Consumer Product Safety Commission (CPSC) passes new regulations on crib design	Parents purchase new cribs that meet the current safety rules

G-PESTELC model and discussed in Chapters 2 and 4; see Figure 4.3 in that chapter. G-PESTELC forces exert their influence on organizations and marketplace expectations. In turn, consumers, who really cannot control those forces, adapt to them through their purchase decisions.

Haute couture (exclusive design firms that create luxury garments for individual clients) and Vaute Couture (a design company that sells eco-conscious, fair trade-made products) designs trickle down (*downward flow*) or across (*horizontal flow*) to influence the marketplace. See the Marketer's Insight feature, "Couture Frenzy."

NEW PRODUCT DEVELOPMENT

Now let's look at how new products are developed and tracked through various cycles.

Question 1: Where do totally unique, previously unknown, brand-new ideas come from? Are they "gifts"—miraculous inventions that can only be conceptualized by geniuses, visionaries, inventors, or artists?

All of the following products were once brand new: chocolate bars, watches, television, mascara, sewing machines, computers, ready-to-wear clothing ... you get the idea.

Question 2: Are all new products actually inventions, or might they have evolved from existing ideas?

People drank chocolate from cups for many decades prior to the invention of the chocolate bar. And before the first watch was invented, there were clocks, and before that, there were sundials.

Questions 3 and 4: Do new products really have to be 100 percent *new* to be classified as such? Or

MARKETER'S INSIGHT: "COUTURE FRENZY"

There's a certain word that's very popular today. It's often used, or should I say, **mis**used, even by those in the fashion industry, who should know better. "And which word is that?" I hear you query.

Couture, my friends…*Couture!!* And its abuse is one of my pet peeves.

Well, okay. Maybe I do have a tendency to let certain things bother me more than I should. And, yes, it's a very "of the moment" kind of word, which is, after all, what fashion is about—what's new … what's current …what's in … what's "now."

But still, it's misleading. It's inaccurate. Couture has become a mere *buzzword*, put into play by marketers, to get your emotions going and make you feel that you're on to something special, that you're *in-the-know*… when you're actually *in-the-NO!*

It's too bad, really, because couture does have an important place in fashion history.

Known for more than 150 years by those who have practiced it as "the art of perfection," it officially began when Charles Frederick Worth, an English designer working in Paris, created a gown for Empress Eugenie, wife of Napoleon III. From then on, *haute couture* became a revered Parisian art, requiring that each piece be an original design, a collaboration with the wearer, entirely made by hand, and executed to perfection.

Now, I ask you, does that sound like the word that is currently used to describe everything from cell phones to doggie duds?

Recently, I've seen/heard couture used in all sorts of ways—to describe frozen treats as in *yogurt couture*; to attract customers to a financial institution by offering *couture bank accounts*; to promote a company that creates "handmade business solutions," calling itself *Couture Business Development*; to reposition a furniture manufacturer that changed its name from Absolute Business Furniture to *Couture Business Furniture & Interiors Ltd.*, etc.

Must I continue?

Yes! Because I'd certainly be remiss if I didn't mention my personal favorite—*Stinky Couture.* It's a cloth diaper company in Colorado that's attempting to provide a solution to the 3.4 million tons of trash made each year by disposable diapers … an admirable undertaking.

Being somewhat of a risk taker and original thinker, I've come up with a few ways to ride the haute couture bus myself, and so, I ask you, what do you think of *bloat couture*, coy cover-ups one can wear when planning to overeat; or *float couture*, a new line of oh-so-chic swimwear with slenderizing life preservers cleverly attached; or *croak couture,* a collection of garments with celestial detailing to wear in the afterlife?

Okay, I'll stop.

To be fair, there are some companies that have used the couture concept in rather clever (and somewhat respectable) ways. One is DHL, the international freight company. Together with German designer Michael Michalsky, and because DHL is a sponsor of Fashion Week Worldwide, the company created a special collection of formal gowns made completely from original DHL packaging materials, to highlight its commitment to special handling of fashion goods. (Think cardboard, plastic bubble wrap, and string, all in the hands of Cinderella's fairy godmother.)

There's also *Vaute Couture*, Chicago designers/ producers of hip pieces made from recycled and vegan materials (hence the V in Vaute). The mission, "to create gorgeous alternatives to animal derived fabrics," has already made the clothes into favorites of young celebs. Vaute Couture is determined to merge ethics and aesthetics, and so far, their efforts have brought them critical acclaim and loyal fans.

All right, I'll say it … Monsieur Worth would be overjoyed, I'm sure.

Source: Stefani Bay, President and Creative Director of Stefani B jewelry (www.stefanib.com), Associate Professor at The Illinois Institute of Art–Chicago, and author of two textbooks about the fashion industry.

can they come in the form of modifications and improvements to already existing products? From the discussion above about new product variations, you know the answer to these questions is no and yes, respectively.

Today new ideas emerge in many ways. They can be new inventions that are named as such by a division of the government, the United States Patent and Trademark Office. If an item has been submitted to the office along with the correct paperwork, drawings, explanations, and so on and ultimately determined to be absolutely new, its inventor will be granted a patent, which is a right granted by the government to an inventor to make, use, sell, or distribute that invention for a specific period of time, generally 20 years. While some countries such as France protect fashion apparel and accessories through copyright, the United States does not at present.

But there are other types of new products that are known as **innovations**; these are products and services that are *perceived* as new by consumers, either because they've never been seen or experienced by the customer, or because they've been successfully positioned as such by marketers.

Some innovations are considered *continuous innovations*, meaning they are simply modifications of an already existing product, like the first widescreen TVs and the slimmer, lighter-weight models that followed.

Others are referred to as *dynamically continuous innovations*. These may require the customer to learn a new behavior because of a particular change that's been made to an existing product. At first, cell phones had dial pads with raised keys; now, many have touch screens, which require a different technique. And there are those we call **discontinuous innovations**, which actually change the way we live; they can be referred to as inventions, because there wasn't anything like them prior to their introduction. Examples include the printing press, the automobile, and the camera. Today it seems that people want what's "new" more than ever. In fact, we seem to be constantly on the lookout for the next big thing. But to really make it in the marketplace, so much time must be spent on research and development, so much testing must precede the introduction of the concept, and so much money must be spent to convince customers to adopt the product that it's not always as successful or as profitable as was anticipated.

Nevertheless, fashion is about continual newness and whatever is of the moment; hence, updated, innovative products and services are critical to the ongoing success of designers, retailers, fashion brands, and other fashion marketers. How can a marketer meet the desire for newness expressed by the purchasers of fashion goods in a timely manner and recover its investments? Perhaps the product initiatives don't have to come in the form of new inventions, but rather through continuous outside-the-box thinking and the improvement of products, services, techniques, presentation methods, and other marketing elements.

Major Stages of Product Development

Essentially, to remain competitive, all companies should encourage and support new ideas. As previously stated, new ideas take time to develop; they must be proposed, discussed, evaluated, revised, and so on.

In the fashion industry, product development largely depends on the type of fashion that's being developed. For example, the methods used in the creation of an haute couture collection are very different than those used to develop a ready-to-wear line. And, in the case of men's tailored wear, the methods used are different, once again. Some designers are inspired by textiles; others find inspiration in art; still others base collections on particular locations. Ideas are everywhere!

Most popular consumer products such as cell phones and iPads go through a seven-step product development process:

1. *Brainstorming/opportunity identification.* This phase is also referred to as idea generation. During this period, new ideas are proposed and explored; sometimes they come from customers, sometimes from employees, and some are the result of research. Those that are in line with the company's other offerings and/or its brand extension/expansion strategies are identified and taken to the next phase.

2. *Concept expansion and screening.* In the second stage, marketers examine the real potential of select ideas. Further exploration is required in order to more completely develop each idea by formulating the actual features and benefits of the prospective products/services and determining which are most likely to appeal to consumers.

3. *Marketing strategy development.* At this point, marketers begin to strategize about effective ways to present the prospective product and engage the target market. The marketing mix tools come into play during this phase, as marketers focus on objectives along with possible tactics they may use to encourage acceptance and adoption of the product.

4. *Business analysis.* The questions during this stage are not about creativity or the excitement

FIGURE 8.6 The retro 1960s look of the popular TV show *Mad Men* has inspired new apparel designs, including a collection for men and women by Banana Republic.

the product might generate; this phase is strictly business. In other words, costs are the primary concern. How much money will be spent to develop and promote the new concept and what is the potential for profit? Accurate estimates regarding demand become the primary focus as marketers try to determine the likelihood of initial and continued success.

5. *Technical development.* During this phase, companies choose the idea that is most likely to succeed and attempt to refine the design. A prototype will most likely be created, followed by decisions about how to go about producing it and where to find suppliers.

6. *Testing.* At this point, marketers may choose a particular geographic area that's reflective of their target market, test the product and the marketing plan on a limited basis, and evaluate the response. Perhaps improvements or changes are indicated. Sometimes a company may decide not to go forward if those in the test market don't react positively. But if the product and the accompanying marketing strategies are successful, the product will be prepared for its launch.

7. *Product launch.* The product/service is introduced to the target market along with carefully planned marketing activities, including promotion and distribution.

The development of a fashion apparel or accessory line is slightly different; unless we're referring to customized garments or accessories, there are generally six steps that take designers and manufacturers through the process:

1. *Product development cycle.* In this stage the team of designers, merchandisers, and marketers researches fashion trend forecasts, new developments in textiles, target market shifts and preferences, past and present sales figures, the current economic and cultural zeitgeist, and so on. It's during this period that new ideas surface, excitement is generated, and efforts are directed toward the creation of a cohesive collection or "story."

2. *Concept creation.* Once the research is completed, interpreted, and integrated, the designers begin the creative process. A basic concept emerges, and either via sketching or computer generation, groups of garments (or accessories) begin to take shape. All lines must have a focus—a harmonious idea that connects all of the pieces. Fabric possibilities are explored, colors selected, and silhouettes developed.

3. *Design development.* Now that the various pieces have taken shape "on paper," actual samples must be made. Expert seamstresses make each garment, and "fit" models, who reflect the average sizes of target market members, try them on. Any problems can be corrected and designs can be tweaked at this point; pieces that didn't turn out as expected or may be too complicated to reproduce uniformly will be deleted. Experts, who understand pattern making's complicated steps, will create new patterns by hand or computer. Also during this stage, fabrics are chosen, technical specifications are determined, and the costs of individual pieces are calculated.

4. *Pre-production planning.* At this point, the concept and direction of the collection is clear, and sample garments are readied for preliminary

showings to important buyers, fashion consultants, independent merchandisers, or other experts in the field—possibly an influential fashion editor or two. The company considers the feedback in order to accurately estimate demand, so that orders for fabric and trimmings can be placed and wholesale pricing can be determined.

5. *Production/manufacturing.* The hands-on phase begins now. Every pattern is graded or sloped—this is a process by which each pattern is adjusted to reflect all the sizes that will be offered. When the fabric arrives, it is carefully laid out on cutting tables, often in layers so that a number of garments can be cut at a time. Copies of the patterns called markers, which are made in lightweight paper, are placed on top of the fabric to mark each part of the garment. The various pieces of the garments are then cut, bundled, and labeled, for example, "right sleeve, #5024, sz. 10," and sent to the sewing staff for assembly.

6. *Distribution.* Garments are inspected, tagged, packaged, and shipped to retailers.[4]

WHAT DO YOU THINK?

Consider the evolution of eco-friendly fabrics, hybrid vehicles, synthetic substitutes, or virtual retail stores. How were these ideas developed and nurtured? What results have you seen?

PRODUCT LIFE CYCLE

Fashion is fickle—this we all know. That's why every marketer needs to ask this question: *How long will this idea retain its popularity*? How long will sky-high platform shoes be adored before kitten heels become the rage? Will the armies of denim ever retreat, or will they hold on, despite attacks from other fabrics, which may be even more durable and comfortable?

PRODUCT LIFE CYCLE

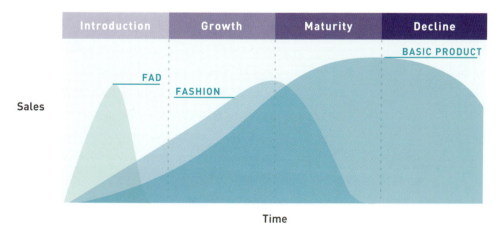

Source: http://courses.cit.cornell.edu/cuttingedge/lifeCycle/03.htm

FIGURE 8.7 BY VANESSA HAN AND ALICIA FREILE

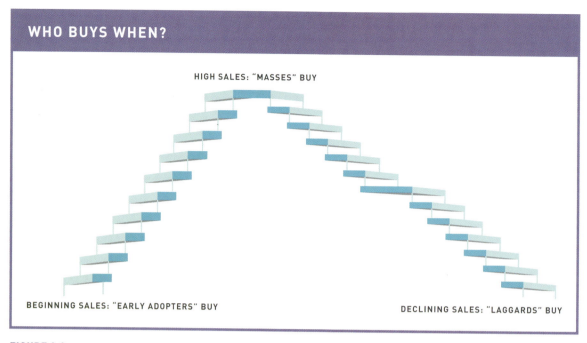

HIGH SALES: "MASSES" BUY

BEGINNING SALES: "EARLY ADOPTERS" BUY

DECLINING SALES: "LAGGARDS" BUY

FIGURE 8.8 BY VANESSA HAN AND ALICIA FREILE

Every product has a life; some may endure for longer periods than others. But whether a passing fad or a beloved classic, each product goes through a cycle that takes it from newness to old news. This is referred to as its **product life cycle**. (See Figure 8.7.)

In the case of fashion, the adoption of a particular style, color, or brand is based on the action of many customers during a particular, and usually limited, time period. When it is no longer deemed current, a fashion product's life cycle ends. Fashion products usually experience a sudden and steep decline once they reach their highest sales, and quickly descend into obsolescence. Different groups of consumers tend to enter the cycle at different points. For example, *innovators* are the first to create and/or identify a new fashion; innovators might be designers themselves or celebrities

like musicians, actors, or other artists. Those who want to be among the first to own/wear what's new and exciting are called *early adopters*; they are often members of a group referred to by consumer behavior experts as "opinion leaders," those to whom people tend to look for direction. The *masses* are the next to embrace a new product; this is the point at which sales are the highest—everyone seems to want the particular style in some form or another. By now, however, innovators have already discovered something else. Soon, more and more people tire of seeing the style everywhere, and sales begin to decline. (See Figure 8.8.)

This is when a group referred to as *fashion laggards* enter the cycle; members of this group tend not to attach a lot of importance to having things that are "of the moment" but prefer to make purchases when pieces go on sale or when they appear at off-price retailers for considerably lower prices. Now you understand the steps needed to drive a new product from idea generation through commercialization.

RATE OF ADOPTION

When the consumer buys and uses a new product, it is called **product adoption**. Five steps are generally used to describe this process: *awareness*, *interest*, *evaluation*, *trial*, and *adoption*. Marketing efforts are very important in each step because some customers along this cycle will be tempted not to stay with it. Just think about how many times you have heard about a new product or service but not bought it. Or maybe you bought it once, but then reconsidered or did not give it any thought the next time. Let's look at each step in the adoption process.

1. *Awareness*. You hear about some new product (an item, service, or idea) but don't really have much information about it.
2. *Interest*. You check various sources to learn more about this new thing.
3. *Evaluation*. You consider its product attributes and think about whether it is really something you want or need.
4. *Trial*. You give it a chance and try it for the first time.
5. *Adoption*. You start using it consistently.

Naturally, exposing a new product to the customer and even getting the customer to use the product does not ensure its continued success. That's why it's important to use coordinated marketing communications *after* consumers have adopted a product. See Figure 8.10, the "Consumer Filtering Process." These follow-up marketing messages may reduce buyer's remorse, reinforce applicable benefits, further educate consumers on related applications, or provide ways to improve the next product generation. Sustaining business profitability in a highly competitive environment necessitates the incorporation of this extra step. For example, say you replaced your current cell phone with one that included new video-chat and global contact features and you thought they worked pretty

FIGURE 8.9 As editor-in-chief of *Vogue*, Anna Wintour (right) not only influences fashion adoption but is herself an early adopter of new fashions.

TABLE 8.4 Product Adoption Steps

Step	Marketing Effort Goal	Example of Marketing Tool Used	Possible Customer Response
Awareness	Get customers' attention	Make product introduction announcement	Notice the product mentioned in a magazine
Interest	Entice customers	Use advertising to describe the product's benefits	Seek more information through friends or online
Evaluation	Encourage customers to weigh key benefits against their needs	Educate consumer through informational Web site	Compare the product's features to those of a previous product used
Trial	Get product in customers' hands	Provide free samples	Try the product
Adoption	Get customer to buy	Use promotions or discounts	Start using it regularly

well but weren't absolutely sure. Then you received follow-up marketing messages or read independent consumer study results validating the effectiveness of these features. You would probably have a big smile on your face and perhaps even tell your friends to try it, while you confirmed to yourself that you made a good buying decision. Smart marketers make these follow-ups consistently happen in order to entice customers for future purchases.

Ethics and Social Responsibility

Knowing what's right or wrong in the workplace and then doing the right thing, while at the same time benefiting stakeholders at multiple levels, is sometimes easier said than done. The phrase **strong moral compass** suggests that when

things get tough and we are under great stress (the economy shrinks; competitors surpass us; our latest product, idea, fashion collection, or invention is not well received), we will continue to follow those positive values and beliefs we followed when things were going well. Imagine this: A salesperson steers his customer to multiple items (blouse, skirt, and outer jacket) that the person does not really need or want and pressures her to purchase them. What of the fashion designer who copies a design and logo style but merely changes the smallest detail to avoid liability issues? How would you respond to the manager who hires an employee because of potential future personal networking opportunities? The term "gray area" refers to decision-making situations where the surrounding circumstances or facts may suggest a response that is not definitely a strong yes or no. For example, a hairstylist may suggest a particular new gel, lotion, or shampoo that is more profitable for the salon to sell, even though the regularly used, less expensive one is probably just fine for the client. On the other hand, a "loophole" is an ambiguous and unclear wording or exception to the law or guideline. Say a city's building code authorized all new retail stores in a shopping complex to be no larger than 8,000 square feet but the developer circumvented this regulation by creating two stores that together totaled more than 8,000 square feet. These actions may not necessarily be illegal but might certainly be unethical.

Greenpeace activists, those who actively support global "green" environmental issues and peace, have long accused companies of mass deforestation when harvesting palm oil. More and more organizations are trying to do the socially responsible right thing. For example, the action by Unilever of using algal oil, a liquid substitute for palm oil, in its foods, soaps, and lotions demonstrates how companies are trying to use ingredients that don't damage the environment.[5] In turn, fair labor laws and anti-sweatshop legislation are critical for socially responsible apparel production companies.[6] Their objectives include creating and distributing fashion items while eliminating labor exploitation and environmental decomposition.

CONSUMER FILTERING PROCESS

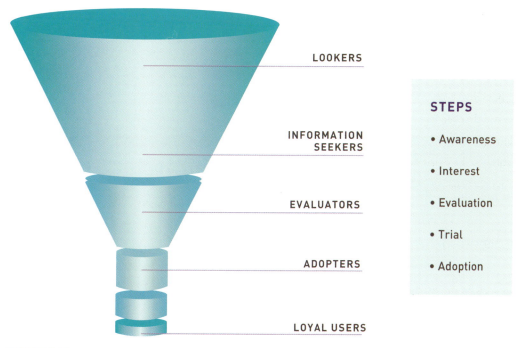

LOOKERS

INFORMATION SEEKERS

EVALUATORS

ADOPTERS

LOYAL USERS

STEPS

- Awareness
- Interest
- Evaluation
- Trial
- Adoption

FIGURE 8.10 BY VANESSA HAN AND ALICIA FREILE

Globalizing Ideas

Globalization happens with new products, services, relationships, or strategic partnering. In today's economy, developing new products and using ideas, raw materials, or services from interdependent global partners, who contribute these lower-cost value bundles, is business as usual. Companies **outsource**—that is, assign jobs to a business entity or individual outside of one's company and often in a different country—various parts of the manufacturing or distribution process to sustain profitability, while encouraging integrated market harmony.

In short, others who complete the process more inexpensively and therefore reduce the company's expenses increase the opportunities for business success. On the product development side, an *MIT Sloan Management Review* article addressed global product development and noted that highly effective product development necessitated cooperation and collaboration among the various departments

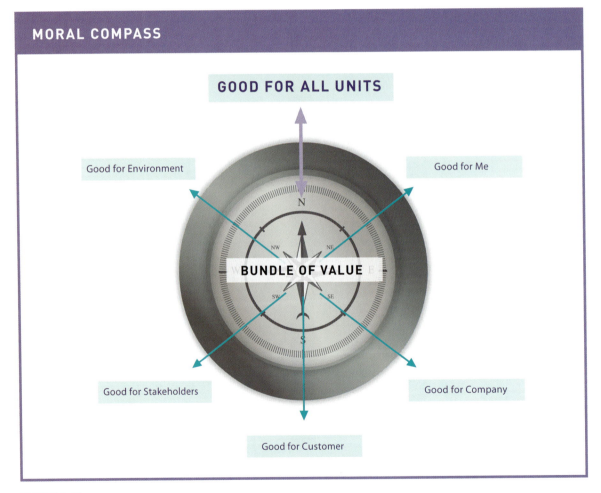

MORAL COMPASS

GOOD FOR ALL UNITS

Good for Environment

Good for Me

BUNDLE OF VALUE

Good for Stakeholders

Good for Company

Good for Customer

FIGURE 8.11 BY VANESSA HAN AND ALICIA FREILE

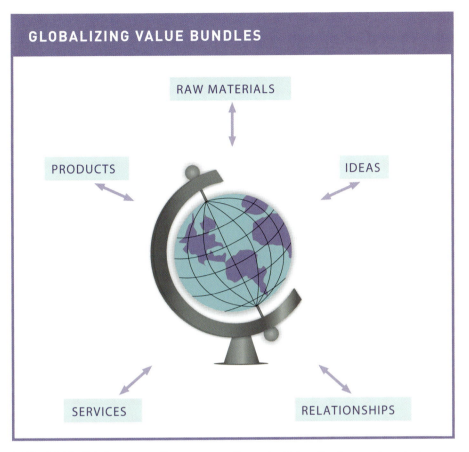

GLOBALIZING VALUE BUNDLES

RAW MATERIALS

PRODUCTS

IDEAS

SERVICES

RELATIONSHIPS

FIGURE 8.12 Global success relies on cooperation and collaboration from each sector in the marketing process. BY VANESSA HAN AND ALICIA FREILE

such as production, manufacturing, operations, marketing, and administration.[7] Consider how Gap, Inc., an international retailer, coordinates its worldwide businesses and product development processes while collaborating with multinational units, as it utilizes both brick-and-mortar and Internet-based shopping portals.

Once companies create their products, global expansion provides access to both developed and newly developing countries. Increasing market share worldwide develops brand awareness, keeps the company viable, and provides a foundation for other product offerings. For example, Walmart aggressively advanced into the Africa market during the fall of 2010 after its U.S. stores open more than a year experienced a revenue drop over the prior five quarters.[8]

Companies then monitor their product life cycles and create appropriate marketing strategies to address marketplace changes. In short, global awareness and subsequent presence are important for the development and growth of products in today's marketplace.

summary

This chapter detailed that what the customer ultimately gets should go beyond basic product benefits. The complete product should include a mix of excellent service, warranty supports, and appropriate extras. Developing a new product, monitoring its progress, and adjusting to the marketplace as needed to exceed customer expectations are key factors for business success.

Once a product proceeds through a development process cycle, the marketer tracks its popularity (from newness to old news) through the product life cycle, continues coordinated marketing efforts during each of the five adoption levels, and even solicits feedback after the customer has adopted a product. Reviewing these processes and adapting to the market are important to sustain profitability.

An organization might also adjust to the marketplace by repositioning itself, communicating extra product uses, incorporating innovation or even appealing to a new target market. Integrated marketing communications are vital because success in today's global economy requires planned cooperation with interdependent partners who co-develop low-cost benefit bundles that can delight and excite customers by providing value-added product solutions. Doing all of the above, following a strong moral compass, and making socially responsible decisions that positively impact stakeholders at all levels are admirable goals.

New Products for a New Business

Lilly had been working in public relations for several years. She worked for a firm that specialized in the image building of new businesses. Her accounts were primarily hip restaurants with owners who wanted to attract the city's most chic and savvy clientele. Her job, in essence, was to position these new restaurants as stylish, "happening" places for after-work gatherings, business meetings, celebrations, and so on, while also promoting the featured cuisine and bringing in celebrities who were in town.

Naturally, this required many late nights, an expensive wardrobe, a lot of smiling, and more eating than anyone should have the opportunity to do.

Lilly enjoyed the prestige and excitement, but she had a secret desire to start her own business. She loved fashion, accessories, and all things sleek and modern. She had always dreamed of opening a boutique where she could be her own boss, interact meaningfully with customers, use her creativity and connections to build something for herself, and do something she loved—providing women with the means to look and feel great at reasonable prices.

But *liking* fashion and *knowing* enough about it to actually develop a business are two different things.

Lilly signed up for a two-year program in fashion merchandising at a local college, which she completed while maintaining her public relations activities. Yes, she was often exhausted but highly motivated. Her brothers, one an accountant and one an attorney, were not only impressed by how much money she'd managed to save during her years as a publicist, but at her determination as well, so they agreed to help her secure the money she would need to start and maintain her business until it took off. It looked like everything was falling into place for Lilly. She'd even chosen a location.

Could her dream actually be coming true?

QUESTIONS

1. Do you think Lilly is ready to open her boutique? Discuss the bundle of benefits that the customer expects. Identify the product essence, real product, and expanded benefit bundle.

2. What kinds of new product variations might she consider in order to differentiate her boutique from others?

3. Considering Lilly's experience and connections resulting from her years as a publicist, the financial support she has in place, and the current zeitgeist, do you think she would do best carrying shopping products, specialty products, or a combination of both? Why?

4. Looking at the rate of adoption process, address the five steps that a customer might experience as she becomes a repeat customer of Lilly's boutique.

KEY TERMS

business products
consumer products
discontinuous innovation
durable goods
expanded benefits
fashion products
innovation
new products
nondurable goods
outsource
product adoption
product essence
product life cycle
real product
strong moral compass

REVIEW QUESTIONS

1. Identify the three components of value that customers receive (described as the "bundle of benefits"), and use one product to provide an example of each of these components.
2. Explain the differences and similarities between business and consumer products. Illustrate with an example.
3. How do nondurable and durable goods differ, and why are these important issues for marketers?
4. Describe the new product development process for a fashion apparel item, and explain how it is different from the development process for a non-apparel item.

5. What are the stages of a fashion product life cycle and what types of consumers purchase a product at each stage?

DISCUSSION ACTIVITIES AND PROJECTS

1. Review Table 8.1, "The Benefit Package," then identify a product or service that you purchased during the last 12 months and explain how the three levels noted in Table 8.1 relate to your specific purchase.
2. Select two subgroups mentioned in the "New Product Variations" section of this chapter, then identify and discuss two products that clearly exemplify that subgroup designation.
3. Contact a local fashion designer and ask that person to briefly explain his or her fashion development process for a specific product. Review that information and compare it to the six steps noted in the chapter. What differences or similarities did you find?
4. Facilitate a 10-minute class discussion on how some new product development business decisions can be unethical but not illegal. Explain how the strong moral compass concept factors into this process.
5. Research an international company that collaborates with multinational units or outsources some of its production, operations, or administrative functions. Why do you think the company does this?

DEVELOPING YOUR MARKETING PLAN

Continuing with the product element of the marketing mix, the next step in your marketing plan is to examine the development of your company's product and its life cycle. Here are steps for you to take:

1. Detail your product's bundle of benefits; that is, identify its product essence, real product, and expanded benefits.
2. Identify what product category applies to your product, and explain why that is the appropriate one.
3. Into which of the six subgroups of new product variations does your product fall?
4. Where does your product fall within the product life cycle?

Refer to the Marketing Plan Outline in Table 1.2 provided at the end of Chapter 1, as well as Appendix A: Sample Marketing Plan.

REFERENCES

1. Neutrogena, "Skin Care Resources, 2011, http://csh.neutrogena.com/skin-cancer-resources (accessed August 27, 2010).
2. Abt Web site, "Move Over, Apple: The World's Largest Electronics Outlets," http://www.abt.com/about/news/prlog_080610.php3 (accessed August 6, 2010).
3. Apple, "Design. Apple TV, Streamlined," October 11, 2011.
4. Michael Solomon, Greg Marshall, and Elnora Stuart, *Marketing: Real People, Real Choices*, 6th ed. (New York: Pearson Education, 2009).
5. Paul Sonne, Marketplace Section, September 9, 2010, *Wall Street Journal*; RadioAustralia, http://www.radioaustralia.net.au/connectasia/stories/201009/s3016309.htm (accessed September 9, 2010).
6. Ann Manser, "Social Responsibility Comes into Fashion," *Messenger*, University of Delaware, vol.14, no. 4, 2006, http://www.udel.edu/PR/Messenger/05/04/Social.html (accessed October 11, 2011).
7. Steven D. Eppinger and Anil R. Chitkara, "The New Practice of Global Product Development, *MIT Sloane Management Review*, Summer 2006 http://www.moderntimesworkplace.com/good_reading/GRColInnov/Global_product_dev.pdf (accessed October 11, 2011).
8. Miguel Bustillo, Robb M. Stewart, and Paul Sonne, "Walmart Bids $4.6 Billion for South Africa's Massmart," *Wall Street Journal*, Marketplace section, Tuesday, September 29, 2010.

CHAPTER 9

Pricing: Identifying and Promoting Customer Value

This chapter defines price and describes its importance to fashion marketers. It then explores the factors that influence marketers' pricing decisions and strategies, and interprets how consumers evaluate price as part of their purchase decision.

WHAT DO I NEED TO KNOW ABOUT PRICING TO IDENTIFY AND PROMOTE CUSTOMER VALUE?

* The meaning of the term price and its importance to fashion marketers and consumers

* What is meant by pricing objectives and the difference between profit- and sales-oriented objectives

* How demand and supply influence price

* The effects of costs on price

* Pricing approaches and the steps in setting price

* Issues related to global pricing

Getting What You Pay For

Susan Tyler, a junior college business teacher in her mid-twenties, walked into her favorite downtown mall and immediately noticed a department store window display with three mannequins, each wearing an in-the-moment fashion dress. One was *moderate* in price, affordable with some basic features. Another was somewhat higher-priced, in what the industry calls the *better* range—still affordable but with more trendy features and detailing. The third was still higher in price, known as the *bridge* level—a range bridging the price levels between designer and better goods. It had even more features and styling that appealed to Susan.

Susan liked all three and hurried to the dress department hoping to find each in her size. Although it was the most expensive of the three and initially her favorite, the fit of the bridge-priced dress disappointed her when she tried it on. Behind glass and on the rack the dress seemed to glimmer like silk with eye-catching embellishments and a flattering neckline. And from the aisle, it certainly had hanger appeal. But once she put it on, the look just didn't work for her, even though the sales associate felt that with a nip here, a tuck there, and the right accessories, it could be perfect. The brand was very well known; however, after a closer look revealed some loose threads, a few skipped stitches, and a coarse fabric, the dress simply failed to live up to Susan's expectations, particularly considering the price tag.

The moderately priced item fit Susan much better, but in her mind, its more basic look lacked a certain appeal. Susan also didn't like how the pink print tones worked with her hair color; as she explained to the sales associate, she just didn't feel transformed. The associate listened attentively and agreed. The moderate-price dress just didn't have the *wow* factor that she was looking for.

But the better-price dress was everything she hoped for: the right size, the right color, the right style, the flattering fabric that fit and draped perfectly. The hangtag described in detail how carefully the dress was made and, last but far from least, named a price that justified what she felt she was getting. Sealing the deal, Susan handed the sales associate her credit card. She smiled as she navigated the revolving door onto the sidewalk, firm in her belief that her shopping bag held her fashion item of the season.

P rice is an especially important part of the marketing mix. It is the easiest component to change, perhaps the most difficult to understand, and it may carry the greatest responsibility for a company's profits. Pricing depends in large part on demand, that is, the amount of a product that consumers want, and supply, the amount of a product that is available. But it is also based on a marketer's costs, its competition, its marketing mix, and a whole range of external elements, including issues of ethics and social responsibility as well as factors in the global economy. Only after considering all these things can fashion marketers develop pricing policies and set prices that coordinate with and help them meet their overall marketing objectives.

What Is Price and Why Is It Important to Fashion?

Price, or the amount one pays in exchange for a product, is important to consumers because it represents what they must spend for the things they need, such as clothing, food, college tuition, bus fare, and in the case of Susan's quest in "Getting What You Pay For," the right image. Most of us have only limited funds to satisfy our various wants and whims,

FIGURE 9.1 Similar fashion looks are available to consumers at several different prices.

so seeking the prices that best meet our goals is a positive way of using the resources we have. Fashion marketers know that price is important because the very success of their business depends largely on their successful pricing decisions.

WHAT IS PRICE?

When something of value is exchanged for something else of value, the amount of money (or its equivalent) for which the item is bought or sold is its price. Currency, credit cards, and checks are common forms of exchange, used worldwide. When Susan used her credit card to purchase her dress, she did so knowing that the price was in alignment with the dress's value to her. Sometimes people use substitutes for money, such as trading products for products, known as **barter**. Bartering is the oldest form of exchange; for example, ancient Romans bartered by exchanging salt for goods and services. Salt was a precious seasoning and preservative in the days before refrigeration. Ancient Roman armies were known to be paid in salt, hence the word "salary." Bartering today, you may trade a friend a sweater for a CD. Each participant in a marketing exchange believes the trade is worthwhile; otherwise, it wouldn't take place. In reality, then, customers are actually purchasing the benefits of a product that amplify the product itself.

Consider buying a blazer: You look at the garment, noting its color, cut, and heft of the fabric. Trying it on and seeing your reflection in the mirror, you can tell that the jacket fits well and makes you look smartly dressed. Your subsequent blazer purchase is based on your satisfaction with your appearance in that product—above and beyond the

FIGURE 9.2 Each of these items is designated by its price.

product itself. In fact, the satisfaction customers gain from buying fashion goods in general, and luxury items in particular, comes from the positive emotions they experience from wearing or using the new product. This is the product essence described in Chapter 8.

WHY PRICE IS IMPORTANT TO FASHION MARKETERS

Fashion marketers pay great attention to setting prices, basing their price levels on the perceived value of the product to their target customers. For example, Ralph Lauren maintains an aura of uniqueness and prestige at a number of price levels, marketing each label according to its level of distinctiveness. The exclusive Purple Label tailored clothing is available in the company's eponymous shops, while the lower-priced Chaps brand is offered at Kohl's. Determining the right emotional appeal to customers shopping each price level has a direct effect on the pricing and the potential success of each particular line.

Price is the assessment of anything of value, whether tangible, such as clothing, or intangible, such as the influence of promotion. Price levels also integrate with the entire marketing mix: the nature and quality of a product, its distribution, and promotion. Compare custom-made shoes by designer Christian Louboutin to a mass-produced pair of Candies shoes sold at Payless. Assessing price also includes the intangible allure associated with a celebrity who walks the red carpet in either shoe. Targeted promotion can sway many potential customers to buy.

Price as Consumer-Perceived Value

In comparing price with value, many customers weigh their perception of every aspect of a good or service, including product quality, raw materials, craftsmanship, the marketer's image, brand name, customer service, and other aspects of both the product and the purchase situation. After totaling all the assessed values, customers will arrive at the price they are willing to pay. The equation for determining this is as follows:

$$\text{Customer perceived value} = \text{Product benefits} / \text{Price}[1]$$

Remember Susan was initially drawn into the department store by a window display. The look, not the price, of the dresses was the initial enticement for her to go in and examine them more closely. She shops this particular store on a fairly regular basis and has developed a perception of the store and its goods. Before reviewing each dress, Susan had created and prioritized a mental list of her essential dress requirements, including a flattering fit, embellishments adding interest to the dress, and an overall attractive image. She examined each dress according to her list and its price tag. Susan had to be convinced as to the value or worth of her selection before deciding on a purchase.

WHAT DO YOU THINK?

Think of an important item you purchased recently, perhaps a cell phone, computer, or item of clothing. What were three of the perceived benefits of the product that influenced your purchase decision?

FASHION MARKETING IN FOCUS:
COMPARISON OF PRICE LEVELS FOR WOMEN'S APPAREL

There are seven recognized price levels for women's apparel and accessories. In descending order, these are *couture*, *designer*, *bridge*, *contemporary*, *better*, *moderate*, and *budget*. Design houses and other manufacturers create merchandise lines within these price levels.

Designers at the highest end, couture, create garments of original design tailored for specific clients in their Paris workrooms. They must also hold two fashion showings a year. The price range for couture can be said to start at around $5,000 and up; $10,000 and more for evening wear; and $50,000 and higher for bridal gowns. (No wonder the number of couture clients worldwide amounts to only a few hundred!) Jean Paul Gaultier designs couture, but because couture by itself is not profitable, he and other couturiers and couture houses also design ready-to-wear (prêt-à-porter), machine-made garments at the designer price level. Some well-known designers and design organizations such as Marc Jacobs for Louis Vuitton, Sonia Rykiel, and Karl Lagerfeld do ready-to-wear in the price range labeled "designer." While designer prices are still expensive (up to several thousand dollars), the looks are made to appeal to a larger target market, one that finds these prices affordable. Recently, to become better known in global markets, designers have created goods for budget markets. Rei Kawakubo started a trend by designing a short-run line for the fast-fashion Swedish budget retailer Hennes & Mauritz (H&M) in 2008. Soon other designers, among them Karl Lagerfeld and Jimmy Choo, followed suit. German designer Jil Sander tied in with the Japanese fast-fashion retailer Uniqlo to create a brand uniquely for that organization.

Retail stores organize their departments according to various price levels. Designer departments, such as Macy's 28 Shop in Chicago, offer ready-to-wear merchandise from the world's top designers including Giorgio Armani, Missoni, Michael Kors, and others. Many of these designers and brands realize they can reach more customers by offering additional merchandise lines at a slightly lower price, or "bridge" level. Originally, the term "bridge" came into use when fewer price levels existed; it was meant to "bridge the price gap" between the designer and "better" levels, at that time the next level down. For example, Donna Karan's designer price level is titled "Collection" (a term adopted by the industry to indicate a designer's most exclusive prices and looks), and the bridge price level brand is DKNY. Although still expensive, bridge merchandise is not as costly as designer goods. Some designers, such as Eileen Fisher, offer goods exclusively in the bridge price range. Banana Republic is another bridge-level brand.

In an effort to capture a younger market, fashion companies created a look and accompanying price range slightly lower than bridge and labeled it "contemporary." One of the best-known contemporary brands is Juicy Couture. Department and specialty stores feature these lines in contemporary departments. The next two price levels are found everywhere and do a large volume of business. These are the "better" level, with brands such as Jones New York, Abercrombie & Fitch, Gap, Ellen Tracy, Anthropologie, and others; and moderate price levels, including brands such as Alfred Dunner, American Eagle Outfitters, Buckle, and more. Budget levels include the Old Navy, Cherokee, and Merona brands, and fast-fashion apparel from Forever 21, Zara, H&M, and Uniqlo.

The Relationship of Price to Profit

Pricing is vital to all marketers for another essential reason: Price is the easiest element of the marketing mix to change but also the most potentially dangerous to adjust because it directly affects a company's **profits**. The money a company brings in—its revenue—comes from the prices it charges. The profit (or loss) a business incurs is calculated by subtracting the costs of running the business (buying raw materials, transporting goods, paying employees, paying taxes, and so on) from the total revenue. Revenue minus costs equals the company's profit. Note the following equations:

$$Total\ revenue = Price \times Quantity\ sold$$

$$Total\ profit = Total\ revenue - Total\ costs$$

$$Profit = (Price \times Quantity\ sold) - Total\ costs$$

COMPETE ON PRICE OR SOME OTHER WAY?

Sometimes marketers and consumers have a hard time distinguishing the benefits of one product over another. In that case, price may be the best way for marketers to gain sales. Macy's may offer diamond earrings or pendants at one price, Kohl's or JCPenney at a lower price, and a seller on eBay at still another level. Although there may be slight differences in quality, consumers have the option of selecting the lowest-priced item. Price competition occurs frequently with commodities like soft drinks

FIGURE 9.3 Fashion marketers—brick-and-mortar retailers and online e-tailers—often compete on price for similar goods.

FIGURE 9.4 Fashion marketers often appeal to emotions by emphasizing elements other than price. Here, appealing to customer-perceived value is the goal.

and snacks but also with fashion goods, particularly at the end of a season. We'll look at various price policies later in the chapter.

When using non-price competition, fashion marketers focus on the other elements of the marketing mix: product, place, or promotion. For example, Todd Howard of Not Your Daughter's Jeans varies the product, adding chinos to the company's selection of jeans of various lengths. Caren Lettiere of Jolt jeans describes another product variation: luxurious fabric labeled Yummy Gummy. The Kardashian sisters, expanding their company's marketing channels, create a private label for Sears. Enhancing its promotion strategy, Ann (formerly Taylor), signs Katie Holmes to appear in an advertising campaign. If fashion marketers can touch the right emotional chords by emphasizing other aspects of the marketing mix, they do not need to depend as heavily on price promotions. Luxury fashion marketers such as Louis Vuitton and Hermès, due to the emotional appeal and distinctiveness of their products, rarely use price promotions. In fact, France limits the times when fashion retailers may offer their goods at sale prices to three-week periods twice a year, in January and July.

Pricing Objectives

Companies [need to] establish their pricing objectives as components of their marketing goals. These objectives need to be realistic, able to be reached, and measurable. Three categories of pricing goals or objectives are *profit-oriented, sales-oriented*, and *status quo.*

PROFIT-ORIENTED PRICING OBJECTIVES

Within the category of profit-oriented objectives there are three types: *profit maximization, target return on investment (ROI)*, and *satisfactory profits.*

Profit Maximization

The goal of profit maximization is to obtain as much revenue as possible. It does not necessarily mean establishing high prices, but rather setting prices at levels where consumers perceive value and make purchases. A company's everyday low price (EDLP) policy emphasizes its interest in appealing to consumers' perceived value. Walmart may be said to operate using profit maximization. Its goal is to increase revenue through low prices and at the same time reduce costs from suppliers.

TABLE 9.1 Pricing Objectives

Pricing Category	Objective
Profit oriented	■ Profit maximization
	■ Target return on investment (ROI)
	■ Satisfactory profit
Sales oriented	■ Market share/sales volume
	■ Sales maximization
Status quo pricing	■ Maintaining prices
	■ Meeting the competition's prices

Target Return on Investment (ROI)

Target return on investment (ROI) is a popular form of pricing objective. Its goal is to determine how well management is using company assets in creating a profit. A high return on investment or assets indicates a profitable company. The equation for return on investment is as follows:

$$ROI = \text{Net profits after taxes} / \text{Total assets}$$

A company sets a target return and then determines how well it has met that goal. Depending on the industry, satisfactory ROIs can range from 5 percent upward. Suppose a company developing apps for smartphones is considering putting several new apps on the market. In planning its offering, the company may decide to determine how much it needs to invest in each app in order to obtain a certain profit. In this case, it would be using the target ROI as a pricing objective.

Satisfactory Profit Objectives

Satisfactory profit objectives are to maintain an adequate level of profit. The meaning of the term "adequate" depends on management's goals and its willingness to take risk. If the industry risk were high, management might call for higher adequate profits, possibly 30 percent. If industry risk were low and profits more or less stable, lower profits would be expected, say 5 to 7 percent. Suppose a fashion designer decided to introduce a radical new look in apparel representing an authentic departure from current fashions. She might decide that to overcome the risk of the look not being accepted, a satisfactory profit objective for this look might be lower than normal. The hoped-for outcome would be adequate for the company to realize a profit.

SALES-ORIENTED PRICING OBJECTIVES

Two types of sales-oriented pricing objectives focus on either an increase in market share or sales volume, or on sales maximization.

Market Share/Sales Volume

The percentage of a total industry market that a particular company holds is called its market share. For example, within the entire athletic shoe industry, Nike is estimated to have a 19 percent market share. Other brands such as adidas, Pumas, Reebok, and unbranded athletic shoes make up the total market. For a long time, conventional wisdom held that an increase in a company's market share would mean an increase in profits. Unfortunately,

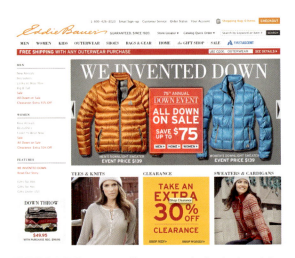

FIGURE 9.5 Temporary discounts at the beginning of the season can help marketers determine which items will be popular, perhaps in time to reorder.

that is not always the case. Other elements of the marketing mix can also have an effect. Product and distribution costs may rise, and promotion strategy may not be effectively communicating product benefits to current and potential target customers.

Sales Maximization

Sales maximization pricing objectives are to increase sales as much as possible. The economic climate, competitors' actions, and even profits are all secondary if sales are going up. To achieve a sales maximization objective, it is often necessary to lower prices. For this reason, sales maximization is a short-term objective. It is frequently used in the fashion field to get rid of end-of-season stock, thus providing funds for new merchandise. Also, it may be used at the beginning of a season to gain an edge on the competition and determine which styles should be reordered. Eddie Bauer, Belks, and Nordstrom are among the fashion marketers employing this objective on a temporary basis.

STATUS QUO PRICING

Maintaining prices or meeting the competition's prices is the objective of status quo pricing. It is a reactive pricing policy, requiring little planning, and is used in situations that necessitate following the price leader. A fashion retailer noting that the store down the street has lowered prices on certain competitive items will meet those prices in order to continue drawing customers.

WHAT DO YOU THINK?

You are opening your own fashion design and marketing business. What two pricing objectives seem the most relevant to you and why?

How Demand and Supply Determine Price

In order to fulfill their pricing objectives and reach their profit goals, fashion marketers establish specific prices that conform to their objectives. Two elements are essential parts of the actual pricing decisions: product **demand** (the quantity customers want at a certain price) and the costs of putting an item on the market. Other considerations also enter into play, such as the state of the economy, the effect of technology, and other elements of the marketing mix. These topics are covered later in this chapter.

WHAT IS DEMAND?

Marketing managers are responsible for determining the extent of consumer demand. Gauging demand is not an easy job, particularly when dealing with fashion goods. For example, the style of a dress or coat may be ahead of its time and, while industry decision makers may believe it will sell, the fashion consumer simply might not be ready yet for that look.

The Demand Curve

To make their predictions more accurate, marketers employ some fundamental concepts about demand. One of these is the **demand curve**, a

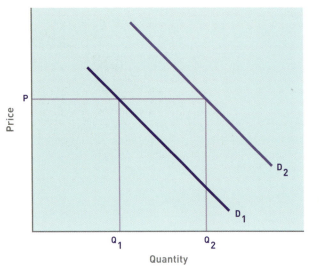

Source: William M. Pride and O.C. Ferrell, *Marketing*, 14th Edition (Boston: Houghton Mifflin, 2008), p. 580, figure 21.1.

FIGURE 9.6 This demand curve illustrates the relationship between price and quantity demanded. In D1, quantity increases as the price decreases, assuming other factors remain constant. If improvements are made in product, promotion, or distribution, a higher quantity may be sold at all prices, as shown in D2. BY VANESSA HAN AND ALICIA FREILE

graph showing the relationship between demand and price. The demand curve in Figure 9.6 indicates the quantities estimated to sell at different price levels. Demand also depends on other elements of the marketing mix. If improvements occur in the product, distribution, or promotion, a company may sell a larger quantity at the same price. For instance, home textile companies that introduced new cotton knit versions of their sheets saw demand increase based on the sheets' softness (the feel of a comfortable T-shirt) and a plug on television by Oprah Winfrey, which also led to more retail outlets carrying the sheets. However, if product, distribution,

and promotion remain the same, a company may also increase the quantity sold by lowering the price. The demand curve indicates the amount of product that is expected to sell at various prices, with price shown on the vertical axis of the graph and quantity on the horizontal axis.

Note the demand curve indicates how lowering prices increases the quantity sold; if prices go down, all else being equal, sales increase. When fashion marketers have had goods on hand for a while,

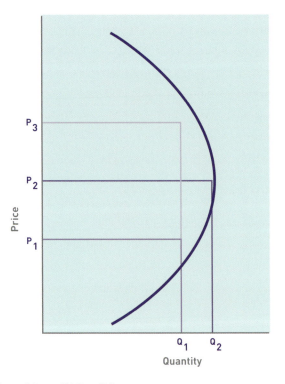

Source: Ibid. page 581, figure 21.2

FIGURE 9.7 For prestige products, the demand curve shows quantity increasing along with price, up to a certain level (P2). If prices go beyond that point, quantity decreases again as consumers judge that the value does not warrant a higher price. BY VANESSA HAN AND ALICIA FREILE

whether it is capri pants or patio furniture, toward the end of the season they will lower the price to close out inventories in order to buy goods for the next season. A new and larger group of consumers unwilling to pay the original price now find the goods an appealing value, causing an increase in sales.[2]

Luxury fashion brands such as Rolex and Cartier have a different demand curve. They tend to be more popular at higher prices, due to their distinctiveness and prestige. Many customers believe that an exclusive brand contains a unique aura that is substantiated by the price. Note Figure 9.7, which shows the relationship between price and quantity for luxury goods. A larger quantity of a given prestige item will sell at a higher price and a smaller quantity when the price is lower, due in part to the customer's view that if the product costs less, its prestige diminishes, lowering its value.[3]

WHAT DO YOU THINK?

How do you account for the difference between the first demand curve and the demand curve for prestige items?

Elasticity of Demand

Marketing fashion goods is subject to **elasticity of demand**, that is, a measure of consumer sensitivity to the change of prices. A demand curve can be either elastic or inelastic. Products that tend to be discretionary purchases—including many fashion items from apparel to electronics, sports cars, and swimming pools—face an *elastic demand*, in which sales volume follows price changes. In a situation of elastic demand, sales tend to decrease when prices

FIGURE 9.8 While the automotive industry faces a fairly inelastic demand for utility vehicles, mid-price sports cars face an elastic demand.

go up and increase when they go down. Products facing an *inelastic demand* are those for which customers need a set amount and that they will buy despite price changes. Gasoline and heating oil are some of the products that face a fairly inelastic demand. No matter how high the price, consumers still need a certain amount of gas for their automobiles and heat for their homes.

SUPPLY AND ITS EFFECT ON FASHION PRICING

On occasion, demand for a fashion product may simply sweep the market and far exceed the **supply**, or quantity of a product available for sale. Sometimes the short supply occurs because the manufacturer produces only a limited amount. This happens habitually with some luxury items such as designer apparel. In this case, a short supply may actually enhance the designer's image by emphasizing the rareness and exclusivity associated with prestige products. Typically, when the supply of a particular fashion product is low, the price will be high. When the supply of goods rises or demand at the original price has diminished, the price comes down and sales increase due to the appeal of the new price. Fashion marketers' closeouts and end-of-season sales illustrate this concept of supply. In addition, when supply costs go up, they can have an effect on the sales of related products. For example, as the price of jet fuel rises, airlines need to raise the ticket price for passengers, as well as the price for shipments of designer collections, fresh flowers, and other products being transported.

Cost-Based Pricing

Setting prices based on the economic theory of demand carries some risk, not the least of which is estimating the size of consumer demand. If consumers do not want a product, no matter what the price, they will not buy it. Therefore, in addition to determining the level of consumer demand, fashion marketers also need to ascertain the costs of developing and marketing a product. Costs are an essential factor both in setting prices and in calculating potential sales and profits, since in order to survive, a marketing organization cannot effectively price its products below their cost.

There are two types of costs that marketers must determine: fixed and variable. **Fixed costs** are those that do not change with the quantity of goods sold, such as rent, insurance, and executive salaries. **Variable costs** are those that do change with the amount of goods sold, such as raw materials, workers' wages, and transportation costs. They are called variable because they must rise as production increases. For example, if a T-shirt manufacturer receives additional purchase orders, it must order more fabric and pay workers for producing the additional garments. In adding its variable costs together with fixed costs, a company can calculate the sum of its cost outlays. The resulting **total costs** combine total fixed and total variable costs.

A company's ability to keep both fixed and variable costs down can contribute substantially to its revenues and profits. Improved technology, ranging from more sophisticated design and production methods to enhanced distribution systems, helps to reduce both fixed and variable costs. In addition, in the late twentieth century, apparel industry manufacturers began to shift production of fashion goods from the United States to factories overseas, in Europe, the Middle East, Central and South America, and particularly in Asia. In these countries, workers' wages were a fraction of those stateside, and the production and transportation costs back to the States were still less than having these same items produced at home. Although domestic apparel organizations decimated U.S. textile and apparel manufacturing jobs, at the same time, consumers received the benefits through stable or lower pricing on goods.

There are three types of cost-based pricing that are useful to fashion marketers: break-even pricing, cost-plus pricing, and standard markup pricing.

BREAK-EVEN PRICING

To earn a profit, a company must bring in revenue to more than cover its costs. To accomplish this goal, some marketing organizations use **break-even**

FIGURE 9.9 Only a limited number of customers have access to couture designs; the short supply enhances the designer's exclusive image and justifies the price.

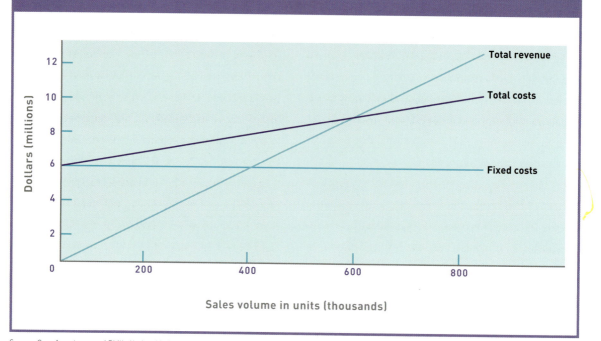

BREAK-EVEN CHART

Total revenue

Total costs

Fixed costs

Dollars (millions)

Sales volume in units (thousands)

Source: Gary Armstrong and Philip Kotler, *Marketing: An Introduction, 10/E* (Boston: Prentice-Hall, 2011), p. 279, figure 1.3.

FIGURE 9.10 To learn at what point it may begin to create a profit, a company creates a break-even chart. About how many units must be sold in this example for the company to break even? BY VANESSA HAN AND ALICIA FREILE

analysis, using an equation to determine the point at which the costs of manufacturing a product equal the revenue from marketing it, or a break-even point. Essentially, a break-even point is calculated by dividing the fixed costs by the price minus the variable costs. If a company manufactured dinette sets at a total cost of $300,000 and sold those sets for a total of $300,000, the company would break even.

The equation is as follows:

Break-even point = Fixed costs / (Price – Variable costs)

In order to determine a break-even point, a company needs to figure out how many items it is going to make. Suppose you manufactured 2,000 raincoats priced at $100, and your fixed costs were $42 per garment while your variable costs were $58 each.

$$42 \times 2000 = 84,000$$

$$(\$100 - \$58) = \$42$$

$$\$84,000/42 = 2,000$$

You would break even at marketing 2,000 units. Marketers determine break-even points at several prices in an effort to ascertain which price will be most advantageous. Break-even analysis is most reliable when the demand for goods is relatively inelastic, since estimating the break-even point is based on deciding on the number of units that can be sold.

COST-PLUS PRICING

Cost-plus pricing adds a certain dollar amount or percentage to the cost of an item. It is used by intermediaries such as wholesalers, and discounters such as Costco and BJ's, among other retailers. Service organizations and marketers with customized products such as wedding gowns favor cost-plus pricing to cover their costs, overhead, and profits. A wholesaler specializing in neckwear and gloves may add a certain amount to the goods it receives from a producer before shipping them on to a retailer. This amount covers the costs of collecting assortments from various suppliers and marketing them to retailers, plus profits.

MARKUP PRICING

A cost-based pricing strategy that adds a certain percentage to a product is **markup pricing**. Fashion retailers typically use markup pricing based on the wholesale price. The **markup**, or amount added to the cost price, varies according to the goods. It can be either a dollar amount or a percentage amount and may be based on the wholesale or retail price of a product. Fresh produce—perishable, just like fashion goods—may be marked up 100 percent on the cost price and even higher. Typically, apparel and accessories may have a markup of 30 to 55 percent based on the retail price, and a lower markup on discount items, say 20 percent or so, based on the retail price. A higher anticipated sales volume permits the lower markup. The markups on higher-priced items, also based on the retail price, are often close to 50 percent and even more for luxury goods. In addition, certain items that are sold to complement a high-priced item—such as carrying cases for tablet computers or mounts for flat-panel TVs—tend to have a high markup because their base price is relatively low and their value to consumers is high. Following are some examples of markup based on cost and then on retail price.

Markup Based on Cost Price. Suppose a gourmet food store that also carries non-food items such as T-shirts, slippers, and sunglasses also stocks scarves. It purchases a group of trendy scarves and pays $8.75 each, deciding to mark them up on cost to sell for $15.00. Subtracting the cost price of $8.75 from the selling price $15.00 results in a markup of $6.25. Dividing the markup by the cost yields a markup of 71 percent:

$$\text{Markup as a \% of cost} = \text{Markup} / \text{Cost}$$
$$= \$6.25/\$8.75$$
$$= 71\% \text{ markup}$$

Markup Based on Retail Price. Say a specialty store buys a scarf costing $12.75 and prices it at $25. Subtracting the $12.75 cost price from the intended $25.00 retail price gives a markup of $12.25. Dividing the markup by the retail price results in a 49 percent markup:

Markup as a % of retail price = Markup / Retail price

= 12.25 / $25

= 49% markup

Markups vary for individual items and may change during a season. Ways of determining profitable markup percentages and when to change markups are covered in buying courses.

As you can tell, the cost of getting shirts, pants, and other fashion apparel from the designer's sketch pad to the selling floor varies with the manufacturer, wholesaler, and retailer. Each has incurred costs in producing and marketing the goods or service. The markup covers all associated costs and the profit that each level of distribution needs to achieve. However, because the retailer provides more services and individual attention when addressing consumer needs and wants, its markup requirements are generally greater than those of the manufacturer and wholesaler. Standard markup pricing does not consider market conditions, competition, or other factors that might impact the pricing decision.

WHAT DO YOU THINK?

You own a fashionable clothing store and decide to use markup pricing. Would you base your markup on the cost price of goods or on the retail price? Why?

Competition-Based Pricing

Sometimes the prices set by competitors play a more important role than costs when a fashion organization is planning prices. This is particularly true when products are fairly similar. In determining prices for electronics such as smartphones and e-readers as well as for much clothing, marketers pay close attention to competitors' prices. For its Jaclyn Smith line, for example, Kmart notes the prices of similar goods offered by Sears, Target, fast-fashion marketers such as Forever 21, and others, and determines its pricing accordingly. With consumers initiating purchases through online searching and shopping, fashion marketers offering fairly similar goods know that many customers are on the lookout for attractive prices and are quite aware of the prices the competitors are charging. The fashion marketer's challenge is to offer a perceived value gauged to overcome competitors' efforts.

Other Factors Determining Price

A number of additional factors enter into fashion marketers' pricing decisions. Some of these include aspects of the marketing mix such as the stage in the product life cycle, and distribution and promotion strategies. External factors also can play a part in a company's pricing strategy; among these are the competition, economic conditions, the impact of technology, the political-legal environment, and societal changes.

FIGURE 9.11 Consumer goods such as LCD and plasma TVs are marketed at competitive prices.

EFFECT OF THE MARKETING MIX ON PRICING

The other elements of a company's marketing mix have an effect on price. These include the nature of the product and the stage of a product in its life cycle, the company's distribution strategy, and its promotion strategy.

Nature of the Product

As you recall, products are classified as convenience or shopping goods, specialty items, and unsought goods. Most fashion goods fall into the category of shopping goods or specialty items. Shopping goods such as sportswear and accessories, some home furnishings, and certain automobiles may be somewhat costly, but consumers tend to purchase them fairly often. They compare shopping goods for style, quality, and workmanship. When marketers find that competing based on these factors is not

possible, and when the end of a fashion season is approaching and they want to make room for new stock, they will lower the price in order to gain sales.

Specialty items are just that: unique, distinctive, and available at destination locations. Fine jewelry, designer apparel, or a vacation at a five-star resort are all specialty items, each bearing a hefty price. For specialty items the high price is an asset, making the item something to be sought after, adding to its prestige and exclusiveness. Although specialty items do go on sale, lower prices are infrequent and short-term. A thriving Internet market on Web sites such as eBay or www.bags.com provides consumers with a means of obtaining specialty items second-hand or by renting them. The consumer is content with the price, and the fashion marketer retains its prestige.

Stage in the Product Life Cycle

As you recall from Chapter 8, products, just like humans, have a certain life span. A product's life span can be long, like Ivory soap (over a hundred years), or short, like cutoff T-shirts (just a season or two). The life span of a product is expressed as its life cycle, consisting of four stages: introduction, growth, maturity, and decline. Introducing a product and bringing it to market can be an extensive and costly process. Think of the iPad and the research and development it took to create the tablet itself, plus the imagination to develop its various apps and capabilities. It takes time and money to create a fashion item. Management must plan ways to meet consumer demand long before promoting a new offering. Because of the cost involved in bringing new concepts to market, businesses want to recoup their investments quickly.

For that reason, many times they put a high price on new products. Think of the electronic reader. When Amazon first introduced the Kindle e-reader, it was priced at around $400, a level indicated in part because the product was unique at the time and the high price added prestige. Some of this price could also be attributed to the expense of the research and development necessary in creating a brand-new product.

A product itself may fizzle out and die anywhere along its life cycle, but let's say that sales increase, as they did for the Kindle. Prices remain constant, and profits begin to show. When sales increase even more, the product is now mature, but profits are not as high because competitors have seen the product's success and have entered the market with their own versions, such as Barnes & Noble's Nook. The original company knows now it must spend more money on

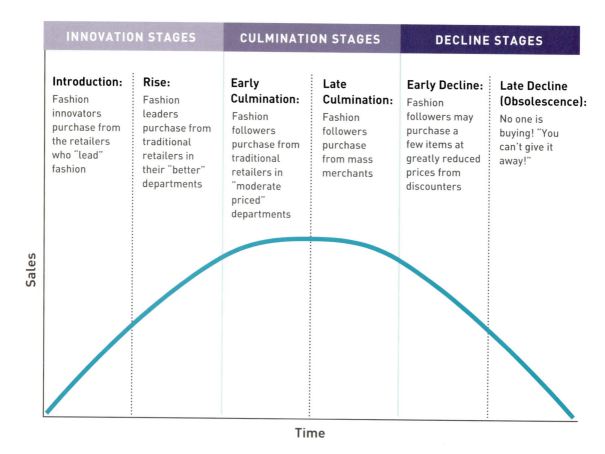

FIGURE 9.12 The stage in the life cycle of a fashion product life has an effect on its pricing.
BY VANESSA HAN AND ALICIA FREILE

promotion to distinguish its product from the rest. The result is that although sales increase in maturity, profits decrease because of the necessary promotional spending. When sales begin to decline, the company starts offering the product through fewer channels, and also lowers the price. Notice how the price of the Kindle reader came down when competitors entered the market and at lower prices, and also when Amazon itself introduced newer, improved versions of the Kindle. Eventually, marketers may close out the item as sales recede below a viable level and the product becomes obsolete. Perhaps another innovation replaces it and the cycle starts anew.

Distribution and Pricing

A fashion marketer may choose to offer goods through one channel, perhaps a retail store or a Web site; through selected intermediaries, representatives, and specialty retailers; or through intense distribution including mass marketers such as grocery, discount, and drug stores. Each of these channels has certain costs and consequent price levels. A Mercedes dealer maintains an attractive and well-designed showroom with a knowledgeable sales staff; a department store offers a wide assortment of goods with a choice of mid-range to designer prices; a drug store provides an assortment of brands at moderate prices. The costs of running these businesses must be covered in the prices set. The exclusive automobile dealer needs to add a high initial markup to cover its sales; the department store, because it is geared to sell greater quantities at various prices, can also vary its markup on the items it carries to cover its costs. The discount store, because it sells large quantities of goods, can afford a lower markup. The higher sales volume justifies its lower prices.

Intermediaries in the marketing channels can gain price concessions from producers through the discounts they obtain for marketing services rendered. Four types of discounts are found in the fashion field: trade, quantity, cash, and seasonal discounts. A **trade discount** is a reduction in the cost price a producer gives to a retailer for reselling its goods. The price on a purchase order of coats a retailer pays the manufacturer is 60 percent of the price the customer sees on the price tag. **Quantity discounts** are reductions from the price that retailers may receive for purchasing in large amounts. **Cash discounts** are price reductions given if retailers pay for their purchases within a specified time. A typical cash discount could amount to 2 percent of a purchase order when paid within 10 days. A **seasonal discount** is a price reduction for buying goods out of season and performing a marketing function such as storing them until the appropriate time. For example, a retail buyer purchases some children's flannel pajamas in April and receives a seasonal discount for holding them until the fall when they could be appropriately put on the shelves for sale.

Some of the discounts granted to intermediaries, such as trade and cash discounts, do not necessarily have an effect on the prices charged to the ultimate consumer. Others, such as the quantity and seasonal discounts, may be passed along in the form of a reduction in the retail prices of certain items.

Promotion and Pricing

A company's promotional activities—including *advertising, personal selling, sales promotion*, and *public relations*—are also factors that affect pricing. Advertising campaigns for fashion goods can be

TABLE 9.2 Discounts Used for Business Markets

Type of Discount	Reasons for Use	Examples
Trade (functional)	To attract and keep effective resellers by compensating them for performing certain functions, such as transportation, warehousing, selling, and providing credit.	A college bookstore pays about one-third less for a new textbook than the retail price a student pays.
Quantity	To encourage customers to buy large quantities when making purchases and, in the case of cumulative discounts, to encourage customer loyalty.	Large department store chains purchase some women's apparel at lower prices than do individually owned specialty stores.
Cash	To reduce expenses associated with accounts receivable and collection by encouraging prompt payment of accounts.	Numerous companies serving business markets allow a 2 percent discount if an account is paid within 10 days.
Seasonal	To allow a marketer to use resources more efficiently by stimulating sales during off-peak periods.	Florida hotels provide companies holding national and regional sales meetings with deeply discounted accommodations during the summer months.
Allowance	In the case of a trade-in allowance, to assist the buyer in making the purchase and potentially earn a profit on the resale of used equipment; in the case of a promotional allowance, to ensure that dealers participate in advertising and sales support programs.	A farm equipment dealer takes a farmer's used tractor as a trade-in on a new one; Nabisco pays a promotional allowance to a supermarket for setting up and maintaining a large, end-of-aisle display for a two-week period.

Source: William M. Pride and O.C. Ferrell, *Marketing*, 14th Edition (Boston: Houghton Mifflin, 2008).

expensive and long running, particularly when ads appear in print media and on television. Signing a celebrity to represent a product is a popular device and can be a long-term and expensive commitment. Michael Jordan for Nike, Julia Roberts for Lancôme, and Audrey Tautou for Chanel are some of the celebrity endorsements that fashion marketers have conducted over several years. These promotions can be costly but obviously contribute to a product's long-term success and are justified in its pricing.

The most expensive part of a promotion strategy is the cost of personal selling. Trained professional sales personnel are essential to marketing top-of-the-line products such as fine jewelry, designer apparel, and interior design services. These people are tuned into consumer needs and quickly learn customers' expectations and values. They are able to explain product benefits to match consumers' expectations. Marketers recognize and amply reward highly skilled professional sales personnel. Their work is the key to marketing luxury goods, in particular.

Sales promotions also incur some costs. Coupons (such as $2 dollars off for a new skin moisturizer) and rebates ($5 check mailed to a consumer from Mr. Coffee after receiving the sales receipt for the appliance) are popular tools marketers use to encourage sales. Others include events such as fashion shows and a cosmetics company's gift-with-purchase (Clinique's free cosmetics bag with samples when the customer buys a product). These promotions' costs are covered in the retail prices of the company's various products. Public relations

FIGURE 9.13 Professional salespeople are skilled at explaining fashion product benefits in terms of customers' perception of value.

activities, such as Microsoft sponsoring a concert or Nordstrom an art exhibit, are expensive and are undertaken to influence the target market and the general public. Publicity, too, engenders some costs: News features, such as the announcement of a vice president's promotion, must be generated by the company before they appear in the media. The costs of all promotion activities are included when a company sets its pricing. (For more on promotion and its elements, see Chapters 12 to 14.)

EFFECT OF EXTERNAL FACTORS ON PRICING

Although fashion marketers can exercise extensive control over the marketing mix, they can exercise relatively little control over their external environment; these include competition, the economy, technology, the political/legal environment, and social changes.

Competition

Much of fashion marketing occurs in a *monopolistic competitive environment*. In economists' terms, this means that the market contains many buyers—we all buy fashion goods—and many suppliers (consider the number of fashion organizations you can name). Succeeding in this kind of competitive environment is not easy, but it can be done. One way is to compete through lower pricing, which can be dangerous when considering a possibility of lower profits. A more effective way that fashion marketers employ is to offer products that stand out distinctly from the competition. Consider the preppy look of Tommy Hilfiger, the urban chic of Sean John, or the uniqueness of Chanel. Each company enhances its image by

FIGURE 9.14 Fashion brands and private labels offer exclusivity, countering the appeals of competitors. Madonna's Material Girl apparel collection is sold only at Macy's.

offering products the others cannot duplicate. This effort can occur at all price ranges, as when Target teams up with Philippe Stark to offer the designer's home furnishings in its stores or H&M contracts with Dolce & Gabbana to create a line designed solely for the retailer's fast-fashion market. In addition to featuring brand names, retailers' private labels are another way of dealing with the competition. Only at J.Crew can consumers buy that brand; Brass Plum is available only at Nordstrom; Inc. is exclusively Macy's. Unique offerings are a major way fashion marketers have found to stand out from competitors. (For more on product branding, see Chapter 7.)

Economic Conditions

When the economy is booming and consumers have substantial funds for discretionary spending, they have the means to satisfy many of their desires for fashion goods and services. The top tier of wealthy people worldwide are able to spend virtually without limit and provide a rich market for luxury goods. Unfortunately, however, half of the world's population lives on less than $2 a day, and discretionary spending is a luxury that many cannot enjoy even in the best economic conditions. As the nations of Asia, the Middle East, Africa, and South and Central America continue to industrialize, increasing job opportunities and the size of the middle class, individual discretionary income should also grow.

Meanwhile, the past few years have seen most of the world experiencing an economic recession and long recovery. Consumers are not able to buy as much, resulting in lower sales volume for businesses and contributing to unemployment in many industries. In hard times, fashion marketers endeavor to design and offer utilitarian products at more desirable prices, replacements for worn-out clothing, or an item a customer might not have, such as a jacket or scarf in an interesting color or pattern to brighten and extend a wardrobe. Marketers tend to offer price promotions sooner and more often, such as a sale in resort wear (for those who still can afford it) early in the season, mid-season reductions on winter coats at all price levels, and a holiday sale on automobiles.

Technology

Technology can affect pricing in a number of ways: Improvements in design and production technology through the use of computer-aided design and manufacturing (CAD/CAM) help speed up production, lowering costs through added efficiency. (See Chapter 2.) In moving goods to market, radio frequency identification (RFID) makes transportation safer and, by reducing the possibility of damage, less costly. These figures can lead to substantially lower prices. The growth of the Internet and social or mobile marketing techniques such as Twitter and Foursquare are perhaps the most dramatic examples of the effects of technology in revolutionizing consumer buying processes. Instead of first planning visits to brick-and-mortar retailers to learn about new products, customers are researching purchases electronically. Their first visits are often to the Web sites of various fashion organizations; here they obtain information on product features, suitability, and the best prices. Shopping Web sites such as eBay and overstock.com, apps on smartphones, and customized e-mail messages offer product information and price incentives (coupons) that help consumers reach informed buying decisions even before they enter a retail store.

Political-Legal Environment

Within the political and legal environment, four major issues have an effect on pricing strategies. These are price fixing, price discrimination, deceptive pricing, and predatory pricing.[4]

Price fixing occurs when businesses get together to set similar prices. *Horizontal price fixing* takes place when two businesses at the same level of distribution, such as retailers, agree to price certain goods at a predetermined level. An example of horizontal price fixing would be if the managers of three competing spas agreed to set the same price for facials, manicures, and pedicures. *Vertical price fixing* takes place when manufacturers require retailers not to sell below a minimum price. This is known as resale price maintenance and is outlawed by the **Consumer Goods Pricing Act**.

Price discrimination happens when different buyers are charged different prices for similar goods, provided the price difference lessens competition. If, as a hat buyer for a retail store, you purchased some caps and matching scarves from a vendor and later learned that another buyer bought the same goods at a lower price, you would be experiencing price discrimination. Several laws, including the **Robinson-Patman** and the Clayton Acts, outlaw this practice.

Deceptive pricing is charging unfair prices to the consumer. An example of deceptive pricing is *bait-and-switch pricing*. If a furniture store customer asks to see an armoire that was advertised at $100 and is told that the armoire is sold out but another, nicer one is available at $475, this is bait-and-switch pricing. The Federal Trade Commission prohibits deceptive pricing.

Predatory pricing is the practice of pricing products so low that it forces competitors out of business. When competitors are no longer in business, the company replaces predatory prices with higher ones. As an example, suppose a regional pie company sold its pies at prices so far below those of a local competitor that the local company could not survive and make a profit; when the local store goes out of business, the regional company raises its prices. This action is clear predatory pricing, and it is illegal under the **Sherman Antitrust Act** and the **Federal Trade Commission Act**.

Social Changes

People tire of the same routines, schedules, and customs and like to experience change. Designers and fashion marketers strive to anticipate societal changes and to prepare for them. In fashion, for example, color experts study the evolution of color palettes five years or so ahead so they can be ready with new color looks for the textile industry to dye and print apparel and upholstery fabrics well in advance of the changes in market demand.

A recent social change is the growing interest in health and physical fitness, starting with children. School administrators and parents are seeing to it that school lunches are more nutritious and contain healthy amounts of fruits and vegetables. (Ketchup is no longer termed a vegetable in school cafeterias!) The movement toward all people being able to obtain healthy diets at reasonable prices continues with discount and drug stores such as Target, CVS, and Walgreens offering food items including produce. The fact that First Lady Michelle Obama made sound eating practices a campaign added strength to the program when she worked with Walmart to obtain its participation. The discount retailer promised to provide fresh fruits and vegetables at prices comparable to those of snack foods in order to promote healthy diets. To do this, Walmart needed to engage the support of its suppliers as well as carefully assess its added markup.[5]

WHAT DO YOU THINK?

You want to put on the market a new item you have designed and can produce. It is a weatherproof storm coat made of a breathable fabric that can be worn year-round. Which three external factors would have the greatest effect on your pricing decisions? What is your reasoning, and how did you prioritize them?

PRICE VIEWS OF THE MILLENNIAL GENERATION Z

"This young group of consumers new to retail started saying, 'This is the new normal, and you have to delight me, engage me, and give me a promotion.' It will be difficult to wean them off that."
—*Catherine Moellering, Tobe Report*

Fashion marketers are most interested in learning what is important to the young, for obviously they are the consumers of tomorrow as well as today. A survey of Generation Z, also known as Millennials—people born between 1990 and 2010—yielded some recession-influenced conclusions. According to the Cotton Council's *Lifestyle Monitor* findings, 84 percent of the Zs surveyed named price as the most important factor in buying clothing. Second was fit (83 percent), style (69 percent), and color (67 percent). Brand names were important to 30 percent of Generation Z, a smaller number than before the 2008 recession. Some brands maintain high loyalty within this age group, among them Apple, Nike, Hollister, Forever 21, and Facebook.

Among older respondents, ages 12 to 29, many brand names were either "very" or just "somewhat important." Their outlook on their own economic condition was more positive (47 percent) than negative (18 percent). The survey reports that 79 percent of Generation Z likes shopping as compared with 58 percent of older shoppers; they shop more, 2.5 times a month as compared to 2 times for older shoppers; and they spend more monthly, $66 vs. $59. Younger consumers also shop more and spend more than older shoppers. Favorite retailers include Old Navy, Kohl's, American Eagle Outfitters, Hot Topic, Charlotte Russe, and Wet Seal.

Nevertheless, this age group is one fashion marketers are still figuring out. Teens sign up on Web sites in order to compare, shop, and get coupons. Many Generation Zers do not pay for most of their own apparel, so marketers are looking to appeal to parents through sound brand names and product features. The key word in marketing to Generation Z seems to be "value."

Adapted from: "The Young & the Restless: Generation Z Shoppers Want It All and Want It Now," *Lifestyle Monitor*, Cotton Incorporated, *Women's Wear Daily*, February 3, 2011, p. 3.

Pricing Decisions

Fashion marketers make pricing decisions to fit their organization's objectives, taking into account customer preferences and their own financial requirements. These decisions can be made using several basic approaches. Two approaches that we will examine are demand-based decisions and cost-based decisions. Marketing managers may incorporate more than one approach when developing an overall strategy.

DEMAND-BASED PRICING DECISIONS

Demand-based pricing strategies focus on customer tastes and preferences and consist of several methods of pricing. These include skimming, penetration, psychological, target, product line, and yield or revenue management pricing.

Skimming Pricing

The **skimming pricing** approach operates when marketers choose to introduce new products at the highest possible price. At this point, customers are not overly concerned about the price, particularly when the item represents a significant innovation. Skimming strategy is endemic in the high-end apparel and home furnishings price ranges. As a new item becomes more popular, the costs of developing and marketing each one are less, enabling the price to go down gradually in an effort to attract more customers who feel they can afford the perceived value at the new price levels.

Apple Inc. revolutionized the electronics industry in 2001 with its release of the iPod music

player priced at $400. The company sold more than 125,000 units in the first three months and nearly 350,000 units in the first year. A few months later, on introducing the next generation, the Nano, with fewer features and a lower price than the original iPod, Apple met with severe criticism due to its initial high price. Original iPod consumers didn't seem to care, and the number of loyal users grew.

The iPod had no real competition, which enabled Apple to develop a product that included its appealing "take your favorite music anywhere" technology, housed in a sleek pocket-size case with distinctive white "earbuds," and available at several price points for just about every income level. The success of the iPod was also due to an innovative marketing campaign. It featured a silhouette in black of a person listening to music on an iPod,

FIGURE 9.15 New products requiring extensive research to put on the market typically employ a skimming pricing strategy, in part to recoup development costs.

an image that seemed to speak directly to everyone, regardless of age, ethnicity, gender, income, or lifestyle. Although a skimming strategy might seem risky, careful research and analysis of the target customer's needs and wants often can enable a company to determine how to build an effective and profitable pricing strategy. Today, the iPod still dominates the digital music player market; by the year 2011, consumers had purchased more than 313 million units.

Penetration Pricing

Penetration pricing is in effect when a new product or service is priced initially lower than the competition in an attempt for the company to gain a foothold in the market. This pricing policy is the opposite of skimming and is used in highly competitive situations where the market is firmly established. Suppose you wanted to introduce a new form of breakfast food to compete with granola and similar popular cereals. Possibly you would start by giving away sample boxes at shopping centers and offering cents-off coupons in newspaper inserts and deals on Web sites like Groupon.com. In order to display your cereal prominently on supermarket shelves, you would pay what is known as a *slotting fee*, a kind of rent for the particular space. You might also attach cents-off coupons at the point of purchase. After consumers start buying your product, over time you would gradually reduce the promotions and raise the price to equal that of competing cereals. All going as planned, your penetration strategy will have obtained your targeted sales or market share.

Sometimes a penetration approach is used to introduce ready-to-wear, as when H&M Canada

introduced "short and sassy" dresses at $6.95. The company sold 3,600 dresses and made a profit. On occasion, new items sold by fast-fashion retailers such as Zara, H&M, and Uniqlo are trendy looks adapted from celebrity tastes and priced to bring consumers into the store in the hope that they will also buy other goods.

Psychological Pricing

Psychological pricing includes several approaches, among them *prestige pricing* and *odd-even pricing*.

Prestige Pricing Setting prices at a high level to convey quality and exclusiveness is called *prestige pricing*. It is automatic for fashion marketers in the designer and certainly couture fields. Distinctive, extremely well made, higher-priced apparel, accessories, and jewelry, as well as travel and entertainment venues, have an appeal to those who want and can afford them that lower-priced goods never match. These consumers affix a value stemming from personal experience in buying and using luxury brands. For them, part of the prestige of ownership is the premium price they pay. Louis Vuitton, a luxury brand enjoyed by fashion-forward consumers throughout the world, concentrates on its exclusivity. Known for its signature monogram and waxed canvas and leather fabrications, the Vuitton organization dates from the middle of the nineteenth century. The merchandise assortment, consisting of luggage, handbags, and small leather goods, supplemented today with apparel by Marc Jacobs, is renowned for its exquisite workmanship. Louis Vuitton consistently ranks as the world's most valuable luxury brand according to Millward Brown Inc.'s annual BrandZ Top 100 Brand Ranking

ostentatious signs of success, but products that offer undeniable intrinsic qualities and timeless values." Clearly, Louis Vuitton customers count the brand's prices among the product's benefits.

Odd-Even Pricing Psychology tries to explain why people behave, think, and feel as they do. Research studies indicate that low or high price points with certain endings heighten the demand for goods and services. Suppose a shopper views two sofas, one retailing at $999 and the other at $1,000. Even though the difference is only $1, the consumer might consider the first sofa more of a bargain, thinking in terms of $900 rather than $1,000. This psychological strategy is known as *odd-even pricing*. Alternatively, the consumer might also perceive the product to be of greater or lesser value when considering the price ending. In some cases the price point ending represents an internal language of the marketing organization, indicating the item is temporarily or permanently reduced in price. The new price ending, often expressed as an odd figure such as $777 in the case of the sofa, indicates a sale price.

Target Pricing

By researching and analyzing consumer behavior, manufacturers and retailers are able to project what consumers will pay for goods and services and apply that to their product, a tactic known as *target pricing*. This approach allows them to build goods and services with features and benefits that satisfy consumers and meet their profit goals.

A manufacturer of men's furnishings developed a new private-label collection of men's knit contemporary shirts for Macy's that addressed a void in the

FIGURE 9.16 Prestige pricing is part of the image of designer goods, such as those of Louis Vuitton.

Report. Antonio Belloni, group managing director of LVMH, stated in the company's 2009 Annual Report that "[Our customers] are enthusiastic and expert, and they are also demanding in terms of quality and durability. They want products that are not simply

MARKETER'S INSIGHT:
PRICE AT THE HIGH FASHION LEVEL

Fashion weeks are glamorous runway events for fashion devotees everywhere. For fashion marketers, they are the heart of doing business. "Part of our job is to put on a beautiful show for the audience," says Yildiz Blackstone, president of the Italian fashion label Luca Luca, "but the critical element of the runway is showcasing our goods to the [attending] store buyers and media editors."

Although designers have previously spent untold hours in developing the line for the runway, the vital work—marketing it—comes right after the show. It is now the time for store buyers and design houses to negotiate terms to obtain merchandise for customers. In deciding what to purchase, store buyers go through their criteria, asking themselves questions such as:

▶ Is the look compatible with our store image?

▶ Can the producer complete the order on time and at the specified cost?

▶ Are the prices within the range our customers will accept?

▶ How much of this merchandise can we sell at full markup before having to reduce the price?

The negotiating strength of a particular retailer depends on its size. A design house needs a certain minimum order before it can see a profit. Incorporating economies of scale, design houses can produce larger orders at lower costs, enabling them to accommodate some retailer requests.

Large retail chains such as Nordstrom or Neiman Marcus have power that smaller stores cannot equal. A large fashion retailer can ask for a style alteration, say a slightly higher neckline for more conservative customers. Big companies can also try to negotiate price on large orders. Here, the retailer's main concern is how much of that order will sell at full price. The purchase can be a gamble. Even after obtaining a lower initial price, if the store orders merchandise that eventually must be marked down in quantity, the retailer may not be able to realize a profit on that particular purchase.

For the design house, too, the financial success of a collection can be determined by the price. According to Blackstone, "If we sell 65–70 percent of the merchandise at full price, sell [others] at a 30-percent discount, and sell 10 percent of the product at sample sales, we consider the season to be extremely successful."

Adapted from: Romy Ribitzky, "Selling the Runway," Portfolio.com February 9, 2011, http://www.portfolio.com/executive-style/2011/fashion-week-is-bargaining-week-for-design, (accessed February 10, 2011).

retailer's shirt classification. Macy's initial purchase was 50,000 units for the first year, and depending on sell-through, additional purchases would follow. The retailer was very optimistic about the success of the new addition and expected that it would become a permanent part of the current program. The manufacturer's investment in the new shirt line was approximately $1 million and included the product development process—planning the line, creating the design concept, planning production, production, and distributing the line. The company determined that the cost of producing one shirt in its China factory was $20. The manufacturer wanted to recoup its initial investment by the end of the first year and submitted a $40 cost per unit to Macy's. Macy's priced its new private-label program at a highly competitive retail price of $80. The contemporary men's knit shirt line became a best seller, and Macy's and the manufacturer exceeded profit goals.

Product Line Pricing

You'll recall from Chapter 7 that companies create a number of product lines in order to reach as many potential target customers as possible. In doing so, they price each line in relation to the others so as to avoid confusion. Product line pricing is setting steps between the prices of the company's various product lines to more clearly distinguish the features of each offering. For example, Polo Ralph Lauren has a number of product lines for men, among them the custom-made Purple Label, Men's Black Label, and Lauren for Men. Along with styling differences, each line is priced differently from the others.

Retail stores also are careful in pricing their product lines. Frequently each department will offer a selection of goods at three different price points. The handbag department at Bon-Ton, for example, might carry a selection of purses priced above $100, with brands such as Dooney & Bourke; a second price level around $79, featuring Tignalli and Nine West, among others; and a third level in the range of $59, with brands such as GAL. The highest price group represents prestige offerings; the middle price range, the volume group where most of the sales occur; and the lowest priced, or promotional group, is most frequently put on sale, hence the name. This three-tiered pricing is often referred to as a "good-better-best" strategy.

Establishing the prices of the related items in a product line in proportion to each other is known as pricing within the product line. Suppose you are responsible for setting the price of coordinated jackets, pants, shirts, and sweaters. The jackets will retail for $88, pants for $78, and the shirts for $35. Pricing coordinated sweaters at $288 would go against the policy of pricing individual line items in proportion to one another.

Another pricing aspect, bundle pricing, involves product lines at least in part. Bundle pricing is combining two or more products as one package at a single price. It is often perceived by the consumer as a better value. McDonald's and other fast-food outlets offer a hamburger with French fries and a beverage at a bundle price, lower than if each item were purchased separately. Bundle pricing is popular among a range of marketing organizations. For example, it has become commonplace for AT&T, Verizon, Sprint, and other communications companies to offer free cell phones and other bundle promotions that combine phone, minutes, and related services under extended contracts.

Marketing underwear and socks often includes bundling. Packaging three pairs of GoldToe socks together with the total price amounting to less than each pair would cost singly is another form of product bundling.

Yield or Revenue Management

Marketers endeavor to have a clearer understanding of consumers in order to anticipate and influence their behavior and thereby maximize their revenue and profit from a fixed resource, such as an airline seat, a hotel room, or car rental. Since 1985 all three of those industries have been extremely active in this type of pricing approach, known as yield or revenue management.

The New York division of a women's apparel retail merchandising team received an e-mail late one Tuesday afternoon requiring that they travel to corporate headquarters in Rome for an emergency strategy meeting at 8:00 the following Thursday morning. At that point, the company had to pay a premium for the six executives' airline tickets. En route, the senior vice president of marketing learned that the person seated next to him had purchased her ticket three months earlier for a third of what the executive paid. The airline was practicing revenue management strategy by pricing its tickets according to anticipated customer behavior. In this case, for the convenience of getting tickets at the last minute in order to quickly seal a business transaction, the buying team had to settle for higher airfares.

The airline, hotel, or car rental agency knows that when the demand exists for expeditious service, customers will pay a price that enables the company to manage its revenues more profitably.

COST-BASED PRICING DECISIONS

Rather than focusing on demand, cost-based pricing focuses on all costs associated with a product. After determining the design, production, and marketing costs of an item, management adds the desired profit margin to meet its goal. Strategies associated with cost-based pricing include customary pricing; above-, at-, or below-market pricing; leader pricing; and flexible pricing policies.

Customary Pricing

Customary pricing occurs when customers are used to paying a certain price for a product, say 50 cents for a candy bar or $3.95 for a certain magazine. Candy bars of a certain weight all cost a predictable amount—unless you purchase them in an airport shop. When marketers depart drastically from customary pricing, unless they offer specific reasons, such as added ingredients or larger product size, some consumers are unwilling to meet the new price and begin to search for alternatives.

Above-, At-, or Below-Market Pricing

Above-, at-, or *below-market pricing* strategies are employed by fashion marketers operating at various price levels. Certain retailers advertise "low cost" or "discount" pricing. These marketers, such as dollar stores, are out to capture a large target market and cover costs through high sales volume. Others, such as department stores, price at the market norm, encouraging consumers to compare goods and buy based on features other than price. Still others, such as luxury fashion marketers, deliberately use above-market or premium prices to attract prestige buyers.

STEPS IN SETTING PRICE

1. Analyze and select pricing objectives
2. Estimate demand, costs, and profits
3. Choose approaches that help determine initial prices
4. Set specific prices; adjust as needed

Leader Pricing

When a retailer drastically reduces the price on an advertised product in order to get customers in the door, in hopes that they will buy full markup products while they are there, it is using a strategy known as *leader pricing*. Every week, supermarkets select different items to put on sale as leaders; one week it may be zucchini, the next week eggplant, a third week apples. When these items are priced below cost, the process is called *loss leader pricing*.

Flexible Price Policies

Flexible price policies operate when fashion marketers offer the same product to customers at different negotiated prices. In marketing automobiles, the negotiations that occur between the dealer and the customer indicate that the company is using flexible pricing. This strategy operates in marketing other high-ticket items such as antiques, art works, furs, jewelry, and yachts.

STEPS IN SETTING PRICES

To summarize the pricing process, fashion marketers can set actual prices once they are armed with knowledge concerning consumer tastes and preferences, as well as a marketing mix to design, inform, and provide goods and services consumers anticipate; alert to internal and external factors affecting the market; and aware of the pricing options available.

The steps in setting prices are (1) analyze and select the most appropriate pricing objectives, (2) determine the target market's evaluation of price and estimate costs and profits, (3) choose pricing strategies that incorporate analyses of competitors and other external influences, and (4) select a specific price. Prices, however, are not static, and marketers adjust them as needed. A newly engineered cell phone may cause competitors to reevaluate their prices. End-of-season merchandise still on the racks signals merchants to reduce prices to move it out.[6, 7]

WHAT DO YOU THINK?

Why are the steps in setting price important? What information does each step yield?

Law, Ethics, and Social Responsibility in Pricing

As discussed earlier in this chapter, a number of laws have an effect on how products are priced. Various regulations and agencies of the federal government address issues including price fixing, deceptive pricing, and discriminatory pricing, among others. In 2007 the Supreme Court ruled that manufacturers and retailers had some leeway in setting prices, however, and that disputes would be settled on a case-by-case basis. Although the Consumer Goods Pricing Act prohibits vertical price fixing, this still occurs sometimes in the fashion field. For example, Nine West paid a hefty fine for insisting that retailers stick by a predetermined price. Although "manufacturer's suggested retail price" is not illegal, manufacturers' insisting that it be maintained is.[8]

As fashion marketers work to offer the most appealing prices to customers, in order to achieve this goal, the industry has been known sometimes to cut corners. Throughout the nineteenth century, sweatshops in New York City's garment district and New England's textile mills were infamous for being demanding, dirty, and dangerous. Employees, mostly women and young girls, worked long hours for pitiful wages. Finally, after a New York blouse factory caught on fire, trapping workers inside and killing many, a social uproar created a favorable climate for recognizing and empowering unions. Speaking in a united voice for workers, unions could now demand and obtain better wages and working conditions. Although unionized garment workers

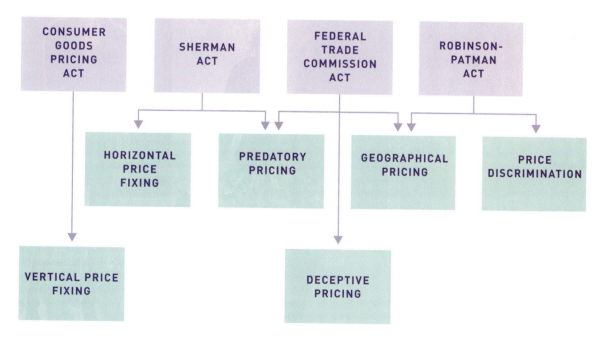

Source: Roger A. Kerin, Steven W. Hartley, and William Rudelius, *Marketing 10/e*, McGraw-Hill Irwin, 2011, p. 364, fig 14-8.

FIGURE 9.17 Selected laws have an effect on pricing of fashion goods. BY VANESSA HAN AND ALICIA FREILE

in the United States benefit from union representation, many other garment workers throughout the world are not as lucky, still working in unsafe conditions, earning a pittance, and living in poverty. Fortunately, a number of U.S. apparel marketers recognize the importance of a decent working environment and are ensuring that their overseas factories and contractors provide these things. Companies such as Gap, Patagonia, and Nike, and celebrities like Bono and Kathie Lee Gifford strive to be socially responsible in their dealings with sources worldwide. In these situations, although price is still important, it becomes secondary to employee well-being.

In addition, to ensure that workers earn fair wages in healthy surroundings, fashion marketers are focusing on creating a sustainable environment, making certain that the effects of production and marketing maintain ecological balance. An example is H&M's recent line of ready-to-wear called the Conscious Collection, made from organic cotton and linen fibers and recycled polyester. H&M's commitment is to use only sustainable cotton (grown so as to produce no negative effect on the environment) by 2020.[9]

Global Pricing

When companies market their goods overseas, they often encounter costs that are higher than at home. For example, consider the transportation necessary for a fashion house in Europe to send its goods to stores in New York, Brazil, and Hong Kong. Higher costs mean that in order to earn a profit, a company must raise its prices. The lower price is a major reason foreign visitors shop for fashion goods in their country of origin: fragrances and apparel in France, leather goods and woolens in Italy, and pearls in Japan.

Sometimes companies want to send their products overseas in order to get a foothold in a certain market. One way is to establish low prices. When the price of an item is lower overseas than it is at home, the practice is called *dumping*. In the late twentieth century, Japanese electronics and automotive industries practiced dumping their newest televisions and cars in the United States, and for a while that tactic worked. More endemic in the fashion industry is the practice of dealing in **gray market goods** (or parallel goods), items not intended for sale in the country where they are being offered.[10] These are legitimate products, but they were manufactured to be sold in another country. A Swiss watch manufactured for Europe but sold in the United States is an example of gray market goods. It may carry a lower price, and the warranty may not be valid in the U.S. market.

summary

Pricing has a direct effect on a company's survival and well-being. Price is important to consumers because it indicates what they must pay for the things they need and want. It is important to marketers because price multiplied by the volume sold equals a company's revenues. By subtracting total costs from total income, a company determines its profit. Consumers often perceive price as the benefits gained from the purchase rather than from the features of the product itself, a phenomenon known as consumer perceived value. The feelings of looking smart and appropriately dressed are the perceived values a customer realizes when buying such items as a well-fitted blazer.

In setting price, companies first determine their pricing objectives or goals. These may be profit oriented or sales oriented. They then consider demand and supply and how in theory those affect price. Next they determine the effects of costs on price

and consider break-even pricing, cost-plus, and markup pricing. In addition, they take into consideration other factors influencing price, including the marketing mix and external factors. They then select suitable approaches from among possible pricing decisions, which may be demand-based or cost-based.

Laws, ethics, and social responsibility are important aspects of pricing for fashion marketers. Certain laws regulate the kinds of prices businesses can charge. Preserving the environment and ensuring fair trade conditions, such as decent wages and working conditions for employees, are issues of concern to fashion marketers. As more consumers worldwide have the interest and means to participate in fashion markets, sourcing and marketing fashion goods globally opens up increasingly viable opportunities.

Forever 21—Really Fast Fashion

What teen fashion fan doesn't love owning the latest trendy look, particularly at a budget price?

Fashion-centered shoppers thrill to the hunt for exciting, new, and—for many teens—inexpensive fashion looks. One of several fast-fashion organizations where consumers can locate just about every trend on the scene is Forever 21. Teen shoppers worldwide have access to vast offerings of trendy and inexpensive original and designer knockoff apparel and accessories. An integrated marketing organization, Forever 21 claims some 477 stores worldwide plus a Web site, employs 35,000 workers, and nets $3 billion dollars annually. In the United States, the company's New York stores include Fifth Avenue and also Times Square. Throughout the country, including California and Las Vegas, and many places in between, Forever 21 stores occupy former Saks, Sears, Mervyns, and other retail locations. Overseas, London's fashionable Oxford Street and Tokyo's Shibuya shopping area are major shopping venues; company plans include opening 75 additional stores in five countries.

Headed by one family, Do Won Chang, his wife, Jin Sook, and their two daughters, Forever 21 grew out of the hard work of the Korean immigrant parents in Los Angeles to build a manufacturing, distribution, and retail network for inexpensive teenage fashions. Mrs. Chang is in charge of obtaining the merchandise, and Mr. Chang handles the other aspects of the business. Daughter Linda runs the marketing department, and her sister, Esther, is in charge of visual merchandising.

A star feature of the company's success is Mrs. Chang's ability to both recognize the latest trends and also negotiate the most favorable prices. She buys goods in relatively small quantities. That way, customers learn to buy when they first see an item because next time it will be gone. An advantage for the company: if a certain look doesn't sell, the loss is minor. Much of the success of Forever 21 stems from Mrs. Chang's expertise in recognizing trends early and the company's agility in swiftly putting them on the market and moving them out. The rapid turnover of merchandise combined with low prices is the key to Forever 21's rapid growth to date.

Featuring the right product is essential. Forever 21 has been known to copy current looks of well-known design organizations such as Diane von Furstenberg, Anna Sui,

Anthropologie, and others. When threatened with legal action, the company tends to settle out of court, counting the settlement as a business cost. (Although U.S. copyright laws currently do not protect designs, the fashion industry is seeking a change in these provisions). Knockoffs are not the company's only business; Forever 21 does have a design team that produces original looks in-house.

Another challenge the company has encountered is the accusation of unfair wages and working conditions. For example, a while back, workers in Los Angeles factories contracting with Forever 21 brought a lawsuit against the company. It was settled in their favor. Other lawsuits, claiming similar violations, typically are settled out of court. From such incidents, Forever 21 created a vendor compliance program requiring the manufacturers they are working with to follow applicable labor laws, and investigating promptly any situations that surface. Currently, about 10 percent of the company's production takes place in the United States, usually items that call for a short lead time. Here, manufacturer compliance can be ascertained fairly easily. As Forever 21 production expands overseas to China, Pakistan, Vietnam, and other countries where costs, wages, and working conditions are less regulated, the question of monitoring and maintaining vendor compliance is cloudier.

Nevertheless, Forever 21 is developing a viable target audience and appeals to it through a marketing mix focused on product appeal, price, presentation, and accessibility.

Sources: Susan Berfield, "Forever 21's Fast (and Loose) Fashion Empire," *Bloomberg Business Week*, January 20, 2011, http://www.businessweek.com/magazine/content/11_05/b4213090559511.htm (accessed March 8, 2012); Forever 21 Web site, HYPERLINK "http://www.forever21.com" www.forever21.com (accessed February 12, 2011).

QUESTIONS

1. If you were consulting with the Changs on selecting the most useful pricing objectives for the company, which objectives would you recommend? Why?

2. Which aspects of the external marketing environment have an effect on the way Forever 21 prices its merchandise? Explain.

3. From the pricing decisions given in the chapter, select two or three that you believe are in effect at Forever 21 right now. Do you see another pricing technique the company might also use? If so, what is it, and why did you select it?

KEY TERMS

barter

break-even analysis

cash discount

Consumer Goods Pricing Act

cost-plus pricing

demand

demand curve

elasticity of demand

Federal Trade Commission Act

fixed costs

gray market goods

markup

markup pricing

penetration pricing

price

profit

quantity discount

Robinson-Patman Act

seasonal discount

Sherman Antitrust Act

skimming pricing

supply

total costs

trade discount

variable costs

REVIEW QUESTIONS

1. What is meant by the term "price" and why is price important to fashion consumers and marketers?

2. Why is creating profit objectives important to fashion marketers, and what is the difference between profit- and sales-oriented objectives?

3. Explain the possible effects of demand and supply on price.

4. Are prestige pricing and skimming pricing the same thing? When might they be different?

5. List and explain each of the steps fashion marketers may take in setting prices.

DISCUSSION ACTIVITIES AND PROJECTS

1. You (alone or as part of a small group) are responsible for recommending the pricing objectives for a new style of competitive running shoe with padding features that other brands do not offer. Your company wants the shoe to appeal to fashion-oriented young men and women who enjoy recreational running as well as races. Select two pricing objectives you would consider, citing your reasons for each.

2. As you set about determining a price for this shoe, explain at least one factor in each component of the marketing mix that could influence the price you are seeking to establish. Write a brief report on your conclusions, and share them with a classmate. Were there duplicates? If so, why? What were they?

3. Go to the Internet and look for the day's news. Select an article having to do with an effect that one part of the external environment could have on the pricing of your running shoe (see

Question 1). Explaining your reasoning, give an oral report on your findings to the class.

4. With one or more classmates, or by yourself, visit a department or specialty store and ascertain three separate price lines within a given department. Identify the top price line, the middle, and the lowest. Which of these lines tends to be featured when there are periodic sales? Which when there are clearance sales? Why?

5. Identify a fashion product you would like to market and set a price for it. Go through each of the steps involved in setting price, describing what you would do and explaining how you arrived at a final price.

DEVELOPING YOUR MARKETING PLAN

.The next marketing mix element for you to address in your plan is pricing. As you consider this element for your product or company, refer back to the four steps to pricing:

1. Start by determining your pricing objectives. Are they profit oriented or sales oriented?

2. Then try to estimate the demand and the costs for your product. Consider possible costs of the other elements of the marketing mix.

3. Analyze the external environment, such as the competitive environment, the economy, and other outside factors.

4. Review available pricing strategies and select the most appropriate.

5. Decide under what conditions you might need to adjust your prices.

Refer to the Marketing Plan Outline, Table 1.2, provided at the end of Chapter 1, as well as Appendix A: Sample Marketing Plan.

REFERENCES

1. Roger A. Kerin, Steven W. Hartley, and William Rudelius, *Marketing: The Core,* 4th ed. (New York: McGraw-Hill/Irwin, 2011), p. 263.

2. William M. Pride and O. C. Ferrell, *Marketing,* 14th ed. (Boston: Houghton Mifflin, 2008), p. 580, Fig. 21.1.

3. Ibid., p. 581, Fig. 21.2.

4. Op cit., p. 364, Fig. 14.8

5. Emily Bryson York and Katherine Skiba, "Healthier Food Focus: Push for Fresher, Better-for-You Grocery Items Takes Big Step as Wal-Mart Plans to Cut Prices, Change Private-Label Goods," *Chicago Tribune,* January 11, 2011, Section I, pp. 23, 24.

6. Op cit., p. 604.

7. Charles W. Lamb, Joseph F. Hair, Jr., and Carl McDaniel, *MKT*, 2010-2011 ed. (Mason, OH: South-Western, 2011), p. 313.

8. Op cit., p. 364.

9. Joelle Diderich, "H&M Launches Sustainable Conscious Collection," *Women's Wear Daily,* February 3, 2011, p. 3.

10. Elaine Stone, *The Dynamics of Fashion*, 3rd ed. (New York: Fairchild Books, 2008), p. 474.

CHAPTER 10

Fashion Marketing Channels and Supply Chain Management

This chapter explores how goods reach consumers and business users. It explains the purpose of marketing channels and describes several channel systems employed in marketing consumer and business goods. Next, it covers the channel decisions fashion marketers must make and the logistics performed in various supply chain activities. Global marketing channels and social responsibility in marketing channel operation conclude the chapter.

WHAT DO I NEED TO KNOW ABOUT FASHION MARKETING CHANNELS AND SUPPLY CHAIN MANAGEMENT?

* The definition of marketing channels and what purpose they serve
* How fashion marketing channels are organized
* The difference between marketing channels and supply chains
* The key role of logistics in supply chain management
* How fashion marketers participate in global marketing channels and in assuming social responsibility

FASHION MARKETING IN FOCUS:
Sean John Rethinks Its Marketing Channels

Recently, Sean John, the fashion company launched by Sean "Diddy" Combs, decided to do what several brand names such as Tommy Hilfiger, Kenneth Cole, Martha Stewart, and others have done—namely, to narrow its retail store customer base and serve more target markets. How did the company go about making this change? By signing an agreement to grant Macy's exclusive distribution for a specific merchandise line, in this case men's sportswear.

In the agreement, Sean John kept the right to offer the line through its own flagship store in New York, plus eight additional outlets. But there was a trade-off. Signing exclusively with Macy's meant that Sean John would lose former retail store customers such as Dillard's, Bon-Ton, Jimmy Jazz, and more, whose combined sales had previously accounted for more than 50 percent of Sean John's total company income. A scary proposition, perhaps, but the opportunity for growth through new marketing channels was judged to outweigh the risk based on a number of facts: The Sean John line had a decade of successful experience with Macy's, plus it would now be available in Macy's 850 stores throughout the country, spotlighted on the retailer's Web site, and featured prominently in several soon-to-be remodeled Macy's flagships.

Adapted from: David Lipke, "Diddy's Big Deal," *Women's Wear Daily,* May 6, 2010, pp. 1, 6, 7.

When customers in Des Moines, Iowa, or Tempe, Arizona, want to buy a new fashion look, they expect to find an assortment in their desired size and color in their local stores or on their favorite shopping Web site. They want that new outfit now, only care to buy one or perhaps two, and expect to take it home or have it shipped right away. Fashion marketing channels and supply chains make it possible for businesses to make this happen. The change in marketing channels that Sean John Combs decided on as described in "Sean John Rethinks Its Changes Marketing Channels" shows how marketing channels are adapted to meet customers' needs.

FIGURE 10.1 Efficient marketing channels enable customers to have a wide assortment of goods and services from which to choose.

What Are Marketing Channels and What Do They Do?

A **marketing channel** (also known as a *distribution channel*) consists of a set of independent business organizations (*channel members*) that help make a product available—in this case fashion goods or services—for consumers or businesses.[1] Members of the marketing channel include **intermediaries** (also called *middlemen* or *resellers*) that work with manufacturers, other intermediaries, and/or ultimate consumers to buy and sell products, and to make the exchange process easier.[2, 3] Intermediaries include **retailers**, organizations that sell mainly to consumers; **merchant wholesalers**, businesses that own the goods they sell to other intermediaries (retailers or other wholesalers); and **agents** and **brokers**, who represent retailers, wholesalers, or manufacturers to customers, making buying and selling easier (agents do not own the goods they are marketing). Finally, marketing channels include *facilitating organizations* such as banks and insurance companies that expedite the marketing process.

THE PURPOSE OF MARKETING CHANNELS

The purpose of channels and their intermediaries is to accomplish what a manufacturer may not be willing or able to afford to do alone. For example, a small sportswear manufacturer may not have the capital to maintain a sales force and so arranges for a wholesaler or broker to sell the company's output. Other tasks of intermediaries include obtaining and distributing the right quantities and assortments of products to retailers and consumers. Manufacturers create products in large quantities, for example, shoes; consumers may require one or two pairs, but they need them in a convenient location, at a certain time, and in a given price range. Intermediaries provide these, collecting and distributing products in ways most suitable to their customers. Instead of offering customers a choice of only one or two shoe styles, shoe retailers such as Nordstrom or DSW collect a wide assortment of styles, sizes, and colors, affording customers a variety from which to choose.

MARKETING CHANNELS INFLUENCE THE MARKETING MIX

A company must select its marketing channels carefully, because the decisions it makes about channels influence every other aspect of the marketing mix. When goods are to be replaced or new products offered, the channels must be in place for customers ready to buy. To create and maintain effective channels, marketers persuade and motivate channel members, and some members require more effort than others. For example, a department store chain may insist on frequent deliveries of handbags

during the season, and the supplier agrees to that arrangement. On the other hand, a small specialty store only needs one or possibly two deliveries during that time and needs less persuasion from the supplier to take on the line. Pricing policies are related to whether the goods are intended for high-end specialty stores, discount stores, or the Internet.[4] Department and specialty stores expect to pay full-cost price and for that they receive complete shipments early in the season, plus services from the supplier such as a trunk show or assistance with advertising costs. Discount stores look to buy at lower prices and are willing to buy goods later in the season and take incomplete assortments. Marketers closely edit the items and prices of products destined for marketing via the Internet.

Because marketing is an ongoing process, successful channel relationships involve a long-term commitment on the part of the members since marketing channel members share certain goals. Each member has unique responsibilities in the channel, knowing that the main common goal is long-term profit, and that profit depends entirely on cooperation within the channel to move the product promptly to the customer.

When intermediaries perform marketing channel services effectively, they contribute to the profitability of each member organization through more efficient operations. Figure 10.2 illustrates the number of contacts individual consumers would have to make to obtain goods if there were no intermediaries.

Imagine being a fashion retailer whose buyer, in order to obtain goods, had to visit every imaginable manufacturer. Or consider a manufacturer that had to send a representative to call individually on each

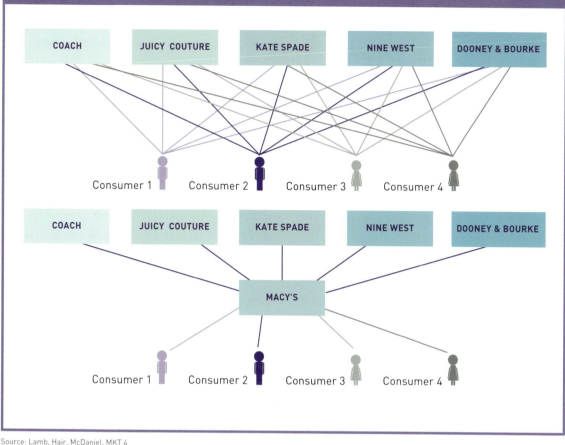

Source: Lamb, Hair, McDaniel, MKT 4

FIGURE 10.2 Intermediaries simplify the buying process. BY VANESSA HAN AND ALICIA FREILE

retailer and each store branch to show new lines. The process would take up an enormous amount of time—time needed to complete the other marketing activities necessary to make goods available to customers in a timely manner. With an intermediary representing both buyers and sellers, the buying process becomes much easier and far less time-consuming and costly.

WHAT DO YOU THINK?

How do marketing channels influence each element of the marketing mix of one of your favorite products?

HOW CHANNELS SERVE THE MARKET

Channels exist to accomplish certain tasks that must be done for fashion marketers to satisfy customers and earn a profit. The specific activities that channel members perform depend on the particular tasks that need to be accomplished and the channel member that can complete them most effectively. Sometimes all channel activities are performed by one channel member, such as Zara and Gap among other fashion marketers, which control their entire marketing channels, as shown in Figure 10.3.

More often, tasks are shared among channel members. For example, a major activity of many fashion goods sales agents is to obtain fashion information from retailers, such as the styles customers want that are not on hand, and pass that information on to manufacturers. In the matter of promotion, most fashion marketers create a long-range plan and gain the cooperation of other channel members, typically retailers, in local advertising. In promoting a new style, J Brand jeans, a division of Fifth & Pacific Companies (formerly Liz Claiborne), will help pay for the J Brand newspaper and magazine advertising that participating retailers such as Bloomingdale's do. See Tables 10.1a and b for a listing of the marketing channel activities that intermediaries perform.

Channel members perform services that add to the value of the product because they make it easier for customers to have the goods they want, when and where they want them. Specifically, some channel members work to bring about transactions by providing information as to customer needs and product availability, locating new customers or suppliers, negotiating price or terms of delivery and payment, indicating desired product modifications or changes, and creating and implementing communications concerning the product. Others work to carry through the transaction by transporting and storing the merchandise, financing the costs of channel participation, or assuming the risks of channel activity.[5]

TYPES OF MARKETING CHANNELS

Fashion marketers create marketing channels to serve their customers most efficiently. Some marketing channels are strictly organized, while others are an informal collection of businesses. What's

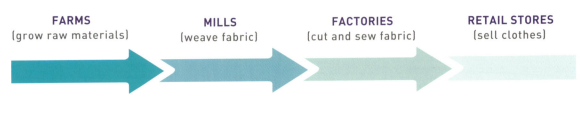

FARMS (grow raw materials) → **MILLS** (weave fabric) → **FACTORIES** (cut and sew fabric) → **RETAIL STORES** (sell clothes)

Source: http://www.gap.com

FIGURE 10.3 Gap closely controls and coordinates each phase of the marketing process. BY VANESSA HAN AND ALICIA FREILE

TABLES 10.1A AND B Marketing Channel Activities Performed by Intermediaries

Some of the activities of channel members help encourage and maintain transactions, while other activities help fulfill completed transactions.

A. ACTIVITIES HELPING TO COMPLETE TRANSACTIONS

Activity	Responsibilities
Gathering marketing information	Obtaining data on sales, product availability, trends, and other relevant marketing factors
Conducting marketing management	Creating strategic plans for developing customer relationships and channel productivity
Facilitating marketing exchanges	Locating product assortments that satisfy customer needs, negotiating terms, fostering cooperation among channel members
Promoting the brand	Utilizing persuasive communications to inform present and potential markets about the product

B. ACTIVITIES FULFILLING COMPLETED TRANSACTIONS

Activity	Responsibility
Physical distribution	Transporting, storing, and assembling product assortments
Financing	Obtaining funds to cover the costs of the channel
Risk taking	Assuming the risks of channel activities

Adapted from: William M. Pride and O. C. Ferrell, Marketing, 14th edition, p. 406, Table 15.1, and Gary Armstrong and Philip Kotler, *Marketing: An Introduction*, 9th edition, p. 295.

more, marketers may use different channels to market their various lines of merchandise. For example, designer Vera Wang uses one channel of distribution to market wedding gowns to Bergdorf Goodman in New York and another for the line the company sells to Kohl's. Tommy Hilfiger sells its line directly to Macy's in the United States but also maintains its own specialty stores.

Some companies such as Amazon and Zappos sell directly to consumers via the Internet, without using intermediaries. Some fashion marketers sell directly to retailers, as Ralph Lauren does with JCPenney and other large fashion retailers, and Sean John Combs with Macy's. Some manufacturers use intermediaries to market their goods directly to consumers. Avon markets its cosmetics

FIGURE 10.4 Fashion forecasters share information on trends with retailers, assisting them in identifying new products for customers.

and skin care products through independent sales-people as well as through catalogues and over the Internet. Other fashion marketers, such as manufacturers that do not want or cannot afford a full-time sales staff, contract with independent wholesalers to show their lines to retailers. Some work exclusively for one fairly large fashion marketer. Other intermediaries, acting as agents, create agreements with a group of small yet complementary designer/manufacturers in order to offer a varied assortment of merchandise to retail customers. For example, Patti McKillop, chief executive officer of the wholesale firm Potluck Paris of Seattle, imports jewelry from Paris designers and others for her retail store customers.[6] Small design companies specializing in apparel such as special-occasion evening wear might connect with a sales representative who shows the lines of 8 to 10 of these designers to various small specialty retailers in several states and takes orders from these store buyers.

Although the goal is the smooth and profitable flow of fashion items consumers want, sometimes **channel conflict**—disagreements over which member should do what and how should each be compensated—can occur because the members are often separate and independent organizations. A *horizontal conflict* can take place among channel members at the same level, say, if Target and Kmart were to charge dramatically different prices for the same chair. To avoid conflict, Nordstrom recently stopped selling Rockport shoes in its stores so as not to compete with Rockport's intensive catalogue marketing efforts. Other disagreements can happen when members in the same channel disagree; this is called a *vertical conflict*. A while ago, Revlon decided to offer its Vital Radiance skin care line to mass marketers such as Walmart and CVS instead of to traditional department stores such as Bon-Ton. When that mass distribution took place, the department stores withheld buying some other Revlon products, and the company lost an estimated $100 million dollars in one year.[7]

FIGURE 10.5 In attempting to reach a wide range of customers, marketers may encounter channel conflicts, which, unless resolved, may result in lost sales.

How Marketing Channels Are Organized

There are three major kinds of marketing channels. One is for consumer products, items that we all use, including fashion goods such as apparel, accessories, home furnishings, electronics, and automobiles. Another is for products destined for business use, for example, airplanes, electronic technologies, industrial sewing machines, and office equipment. The third is for services ranging from haircuts to legal advice. While the main concern of this study is the marketing of consumer fashion goods, marketing business products and services is also described.

MARKETING CONSUMER GOODS

Four marketing channels are used for marketing consumer goods; one is direct, and the other three, which involve one or more intermediaries, are indirect.

Direct Marketing Channels

Since consumer needs for goods require efficient delivery, and because product marketing requirements vary, a channel suitable for one product may not be appropriate for others. To accommodate the variety of needs, consumer goods marketers have created several different types of marketing channels. Looking at Figure 10.6, you will see four major marketing channels for consumer goods that range in length and complexity. Each level of intermediaries is organized most effectively for the kinds of products it moves along to the ultimate consumer. The length of each channel is shown by the number

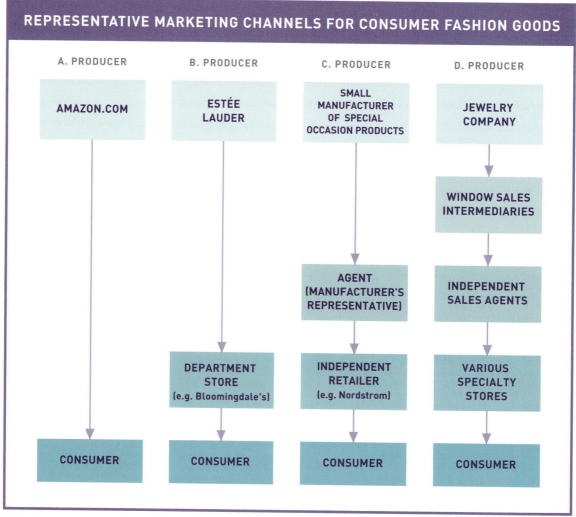

REPRESENTATIVE MARKETING CHANNELS FOR CONSUMER FASHION GOODS

A. PRODUCER	B. PRODUCER	C. PRODUCER	D. PRODUCER
AMAZON.COM	ESTÉE LAUDER	SMALL MANUFACTURER OF SPECIAL OCCASION PRODUCTS	JEWELRY COMPANY
			WINDOW SALES INTERMEDIARIES
		AGENT (MANUFACTURER'S REPRESENTATIVE)	INDEPENDENT SALES AGENTS
	DEPARTMENT STORE (e.g. Bloomingdale's)	INDEPENDENT RETAILER (e.g. Nordstrom)	VARIOUS SPECIALTY STORES
CONSUMER	CONSUMER	CONSUMER	CONSUMER

Source: Roger A. Kerin, Steven Hartley, and William Rudelius, *Marketing the Core*, 2nd edition, pp. 288, 290, figure 13.3 and 13.5.

FIGURE 10.6 Representative marketing channels for consumer fashion goods. BY VANESSA HAN AND ALICIA FREILE

of participating intermediaries; the more intermediaries, the longer the channel. Notice that because the marketing organizations in the shortest channel have no intermediaries but reach out directly to consumers, they are using what are known as **direct marketing channels**. For example, custom apparel and furniture designers work directly with consumers, creating designs and products for clients in their workrooms. Seattle Sutton markets controlled diet weight loss plans directly to consumers, and companies such as Travelocity and Amazon.com market their goods and services directly to customers over the Internet. In using direct marketing channels, the main marketing organization, such as Nike or H&M, assumes all of the marketing channel activities noted earlier. In longer channels, various intermediaries take on some of the marketing activities. For example, retailers send information to suppliers concerning the sales of both popular and slow-moving styles. Manufacturers and intermediaries keep retailers posted on new products as well as discontinued items.

Indirect Marketing Channels

Longer marketing channels containing one or more intermediaries (refer again to Figure 10.6) are known as **indirect marketing channels**. The shortest of these, from manufacturer to retailer, is used by large fashion marketers such as Estée Lauder, Levi Strauss, and Nike, selling directly to large retail organizations such as Bloomingdale's, Dillard's, and Target. Smaller manufacturers may not want the expense of a full-time sales force, and so decide to use an independent agent, called a sales representative (or sometimes *manufacturer's representative*) in the fashion industry. Sales representatives may represent one or several manufacturers, and they sell to a number of retailers, usually in a given geographical area. Joan Prikos is a sales representative who deals in marketing women's apparel for special occasions.

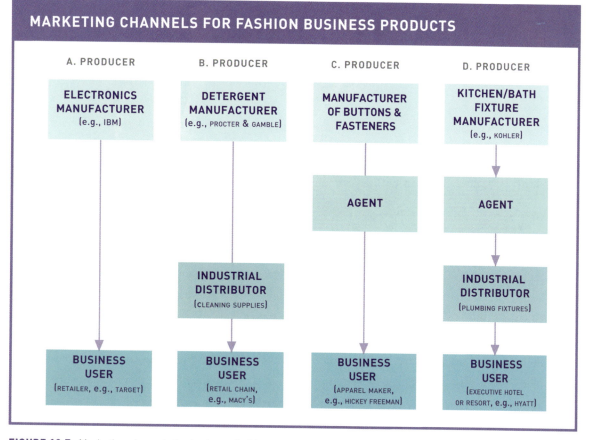

FIGURE 10.7 Marketing channels for business fashion products are similar to those for consumer fashion goods, but with some differences. BY VANESSA HAN AND ALICIA FREILE

The products she offers are created by several small manufacturing and design organizations, and her territory is limited primarily to Midwestern specialty stores and independent boutiques and shops. Other manufacturers, such as the Belgian jewelry firm Mansar Products, Ltd., sell their products to import intermediaries, which then use independent sales agents to connect with fashion retailers.[8] The specific types of channels for each kind of merchandise have come into being because they are each more efficient than an alternative, but they must remain so in order to stay in business. Together, the organizations in each channel are responsible for the flow of products through the channel, the flow of ownership, the flow of payment, and the flow of information and promotion.[9]

MARKETING CHANNELS FOR BUSINESS GOODS AND SERVICES

Business marketing channels are similar to those for consumer goods in that they may be either direct or indirect, as seen in Figure 10.7. When businesses are purchasing expensive products such as copying machines for the office or sewing machines for the factory, they want to deal directly with the manufacturer. A large fashion marketing organization seeking a copier will go right to Xerox and other manufacturers to obtain the most complete product and service information. That same company, when looking for a delivery truck, will work with an industrial distributor, in this case an automobile dealer specializing in business products, to find the most suitable vehicle for the company's purposes. When a fashion business such as an apparel manufacturer is looking for buttons or zippers, it will call on the services of an agent who offers an assortment of these products from a number of manufacturers. When the fashion organization's office manager needs new supplies, he or she is quite likely to look in a catalogue offered by an industrial distributor who obtains products from various agents and manufacturers and so is able to offer a varied selection of paper, ink, staplers, envelopes, and so on.

Services for both consumers and businesses include many products from lawn mowing and dog grooming, to interior design and fashion trend analysis, to legal and financial services. Services are unique in that they are often customized and inseparable from their provider. The look that your hair stylist creates for you is distinctly yours. Another stylist may try to copy it, but the results won't be the same. Services are also perishable. Airline and concert tickets are gone once the flight or concert is over. Because services are from one provider, the quality can vary—remember the last bad haircut you had? Because of their characteristics, then, services are generally marketed through direct channels.

CONVENTIONAL MARKETING CHANNELS

Marketing channels developed in an informal way. Each independent business—manufacturer, intermediary, facilitator—sought to maximize its short-term profits through individual transactions rather than consider the marketing process as a whole: a continual flow of goods and services to satisfy changing consumer demands. Today businesses realize that in order to satisfy a variety of target consumers, their products need to be available through a number of channels. Some are **conventional**

marketing channels composed of independent manufacturers and intermediaries working for each organization's own benefit, without coordination or leadership. Each transaction is unique and no continuous arrangement exists to move the goods from producer to users. This situation does not maximize opportunity for profitability among its participants because without coordination it is often inefficient. Other marketing channels working with greater control and direction can realize greater efficiency. These include vertical marketing systems.

VERTICAL MARKETING CHANNEL SYSTEMS

When manufacturers and intermediaries participate in a coordinated effort, they are taking part in a **vertical marketing system (VMS)**. One channel member may own the others, create contracts with them, or have sufficient control that the others must cooperate.[10] There are three types of VMS: *corporate*, *contractual*, and *administered*.

FIGURE 10.8 A typical marketing channel for large retailers often includes buying directly from a manufacturer such as Juicy Couture.

FIGURE 10.9 Walmart typically establishes a vertical marketing system (VMS) with its suppliers, enabling the company to serve customers quickly and at low prices.

Corporate Marketing Systems

A **corporate vertical marketing system** brings the entire channel under one ownership. Both Uniqlo, the Japanese fast-fashion marketer, and IKEA, the Swedish home furnishings marketer with stores throughout the United States, Europe, Asia, and South America, are able to design, create, and market fashion goods efficiently due to their corporate vertical marketing systems that control the manufacturing and worldwide distribution of their goods.

Contractual Marketing Systems

A **contractual marketing system** exists through written agreements between manufacturers and intermediaries. Coca-Cola maintains agreements with its bottlers and dealers throughout the world. The Ford Motor Company maintains agreements with its local dealers. McDonald's has contracts with its suppliers, not only for food products but for the wrappers, beverage containers, straws, and other needed store items, as well as contracts with its local store owners. Perhaps the best known form of contractual marketing system is the **franchise**, in this case an agreement (franchise) between a large marketing organization with a well-known name (a *franchisor*) and a local business (*franchisee*) to market the franchisor's product exclusively. To do this, typically the franchisee must meet the franchisor's requirements in buying, displaying, and selling the product. In return, the local business may receive the support of the franchisor in areas such as training, promotion, and sometimes financing. The best known franchise businesses are fast-food companies such as Subway and Dunkin' Donuts, but other businesses such as Coldwell Banker Real Estate, Holiday Inn, and Jiffy Lube are also franchises.

Apparel organizations such as Ralph Lauren also make use of agreements similar to franchises, often in overseas retail ventures. An investment group located in another country may be interested in marketing the goods or opening local retail stores offering a well-known brand and enters into an agreement with the parent company. Under this *international licensing agreement*, the investment group may promote and market the company's goods and agree to own and operate the brand's stores in a specified geographic area. Polo Ralph Lauren Corporation has international licensing agreements with several overseas groups located in Central and South America, Asia, and Australia, among others.[11] (Note that the *international licensing agreement* described here is different from a *product licensing agreement* where a marketing organization agrees to have a manufacturer create certain items exclusively for the company. For example, Hanes Brands makes men's Polo Ralph Lauren underwear and sleepwear under a product licensing agreement.)

Administered Marketing Systems

When one member of a marketing channel wields more power than the others, an **administered marketing system** may result. For example, Walmart—even without formal contracts in certain instances—has the clout to control the marketing activities in its channels. Among its directives to channel partners, the company now requires suppliers to think green in product creation and packaging, reducing the size of packages and using biodegradable materials wherever possible. Nike promotes the concept of sustainability throughout its marketing channels. One part is what the company calls Considered Design, including minimizing the impact of product ingredients on the environment and, after use, returning the product safely to nature.[12]

MULTI-CHANNEL MARKETING

Today, marketers are interested in reaching as wide a range of potential customers as possible, and they make use of a variety of channels to accomplish their goals, a concept known as **multi-channel marketing**. For example, note some of the ways paperback books are marketed: through bookstores, newsstands, supermarkets and drug stores, via catalogues and mailers, and electronically, among other ways. Apparel, accessories, and home furnishings marketers use multi-channel marketing extensively. For example, active sportswear marketers Columbia and North Face sell through full-price department and specialty stores, discount retailers, catalogues, the Internet, and through mobile marketing such as iPhone apps. Beyoncé Knowles sells the House of Deréon label to Bloomingdale's, Neiman Marcus, Saks, and Nordstrom, while the sister label for juniors, Deréon, is sold to Macy's, Dillard's, Dr. Jay's, and Akira. Michael Kors distributes the Michael Kors Collection in the company's own stores, as well as to Saks, Nordstrom, and Bergdorf Goodman, while the Michael Kors label goes to company stores and also to Macy's, Nordstrom, Lord & Taylor, and Dillard's.[13]

HOUSE OF DERÉON

FIGURE 10.10 Most fashion marketers today, including Beyoncé and Tina Knowles with their House of Deréon and Deréon labels, use multi-channel distribution to reach target customers.

What are some of the marketing channels you've observed for a favorite product of yours?

Channel Decisions

Selecting the most appropriate channels is essential to maximizing profitability. In reaching channel decisions, marketers need to consider a number of factors, including analyzing customer demand, establishing company channel goals, determining appropriate channels, and dealing with competition. (See Figure 10.11.)

FIGURE 10.11 Some of the factors marketers want to consider when selecting appropriate channels. BY VANESSA HAN AND ALICIA FREILE

ANALYZING CUSTOMER DEMAND

Customers have a variety of product needs that marketers work to satisfy. In order to determine the best ways to fulfill those needs, fashion marketers analyze consumer wants. For example, does a family moving to a new home or apartment seek the services of an interior design specialist who will suggest décor for the entire space, or is it interested in furnishing each room piecemeal, seeking out the best furniture, drapery, and floor covering values for the money? In the first instance, the family looks for coordinated offerings and services available through established independent designers or department and furniture stores. In the second instance, the family creates its own interior design plans and visits discount stores, secondhand stores, and antique shops to locate suitable home furnishings. Other consumer needs include services such as credit, delivery, installation, and so on. The more services consumers demand, the greater the level of services that marketers need to be ready to offer.

FIGURE 10.12 Fashion marketers do not offer services such as special orders when offering goods via television.

ESTABLISHING CHANNEL GOALS

After identifying the intended customer and taking into consideration the nature of the product, its size, and value, companies are ready to establish marketing channel goals. These are generally set up in terms of customer service levels (how often customers want delivery and what other services, such as credit, they require), the size of the company (larger companies have greater power in the channels), and external marketing factors (such as the economy, or sometimes the weather).

Customer Service Levels

Companies often have several target markets requiring different service levels. For example, the Isaac Mizrahi New York line marketed to Bergdorf Goodman, Saks, and Neiman Marcus calls for a more personalized level of service with attention to individual store and customer needs, while the Isaac Mizrahi Live lifestyle brand of apparel, accessories, and housewares marketed on QVC is offered as available until sold out. Customers place their orders and are shipped the merchandise. Requests for services such as alterations or special orders are not part of this channel. The top-of-the-line Calvin Klein Collection for men and women receives a high level of service on the part of management when the brand's retailer is London's fashionable Harvey Nichols or Paris's Galeries Lafayette; the level of customer service is lower for the designer's Home and Bedding lines marketed through Macy's and Dillard's.[14]

The Size of the Company

The size of the company plays a role in its marketing channel objectives. A large organization such as Coach, facing competition from other handbag and leather goods manufacturers, is able to offer customers a free rebinding service for the leather trim of its handbags and briefcases for the life of the product. The owner simply takes the product to the store, where it is then sent to the manufacturer, and after a while, the freshly bound item comes back to the customer free of charge. A smaller manufacturer or one on foreign soil would be hard put to duplicate this service.

External Marketing Factors

External marketing factors also influence channel objectives. In times of economic downturn, companies tend to utilize the shortest channels of distribution and offer fewer services in the hope of lowering costs.[15] Take the accessories and gift shop owner who found that the costs of rent and employee wages were mounting when store revenue was not. She decided to change her marketing channel, close the store, and move her business to a Web site. As a result, her operating costs dropped dramatically at the same time her sales rose, because on the Internet she was reaching a far greater target market than she ever could in her single store location.

Storms, floods, and acts of extreme violence can have an effect on how well channel members are able to meet contract deadlines. For example, suppose a blizzard or hurricane keeps trucks from delivering goods to warehouses and stores for a week, disrupting the efficiency of the distribution system and causing retailers to lose sales. Channels need to be prepared to deal with unexpected external factors.

DETERMINING DISTRIBUTION INTENSITY

The type of product being marketed influences the selection and intensity of a company's distribution channels. Some fashion organizations want their marketers and products to be exclusive, others want their products to be available for comparison with the competition, and still others want their goods to be found in as many locations as possible. Note the various levels of distribution intensity in Figure 10.13.

Exclusive Distribution Strategy

Luxury fashion brands are marketed through short channels. Burberry, Jimmy Choo, and Louis Vuitton use the Internet to reach customers directly, sell in their own stores, or sell to a very few retailers

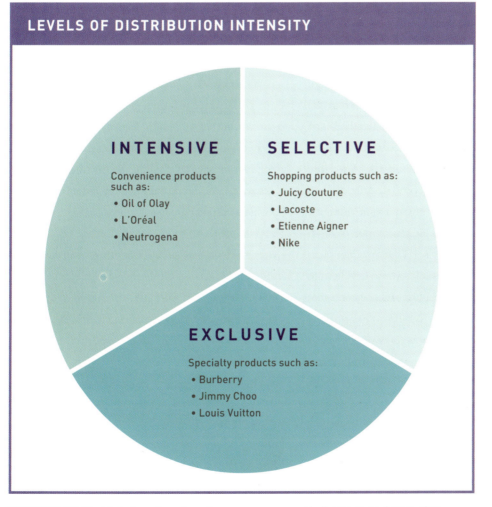

LEVELS OF DISTRIBUTION INTENSITY

INTENSIVE

Convenience products such as:
- Oil of Olay
- L'Oréal
- Neutrogena

SELECTIVE

Shopping products such as:
- Juicy Couture
- Lacoste
- Etienne Aigner
- Nike

EXCLUSIVE

Specialty products such as:
- Burberry
- Jimmy Choo
- Louis Vuitton

FIGURE 10.13 The kind of goods and services consumers want indicates to marketers what intensity of distribution to use for their products. BY VANESSA HAN AND ALICIA FREILE

that are expert in showing customers just how the product enhances their lifestyles. Marketers of products such as designer apparel, Rolex watches, Cartier fine jewelry, and Bentley or Mercedes-Benz automobiles choose a marketing strategy known as **exclusive distribution** using one or just a few retailers in a given area. Exclusive distribution is suitable for expensive goods that are purchased infrequently and that may require detailed information along with personal attention and service to help customers in their purchase decision.

Selective Distribution Strategy

When marketing goods that need some explanation or that customers want to compare with similar goods, marketers often choose a **selective distribution** strategy. Popularly priced apparel such as Juicy Couture and Lacoste, accessories such as Echo neckwear and Etienne Aigner handbags, and home furnishings and accessories such as the Martha Stewart collections are marketed using selective distribution, as are many televisions, cell phones, and computers. In seeking out shopping goods, customers frequently want to take the time to visit Web sites and competing stores to compare product features, styles, and price.

Intensive Distribution Strategy

For relatively inexpensive products that consumers buy frequently (magazines, lip gloss, soft drinks, or paper cups) and that do not need to be explained, marketers use an **intensive distribution** strategy that places their products in many locations. Some skin care and cosmetics fashion brands such as Maybelline, L'Oréal, and Neutrogena make use of intensive distribution so that consumers will find the products in a variety of shopping venues, including supermarkets, drug and discount outlets, and convenience stores.

DEALING WITH COMPETITION

It is no news that fashion operates in a competitive environment. For many businesses it is essential that their new looks be the first on the market. The whole concept of "fast fashion" practiced by organizations such as Zara, H&M, Forever 21, and

FIGURE 10.14 When one company acquires another, it often increases its marketing channels, as happened with Shiseido when it acquired Bare Escentuals.

Uniqlo, where design, production, and marketing are coordinated into one system created to bring new goods to consumers as swiftly as possible, is based on beating the competition to the marketplace. While large companies such as Walmart have an edge because of their vast size and low cost structures, smaller marketers (everyone else) can seek out channel strategies that will work for them and help keep costs down. For example, smaller fashion goods marketers may work with independent *freight forwarders*—that is, businesses that consolidate shipments from various sources—and obtain lower transportation costs.

Channel Management

When companies decide on the most useful marketing channels for their purposes, they first select, then motivate, and continually evaluate their choices.

SELECTING CHANNEL MEMBERS

When the U.S. Time Company first introduced its inexpensive Timex watches, the company approached fine jewelry stores to carry the product line, but these stores were not interested in carrying lower-priced watches next to their pricier lines. The company then turned to mass merchandisers and succeeded in placing the Timex brand there. The results could not have been better, because at the time, mass merchandising outlets were growing rapidly.16 More recently, the Japanese cosmetics firm Shiseido Co. Ltd. purchased the mineral makeup company Bare Escentuals, Inc., partly in order to

increase Shiseido's own marketing channels. Bare Escentuals products are offered through a number of marketing channels, including moderate-priced department and specialty stores such as Ulta and Sephora, TV shopping, and the company's own stand-alone boutiques.17 Shiseido now has access to these channels as well as its existing ones such as Nordstrom.

MOTIVATING CHANNEL MEMBERS

Fashion marketers motivate their channel members in a number of ways. Some of these are helping foot some advertising costs in local media, offering sales training seminars to intermediaries, and arranging for special events to promote their brands, such as celebrity appearances by Sarah Jessica Parker, Beyoncé, Karl Lagerfeld, and others. These activities can draw attention to the marketer's newest products, raise sales, and engender enthusiasm among channel members as well as final customers.

EVALUATING CHANNEL MEMBERS

One of the businesses keeping close watch on its marketing channels is Walmart. In order to maximize efficiency, one of Walmart's major suppliers, Procter & Gamble (P&G), decided to set up an office near Walmart's corporate headquarters and purchasing department in Bentonville, Arkansas. With a wide range of its products including detergents (Tide, Cheer), deodorants (Old Spice, Secret), and shampoos (Head & Shoulders, Pantene) being sold in Walmart stores, P&G felt it could best oversee its marketing channel partnership with Walmart from

FIGURE 10.15 Marketing channel promotions may include celebrity endorsements of fashionable products.

a close proximity. Whenever a P&G item sells in Walmart stores, an electronic replenishment system ensures the prompt delivery of new stock, creating greater efficiency, lowering costs, and increasing customer satisfaction. A smoothly operating plan and constant supervision maintain this system.[18]

Marketing Logistics and Supply Chain Management

For marketing channels to justify their existence, they must ensure a continual flow of products to consumers. To accomplish this goal, organizations work to make certain that products are ready, shipped, stored, and made available when, where, and in the quantity that customers demand. The activities involved here are known as **marketing logistics** (or *physical distribution*); they include planning, initiating, and controlling the physical flow of products from producers to consumers. Marketing logistics activities are conducted by one or a series of businesses, which form a **supply chain.** A supply chain differs from a marketing channel in terms of the companies involved. Supply chain firms are engaged in moving products to intermediaries and consumers.[19] A marketing channel includes other facilitating organizations such as financial institutions and insurance companies. Supply chains are concerned with *outbound distribution*, the flow of goods from the point of origin to the consumer, plus *inbound distribution*, moving materials and products from suppliers to the manufacturing company, and *reverse distribution*, the return of unwanted, surplus, or broken goods by intermediaries or consumers to the producer.[20] (See Figures 10.16a and b.)

Effective supply chain management, aided by today's technology, enables businesses to coordinate worldwide planning, sourcing, and delivery, and to cultivate profitable long-term customer relationships.

THE ROLE OF MARKETING LOGISTICS IN THE SUPPLY CHAIN

Marketers in general, not the least among them fashion marketers, are closely scrutinizing logistics today largely because opportunities exist in this area to lower costs. While product and selling costs remain high to maintain quality, logistics costs can often be trimmed with little or no negative outcome. For example, a producer might combine many small shipments into one load sent at a far lower cost than shipping each order individually. Automated merchandise replenishment systems permit retailers never to be out of basic Levi's jeans or Jockey underwear, thus saving sales otherwise lost. Using the Internet, logistics systems can electronically receive and fill orders, track shipments, handle finances, and transfer information swiftly and inexpensively.

The purpose of marketing logistics is to provide customers with the level of service that they want and a cost they are willing to pay. A high-volume discount retail chain may want weekly warehouse

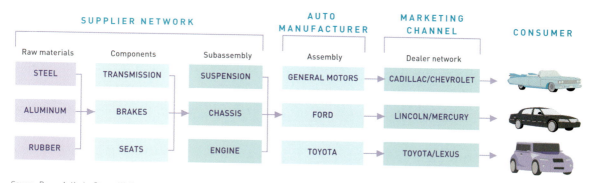

Source: Roger A. Kerin, Steven W. Hartley, and William Rudelius, *Marketing The Core 4/e*, McGraw-Hill Irwin, 2011, p.302, fig. 13-8.

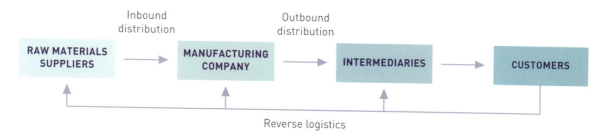

Source: Gary Armstrong and Philip Kotler, *Marketing: An Introduction*, 10th edition (Prentice Hall, 2011), p. 328, figure 10.5.

FIGURE 10.16 Marketing channels use logistics in creating supply chains. BY VANESSA HAN AND ALICIA FREILE

deliveries of T-shirts, while a small specialty store finds that once or perhaps twice a season is most suitable for its customers. Because of the volume ordered, the large retailer sustains a higher delivery cost, but the ability to sell more T-shirts justifies the cost of the more frequent deliveries.

MARKETING LOGISTICS ACTIVITIES

Supply chain managers work to provide logistics systems that meet the levels of service at the cost each customer is willing to incur. The major marketing logistics systems activities include transportation, warehousing and storage, inventory management, and information processing.

Transportation

Marketers choose among the various methods of transportation that suit the product and the needs of the customer. For fashion goods, common transportation methods used are motor vehicles, railroads, water carriers, and airways. (Another

FIGURE 10.17 Motor vehicles are the most popular way of transporting goods domestically.

method of transportation—pipelines—used mainly for oil, gas, and chemicals, doesn't quite work for fashion goods.)

Motor vehicles carry the largest amount of goods in tonnage and value. Each year around $8.4 trillion in goods are transported domestically approximately 1.4 trillion ton-miles, amounting to 42 percent of all goods shipped. Trucks are useful for shipping fashion products, including furniture, clothing, and electronics, due to their advantages (door-to-door delivery and flexible scheduling) over other transportation modes. Increasingly, shippers make use of **intermodal transportation**, combining more than one type of transportation, such as truck and train or ship. Intermodal transportation is possible because of **containerization**, shipping goods in standard containers (up to 80 feet long) that do not need to be opened from point of origin to destination, thus avoiding the possibilities of damage or theft. The contents are left sealed en route (including passing through Customs) because **radio frequency identification (RFID)** chips—tiny electronic chips that can be scanned with special equipment to provide detailed information about the product at any point throughout the supply chain—are placed on the goods at the factory and remain attached throughout the trip to the retailer.

Railroads are used for long-distance movement of many commodities such as coal, grain, livestock, heavy manufactured goods including automobiles, perishables carried in refrigerated cars.. Some furniture and apparel move via rail, particularly cross country and other long distances. Travel by rail is said to be ten times less polluting than motor vehicle transport.

MARKETER'S INSIGHT:
TRANSPORTATION: DEFEATING THE DEADHEAD DOWNER

A condition that for years has cut deeply into the profits of truckers and shippers is known as *deadheading*. It happens when a truck has delivered goods to its destination and then is forced to return home empty, without any paying cargo. Deadheading is highly unprofitable because it wastes truckers' time, shippers' money, and contributes needlessly to air pollution. And the trucking industry estimates that more than 25 percent of all trucks traveling home are deadheads.

Now, industry has its eye on the problem and is working to alleviate it. A number of large retailers, truckers, and manufacturers are developing a program called Empty Miles, designed to share information on trucking routes, create a system that identifies goods ready to be shipped, and put those goods onto otherwise empty trucks. The program is under the auspices of the Voluntary Interindustry Commerce Solutions Agency (VICS), a non-profit organization made up of major corporations. With the price of diesel fuel high, growing public interest in business demonstrating sustainability, and deadheading often meaning the difference between profit and loss, VICS was created with one of its purposes being to develop a more efficient supply chain for consumer goods.

In cooperation with GS1 US, the group that created the barcode, VICS put a portal in place where trucking companies and shipping organizations such as Levi Strauss, JCPenney, and Macy's can display their empty truck routes. While some companies needed to install new technology to take part, the overall cost of access to the Empty Miles Web site is only $1,600 annually. One problem, however, is that companies traditionally prefer not to divulge their shipping routes in case they inadvertently expose trade secrets to competitors. The fact that large companies such as Macy's are taking part helps to alleviate the fears of others. In addition, the Web site hides company names until negotiation is complete in order to prevent trucking companies from contacting shippers unnecessarily.

Although the system is young, it shows promise of substantial savings. A shipper usually pays for a round trip, even if the return is deadhead. When other shippers can be found to pay the return trip, the companies save money. Macy's has already found 70 shippers for its 328 empty routes and estimates an annual savings of $25,000 a year for each empty truck route used by another shipper. Officials at Schneider National report that in less than two years the large trucking company has saved more than 5,500 gallons of diesel fuel and reduced carbon dioxide emissions by just under 62 tons. Programs such as Empty Miles, reducing deadheading, work to lower costs and make the entire supply chain more efficient.

Adapted from: Ken Belson, "Keeping Trucks Full, Coming and Going," *New York Times*, April 22, 2010, p. F2.

FIGURE 10.18 Intermodal transportation reduces the risk of damage or theft when goods are shipped in containers and contents recorded by RFID.

Water carriers ply the oceans and the rivers and bring large quantities of imported goods. Fashion goods made in China and other Asian countries—including electronics, home furnishings, moderately priced apparel, and accessories for women, men, and children—travel on container ships to Los Angeles and Long Beach, California, the world's largest port system. Large container ships can carry up to 5,000 containers, and super container ships can hold up to 15,000 containers.[21] On arrival, they pass through Customs and then (through intermodal transportation) are loaded onto trucks or trains for delivery across the nation. In comparison with other transportation modes, marine shipping is relatively low cost; commodities such as sand and gravel travel inexpensively along the nation's many coastal waterways and rivers.

Airways are the most expensive method of transportation and are used for costly and perishable fashion goods: designer apparel, fine jewelry, fine leather handbags, shoes, and fresh flowers. Designer gowns and accessories from Europe and Asia destined for high-end stores such as Bergdorf Goodman and Neiman Marcus are habitually shipped via air transport. Again, intermodal transportation plays a part when airfreight is transferred to motor vehicles. Companies such as FedEx and J.B. Hunt are major players in combining transportation modes.[22]

Warehousing and Storage

The purpose of a profitable supply chain and effective logistics system is to have goods accessible to consumers just before they ask for them. This includes receiving, storing, sorting, and reassembling for delivery to retailers.[23] To stay profitable, marketers want to store goods for as short a time as possible. They locate their warehouses at optimum distances from where the goods will be sold or shipped. Walmart plans its warehouse locations to be no farther than 200 miles from its stores. In fact, a number of companies rename their warehouses, calling them *distribution centers* or *retail support centers.* The idea is that goods will not stay around for any length of time. Again, Walmart, an industry leader in supply chain management, practices a *cross-docking system* at its warehouses. Here, large shipments coming into one dock of the warehouse are swiftly broken down into smaller quantities and assortments for individual stores, moved across the warehouse, and loaded in trucks bound for regional Walmart stores.

Inventory Management

Managing the inventory means maintaining an assortment of goods to fulfill store requirements and meet customer needs. If warehouses contain too many items, the inventories risk damage and theft, and what's worse for fashion goods: obsolescence. If too few goods are on hand, stores risk *stockouts,* lost sales due to lack of merchandise. The goal of inventory management is to keep an adequate amount of merchandise on hand; this calls for appropriate assortment buying and delivery timing.[24] For further information on this topic, see Chapter 11, "Fashion Wholesaling and Retailing."

Information Processing

Receiving merchandise orders, locating the goods, and tracking their shipment to the retailer are the main functions of information processing in the logistics of physical distribution. **Order processing**—that is, receiving and transmitting information concerning merchandise orders such as quantity, style, and price—consists of three related activities: order entry, order handling, and order delivery.[25] Today, computerized systems have largely replaced paper documents. One of these systems is electronic data interchange (EDI), introduced in Chapter 2, which transmits the information needed for order entry such as style numbers, quantity, and delivery instructions. EDI messages can be read by computers and are usually sent on private company networks or *intranets.* Large organizations such as Target use EDI extensively.[26]

Another electronic order processing method introduced in Chapter 2 is Quick Response (QR), a system used by VF Corporation and other large manufacturers with their large quantity of retail customers. Let's follow a customer buying a pair of

FIGURE 10.19 Electronic technology greatly speeds up order processing at home and around the world.

Wrangler jeans at a local Walmart. Through Quick Response, the sales transaction is recorded not only at the store but also at the Walmart buying office and the Wrangler factory. And it's not just the fact that a pair of jeans was sold, but the style number, size, color, and other pertinent information are electronically transmitted to the manufacturer, which can then put the replenishment process into action, creating and furnishing additional jeans of that style, thus making sure that the retailer experiences no stockouts of this item.

With logistics activities appropriately coordinated, supply chain management can aim to function effectively, supplying consumers with desired goods and balancing distribution costs with the levels of service intermediaries require.

WHAT DO YOU THINK?

What do fashion marketers gain by paying attention to supply chain management and logistics in particular? How do consumers benefit?

Global Marketing Channels

Businesses grow by finding more customers. They may begin by expanding into new markets in their own country as many, including Macy's, JCPenney, and Nordstrom, among others, have done. When domestic markets become saturated—as is the case with a number of large corporations such as Coca-Cola, Holiday Inn, and IBM—management looks for expansion possibilities in other parts of the world. Today, in fact, companies such as these derive more

of their income from overseas operations than domestically, through direct investments in internationally located businesses, and through **exporting**, or marketing their products in other countries.

SOME EXAMPLES OF GLOBAL CHANNELS

Fashion marketing is a global endeavor, not only for U.S. businesses but for companies in Europe and Asia, as fashion customers live almost anywhere in the world. Some businesses engage in *international marketing*, selling products in other countries through marketing channels similar to those used domestically. Williams-Sonoma supplies cooking utensils, tabletop furnishings, and home decorations to its Canadian retail stores this way.[27] Other companies participate in *multinational marketing* activities, forming marketing channels specifically for each country and at times for particular product classifications. For example, the Giorgio Armani organization is developing several new marketing channels including opening A/X Exchange stores in Brazil, China, India, and Eastern Europe; operating a luxury hotel in Dubai; signing an exclusive agreement with Macy's to promote the Armani Jeans line in the retailer's U.S. stores; and creating a men's and women's activewear collection with Reebok to be sold in Reebok and Emporio Armani stores.[28]

Chanel is opening stores in China, Vietnam, Lebanon, and Turkey, in addition to its present locations throughout the world. The fashion marketer is also lengthening its supply chain by acquiring some of its suppliers, such as the embroidery company Lesage and the feather-maker Lemarié, in order not only to preserve the couture process but also to locate

FIGURE 10.20 Michael Kors has stores worldwide, including one in Paris that opened in 2011.

finer (harder to duplicate) materials for its handbags and garments to discourage counterfeiting.[29] Among its many ventures, Calvin Klein, while marketing its namesake better label to stores in the United States, Canada, and Mexico (as well as other products overseas), is expanding its more popularly priced G-III Calvin Klein brand of women's suits, dresses, sportswear, and outerwear to Lord & Taylor stores domestically before considering additional markets.[30]

Many fashion designers and marketers develop overseas channels either by opening their own shops and boutiques or by establishing distribution agreements with intermediaries. Recently, Marc Jacobs opened stores in Madrid, London, and Bahrain. Tory Burch set up boutiques in Japan and the Philippines, London, and Rome. Oscar de la Renta formed a partnership with Retail Arabia International to operate signature shops in Qatar, Saudi Arabia, and the United Arab Emirates. Kate Spade signed an agreement with Kate Spade Japan, a distribution partner, to open shops throughout Japan and other Asian markets including Hong Kong and Mainland China.[31]

HOW GLOBAL FASHION CHANNELS AND SUPPLY CHAINS SERVE CONSUMERS

Large marketing organizations such as Target, Gap, and Nike forge strong supply chains to meet customer needs. Among the most adept supply chain managers are the fast-fashion organizations including Sweden's H&M, Spain's Zara, and Japan's Uniqlo. The secret to Zara's success is the company's close control over its global marketing channels through its corporate vertical marketing system, ownership of supply chain members including the design, production, and distribution segments. Zara also divides up its sourcing, ordering basic products from China with a four- to six-month lead time (similar to competitors) and obtaining fashion-forward merchandise in Spain near headquarters with a two-week lead time. Zara also believes the expense of air freight for fast-fashion goods is worth the cost to speed distribution to its worldwide stores.[32] Zara and other savvy fashion marketers are able to anticipate global consumer fashion desires and respond rapidly with suitable products because of coordinated supply chain management aided by today's advanced technology. In addition to EDI and QR, other technologies (as described in Chapter 2) include *computer-aided design (CAD)*, which transmits design styles and details around the world instantaneously; *computer-aided manufacturing (CAM)*, which includes computerized sewing, patternmaking, and cutting machines; and *computer-integrated manufacturing (CIM)*, which links the entire design and manufacturing process.[33] With the use of technology, efficient marketing channels and supply chains can provide consumers with the goods they want when and where they want them, striving to hold down costs in order to maintain the profitability of the fashion marketing organization.

Ethics, Law, and Social Responsibility in Marketing Channels

In order to remain in business and maintain goodwill, fashion channels work to eliminate conflicts, as described earlier, and to avoid conditions that restrict business. Some of the situations that can arise, requiring the attention of management, involve ethics, the law, and a company's responsibilities to society.

ETHICS AND LAW IN CHANNEL MANAGEMENT

The kinds of ethical and legal situations that may come up for channel members include the following:

▶ *Dual distribution*: Marketing the same line through competing channels such as through a retail store and over the Internet. It happens all the time and is part of doing business, but channel members need to be informed.

▶ *Restricted sales territories or outlets*: Either the geographical area or the retail outlets permitted to sell a line are limited by the marketer. For example, luxury watch manufacturer Omega wants to restrict discount retailer Costco from carrying the brand in its stores, a case that went all the way to the Supreme Court.[34]

▶ *Tying agreements*: Sources demanding that in order for retailers to carry popular items, they must also buy less marketable goods. This practice is illegal.

MARKETER'S INSIGHT:
WHERE ARE THE CUSTOMERS FOR UNSOLD GOODS?

Unlike most firms with the word "bank" in their titles, the New York Clothing Bank is not in the business of lending money; rather it is a non-profit organization whose goal is to distribute clothing and other goods to those who need them. This bank came about when its founder, Suzanne Davis, appealed to a friend for leftover goods that could be given to homeless men. Her friend happened to be Larry Phillips, president of apparel marketer Phillips-Van Heusen. A little while later, the company shipped 100 boxes of windbreakers to be used by the homeless.

The word got around among apparel marketers, and soon London Fog sent 750 trench coats, and Jockey shipped off a supply of underwear. As Davis remarked, "All of this merchandise they weren't going to sell, so what were they going to do with it?"

As more companies learned about the project, manufacturer and retailer donations began to pour in, amounting currently to $10 million annually. By this time, Davis was able to set up a warehouse in Brooklyn, and a JCPenney executive installed an inventory procedure. Among the goods in the warehouse during a typical week might be quantities of women's sweaters, boys' coats, and girls' blouses.

Still, many fashion marketers everywhere go on destroying clothing needed by someone. A graduate student in New York found that one H&M store was cutting up unsold apparel and throwing it out with the trash. When the fast-fashion retailer's headquarters learned of this, it stated that company practice is to donate unsold inventory. Why would some businesses continue to destroy new garments? There are a number of reasons, among them that stores do not care to see people coming into the store wearing discarded garments, or worse yet, trying to return them for credit. Prestige fashion businesses do not care to see the brands (on which they've spent millions of dollars to create and market) worn by the poor.

The tax deductible donations, however, are valuable not just to the recipients. Like a commercial bank, the New York Clothing Bank protects its assets carefully. Established practices keep the warehouse and its contents secure. The building is guarded to prevent theft; labels are removed from garments to preserve company image; and the goods are sent only to non-profit organizations and never to individuals. In addition to the donor companies mentioned, other companies that participate in the program include Macy's, Gap, and Toys "R" Us.

Adapted from: Jim Dwyer, "Where Unsold Clothes Meet the People Who Need Them," *New York Times*, January 10, 2010, p. 33.

▶ *Exclusive agreements*: Banning competing retailers from selling the brand. In fashion, exclusivity is an important factor in marketing prestige and highly popular items. It is the custom for large or prestigious retail organizations with sufficient buying power to negotiate with suppliers to limit specific styles to their trading area for a certain time.[35]

SOCIAL RESPONSIBILITY

Fashion marketers realize that consumers today want to buy from businesses that demonstrate strong ethical principals and good citizenship by assuming responsibility for sustaining a sound environment and society's well-being. Increasingly, marketers are demonstrating social responsibility, including Walmart's plan to power its operations 100 percent by renewable energy and to create zero waste; Eileen Fisher's grants to nonprofit organizations in local communities; and various manufacturers donating surplus goods to the homeless. (See Marketer's Insight, "Where Are the Customers for Unsold Goods.")

In 2010, for the fourth year in a row, Gap, Inc. was awarded the "World's Most Ethical Company" in specialty retailing by the Ethisphere Institute, an international research organization. Best Buy, IKEA, and Target were also among the winners. As one of its activities, Gap collected 270,000 pairs of old jeans to be turned into cotton fiber for insulating 500 homes in underserved communities. Another of Gap's activities was to provide education and training for women textile workers in India to help them move ahead in their careers. These and other activities placed Gap on the 100 Best Corporate Citizens list, published by *Corporate Responsibility* magazine.[36]

Summary

Marketing channels consist of individual businesses that help make products available to consumers. They include intermediaries such as retailers and wholesalers, plus businesses such as financial institutions and transportation companies that help facilitate the marketing process. Marketing channels exist to accomplish certain tasks such as assuming the selling duties of a small manufacturer that cannot afford its own sales force. Direct fashion marketing channels reach out to consumers without intermediaries. Indirect marketing channels are of various lengths, depending on the needs of the market and the resources of the fashion marketer. Some marketing channels are conventional, each member working independently. More organized channels tend to be more efficient and may be set up as corporate, contractual, or administered systems. In order to reach a range of target markets, many fashion organizations today practice multi-channel marketing.

In selecting channels, fashion marketers first analyze consumer demand and then determine channel goals, based first on the level of service their customers want, but taking into consideration the size of the company and external marketing factors such as the state of the economy. In determining how heavily to saturate the market, fashion organizations have a choice of exclusive, selective, or intensive distribution strategies, based on the nature of their products. In marketing channel management, fashion marketers select, motivate, and evaluate channel members in a continuing process to maximize customer service and profitability. To make certain a constant flow of goods reaches consumers, fashion marketers carefully monitor the logistics, or physical distribution, of their goods. Marketing logistics are conducted by businesses that become part of a supply chain—organizations that plan, create, and move goods to consumers. Supply chains differ from marketing channels in that the latter contain facilitating organizations such as banks and businesses that make buying and selling easier. Marketing logistics activities include transportation, warehousing, storage, inventory management, and information processing.

Many fashion organizations engage in global marketing. Some of the most visible are fast-fashion companies such as Forever 21, H&M, Uniqlo, and Zara, whose retail stores are found throughout the world. The success of these organizations is attributable to their efficient and coordinated marketing channels. Businesses today realize that customers want to patronize those organizations that give something back to the community, and many fashion companies practice acts of social responsibility, such as Gap's helping textile workers in India advance in their careers and a number of U.S. apparel manufacturers donating surplus clothing to organizations for the homeless.

Coach Expands Its Marketing Channels

Coach, an American accessories giant, recently decided to expand its marketing channels further beyond its borders. Already established in Asia, Coach decided to enter into a partnership with France's renowned department store Printemps. In addition, Coach was forming an agreement with Hackett, Ltd., a British men's wear company, to distribute Coach products in the United Kingdom, Ireland, Spain, and Portugal. The company sees its expansion into Europe as a real opportunity for growth. "We really see a multichannel distribution approach throughout the key western European markets," noted Ian Bickley, president of Coach, Inc.'s international division. Also on the list for expansion are Italy and Germany, stated Bickley in an interview.

Coach was aiming for a 3 percent market share in the area within the next five years. The company estimates that the brand accounts for 25 percent of the world's luxury handbag and accessories business, with the United States and Japan contributing half of that total. The price range of Coach, the equivalent of around $300 to $900 in local currency, also fills a void in the European market. Although the brand is not well known in Europe and prominent logos are not as important as in the United States and Japan, Coach management believes that customers there recognize the value for the price.

According to the distribution agreement in France, Printemps was placing a shop-within-a-shop in 14 of its department stores throughout France. In the Paris Boulevard Haussmann store, a special shop on the first floor offers Coach products for women and men. In addition to handbags, other items include small leather goods, outerwear, scarves, jewelry, and travel accessories. The décor consists of white paneled walls, fixtures in nickel and lacquer, antique furnishings, and walnut floors. In addition, Printemps planned to have branch stores offer Coach goods in the French cities of Rouen, Lille, and Deauville.

Coach, a U.S. company formed in 1941, began overseas marketing in 1988 after noticing many Japanese consumers shopping in its New York and Seattle stores. Signing a distribution agreement with the Mitsukoshi department store organization seemed appropriate. And it was. Business grew, and today Coach estimates that in Japan, it is the second largest importer of high-end handbags and accessories, with a 14 percent market share and significant brand awareness. Newer marketing channels for Coach include China, with an estimated 3 percent market share, as well as emerging plans for representation in Korea, Taiwan, and Malaysia.

Adapted from: Miles Socha, "Taking Coach to Europe: Brand Inks Major Deals for France and the U.K.," *Women's Wear Daily*, April 20, 2010, pp. 1, 13.

QUESTIONS

1. What is your impression of the likelihood of success for the new marketing channels that Coach was opening up in France? What elements should contribute to their success? What might be improved?

2. In addition to plans for expanding further into China and other East Asian countries, what other countries or regions would you suggest for Coach to expand its distribution? What problems might Coach encounter threatening its marketing channels?

KEY TERMS

administered marketing systems

agents and brokers

channel conflict

containerization

contractual marketing system

conventional marketing channel

corporate vertical marketing system

direct marketing channel

exclusive distribution

exporting

franchise

indirect marketing channel

intensive distribution

intermediaries

intermodal transportation

marketing channel

marketing logistics

merchant wholesaler

multi-channel marketing

order processing

radio frequency identification (RFID)

retailer

sales representative

selective distribution

supply chain

vertical marketing system (VMS)

REVIEW QUESTIONS

1. Define marketing channels and state their purpose.
2. Explain how fashion marketing channels are organized, and cite three initial decisions managers must make.
3. State the difference between marketing channels and supply chains.
4. Describe the key role of logistics and its activities in supply chain management.
5. Cite two examples each of fashion marketers' participation in developing channels for global marketing and in assuming social responsibility.

DISCUSSION ACTIVITIES AND PROJECTS

1. Think of a well-known fashion marketing organization such as Donna Karan, Nike, Zappos, or one of your choice, and explain how the marketing channels it uses influence the marketing mix.
2. Mark Hamilton and Tony Guerrero have a small gift shop in a trendy and expensive urban shopping area. The items they offer—home décor accessories, small leather goods, scarves, jewelry, and designer furniture and outfits for pets—sell well, but the costs of running the retail store (particularly salespeople's wages and rent) are continually rising. What three or four alternative marketing channels might you suggest to eliminate the high operating costs?

3. You have decided to market your own line of custom-made shirts. Explain how you would go about reaching major decisions concerning your selection of channels, including analyzing customer demand, establishing channel goals and distribution intensity, and dealing with the competition.

4. You and several classmates are a team in charge of shipping for a large European organization marketing cashmere sweaters for men and women. Although cashmere apparel does sell almost year-round in the United States, the biggest selling season is the fall, with the season's new fashion looks and Christmas both on the calendar. The luxury brands are produced in Scotland, but most sweaters come from China. This year, production there has been slow. One cause was a severe earthquake that hit a major Chinese manufacturing center in March, but it is now August, and production is finally restored to normal. The problem is that regular marine shipping takes 8 weeks or so to reach U.S. retailer customers, which will only buy sweaters from now through December. Explain what you would do to solve this logistics problem, and state the effect this emergency has on the entire supply chain.

5. Search the Internet for the home page or official Web site of two well-known fashion organizations not described in the text for the purpose of determining their company's participation in programs demonstrating social responsibility. Report your findings to the class.

DEVELOPING YOUR MARKETING PLAN

As you turn your attention to the "place" element of the marketing mix, think about the product you have selected and determine the major participants in its marketing channels:

1. Does the company use a vertical marketing system? If so, describe it.

2. Explain the decisions management faces concerning consumer demand, company goals, and distribution intensity.

3. Explain the role of logistics in the supply chain for your product.

Refer to the Marketing Plan Outline, Table 1.2, at the end of Chapter 1, as well as Appendix A: Sample Marketing Plan.

REFERENCES

1. Gary Armstrong and Philip Kotler, *Marketing: An Introduction,* 9th ed. (Upper Saddle River, NJ: Pearson Prentice Hall, 2009), p. 294.

2. Charles W. Lamb and Joseph F. Hair Jr., and Carl McDaniel, *MKTG 4,* (Mason, OH: South-Western Publishing Company, 2010), p. 197.

3. William M. Pride and O. C. Ferrell, *Marketing*, 14th ed., (Boston: Houghton Mifflin Company, 2008), p. 405.

4. Op cit., p. 294.

5. Ibid., p. 295.

6. Rosemary Feitberg, "Mix and Match," *Women's Wear Daily Magic Supplement to Women's Wear Daily.* February 7, 2010, p. 8.

7. Op cit., p. 297.

8. Roger A. Kerin, Steven W. Hartley, and William Rudelius, *Marketing: The Core,* 2nd ed., (Boston: McGraw-Hill/Irwin, 2007), p. 289.

9. Op cit., p. 296.

10. Ibid., p. 298.

11. *R L –09,* Polo Ralph Lauren Corporation Annual Report, 2009, p. 13.

12. Nike website http://www.nikeinc.com (accessed March 8, 2012).

13. Women's Wear Daily Staff. "The Multi-Channel Road Map to Fashion," *Women's Wear Daily,* December 30, 2009, pp. 8–10.

14. Ibid., p. 8.

15. Op cit., p. 306.

16. Ibid., p. 309.

17. Molly Prior, "A New Beauty Deal: Smashbox Cosmetics Said in Play," *Women's Wear Daily,* April 27, 2010, pp. 1, 8.

18. Op cit., p. 416.

19. Op cit., p. 297.

20. Op cit., p. 311.

21. Len Lewis, "Delivering the World: Navigating Obstacles in Pursuit of Global Supply Chain Optimization," *Stores,* February 2010, pp. S4–S6.

22. Bureau of Transportation Statistics, Research and Innovative Technology Administration (RITA), U.S. Department of Transportation "http://www.bts.gov" www.bts.gov (accessed March 8, 2012).

23. Op cit., p. 446.

24. Ibid., p. 444.

25. Ibid., p. 442.

26. Op cit., p. 220.

27. Harvey R. Shoemack and Patricia Mink Rath, *Essentials of Exporting and Importing: U.S. Trade Policies, Procedures, and Practices* (New York: Fairchild Books. 2010), p. 274.

28. "What Now!" *Women's Wear Daily,* May 5, 2010, p. 8.

29. Ibid.

30. Ibid., p. 11.

31. Kristi Ellis, "Challenges and Opportunities," *Women's Wear Daily,* January 28, 2010, p. 15.

32. Op cit., p. S5.

33. Elaine Stone, *The Dynamics of Fashion,* 3rd ed. (New York: Fairchild Books, 2008), p. 564.

34. Kristi Ellis, "Supreme Court to Hear Costco-Omega Case," *Women's Wear Daily,* April 20, 2010, p. 3.

35. Op cit., p. 513.

36. Heidi Malhotra, "Gap's Social Responsibility Driving Retail Growth," The Epoch Times, May 3, 2010, http://www.theepochtimes.com/n2/business/gaps-social-responsibility-driving-retail-growth-34620.html (accessed March 8, 2012).

CHAPTER 11

Fashion Wholesaling and Retailing

This chapter focuses on the different types of wholesalers and retailers operating in the fashion marketplace today, examining their roles in the supply chain, how they help deliver goods and services to consumers, and what they contribute to the marketing environment.

WHAT DO I NEED TO KNOW ABOUT FASHION WHOLESALING AND RETAILING?

* The services fashion wholesalers provide to manufacturers and retailers
* How merchant wholesalers and agents differ from each other
* The different ways retail store organizations can be classified
* What non-store retailing and multi-channel retailing mean
* Some ways in which fashion retailers are addressing environmental concerns

FASHION MARKETING IN FOCUS:
Getting Fashion to Fashion Consumers

To be able to shop for fashions at any time of the day or night—whether you're browsing at the mall or sitting at home in your PJs—is a fashionista's dream come true. And in today's world, that dream is clearly a reality.

Maybe you're dying to have the look you just saw Rihanna wearing in a new photo on her Facebook fan page, but you know none of the stores in your town would carry the style and you don't have time to travel to the nearest city to shop. Not a problem, because chances are the store can come to you, via the Internet, a smartphone, the television, or even an "old-fashioned" printed catalogue. Or maybe you need a good-looking new sport coat for an upcoming job interview but can't afford to spend a lot of money. Fortunately, there are most likely a half dozen stores (or more) nearby that you can check out in person, comparing prices on a variety of up-to-date styles, feeling the fabric, checking the fit, and making your choice—and perhaps even enjoying some great music or videos that are playing while you shop.

Consumers accessing the enormous selection of products that are readily available today, along with a host of ways to shop for them, would not be possible without two key players in the fashion marketing supply chain: wholesalers and retailers. Both fill a key role in getting fashion goods into consumers' hands, and both are constantly evolving and transforming themselves to keep pace with new trends and forces in the global marketing environment.

ooking back in time, even just a couple of decades, the way fashion marketers distributed their goods and the way consumers acquired them was very different from today. The overwhelming proportion of purchases were made in a physical store; and while customers *could* shop from home, that generally meant browsing through a printed catalogue, placing an order by phone or through the mail, and then waiting sometimes two or three weeks for their purchase to arrive.

Today not only has the Internet transformed the way consumers shop, but technology and advanced systems throughout the supply chain have enabled fashion goods to reach customers in record time,

FIGURE 11.1 Retailers and wholesalers are responsible for helping fashion goods reach consumers, wherever and however they choose to shop.

wherever they choose to purchase them. This transformation has spawned the growth of new types of fashion retailers, and forced traditional retailers to examine their business model and adapt to new trends. It has also created new opportunities for wholesalers of fashion goods to service a growing roster of retailer customers.

Clearly retailers are the fashion businesses with which consumers have the most direct contact; but in many cases, the variety and assortment of goods you see on store shelves and racks are there because of independent wholesalers that facilitate the delivery of products from the manufacturer to the retailer. In this chapter, we'll look at both the wholesaler and the retailer level of the supply chain, exploring how each contributes to the marketing of fashion.

What Is Wholesaling?

As discussed in Chapter 10, most manufacturers do not normally sell directly to consumers, using instead an indirect marketing channel that relies on intermediaries between them and the consumer. A retailer is one such intermediary, but in many cases, there is another entity between the manufacturer and the retailer, as well: the wholesaler.

Wholesaling is defined as all the activities involved in selling goods that are intended for resale or for business use. A **wholesaler**, then, is an enterprise engaged in wholesaling—typically a business that buys large quantities of products from manufacturers and sells them in smaller quantities, for a profit, to various retailers or other resellers, or sometimes to institutional or industrial users. For this reason, a wholesaler is sometimes referred to as a *intermediary* or *middleman*. Because wholesalers do not normally interact with consumers, most of us would not recognize even large wholesalers by name, even when they are selling famous brands to well-known retailers. For example, have you ever heard of Doba? That company name is most likely unfamiliar to you, although you would surely recognize the brands that Doba handles; these include Skechers, Hanes, and Ralph Lauren. (See the Marketer's Insight feature, "Doba Clicks with Online Wholesaling Business.")

WHOLESALERS' ROLE IN FASHION MARKETING

Not all fashions arrive in stores via a wholesaler. Some fashion retailers, such as Zara, Gap, and Forever 21, own their own factories or maintain long-term contracts with their manufacturers to receive goods directly. Other fashion merchants are large enough to buy directly from manufacturers. Walmart, for example, buys Wrangler jeans from that brand's producer, VF Corporation, and Macy's purchases Tommy Hilfiger merchandise straight from the designer's company. Most smaller retailers, however, are not able to obtain merchandise by direct means, so they rely on wholesalers to supply their goods.

The role of wholesalers in the fashion marketplace is an important one—and one that goes well beyond simply "moving boxes" between manufacturers and retailers. Wholesalers often act as partners to the companies they buy from and the stores they sell to, providing key services and facilitating a flow of information as well as merchandise.

They can offer expertise that adds value to the supply chain, and generally perform certain functions more efficiently and cost-effectively than most manufacturers or retailers could on their own.

The extent of a wholesaler's role depends on the specific marketing situation and the individual needs of their supply chain partners. A small retailer, for example, might rely completely on wholesalers to supply the goods it sells in the store, while a retailer large enough to buy directly from vendors might use a wholesaler only for quick fill-ins or for lines it doesn't carry in depth. By the same token, a manufacturer might enter an agreement to sell directly to certain national retail chains, but use a wholesaler to handle sales to individual stores or small regional chains. Overall, however, wholesalers fulfill some or all of these functions:

▶ *Wholesalers help get manufacturers' goods to the widest possible customer base.* Whether they operate on a national or regional level, wholesalers strive to have a thorough knowledge of the markets they serve and to develop relationships with smaller retailers that manufacturers simply don't have the resources to cultivate. A wholesaler's sales force is able to reach many retail customers that would be too costly for manufacturers to contact themselves, or that are too small to purchase in sufficient quantity for the manufacturer to ship to at a reasonable cost.

▶ *Wholesalers are a key informational link in the supply chain.* With the multitude of fashion products continually being introduced, it is not always easy for retailers to keep up with what's new. Wholesalers help by conveying information about available products, trends, promotions, pricing changes, and competitors' activities to their merchant customers. For example, a wholesaler of children's wear might alert its retailer customers that a manufacturer they hadn't previously carried was launching apparel with a hot new movie license they might want to add to their mix. Or an electronics wholesaler might notify its customers when a computer manufacturer was planning a special promotion that bundled a free fashion tote with a laptop purchase, so that retailers could feature the offer to their customers. That sharing of information goes both directions. Because wholesalers work closely with their retailer customers, they get constant feedback on what consumers are looking for and what is selling, and can relay information about consumer preferences back to their manufacturer partners. This feedback can be invaluable to manufacturers in their product planning and other marketing efforts.

▶ *Wholesalers can assist in selecting suitable merchandise assortments for their retail customers.* Some wholesalers offer a specific specialty that their retail customers can count on for filling a niche in the store; other wholesalers carry a wide range of goods, enabling them to be a convenient one-stop shop for their retail partners. For example, a men's wear wholesaler in Chicago specializing in German-made outerwear travels regularly to Germany to select the latest styles. Back home, he displays the collection in his showroom for his Midwest retail store customers. The pre-selected assortment he offers saves time for the retailers and—because of the wholesaler's

FIGURE 11.2 Wholesalers help retailers stay up-to-date on the latest trends and product introductions.

market expertise—provides appealing merchandise for these clients and their customers. Or, an accessories wholesaler might organize seasonal merchandise catalogues featuring a wide array of scarves, gloves, handbags, and other accessories for the company's 18 agents to show boutique owners throughout the country, allowing retailers to select goods appropriate for their customers without having to leave their stores.

▶ *A key function of wholesalers is the warehousing and transporting of goods.* Wholesalers generally maintain local or regional warehouse facilities or distribution centers where they can store goods in large quantities and ship them quickly to retailers as needed. This relieves both manufacturers and retailers of the cost, risk, and responsibility of carrying a large inventory themselves. In addition, wholesalers can generally transport goods at lower prices than their retail customers could obtain on their own. Because most wholesalers carry goods from multiple manufacturers, retailers are also able to place a single order that might include merchandise from a number of different lines, further saving time and cost.

▶ *Many wholesalers provide financing for retailer customers.* To assist their retail partners with cash flow, most wholesalers extend credit to customers, enabling them to purchase goods and pay for them within a designated time period, or sometimes spread their payments over several months. This can be particularly helpful to smaller retailers that may not have the financial resources to prepay an order, or to retailers unable to obtain credit from a bank—which can be a serious problem during recessionary times, even for retail businesses that are considered creditworthy.

▶ *Wholesalers provide continuity of a manufacturer's marketing message.* Over the years, wholesalers have expanded their offerings to become almost like a marketing arm for their manufacturer partners. Manufacturers count on their wholesalers to preserve their marketing message and goals, including restricting sales to certain types of retailers if that is part of the marketing strategy for some or all of the line. For example, a wholesaler representing a prestige fragrance line will not sell it to mass merchants, because they clearly do not fit the company's marketing plan. In addition, some wholesalers train retail sales staff about new products so they can present them accurately to consumers, and some offer merchandising and display assistance as well. Many wholesalers also work with retailers on advertising and special promotions, either passed along from the manufacturer or sometimes created by the wholesaler itself.

WHAT DO YOU THINK?

If you were a wholesaler of fashion accessories, what marketing services would you offer your retail store customers? Would the marketing services you provide large customers such as department stores vary from those you give smaller stores? If so, in what ways would they differ?

TYPES OF WHOLESALERS

In some situations, a manufacturer's own sales office or branch undertakes wholesaling activities by selling directly to retailers or other customers. Large companies such as Levi Strauss, headquartered in

California, maintain showrooms in various cities such as New York and Chicago, where retail buyers may place orders during market weeks or at other times of the year. Other industries, including real estate and insurance, often use *brokers*, a type of wholesaler that negotiates deals between buyers and sellers. Brokers are not prominent in fashion goods marketing, however.

Here we examine the two categories of independent wholesale organizations that are most active in the fashion industry: merchant wholesalers and agents. These types of wholesalers differ from each other based in part on whether or not they take title to the goods they are marketing—that is, whether or not they take actual ownership of the products before reselling them.

FIGURE 11.3 Many wholesalers offer quick shipment of goods from their fully stocked warehouses, relieving retailers and manufacturers of the cost involved in carrying a large inventory.

Merchant Wholesalers

The first and largest group is merchant wholesalers, one of the marketing channel intermediaries you'll recall from Chapter 10. Merchant wholesalers are independent businesses that purchase and usually take physical possession of the goods they are reselling, making their profit by marking up the price. Approximately half of all wholesaling businesses are in this category. Depending on the industry, merchant wholesalers are sometimes called *jobbers* or *distributors*. Importers and exporters are merchant wholesalers that purchase goods in one country for resale in another.

Merchant wholesalers are one of two types: *full-service wholesalers* or *limited-function wholesalers*. Full-service wholesalers perform a complete range of marketing functions, including merchandising, maintaining inventories, warehousing, providing market information, and financing, among others. (See Table 11.1.) There are three types of full-service wholesalers, based on the breadth of their product offering: *general merchandise wholesalers*, *limited-line wholesalers*, and *specialty merchandise wholesalers*. Some merchant wholesalers in the clothing industry are general merchandise wholesalers, meaning that they offer a wide variety of merchandise from many manufacturers, sometimes within broad categories such as shoes, children's wear, and accessories. Limited-line wholesalers provide a narrower selection of goods, for example, only jewelry from a few key manufacturers. Specialty merchandise wholesalers specialize in a single product line or just part of one, such as health foods, and are found more often in the food industry than the fashion field.

Limited-function wholesalers, as the name implies, perform fewer services than their

TABLE 11.1 Marketing Services Performed by Full-Service Wholesalers

Service	Benefit to Manufacturer or Retailer Partners
Expand manufacturers' market	Service retailers too costly for producers to reach and too small to order direct
Provide market information	Keep retailers informed of trends and new products or pricing changes
Gather market data	Provide manufacturers with feedback from store level to assist in product and production planning
Build assortments	Assist retailers with pre-edited merchandise selections
Warehouse goods	Absorb cost and risk of maintaining large inventory
Ship goods	Transport any size order cost-effectively and quickly to retailers as needed
Offer financing	Provide credit programs to retailers
Provide training	Offer product and sales training to retail staff
Help promote	Develop advertising and promotion programs in conjunction with partners
Maintain marketing message	Ensure that manufacturers' marketing message is consistent throughout the channel

full-service counterparts. There are several types of limited-function wholesalers. *Cash-and-carry wholesalers* sell for cash, do not extend credit, and do not deliver goods. They tend to carry limited lines and sell to small fashion businesses, such as mom-and-pop stores in urban neighborhoods, which would not be profitable for larger wholesalers to service. *Drop shippers* arrange for goods to be sent directly from the factory to the customer, so they do not take physical possession of the goods, although they do take title to them. Carpeting is one product handled

through drop shippers. The drop shipper obtains orders from retail furniture and department stores and relays them to the carpeting factory to fill. In some cases, full-service wholesalers also offer drop shipping for large items or for goods ordered online.

Rack jobbers (also called service merchandisers) work primarily with supermarkets and drug stores selling non-food items such as hosiery, health and beauty aids, and cooking utensils. They own the products and bill the retailers when the goods sell. Rack jobbers not only handle delivery but also stock the shelves, set up displays, and track inventory of their goods for the retailer. A typical rack jobber will have a territory consisting of a dozen or so supermarkets and drug stores. *Truck jobbers* market fast-moving food items such as milk or baked goods to restaurants, grocery stores, and other customers, primarily selling and delivering only. *Mail-order wholesalers* issue catalogues and/or set up Web sites for retail, wholesale, or industrial buyers. Some mail-order houses offer cosmetics, jewelry, and similar small fashion goods; others specialize in maintenance, repair, and operating products (MRO items), such as tools, parts for electronic equipment, and cleaning supplies. These wholesalers fill customer orders and ship them via United Parcel Service (UPS), the post office (USPS), or other inexpensive transportation means.

Agents

Differing from merchant wholesalers are agents, also known as *manufacturers' representatives* or *sales representatives* ("reps" for short). **Agents** are wholesalers that represent either buyers or sellers, generally on an extended contractual basis, and that do not take title to the goods they are selling. A manufacturers' agent handles non-competing but related lines of goods, and earns money through a commission on sales. Agents often sell within an exclusive territory, and they have limited authority with regard to prices and terms of sale. Some agents are import or export agents and specialize in international trade.

Agents in the fashion fields typically offer the merchandise lines of up to a dozen or so designers and manufacturers. An agent in the toy business, for instance, might represent several high-quality lines encompassing wooden toys, collectible dolls,

and building sets that target independent specialty stores. A rep for women's sportswear would make certain that the brands she represents are complementary in style and price range for a certain target customer. For example, that rep might offer retail store buyers brands such as Nautica, Ruff Hewn, and Columbia, among others. These fashion looks convey a certain image but do not compete directly with one another. In fact, they can offer the retailer an edited selection that saves time in planning an assortment.

MARKETS

For some fashion categories, wholesaling activities may take place in locations designated as **markets**, or venues where manufacturers selling the same type of product have a significant presence and where retailers can conveniently see a range of new goods and place orders for merchandise. Most often located in large cities, markets generally consist of manufacturers' showrooms, which are often grouped together in dedicated buildings called *merchandise marts*. All markets are open during market weeks (see the section that follows), and some are open year-round.

Some cities are home to several different markets. New York, for example, is not only a key market for women's ready-to-wear but also for

MARKETER'S INSIGHT:
DOBA CLICKS WITH ONLINE WHOLESALING BUSINESS

Just as consumers can use the Internet to shop at their convenience, so can retailers shop online for fashion goods to fill their store displays—whether those displays are in a physical store or a virtual online store. Most independent wholesalers maintain B2B (business-to-business) Web sites where their retailer customers can view merchandise, check product pricing and availability, and place an order 24/7. Doba goes a little further: The wholesaler operates exclusively online and sells strictly to online retailers, who pay a membership fee to take advantage of all the products and services Doba offers.

Doba describes itself as a *"product sourcing marketplace"* or *"drop-ship aggregator."* Its members are online retail merchants that buy products at wholesale prices and sell them at retail prices without having to deal with the hassle and expense of storing products, managing inventory, packing and shipping products, and handling returns. Doba members can select from more than 1.2 million products from hundreds of suppliers—including such fashion brands as adidas, Bulgari, Nautica, LG, Sony, Skechers, and Polo Ralph Lauren. The retailers market and sell the products to online shoppers, collect payments, and place an order on Doba's site to have the merchandise drop-shipped directly to their customers.

More than 20,000 retailers use Doba to transact millions of dollars of e-commerce on an annual basis. In addition, Doba complements its product catalogue with premium services for retailers and suppliers, including advanced tools, resources, and training and education that are designed to help them maximize sales and profits and manage their businesses more effectively and efficiently.

Source: Doba, www.doba.com (accessed March 6, 2012).

---

men's and children's apparel, as well as for home goods: 41 Madison Avenue, also known as the New York Merchandise Mart, has 23 floors of tableware, tableware housewares, and gift products showrooms, while 7 W New York is a destination for the gift, home, tabletop, and textiles industries. Many regional markets have their own specialties. The California Market Center in Los Angeles is known for sportswear, the Dallas Market Center for men's wear and western wear, and Miami for children's wear, among other categories. High Point, North Carolina, is the primary market for the furniture industry. Chicago and Atlanta, as well as some smaller cities, also have market centers, enabling retailers from the surrounding states to view lines and order new merchandise without having to incur the expense of traveling to New York, California, or Las Vegas.

FIGURE 11.4 Some markets are home to merchandise marts (such as the Chicago Merchandise Mart, shown here), where manufacturers and agents maintain showrooms and where retail buyers can view lines and place orders.

MARKET WEEKS AND TRADE SHOWS

Much of the wholesale business for fashion goods is done at **market weeks**, times designated by the fashion industry to show retail buyers new merchandise for the coming season. During market weeks, store buyers from all over the country visit the markets to meet with the manufacturers' and wholesalers' personnel gathered there, view their merchandise, and place orders for goods for the coming season. Much of the business takes place in manufacturers' showrooms, but companies that don't maintain a permanent showroom in the market can often participate in a temporary exhibit space at the merchandise mart or other nearby location. Retailers, depending on the kinds of goods they carry, may attend several different market weeks in various locations.

Related to market weeks are **trade shows**, or temporary exhibitions organized to showcase to retail buyers products from a wide array of manufacturers in a particular industry. Trade shows usually take place in a secondary venue, such as a convention center or hotel, where exhibitors set up booths to show their goods, usually for three to four days. In some cases, manufacturers with nearby showrooms will also meet with buyers at their own site during the show. One of the most famous apparel trade shows is MAGIC (Men's Apparel Guild of California), held twice yearly in Las Vegas. Over the years MAGIC shows have grown to include women's and children's wear as well as men's apparel. The consumer electronics industry also holds its annual trade show, the International Consumer Electronics Show (CES), in Las Vegas, while the toy industry's American International Toy Fair takes place every February in New York.

Fashion Retailing Today

While wholesalers supply goods and services to other businesses, retailers deal directly with consumers, that is, the final users of a product. **Fashion retailing** is the business of sourcing and selling apparel, accessories, and other designed products to individuals and households.

With the rapidly expanding ways in which consumers are able to shop for fashion goods today, manufacturers must look at more variables than ever when they decide which retailers will best help them meet their marketing goals. Because fashion retailers are themselves marketers—and develop their own specific marketing strategy—producers of fashion seek out retailers whose target customer aligns with their own. For example, Neiman Marcus targets customers who are interested in new, exclusive fashion looks and are willing to pay for them, so the retailer is a good venue for top brands and well-known designers such as Stella McCartney, Jimmy Choo, and others. Kohl's, on the other hand, targets customers seeking brand names and stylish looks at reasonable prices, so the retailer is a good fit for manufacturers offering affordable fashions, as well as for designers such as Vera Wang and Ralph Lauren who are interested in creating exclusive lower-priced collections.

The process of identifying appropriate retailers for a manufacturer or designer may begin by looking at the broad classifications into which a retailer falls, since that provides an initial indication of who their primary customer is and how they meet that customer's needs.

CLASSIFYING RETAIL STORES

There are a number of ways of classifying retail organizations. The most frequently used methods are according to *form of ownership*, *level of service*, *pricing strategy*, and *product assortment*. How a retail enterprise is owned is a clear-cut method of classification. But because every successful retailer has a distinct brand identity that sets it apart from its competition and offers value to its target customers, the lines among the other three methods of classification sometimes blur. In most cases, a retailer will position itself in the marketplace through the combination of its choices regarding service level, price,

and products carried. For example, a retailer selling inexpensive costume jewelry on a self-serve basis is clearly positioned differently than a retailer selling fine gold and gems that are displayed in locked cases only a salesperson can access.

Form of Ownership

The greatest number of stores in operation are **independent retailers**, which are stores owned by a single person (sole proprietorship), by a partnership among two or more individuals, or by a private corporation. A **corporation** is an organization of individuals authorized by law to act as a single entity; a *private corporation* is one whose shares (units of ownership) are not publicly traded and are held by a small number of shareholders, sometimes members of a family. One of the advantages of being incorporated is that the shareholders do not personally bear all of the financial risks of the business, as do sole proprietors and partners.

Smaller independent retailers are often referred to as "mom-and-pop stores" and generally have one or maybe a few stores in their local area. Some become successful enough that they eventually expand to additional markets, usually changing their ownership structure as they grow. Lord & Taylor and Brooks Brothers are two such examples, both having originated as partnerships. Independent fashion retailers, such as shoe stores and clothing stores, traditionally filled neighborhood and downtown shopping areas in towns across the country. Today, they have become fewer in number as larger retail operations with bigger marketing budgets have moved in and forced some smaller retailers out of business. Independent stores still play a vital role in local markets, however, frequently offering

MARKETER'S INSIGHT:
MANDEE STORES GET BOLD MAKEOVER

Before there was Forever 21 or H&M, there was Mandee. The value-priced juniors chain was doing fast-fashion decades before the phrase became a retail buzz term. Now the specialty chain is putting itself back in the spotlight with a new store prototype, designed to evoke a nightclub feel and to give a more dramatic focus to its merchandise. The redesign is also part of a bigger master plan for the retailer to expand not only beyond its primarily Northeast locations, but internationally as well.

Mandee targets a core customer base of 17- to 25-year-old women with an assortment that includes apparel, footwear, lingerie, and accessories. To better highlight its merchandise, the retailer de-cluttered the store space and crafted a high-energy, bright, open shopping environment—including, in a revamped Manhattan store, a space designed to resemble a runway, where fully accessorized mannequins are draped in Mandee apparel and accessories. Bold, graphic photos of models styled in the retailer's outfits pepper the walls, and merchandise focal points have been created throughout the store. The shoe department was also reworked to artfully display brands like XOXO and Steve Madden, and new colorful tables were added to highlight handbags, Mandee-branded jewelry, and beauty products like e.l.f. cosmetics.

Mandee is always scouring the globe for exciting new merchandise, receiving shipments of new goods three or four times a week. The assortment has traditionally been about an equal mix of brands like Almost Famous and Hydraulic Jeans with exclusive and private-label goods, but the plan is for the retailer to design more products in-house and work with suppliers on more exclusive styles. It is all coming together as Mandee expands further west and south in the United States—and eyes markets in Asia, Eastern Europe, and the Middle East, with the goal of being a global company within five years.

Adapted from: Barbara Thau, "Old School, New Fashion," *Stores*, September 2010, www.stores.org/STORES%20Magazine%20September%20 2010/old-school-new-fashion (accessed March 6, 2012).

consumers a high level of service and specialized, niche, or artisanal products that cannot be purchased in their competitors' stores.

Many of the larger retailers that now dominate most markets began as single-store independent retailers, and over the years, they grew to become **chain stores**, or multiple retail outlets owned and managed by a single organization. The owner of a chain store is generally a *public corporation*, or one whose shares are publicly traded and owned by a large number (hundreds or thousands) of shareholders.

FIGURE 11.5 Independent retailers compete with corporate-owned chain stores by offering a higher level of service and/or specialized, niche products.

Chain stores can be regional or national in scope, but all operate under the control and administration of a central headquarters office. Examples of regional chains are Wolf Furniture, which operates 11 furniture and mattress stores in Pennsylvania and Maryland, and P.C. Richard & Son, a 65-store electronics and appliance chain operating in four Northeast states. Macy's, Sears, Walmart, and JCPenney are among the largest of the national chains, all with stores located across the country. Some retail corporations operate multiple chain store brands. Banana Republic, Gap, Old Navy, and Athleta are all chain stores owned by Gap Inc., while Bon-Ton, Bergner's, Boston Store, Carson Pirie Scott, Elder-Beerman, Herberger's,

and Younkers are all under the corporate umbrella of The Bon-Ton Stores, Inc.

Yet another form of retail ownership is the franchise. As you'll recall from Chapter 10, a retail franchise is a contractual agreement between an organization (the franchisor) and an independent entrepreneur or group (the franchisee) that allows the franchisee to own and operate one or more stores under the organization's banner and set of business procedures. The major strength of a franchise is generally its widely recognized trade name—think Benetton, Dollar General, McDonald's, Subway, or Holiday Inn. In addition, the franchisor provides new store owners with a comprehensive business plan that's been tested and proven in other markets, along with a full range of marketing support, dramatically reducing the risk that normally accompanies a new retail venture. In exchange, the franchisee pays an upfront fee and shares a portion of the profits with the franchisor.

Franchising can be an effective way for fashion marketers to test new markets. In planning for global expansion, Polo Ralph Lauren developed a number of agreements for franchised stores in Asia and Russia, among other places. This enabled the company to enter international markets without the expense of opening and running a business from corporate headquarters, possibly half a world away. Other fashion companies that use a franchise-type system for retail operations include La-Z-Boy and Norwalk Furniture.

Level of Service

Classifying retailers by their level of service runs the gamut from full service, which may include amenities such as complimentary refreshments and gift wrapping, to self-service, where customers browse and select merchandise on their own, sometimes to the point of ringing up their own purchases at a self-checkout counter. The amount of service that retailers offer depends on what their customers expect and how much they are willing to pay to cover the additional cost that service entails.

Over the years, the number of fashion retailers providing a high level of service has diminished, and consumers have become accustomed to unassisted shopping, often appreciating the lower prices that go along with less service. In some cases, a store may have salespeople available to answer questions or help find a particular item, but in other cases, employees are primarily on hand simply to replenish merchandise on the selling floor or complete purchase transactions.

FIGURE 11.6 Personal shoppers provide customers of some high-end apparel stores with the ultimate level of individualized service.

Most apparel boutiques and high-end department or specialty stores still fall at the full-service end of the spectrum, since they cater to a more affluent customer to whom service and ambience may be almost as important as the merchandise. Alterations and delivery are among the services that these fashion retailers offer. In addition, at some retailers, service options may include the personalized advice of a knowledgeable fashion expert. Known as **personal shoppers**, these are salespeople who devote their time to meeting the fashion needs of select customers, referred to as clients, by supplying fashion information and choosing merchandise tailored to them in their business and social lives. A personal shopper keeps a client list, calls clients to notify them of the arrival of new merchandise, collects an assortment of items to present at a specific client appointment, and steers each client toward purchases that enhance his or her image. To do this work successfully, the personal shopper may visit the client's home to analyze the contents of his or her closet in order to advise about useful additions among the current season's offerings. Retailers such as Nordstrom, Bloomingdale's, and Macy's, as well as smaller boutiques, offer personal shopper services at no charge to the customer. Most personal shoppers earn a percent of the merchandise they sell, and the incomes for some can rise above $100,000.

Pricing Strategy

Fashion retailers can also be classified by the way they price their merchandise. Some stores regularly apply a full markup (see Chapter 9) to the goods they're selling, then hold periodic sales events where prices are temporarily lowered. Other stores take a smaller markup in order to offer their customers "everyday low pricing."

In general, a retailer's pricing strategy is linked closely to both the level of service it offers and the product assortment it presents to consumers. For example, the relatively high prices at a store such as Saks correspond to its merchandise from top brands and designers and its high level of service. By contrast, the low prices at Kmart relate directly to the retailer's selection of mass-market brands and its self-service environment.

Product Assortment

Perhaps the most common way to classify retailers is by the kinds of merchandise they offer. For fashion goods, the major classifications are department stores, specialty stores, discount stores, wholesale clubs, and off-price stores.

▶ **Department stores** offer a wide selection of apparel and accessories for women, men, and children, as well as cosmetics, home textiles and other home décor, small appliances, gifts, and sometimes furniture or other product categories. Each department has its own managers and buyers. *General department stores* such as Macy's and Sears carry a broader assortment of products than do *specialty department stores* such as Neiman Marcus and Nordstrom. Department store prices range from moderate, such as JCPenney, to high end, such as Bloomingdale's.

▶ **Specialty stores** focus on a specific type of merchandise, such as apparel, footwear, furniture, or toys. Stores offering a wide assortment of merchandise in a basic category, such as sporting goods and apparel at Sports Authority, are known as *single-line stores*. A store specializing

in a narrower product line, say children's shoes at Stride Rite, is called a *limited-line store*. Specialty stores may be single-unit operations or part of a chain. Jolie Femme, which sells women's apparel, and Abt Electronics, which specializes in home theaters and kitchen designs, are both single-unit specialty retailers in the Chicago area. Chain store specialty retailers include Pottery Barn, J.Crew, Abercrombie & Fitch, Buckle, and many others. Specialty store prices run from budget, such as Old Navy, to expensive, such as Bergdorf Goodman.

▶ Traditional **discount stores**, sometimes referred to as *discount department stores*, offer a broad assortment of merchandise, ranging from budget-price apparel, accessories, and household items to automotive and garden supplies, in a departmentalized setting. The stores emphasize brands, sometimes teaming with designers and celebrities to promote certain fashion looks. Jaclyn Smith has had a line of apparel at Kmart for many years, and Target creates seasonal agreements with designers such as Mossimo and Isaac Mizrahi, among others, to provide women's wear. Walmart is the largest of the three major discount retailers, with more than 4,000 stores worldwide. Some discount store chains, including Walmart, Target, and Meijer in the Midwest, have created an even larger format for stores called *supercenters*, which offer a combination of general merchandise including apparel and accessories plus groceries, pharmacies, portrait studios, optical shops, and other services.

In addition to traditional discounters that sell a wide range of merchandise, there are a number of *discount specialty stores* that focus on a single

FIGURE 11.7 Specialty stores offer merchandise of a specific type, such as children's apparel.

line and rely on huge volume to sell products at a low cost. These retailers are often referred to as *big-box stores* or *category killers*, and include such chains as Bed Bath and Beyond, Staples, Best Buy, Toys "R" Us, and Home Depot. Discount store prices generally fall significantly below those of regular department and specialty stores.

▶ **Wholesale clubs**, also called *warehouse stores*, are discount operations that offer a variety of low-cost items such as food, apparel, home furnishings, and health and beauty aids to their member customers. The two best known are Sam's Club, a division of Walmart, and Costco. In order for consumers to shop there, they must pay an annual membership fee, thus creating a "club." Wholesale clubs' fashion goods assortment changes continuously, and may include fine jewelry, gold, diamonds, and other gems, and from time to time, closeout or specially created sportswear from brand-name manufacturers such as Calvin Klein, Columbia, Ellen Tracy, Perry Ellis, and others. Wholesale club prices are traditionally low because the retailers buy in bulk and take advantage of closeouts and other opportunistic buys.

▶ **Off-price stores** sell brand-name merchandise that is at the peak of its life cycle, buying the goods at below regular wholesale prices so they can sell to consumers at a greatly discounted price. A typical off-price organization buys its merchandise later in the season than do the store buyers paying full price. Off-price merchandise might not contain a complete size or color assortment, and might include irregular merchandise, closeout merchandise, or manufacturers' overruns (merchandise produced in excess of what a company's regular retail customers order). Examples of off-price chains include T.J.Maxx, Marshalls, Ross Stores, and Springfield, a Spanish fast-fashion retailer for men.

Two variations of off-price retailers are *manufacturer's outlet stores* and *retailer's closeout stores*. These two types of stores are often found together in factory outlet malls, or specialized shopping centers that group the retailers in one location to draw consumers looking for bargains in brand-name merchandise. Typically, factory outlet malls are located away from full-price downtown and suburban shopping centers so as to avoid extreme price competition; examples include Premium Outlet Centers, with dozens of locations throughout the United States, as well as in Japan, Korea, and Mexico. Among the manufacturers that operate outlet stores to sell their end-of-season fashion goods—or sometimes new goods created specifically for the outlets—are Coach, Nautica, Calvin Klein, Totes, Mikasa, Creuset, and OshKosh B'Gosh. Retailers' closeout stores, featuring reduced-price goods gathered from their regional full-price stores, include Last Call by Neiman Marcus and Saks Fifth Avenue Off 5th. Some retail closeout stores, including Nordstrom's Rack and Brooks Brothers Outlet, combine clearance goods from their full-price stores with merchandise created for their outlets to create a hybrid manufacturer's outlet/retail closeout store. Off-price store prices, while always less than regular price, can range from budget to high depending on the original price of a given product. For example, a designer gown may have been priced originally at $3,500, meaning that even at half price, it's still beyond the range of many consumers' budgets.

WHAT DO YOU THINK?

If you were to own a retail fashion business, what form of ownership would you select? Why? What service levels would you offer your clients, and what price range would you choose to cover those services?

FIGURE 11.8 Factory outlet malls may feature manufacturers' outlet stores, retailer closeout stores, or both. Which type do you see here?

MULTI-CHANNEL RETAILING

The majority of retailers that are most familiar to consumers are brick-and-mortar retailers; that is, they have a physical store presence in one or more markets. But, as discussed at the beginning of this chapter, there are more ways than ever for consumers to shop, and therefore more avenues that retailers are using to reach customers. In many cases, this involves **non-store retailing**, in which consumers can make purchases without setting foot in an actual retail store.

Most brick-and-mortar retailers today have expanded their marketing efforts to include one or more forms of non-store retailing—not only to maintain the loyalty of existing customers who might like the option of not having to visit the store to make a purchase but also to extend their exposure to as wide a target market as possible. And while there are some fashion retailers that function strictly as non-store merchants, they may also use more than one method to reach target customers. This strategy of selling to consumers through multiple store and/or non-store means is called **multi-channel retailing**. A large proportion of retailers today are multi-channel retailers, meaning they treat their physical store, Web store, catalogue, and other sales vehicles as integral parts of a marketing whole, allowing customers to use them all interchangeably and seamlessly.

E-tailers

E-tailer is the name commonly given a retailer that engages in e-commerce (the "e" being short for "electronic"), that is, conducting sales over the Internet. As consumers have become more comfortable with online shopping, and as the number and variety of shopping Web sites have grown, total online retail sales have skyrocketed—reaching some $173 billion in the United States alone in 2010, and forecast to hit $249 billion by 2014.[1] Within that total, the fashion category, including apparel, accessories, and footwear, represents one of the largest and fastest-growing segments that consumers are shopping for online, recently surpassing airline tickets and second only to books.[2]

You would be hard-pressed to find a major brick-and-mortar retailer that does not also have a sales presence on the Web featuring merchandise that mirrors, or is sometimes more extensive than, the selection available in the store. The term "click-and-mortar" is sometimes used to identify these retailers. As part of their multi-channel operation, many retailers offer customer conveniences such as free delivery of an online order to the local store, or the ability to return merchandise bought online to a store branch.

There are also many thousands of online-only retailers that operate without a physical store. These e-tailers create "virtual storefronts" on their Web sites and ship purchases directly to consumers' homes. By far the largest Web-only retailer is Amazon.com. Originally founded as an online bookstore, Amazon quickly diversified and now offers an inventory that encompasses everything from music and movies, to electronics, accessories, jewelry, clothing, and more. Some of its expansion has come through acquisitions of other e-tailers, such as Shopbop, which specializes in designer clothing and accessories for women, and Zappos, which offers shoes and apparel for women, men, and children, as well as accessories, beauty products, and

NORDSTROM LINKS REAL AND VIRTUAL STORES

Multi-channel retailing is all about providing an integrated, seamless shopping experience for consumers, wherever and whenever they choose to shop. But truly melding a Web site and physical store is surprisingly rare in the retailing world. That's why Nordstrom drew applause when it found a way to increase consumer spending by simply changing the way it handles inventory.

Say that a shopper was looking at a blue Marc Jacobs handbag at Nordstrom.com. She could see where it was available at nearby stores and reserve it for pickup the same day, or order it for delivery from the retailer's online inventory. But what if the nearby stores and the Web warehouse were out of that bag? With the new system, it wouldn't matter. Inventory from Nordstrom's 115 regular stores would also be included in the available stock—so even if there was just one handbag left in the entire company, sitting forlornly in the back of the Roosevelt Field store, it would be displayed online and store employees would ship it to the Web customer.

Nordstrom began overhauling its online approach several years ago, adding the option to shop and buy online and pick up the item in a store, partly to address a common customer request. The company was also trying to increase the number of people who shopped at Nordstrom in more than one way, since those so-called multi-channel shoppers spend four times, on average, what a one-source shopper does, the company found.

The result of weaving individual stores' inventory into the Web site had an immediate effect on the percentage of customers who bought merchandise after searching for an item on the site: The percentage doubled on the very first day. What's more, the system change has helped inventory to move faster, and often at higher prices, since less merchandise is left on store shelves late in the season, when it would likely be sold at a marked down price.

Adapted from: Stephanie Clifford, "Nordstrom Links Online Inventory to Real World," *New York Times*, August 23, 2010, www.nytimes.com/2010/08/24/business/24shop.html?th&emc=th (accessed March 6, 2012).

home goods. Many of the fashion products sold by Amazon are from well-known brand names such as 7 For All Mankind, Alfred Dunner, Armani Exchange, Guess, Juicy Couture, and Steve Madden, among many others.

Catalogue Retailers

Catalogue, or mail-order, retailing has been around since 1872, when Montgomery Ward saw an opportunity to sell a wide variety of needed goods at a fair price to remote farmers. For much of the twentieth century, the Ward's and other general merchandise catalogues such as Sears were staples in many homes. Today, most catalogues tend to be more specialized, targeting a particular consumer segment, such as new mothers or outdoors enthusiasts, or highlighting an edited selection of merchandise that a retailer may be introducing or offering on sale.

Some retailers augment sales at their physical stores via periodic catalogue mailings to customers. Victoria's Secret, for example, publishes a merchandise catalogue four or five times a year, and Neiman Marcus mails customers a variety of fashion, gift, and other catalogues throughout the year, culminating with its famous Christmas Book, which features extravagant items such as a seaplane with

FIGURE 11.9 Catalogues, whether in printed or electronic form, remain an important channel by which retailers reach their target customers.

his-and-hers flying lessons or a $15,000 edible gingerbread playhouse. Other retailers that originally launched their business as catalogue-only have become multi-channel by replicating their catalogues on Web sites, and sometimes by opening physical stores as well. Hanna Andersson, a children's clothing catalogue that began in Sweden, now sells its merchandise online and has rolled out more than two dozen retail stores across the United States. Similarly, Coldwater Creek originally sold its line of women's apparel, gifts, jewelry, and accessories strictly through its catalogues, but now has a complementary Web site as well as more than 370 stores nationwide. Lands' End, which had already added a Web site and launched sales of its clothing through Sears and its own "inlet" stores (outlets within a store), went even further by creating a free app for iPad, iPhone, and iPod Touch that lets shoppers browse a digital, interactive catalogue that is available days before the paper version arrives in the mail.

Direct Sellers

Fashion retailers that use commissioned sales representatives to sell apparel, accessories, and other fashion goods directly to consumers are known as **direct sellers**. Direct sellers work with a network of self-employed salespeople who market to consumers in their local territory. Avon and Mary Kay cosmetics are among the best-known direct-selling organizations, along with Pampered Chef and Tupperware. In addition to its network of sales representatives in the United States, Avon has built a sales organization of nearly 6.5 million representatives in more than 100 countries worldwide. It also now sells its merchandise online, as do a number of other direct sellers, sometimes by submitting the order to one of their representatives.

While early direct selling involved salespeople going door to door to individual homes, today the technique has shifted primarily to other venues or group selling, often using a party plan system. A Mary Kay representative, for example, enlists friends or customers to host parties and invite other friends; at the parties, the representative demonstrates a variety of Mary Kay cosmetics to the guests and takes orders from those who want to make a purchase. Examples of other fashion goods that are sold via the party plan system include Lia Sophia jewelry and Longaberger baskets. New York-based Carlisle employs a slightly different technique in marketing its designer dresses, suits, separates, and accessories to a very upscale target audience. The company trains regional Carlisle "wardrobe consultants" who take orders for merchandise at trunk shows they hold by appointment four times a year in their own homes.

Television Home Shopping

Home shopping channels have been a part of the television lineup for three decades, enabling midnight shopping sprees long before PCs and the Internet were common household items. Home Shopping Network (HSN) first broadcast in 1982, followed by QVC in 1986. Since then, both those networks have expanded their broadcasting internationally—HSN to six other countries and QVC to four—and have been joined on the airwaves by a number of other TV shopping channels, including Shop NBC and HSN2, among others.

Home shopping networks feature a variety of fashion merchandise for consumers to purchase, including jewelry, apparel, accessories, beauty products, and electronics. QVC shows more than 1,000 products a week, some from fashion brands including Bob Mackie, Isaac Mizrahi, Dooney & Bourke, Apple, and Bose. Shop NBC emphasizes lifestyle brands, featuring such names as Adrienne Vittadini, Ed Hardy, and Pandora Beads, among others. Like other fashion retailers, the television shopping networks have gone beyond their original format to reach customers, including establishing e-commerce sites. In addition, both HSN and QVC operate several outlet stores; and HSN's Cornerstone division markets luxury home and apparel goods online and through catalogues for brands such as Territory Ahead, Frontgate, and Garnet Hill, among others.

Mobile, Social, and Pop-Up Retailing

The growth of social networks such as Facebook and Twitter, along with the advent of smartphones, iPads, and other portable devices, is helping open the door to additional, brand-new forms of retailing that are only beginning to be tapped. As these new retailing approaches develop, they share one common goal: to connect with customers wherever they are and to convey a marketing message with the greatest possible impact.

Chances are you're familiar with flash mobs, which appear seemingly out of nowhere, perform a dance or song, and just as quickly disperse. Retailing has its own version of the concept: **pop-up stores**, or temporary shops that open in a major city or mall for a few days or weeks and then disappear. Examples include Halloween stores that appear in late September and are gone the first of November. Although pop-up stores are not new, they have

FIGURE 11.10 Pop-up stores generate buzz and a sense of urgency to buy, since consumers don't know how long they'll be open.

become much more commonplace in recent years. Not only are they a way for fledgling retailers to test the waters of a market before committing to permanent space, but they are also used to create excitement and demand, since consumers know that if they don't make their purchase quickly, it may be too late and the shop may be gone.

Target has used pop-up shops to generate buzz about new merchandise or collaborations before they hit its stores, such as a 24-hour Zac Posen for Target pop-up store and a two-day Liberty of London for Target pop-up store the retailer opened at different times in New York City. Luxury brand Louis Vuitton created a pop-up shop next to its permanent store in Cannes, France, to remain open throughout the Cannes International Film Festival, with the goal

of luring the festival's wealthy, high-profile visitors inside to view the company's evening wear.[3] Taking a slightly different twist, Munich-based Clemens en August, a luxury apparel line known for its minimalist style and subdued elegance, avoids the "pop-up" label and instead takes its collection "on tour" to a dozen world cities each year, setting up shop in contemporary art galleries or museums for two or three days. Information on the tour stops is by e-mail invitation or word of mouth only; and by avoiding normal retail markups, the company can sell its clothing at prices substantially lower than most luxury apparel.[4]

One online relative of the pop-up store is the **flash sale**, a limited-time (typically 36 or 48 hours) discount on high-end brand merchandise, usually offered by a retailer or a Web site specializing in online private sales. Among the sites offering flash sales are Gilt Groupe, Rue La La, Ideeli, and HauteLook, which was acquired recently by Nordstrom but was to be continued as a stand-alone subsidiary. The daily "deals" offered by Groupon and other similar marketers are another form of flash sale.

Fashion retailers are also exploring ways to tie shopping into the social networking habits of consumers using Facebook and Twitter. While numerous fashion companies maintain a fan page on Facebook to share information with and get feedback from consumers, actual selling from the site has so far remained somewhat limited, partly due to Facebook's own restrictions. Among the first fashion companies to set up commerce at the site is Nine West, which initiated a Facebook shopping app that's accessible to fans who "like" the brand.

FIGURE 11.11 Retailers including American Eagle Outfitters are incorporating various forms of m-commerce in their ongoing effort to connect with consumers and motivate them to shop.

As an increasing number of consumers rely on smartphones and tablet computers for all types of communication and information, retailers are entering the new arena of **m-commerce**, or selling to consumers via their mobile device. Some retailers use mobile apps to offer consumers real-time coupons, discounts, or exclusive merchandise offers. Bergdorf Goodman, for example, has a mobile app called the Shoe Salon, which features a different pair of shoes each day and gives shoppers 24 hours to buy them, with free, expedited delivery included.[5] Others, such as Sears and American Eagle Outfitters, have full mobile shopping sites that consumers can use to get product specifications or read reviews as they browse the store; with Target's mobile app, consumers can even find out which aisle to go to for, say, nightgowns. Norma Kamali takes it a step further at her boutique in Manhattan, where shoppers can point their phone at merchandise in the window and buy it, even when the store is closed.[6] In addition, a growing number of marketers are using QR codes (bf), two-dimensional bar codes that consumers can scan to view Web-based content and marketing information on their smartphone. (Have you tried scanning the QR code on this book's cover?) Some retailers are placing the codes on their storefront windows, on product displays, at cash registers, or even in fitting rooms, inviting consumers to instantly retrieve additional product information and further cement their loyalty to the marketer.[7]

Fashion magazines are helping facilitate m-commerce as well. *Vogue* introduced an iPhone app called Vogue Stylist, which lets users click on an electronic ad, which then takes them to a retail Web site where they can buy some or all of

SOME WAYS FOR RETAILERS TO OPTIMIZE MARKETING THROUGH DIGITAL CHANNELS

1. Use "sticky" programs enabling viewers to connect further with channels that interest them.
2. Listen to what customers say on social media.
3. Explain the unique qualities of their business.
4. Distinguish the special characteristics of each of the social and mobile channels: Facebook, Twitter, Tumblr, YouTube, and Instagram.
5. Tailor their message to take advantage of each channel's strengths.
6. Utilize Facebook as a marketing tool.
7. Develop creative ways to use social media to drive in-store traffic.

Adapted from: Rachel Strugatz, "Retail's Social Media Wave, Next Step: Driving Sales," *Women's Wear Daily*, September 6, 2011, pp. 6 and 7.

the pieces in the look.[8] An even more ambitious project was undertaken recently by *Glamour*, which produced an original reality series called "Glamour Girls," viewable exclusively on the iPad. Viewers could pause the program at any point with the tap of a finger, scroll through the Gap outfits worn by each character in the episode, and with another tap of the finger, go directly to Gap.com to buy the clothing.[9]

Global Fashion Retailing

Just as producers of fashion goods have taken an increasingly global approach to their marketing, many fashion retailers also have an international presence. A recent newspaper article entitled, "The Americanization of the Rue St.-Honoré,"[10] described how American designers and brands are influencing the fashion capitals of the world, in

this case, Paris. Impetus for the article came from the opening of a Michael Kors boutique on the famous fashion street, but Kors is far from the only American brand found in Paris. Abercrombie & Fitch, Ralph Lauren, Gap, and Tommy Hilfiger are just some of the U.S. companies that have established retail locations there.

It's not only France that reflects the globalization of fashion retailing. Upscale department stores Saks Fifth Avenue and Bloomingdale's have stores in Dubai; Target and Williams-Sonoma, among others, have opened locations in Canada; and you can shop in a Gap store in locales from Sydney to Rio de Janeiro, just to give a few examples. In return, retailers from other countries are bringing their brand of shopping to the U.S. market. Sweden's IKEA and H&M are already well established in America, as are Spain's Zara and Japan's Uniqlo. Additional companies entering the U.S. market include South Korea's Who.A.U, Canada's Garage, and Britain's

Topshop, as well as Russia's teen retailer Kira Plastinina.[11] What's more, through the Internet, consumers can shop virtually anywhere in the world without leaving their chairs, which is leading some U.S. fashion retailers to target international shoppers by creating versions of their Web site in Spanish, German, Arabic, and other languages.

Social Responsibility in Fashion Retailing

Consumers today are asking retailers for more information than just the color, size, and price of a garment. For example, some consumers are learning about the damaging effects to the environment from the dyes used on jeans, and want to protect their surroundings from the effects of pollution. Some are also interested in conserving resources and reducing waste. Many fashion retailers are addressing these concerns and taking steps to improve their own environmental impact—such as installing solar panels and offering reusable cloth bags—as well as to ensure that the merchandise they sell is manufactured in an environmentally responsible manner.

A group of retailers including JCPenney, Walmart, H&M, Patagonia, and Timberland is working with manufacturers, universities, the Environmental Defense Fund, and others to create standards that would show consumers the level of sustainability of a garment by giving it a rating. Called the Sustainable Apparel Coalition, the group is developing a database showing the environmental impact made by the creation of each part of a garment, including fabrics, dyes, threads, buttons,

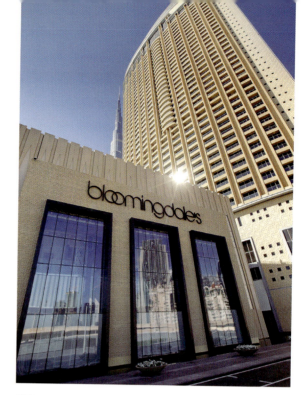

FIGURE 11.12 Fashion retailing is increasingly global, with many U.S. retailers opening stores in countries around the world, as evidenced by Bloomingdale's-Dubai in the United Arab Emirates.

and other embellishments. Results from the database will be the basis for the sustainability rating. Because individual components of apparel and shoes may come from a number of different locations around the world, the first step is to trace a product's supply chain and determine the impact of each of its components.

Once the data are collected and assembled, a rating can be created for each item of apparel, enabling store buyers to include sustainability among the factors they weigh when deciding whether or not to purchase a particular line of goods. Consumers, too, will be able to make an informed decision about their purchases by being able to see a garment's sustainability rating on its hangtag.[12]

summary

Wholesalers and retailers fill a key role in bringing fashion products to consumers. Wholesalers are intermediaries that typically buy goods from manufacturers and resell them for a profit to retailers. Wholesalers provide a variety of services that include reaching a wider customer base than manufacturers could on their own; providing product information to retailers and consumer feedback to manufacturers; assisting retailers with product assortments; warehousing and transporting goods; offering financing; and providing continuity of manufacturers' marketing message. The two types of wholesalers most active in the fashion industry are merchant wholesalers, which own the goods they resell, and agents or manufacturers' representatives, who represent buyers and sellers but do not own the goods they sell.

Wholesaling activities often take place in markets, usually major cities where manufacturers in a particular business have a significant presence and maintain showrooms that may be grouped in one building called a merchandise mart. Market weeks are designated times when new fashion looks are presented to retail buyers. Similarly, trade shows are temporary exhibitions organized to showcase new products for retailers from manufacturers in a specific industry.

Fashion retailing is the business of sourcing and selling designed products to target customers. Retailers may be classified according to form of ownership, level of service, pricing structure, and product assortment. The most common identification of retailers is by product assortment, with the major classifications of fashion retailers being department stores, specialty stores, discount stores, warehouse clubs, and off-price stores. Most fashion retailers today are multi-channel retailers, meaning that they employ a combination of store and non-store means to sell to their customers. Among the non-store retailing methods are e-tailing, catalogues, direct selling, television home shopping, and a growing variety of mobile, social, and pop-up retailing.

Fashion retailing is global in scope. Many U.S. retailers operate stores in countries around the world, and a number of international retailers have established a presence in the United States. Fashion retailers are also addressing environmental concerns. One group of retailers is part of a coalition working to create a sustainability rating for apparel.

Retailers Reap Rewards with Exclusive Lines

So you want to buy a tank top from Miley Cyrus's clothing line. Or maybe you want a T-shirt from the Tony Hawk collection. Unless you know which retailer has the exclusive agreement for those apparel lines, you're out of luck. That's because, in an effort to avoid rounds of price-slashing with competitors over the same brands, retailers are increasingly relying on merchandise that can't be found anywhere else. So to buy Miley Cyrus clothing, you have to head to Walmart. For Tony Hawk apparel, Kohl's is your destination.

Exclusive merchandise lines like these have existed for years, but the recent recession made them more prevalent as even top designers became willing to cut exclusive deals rather than risk being cut from store floors altogether. Sometimes it's an entire collection; sometimes a specific color or material. Saks, for instance, has the exclusive on the "taupe" color of a Christian Louboutin ankle boot, while a metal-heeled Louboutin in beige is available only at Neiman Marcus. For retailers, these exclusives provide differentiation from the competition. Also, markups and mark-downs can be made at their own discretion and pace, resulting in a far more profitable outcome than with a national brand.

So what is the downside? For one thing, it can be dizzyingly hard for consumers to keep track of what line is sold at what store. In addition, celebrity lines are tricky, since a star can wane in popularity almost overnight—or a scandal can hurt clothing sales. Nonetheless, the move to exclusive designer and celebrity lines will doubtless continue, both for the sake of retailers and of consumers who are tired of seeing the same clothes everywhere.

Of course, it has to be the right match. Designer Paul Sinclaire felt that way when he signed an exclusive deal with Saks, saying, "It's focused—it's one group of stores, it's one vision, and you build the business together. Every step of the way, from press, to merchandising, they are kind of the co-creator of the line." Or as noted Jeffrey Gennette, chief merchandising officer for Macy's, which has exclusive lines from Martha Stewart, Madonna, Donald Trump, and Sean John, among others, "When you get a great celebrity that has an authentic vibe that caters to a particular customer base, that can be really potent. [Customers] get the celebrity, and they get the product."

Adapted from: Stephanie Clifford, "To Stand Out, Retailers Flock to Exclusive Lines," *New York Times*, February 14, 2011, www.nytimes.com/2011/02/15/business/15retail.html?scp=1&sq=departmentstore&st=cse (accessed March 6, 2012).

QUESTIONS

1. What other celebrity merchandise do you remember seeing or buying? Can you remember what store or stores carried the line? If only one retailer was selling apparel by a celebrity you admired, would you go out of your way to visit that store to see and purchase the clothing?

2. Suppose you are the designer of an apparel line for college students, but you are not a celebrity (yet). What marketing strategies would you use to enlist the aid of your wholesalers and retailers in reaching your target market? Would you consider an exclusive agreement with a retailer that you thought reached your target customers well?

KEY TERMS

agents

chain stores

corporation

department store

direct seller

discount store

e-tailer

fashion retailing

flash sale

independent retailer

m-commerce

market weeks

markets

multi-channel retailing

non-store retailing

off-price store

personal shopper

pop-up store

QR code

specialty store

trade show

virtual retailer

wholesale club

wholesaler

wholesaling

REVIEW QUESTIONS

1. Explain why the work of wholesalers is important, and describe three or four marketing tasks they might perform.

2. What are two key differences between a merchant wholesaler and an agent?

3. Name the five major classifications of fashion retailers based on product assortment. What are the price levels each one encompasses?

4. What is the definition of multi-channel retailing? Give examples of three or four different types of non-store retailing.

5. How has fashion retailing become a global business? Name two U.S. retailers that operate internationally and two foreign retailers that have stores in the United States.

DISCUSSION ACTIVITIES AND PROJECTS

1. Are the marketing services wholesalers perform necessary? Are there some functions that could be eliminated without impacting their supply chain partners? With a classmate or alone, prepare a brief report on your view of these two questions and present it to the class.

2. Search the Web for apparel and accessories wholesalers. Select a fashion goods wholesaler not mentioned in the chapter that appeals to you. Explain this wholesaler's function. Is this a merchant or agent wholesaler? How can you tell?

3. Imagine you are the owner of a retail business. Cite three items you would purchase from the wholesaler you chose in Question 2. State why you chose these specific items for your customers. Give a brief oral report to the class on the reasons for your selections.

4. You want to work in fashion retailing. How would you start? Would you set up a Web site? Open a retail store? Become a representative for a direct-selling fashion organization such as Lia Sophia? Write a brief report on the kind of fashion operation you would have, citing the reasons for your choices and including the form of business ownership you would choose and why.

5. Select your favorite designer or fashion marketing organization and go to its Web site. See if you can determine whether or not it has an international retail presence, and if so where. Then look to see what its activities are in the area of social responsibility. Prepare an oral report or a short PowerPoint presentation for your class describing what the company of your choice is doing in these areas.

DEVELOPING YOUR MARKETING PLAN

Going a step further, use what you've learned in this chapter regarding the role of wholesalers and the different classifications of retailers to plan how your company's product will get to market. Thinking about your target customer, determine the best channels of distribution:

1. Which type or types of retailers would target the same customer in terms of their product assortment, price strategy, and level of service?

2. Identify four or five specific retailers that fit your company's marketing goals. Would you sell to them direct or work through a wholesaler? Explain why.

Refer to the Marketing Plan Outline, Table 1.2, provided at the end of Chapter 1, as well as Appendix A: Sample Marketing Plan.

REFERENCES

1. "E-retail Will Influence 53% of Purchases by 2014, Forrester Says," *Internet Retailer*, March 8, 2010, http://www.networkworld.com/news/2008/052208-mit-researchers-morphing-web-sites.html (accessed November 28, 2011).

2. "Fashion Outsells Airline Tickets Online," FashionMag.com, August 9, 2010, http://us.fashionmag.com/news-117386-Fashion-outsells-airline-tickets-online (accessed September 8, 2010).

3. "Louis Vuitton Goes for Pop Up Store During the Cannes International Film Festival," Elite Choice, April 15, 2010, http://elitechoice.org/2011/04/15/louis-vuitton-goes-for-pop-up-store-during-the-cannes-international-film-festival/ (accessed March 7, 2012).

4. "High-End Clothing Brand Only Sells on Tour Dates," Springwise, April 16, 2010, www.springwise.com/retail/clemens/ (accessed March 7, 2012).

5. "Bergdorf Goodman Steps into M-Commerce with Luxury Shoe App," *Internet Retailer*, February 26, 2010, http://www.internetretailer.com/2010/02/26/bergdorf-goodman-steps-into-m-commerce-with-a-luxury-shoe-app (accessed March 7, 2012).

6. Stephanie Rosenbloom, "Cellphones Let Shoppers Point, Click, and Purchase," *New York Times*, February 27, 2010, http://www.

nytimes.com/2010/02/27/business/27shop. html (accessed March 7, 2012).

7. Christina Binkley, "Vogue App Turns Ads into Shopping Links," *Wall Street Journal*, February 25, 2010, http://online.wsj.com/article/SB100 0142405274870424000457508567315252 39 04.html (accessed March 7, 2012).

8. Jeremy W. Peters, "Media Decoder, As Seen on iPad," *New York Times,* March 7, 2011, p. B5.

9. Guy Trebay, "The Americanization of the Rue St.-Honoré," *New York Times*, March 10, 2011, pp. E1, E6.

10. Jennifer Saranow and Kris Hudson, "Apparel Retailers from Overseas Are Hitting the Malls in the U.S.," *Wall Street Journal*, July 28, 2008, http://online.wsj.com/article/ SB121721046373988983.html (accessed March 7, 2012).

11. Tom Zeller Jr., "Clothes Makers Join to Set 'Green Score,'" *New York Times,* March 11, 2011, pp. B1, B4; Evan Clark, "Sustainable Apparel Coalition Created," *Women's Wear Daily,* March 1, 2011, p. 7.

Part IV

COMMUNICATING FASHION'S VALUE THROUGH PROMOTION

IN ORDER FOR fashion products to sell, customers need to know about them. Marketers must set fashion promotion objectives, make customers aware, and persuade them to buy. The promotion mix offers a number of ways to reach customers. Effective personal selling in high-end fashion marketing and direct marketing programs are key strategies. Creating awareness and customer demand through advertising, sales promotion, and public relations are also fashion marketing essentials. These promotional elements, when effectively coordinated in an integrated marketing communications strategy, convey a consistent message and communicate a product's value to target customers, thereby helping fashion companies achieve their marketing goals.

Promoting Fashion Goods and Services

This chapter explores the role of promotion in the marketing of fashion products, and describes the elements of a promotion mix, as well as factors that influence how marketers create and integrate their marketing communications strategy.

WHAT DO I NEED TO KNOW ABOUT PROMOTING FASHION GOODS AND SERVICES?

* What the goals and uses of promotion are
* The different elements that make up a promotion mix
* Factors that influence how marketers develop their promotion mix
* The importance of integrated marketing communications
* Global and ethical issues that apply to promotion

375

Promotion Is Everywhere

A few years ago, toning shoes burst onto the fashion scene, promising to turn ordinary walking into a body-sculpting session for wearers' legs and behinds. Maybe you bought a pair, or if you didn't, you probably know someone who did. But stop and think for a minute: How did you first hear about this type of shoe? Did you see a commercial on TV or an ad for toning sneakers on a Web site you were browsing? Did you notice them in a circular or catalogue that came in the mail? Maybe there was a store display of the footwear with special signage that caught your eye, or a shoe department salesperson assisting you with a purchase suggested that you try a pair.

There could be other ways that you were either made aware or kept aware of the shoes. Perhaps you receive e-mails or text alerts about new arrivals or sales at your favorite store and got a message that a particular style of toning sneakers was on sale. You might have seen a friend "like" a brand of the shoes on Facebook, or you follow someone on Twitter who tweeted about how well the shoes trimmed her hips. Maybe you read an article in a newspaper or online explaining the shoes' technology and design, or watched a TV segment or video on YouTube demonstrating how the shoes work. Or you could have seen reviews on a shopping site or fashion blog—or maybe even noticed a character in a TV show or movie wearing a pair of the shoes.

As you can see from reading this chapter's Fashion Marketing in Focus, "Promotion Is Everywhere," there is a multitude of ways by which consumers can learn about a fashion product—and most of them, even when it's not obvious, are in some way planned and initiated by marketers. The reason? Marketers know that no matter how meticulously a fashion product or service has been researched, designed, developed, and distributed, if potential customers don't know about it or don't understand what differentiates it from other similar products and services, it will not be successful. This is where the final element of the marketing mix comes into play: namely, promotion.

The Role of Promotion

FIGURE 12.1 Promotion is the marketing tool that makes—and keeps—consumers aware of a company's products.

In preceding chapters, you learned how fashion marketers go about developing the product, price, and place elements of the marketing mix in order to create value for customers with their goods and services. The purpose of promotion is to communicate that product value so that consumers will be motivated to make the purchase. Specifically, **promotion** refers to the variety of activities that are designed to inform target customers about the features and benefits of a product and to persuade those customers to buy. Promotion can also be used to inform the broader public about a company or brand itself, to enhance its image, and to create and maintain positive relationships between the company and its various publics, including customers, suppliers, the government, and others. Because conveying information is its central goal, promotion is often referred to as *marketing communications*. Promotion works hand in hand with the other elements of the marketing mix, but it could be described as the "icing on the cake," since the actual promotional activities generally occur after the other marketing mix elements are in place.

Although the purpose of promotion has not changed over the years, its execution has been impacted dramatically by the growth of technologies that enable marketers to reach consumers in new and different ways—and to deliver their marketing message virtually instantaneously to customers in all corners of the world. In the past, most marketing communications involved **mass communication**, or the delivery of impersonal messages to a general public utilizing communications vehicles that reach a broad audience. These vehicles are called **mass media**, the various channels by which information can be communicated to a large number of people all at one time. Television is an example of the mass media, as are newspapers, radio, and general information Web sites such as Yahoo. Marketing messages conveyed via mass media are impersonal and cannot be targeted to a specific consumer segment; this is sometimes

FIGURE 12.2 Marketers today have an increasingly wide range of media through which they can reach customers with their promotional message.

referred to as a *shotgun approach*, where the aim is to cover as wide an area or population as possible, knowing that the information will reach consumers who are not necessarily part of a target customer base as well as those who are.

Even with mass communications, marketers have always been able to narrow their audience to some degree, using demographic and psychographic information to choose specific methods or media to carry their message. For example, a luxury brand such as Louis Vuitton might focus its marketing communications efforts primarily in major cities that tend to have a higher number of affluent consumers than smaller towns or secondary cities. Similarly, with television, marketers can use audience statistics to focus on specific networks that are most appropriate for their promotional activities, or can choose specific programs during which their commercials will air, based on the general characteristics of the viewers of that show. Fashion companies such as H&M or Target that want to communicate their marketing message to 18- to 34-year-old female consumers might run commercials during the TV show *Glee*, for example, since its total audience includes a high proportion of young women.

Today, with the Internet and mobile communications, there are many more avenues by which marketers can communicate with their target customers. Some of these media enable more personalized communication with smaller and more narrowly targeted groups, such as a company's brand page on Facebook. Some even permit one-on-one communication in which individual consumers can offer feedback and perhaps even influence the marketing message, as when customers respond to a conversation on a marketer's Twitter feed.

In addition, technology is advancing so that more individualized messaging can be accomplished through what used to be strictly mass communications channels. For instance, cable television set-top boxes are being developed that will allow different commercials to be broadcast to different homes, customized to consumers' specific tastes and lifestyles. When fully implemented, this "addressable" television marketing would enable a commercial for a hot new toy to be transmitted to a home with children, while across the street, the young couple without kids might see an ad for a sleek new e-reader. In other words, promotion today is taking place in a rapidly changing environment—one in which fashion marketers must be nimble and constantly ready to adapt to new trends, in order to ensure that their marketing messages are reaching target customers in a way that makes the most impact.

WHAT DO YOU THINK?

Think of a new fashion product you recently became aware of—maybe a tablet computer, trendy restaurant, or style of jeans. Do you remember whether you first heard about the product in the mass media or through social media? If you were introducing a product of your own that targeted consumers like you, which would you use to promote it initially? Why?

GOALS OF PROMOTION

As stated above, promotion for a fashion product is meant to inform target customers about the product's features and benefits, as well as to persuade

- ▶ Create awareness of a new product.
- ▶ Increase sales among current customers.
- ▶ Identify and gain new customers.
- ▶ Solidify customer loyalty.

- ▶ Support resellers by increasing consumer demand.
- ▶ Counteract promotions by competitors.
- ▶ Reduce fluctuations in sales.
- ▶ Communicate a brand repositioning.

them to make a purchase. To accomplish that goal, fashion marketers sometimes refer to the **AIDA model**, a concept that delineates four steps—*attention, interest, desire,* and *action*—through which a marketing message should lead consumers in order to achieve the intended result.

- ▶ *Attention.* The first objective of promotion is to capture consumers' attention and make them aware of a product. A billboard in New York City's Times Square, for example, might catch the eye of passersby with a giant photo of Sean "Diddy" Combs wearing the latest Sean John outfit.
- ▶ *Interest.* Once marketers have consumers' attention, they need to generate interest in their product by touting its features and benefits and differentiating it from competitive products. Coty might place scent strips of the newest Jennifer Lopez fragrance in magazines or position a representative in a department store to offer a sample spritz to consumers, so they can experience the scent for themselves.
- ▶ *Desire.* When interest has been generated, marketers need to go a step further by creating desire among consumers for their particular product. That desire might be inspired when a fan of Tina

Fey admires a Michael Kors gown the comedienne is wearing at the Academy Awards, or when a consumer sees a photograph of actress Emma Watson carrying a Burberry Prorsum leather tote bag and longs to emulate the look.

- ▶ *Action.* Consumers' desire for a product is not enough. Marketers must then use promotion to motivate customers to take action—usually meaning to buy the product. When Apple introduces a new iPod in a limited-edition design or color, when fast-fashion retailer Zara changes its assortment and displays every week, or when Nissan offers short-term sale pricing on a new model car, all are providing an impetus designed to encourage consumers to take action and buy quickly.

Not all promotional efforts require that consumers go through all four steps of the AIDA model. A consumer who has previously purchased a particular shade of Cover Girl lipstick and liked it does not need to have her attention captured or interest and desire piqued, but she might take action in response to a buy-one-get-one-free offer. By the same token, getting consumers' attention for a product will not necessarily lead to a desire for the product or

FIGURE 12.3 Fashion retailers' display windows use merchandise and creative design to both capture attention and generate interest and desire, as well as to encourage action, as when goods are on sale.

a purchase action. A sexy Victoria's Secret lingerie ad, for example, might draw the eye of female consumers who notice and even admire the brand's newest styles, but who prefer other choices in intimate apparel for their personal style or budget.

USES OF PROMOTION

As a key element of the marketing mix, promotion must be incorporated into a company's marketing plan from the early stages so that it is tied in to the overall marketing goals. Indeed, how the promotion itself is planned and implemented relates directly to the company's overall marketing objectives. For example, one of the primary uses of promotion is to introduce a new product. In this situation, the marketing communications are designed to let consumers know not only that the product is available, but to convey its benefits in a way that tells consumers why they should choose it over other similar products from other companies.

Promotion may also be used to gain new customers for an existing product. A fledgling designer selling his sportswear to a core group of devotees in a handful of local shops could use promotional tools to showcase his designs to a wider range of consumers in additional markets. Or, a fashion marketer might use promotion to increase sales of its product among current customers, perhaps by offering special pricing for a limited time, or by raising the product's profile through special events or celebrity appearances. Promotion is also a key tool when a marketer makes the decision to reposition its brand, perhaps to address changes in the marketplace or in its target customer base. Even if you weren't around or aware in the late 1980s when Oldsmobile attempted to change its image as an "old man's car" and reposition itself to appeal to a younger consumer audience, you have probably heard the iconic slogan (or a variation of it) that the now-defunct car brand used: "This is not your father's Oldsmobile." The promotional slogan was arguably more successful than the repositioning, since the catchphrase remains in popular culture while the automobiles have long stopped rolling off the assembly line.

"PROM REPS" PROGRAM PROMOTES MEN'S WEARHOUSE

Building customer goodwill is sometimes as important a goal of promotion as building brand awareness and sales—and Men's Wearhouse accomplished both with a special promotion that let high school students become "Prom Reps," earning a free tuxedo rental if they recruited ten friends to rent one.

In the multifaceted promotion, kids who signed up as prom reps could use a personal Web page, or "PR Dashboard," as the company called it, to keep track of their sales referrals. The site gave registrants a prom rep ID number to distribute to their friends via more than 200 social media channels including Facebook, Twitter, and SMS messaging. In addition to the free rental, reps could earn as much as $100 cash and have the chance to win a new Chevy Camaro; and girls who wanted to participate could accept either a $100 Visa gift card or give the free tuxedo to a friend.

To kick off the promotion, Men's Wearhouse ran paid search ads via Google, Bing, and Yahoo, as well as display ads at teen-oriented sites like Gala.com, myYearbook.com, Pandora.com, and Takkle.com. Sponsored articles and contests also appeared at some of those sites, while a New York-based agency coordinated outreach to teen-focused blogs. In addition, the brand's Facebook "fan" page was updated to include a "Tuxedo" tab that viewers could click and see a button for a "Build-A-Tux" app that let them virtually create a specific look.

Off line, the retailer's more than 500 stores were supplied with "Prom Reps" marketing materials and their sales teams were instructed on how to help people get registered.

Adapted from: Christopher Heine, "Social Media Helps Men's Wearhouse's 'Prom Reps' Get to the Dance," *ClickZ News*, March 9, 2010, http://www.clickz.com/3639733 (accessed March 6, 2012).

Elements of the Promotion Mix

In developing a marketing strategy, fashion companies consider all elements of the marketing mix and how they will work together to accomplish the marketing goal. Similarly, there are multiple elements that make up a marketer's promotional toolbox, and depending on the product and the purpose of the promotion, a fashion company might use some or all of them to varying degrees. These promotional elements are *advertising*, *public relations*, *sales promotion*, *personal selling*, and *direct marketing*—and the combination of these techniques that a marketer uses to achieve a specific goal is called the **promotion mix**. Each of these individual elements will be explored in more detail in the following two chapters, but let's look here at the basic concept of each type of promotion.

ADVERTISING

Advertising is the placement in any of the mass media of paid, nonpersonal announcements or messages in which the sponsor is identified and is seeking to inform and/or influence the audience about its products or organization. Advertising can appear in broadcast media (television and radio), in print media (newspapers and magazines), on billboards, in banners or pop-ups on a Web site, and other places. Marketers select the media in which to advertise based on the audience they want to reach, the suitability of their message to a given medium, as well as their budget, since the cost of purchasing advertising varies dramatically, with network television being the most expensive.

The advantage of advertising is that, because advertisers pay for the space or time, they can control the message completely. Advertising also has the potential to reach a vast number of consumers spread over a wide geographic area, making the cost per exposure (each viewing of the ad by one individual) relatively inexpensive, even if the total cost is high. The disadvantage of advertising is that it is impersonal and cannot be tailored to an individual audience. It is also clearly designed to give only the marketer's point of view, which can diminish its power of persuasion, particularly with today's savvy consumers.

PUBLIC RELATIONS

Public relations (PR) is the marketing function whose aim is to generate goodwill and a positive image for the marketer and its products among all its various publics, including consumers, shareholders, government, and the media. One component of public relations is **product publicity**, the placement of unpaid articles or announcements about a product in the media to gain positive exposure. In addition to initiating media coverage for the company, the brand, and individual products, public relations activities can also include planning and executing special events, creating newsletters and other informational materials, counteracting negative publicity that may appear, and addressing other issues that impact the company's public image.

Public relations holds certain advantages over advertising because items that appear in the media are viewed by the public as more objective and less self-serving than an advertisement. A positive feature story or mention of a product or company can also be perceived as an endorsement by the medium,

FIGURE 12.4 Advertising can reach a wide audience at a relatively low cost per exposure, but its message is impersonal and cannot be tailored to individual consumers.

further earning consumers' confidence. The disadvantage is that the marketer does not control when or whether a message will actually appear, nor how the media will present it to their audience.

SALES PROMOTION

Sales promotion includes marketing communications activities that take place for a predetermined, limited time with the purpose of increasing demand and stimulating sales. A marketer can target sales promotion to consumers, or to retailers or wholesalers. Among the common vehicles used for sales promotion are free samples, discounts, coupons, gift-with-purchase, purchase-with-purchase, contests, giveaways, and other special offers that encourage an immediate purchase.

Sales promotion can be very effective in boosting short-term sales, but it may not have an impact on long-term marketing goals. In some cases, if a marketer overuses sales promotion techniques, customers learn to "wait for the sale" so that everyday purchases between promotions actually suffer. (See Chapter 14 for more detailed discussion of advertising, public relations, and sales promotion.)

PERSONAL SELLING

Personal selling involves a one-on-one, often face-to-face interaction between a marketer's representative and an individual or small group of customers with the goal of generating a sale. Personal selling is used most often when there is a strong need to persuade the customer to buy, such as with a high-cost item or product that requires more extensive explanation of its competitive advantages.

FIGURE 12.5 The promotion mix element of personal selling is particularly suited to expensive or complex products, such as automobiles.

The biggest advantage of personal selling as a promotional tool is the relationship that can be established between the salesperson and the customer. When the customer develops confidence in the salesperson's expertise and trustworthiness, repeat sales become more likely.

DIRECT MARKETING

Direct marketing is a promotional strategy in which the seller initiates direct contact to carefully chosen individual customers by one or more channels in order to cultivate a relationship and solicit a response, usually in the form of a purchase. Direct marketing takes many forms, including direct mail, catalogues, telemarketing, e-mail marketing, and shop-at-home selling.

The advantage of direct marketing is that it can be customized to a targeted customer, and it provides a method for the customer to respond immediately, whether by phone, by mail, at a Web site, or by clicking a link in an e-mail. In addition, based on a customer's response, marketers can adapt their next direct contact, tailoring it further to the customer's preferences. (See Chapter 13 for further discussion of personal selling and direct marketing.)

WHAT DO YOU THINK?

Think of an example of a promotion that got your attention and piqued your interest in the product. Which element of the promotion mix did it involve? As a consumer, do you think you respond more positively to one type of promotion over another? Does it depend on the product being marketed?

Creating a Promotion Mix

Each of the elements of promotion has its own distinct objective and role in conveying a marketing message to consumers. Because of that, fashion marketers must develop a promotional strategy that delineates how—and whether—each element will be used to accomplish a specific marketing goal. The promotion mix for one product may well be very different from the promotion mix for another product marketed by the same company at the same time. Let's look first at some of the factors that help shape the ways in which fashion marketers decide how a product will be promoted, and then discuss how companies coordinate the promotional elements to ensure that the parts of their marketing communications work together as a cohesive whole.

FACTORS THAT AFFECT THE PROMOTION MIX

As you can see in Table 12.1, each type of promotion varies in effectiveness at different steps of the AIDA model. Understanding this can help a fashion marketer select which elements to use based on its promotional objectives. In addition, there are a number of other factors that influence how marketers develop their promotion mix, including the available budget, the characteristics of the product, the characteristics of the target market, and whether a push or pull strategy (discussed later in this section) will be employed.

Available Budget

One of the most basic factors that affects the promotion mix is how much money the marketer has available to spend for a specific promotional effort. Promotional vehicles vary greatly in cost, and marketers must weigh the expense against the projected benefit they will gain. Sometimes that benefit can be directly measured, as when a personal selling contact results in an immediate sale, or when a desired number of consumers redeem a sales promotion coupon when they buy a product. But in many other cases, the effectiveness of a promotion is less clear-cut. Public relations efforts and advertising campaigns that generate exposure for a product may well inspire consumers to make a purchase, but the direct cause-and-effect dynamic is difficult to measure.

TABLE 12.1 Effectiveness of Promotion Mix Elements

Promotion Mix Element	Attention	Interest	Desire	Action
Advertising	✳	✳	○	■
Public relations	✳	✳	✳	■
Sales promotion	○	○	✳	✳
Personal selling	○	✳	✳	✳
Direct marketing	✳	○	○	○

Key: ✳ = Very effective   ○ = Somewhat effective   ■ = Not very effective

Adapted from: Charles W. Lamb, Joseph F. Hair, Jr., and Carl McDaniel, *MKTG* 2007/2008 ed. (Mason, OH: Thomson South-Western, 2008), p. 216.

Advertising tends to be the most costly of the promotion elements, and in general, only the largest marketers have a big enough promotional budget to afford advertising on national network television, and particularly on the most-watched programming, which commands the highest rates. Buying advertising in top magazines may also be out of reach for most smaller marketers. For example, the cost of a 30-second commercial on the Super Bowl is more than $3 million,[1] and a single full-page ad in *Vogue* costs upwards of $150,000.[2] Even though the cost per exposure for those advertisements may be relatively small—some 111 million people watched the Super Bowl in 2011, meaning it cost advertisers less than three cents to reach each potential viewer[3]—without a hefty enough budget for the initial outlay, most marketers must rely on less expensive promotional vehicles, maybe an ad in a regional magazine or on a local TV channel. Whether they are using a limited public relations effort to generate free publicity or have the financial means to combine several promotional elements in their mix, marketers of all sizes try to maximize their dollars to achieve the greatest impact with target customers.

Product Characteristics

Marketers must create a promotion mix that also takes into account the product's characteristics, including the price of the product, the type of buying decision it entails, and its stage in the product life cycle. Looking at price, inexpensive fashion products, such as costume jewelry, do not generally require personal selling to persuade consumers to make a purchase; and unless the sales volume is high enough, they might warrant only a minimal expenditure on advertising, sales promotion, or other promotional activity. On the other hand, luxury goods, such as a Kate Spade handbag, benefit from personal selling to explain to consumers why the product offers value for the high price. At the same time, these products would not require mass advertising that reaches customers well beyond the target market. Similarly, marketers of fashion products that are low-involvement purchases, such as hosiery or mascara, would most likely use advertising and sales promotion as their primary tools, whereas marketers of high-involvement purchases, such as automobiles or wedding apparel, would lean more heavily on personal selling as a larger proportion of the promotion mix.

A fashion product's stage in its life cycle also influences the promotion mix a marketer chooses—and usually a marketer will adjust the mix as the life cycle progresses. At a product's introduction, the main goal of promotion is to raise awareness among target customers about the product's availability, features, and benefits, so advertising and public relations play a key role. Personal selling to retailers and distributors is also employed to garner wider distribution for the product at its launch; and sales promotion and direct marketing may also be used to encourage initial customers to buy. As the product enters its growth stage, sales promotion may become less important as a tool to encourage sales, while advertising, public relations, and direct marketing continue in order to keep interest strong, capture new customers, and build brand loyalty. At the product's maturity, marketers generally reduce their advertising and public relations efforts somewhat, but may continue direct marketing and reintroduce sales promotion to maintain or increase their market share. When the product

FIGURE 12.6 The most prestigious fashion magazines can charge hefty rates for advertising, putting them out of reach of many marketers' promotional budgets.

enters the decline stage, all promotional activity tends to be dramatically reduced, particularly advertising, although some sales promotion efforts may continue, for instance, as retailers work to clear inventory to make way for new arrivals.

Target Market Characteristics

The promotion mix is also shaped by the characteristics of the target market—including its demographics, geographic distribution, and size. Marketers of fashion products that have potential

FIGURE 12.7 When a fashion product is in its introduction stage, a major goal of promotion is to raise awareness and encourage consumers to try it, sometimes by offering free samples.

appeal to a wide variety of consumers, such as flat-panel televisions or athletic shoes, have greater options in choosing their promotion mix, since a greater variety of vehicles will reach the target market. If the budget permits, national or regional advertising, broad public relations outreach, direct marketing, and sales promotion might all be employed to reach as many consumers as possible.

Products with a narrower target customer base need a more focused promotion mix, whether it means concentrating on a specific geographic area or emphasizing promotion vehicles that reach a particular age group or income level. The promotion mix for designer apparel, for instance, would use a high proportion of personal selling to reach its very affluent customer base, and would not normally employ sales promotion techniques. Products aimed at young consumers, such as licensed clothing based on a popular new movie, would have a very different promotion mix, leaning toward advertising and sales promotion but using vehicles known to reach that demographic, including youth-oriented TV shows, teen magazines, and social media, among others.

Push and Pull Promotion Strategies

In determining their promotion mix, marketers also consider whether to use a push strategy or a pull strategy. In a **push strategy**, the marketer promotes a product only to the next level along the supply chain—in other words, a manufacturer aggressively sells to the wholesaler, the wholesaler to the retailer, and the retailer to the end consumer. This type of promotional strategy relies heavily on personal selling, sometimes with additional support from advertising and sales promotion to help "push" the products through the channel. A small toy

For three months recently, Jimmy Choo sprinted into athletic shoe production and social media with a promotional splash: The luxury shoe vendor dreamed up CatchaChoo, a "trainer hunt" that merged the real and digital worlds in a quest to capture a free pair of sneakers.

The promotion took place in London, where consumers were invited to follow CatchaChoo on Facebook, Foursquare, and Twitter. Once on the sites, followers would see an anonymous Jimmy Choo representative release hints about her activities—and occasionally see her "check in" at a public London venue. The objective was to race over and find the representative, who'd be carrying a pair of shoes. The first to approach her and say "I've been following you" received a pair of Jimmy Choo trainers.

For the Jimmy Choo brand, CatchaChoo accomplished several promotional objectives. For one, it spurred activity on the part of select digital users interested in the brand, and rewarded them not just with free shoes, but with interaction with a friendly and respectful personality on the social sites. The promotion also demonstrated that Jimmy Choo was not only daring and new, but also engaging—a quality crucial to developing long-term social-media relationships, thereby paving the way for future experiments. And finally, it was completely relevant to the product. After all, what better way to promote new sneakers than to get people on their feet and on a quest through the streets to "catch" a pair?

Adapted from: "How Jimmy Choo Boosted Its Brand with CatchaChoo," MarketingProfs.com, September 16, 2010, www.marketingprofs.com/short-articles/2024/how-jimmy-choo-boosted-its-brand-with-catchachoo (accessed March 6, 2012).

company, for example, might use personal selling at trade shows and through manufacturer's reps to get its products into wholesalers' and retailers' assortments, relying on those channel partners to push the products on through to consumers.

A **pull strategy**, on the other hand, focuses the promotion mix on the end consumer, with the goal of stimulating enough consumer demand that retailers will be eager to carry the product to sell to their customers and order it from wholesalers, who in turn will place orders with the manufacturer. This type of strategy uses a heavy mix of advertising, public relations, and sales promotion, with the idea that generating strong demand at the consumer level will result in the product being "pulled" through the supply chain. An electronics company, for example, might launch a sleek new smartphone with an aggressive advertising and public relations campaign, including a limited-time sales promotion to further pique interest and desire, and then

FIGURE 12.8 Promotion is most successful when the promotional elements are coordinated as an integrated marketing communications strategy. Skechers used complementary promotional tools for its Shape-ups campaign with Kim Kardashian.

count on consumers to go to their favorite retailer to ask for the phone.

In most cases, marketers do not use a push or pull promotion strategy exclusively, but rather combine elements of the two approaches to achieve the desired marketing goal. Many fashion designers, for instance, use personal selling to boutique owners to widen their distribution but also place product publicity or product advertising in key media to heighten consumer interest in their designs.

INTEGRATED MARKETING COMMUNICATIONS

Whatever the product and whatever the promotional goals of the marketer, presenting a clear message about the product to consumers is crucial to ensuring marketing success—particularly with today's rapidly changing media landscape. That is

why fashion companies are increasingly pursuing a strategy of **integrated marketing communications**, in which all elements of promotion are carefully coordinated in order to deliver clear and consistent information across all channels.

In the past, each element of promotion might have been handled by a different department within a company or even by an outside agency under the direction of a company manager. As a result, a print ad might have given a different impression to consumers about a product than a direct marketing piece, which in turn might have been different from a personal selling pitch. Not only can this type of disjointed approach create consumer confusion, it can detract from the strength of a company's brand identity and cause different elements of the promotion mix to actually work against each other. This is particularly true with the growth of digital communications, which has lessened the impact of promotion through mass media and dramatically changed the ways in which consumers learn about products and companies.

With integrated marketing communications, all aspects of promotion are planned in tandem, enabling marketers to create a cohesive strategy both in terms of the message and the plan's implementation. Each contact with consumers is designed to have a consistent look and feel—whether it's a television commercial, a press release, a catalogue, or a Web page—so that each contact reinforces the others and establishes a specific image in consumers' minds. Not only does this integrated approach help foster brand loyalty, but it allows the promotion elements to work synergistically, improving the effectiveness of the entire promotion mix.

Ethical Issues in Fashion Promotion

As do other aspects of the fashion business, promotion sometimes raises issues regarding ethics and social responsibility. Some critics believe that heavy promotion creates artificial needs and leads consumers to purchase products that aren't really necessary to their lives—or that maybe they cannot really afford. This could be said to apply particularly to fashion products, whose success rests on the eagerness of consumers to own the newest style or latest technology, whether or not their existing possessions are still usable. Indeed, some consumers may be swayed by promotion to purchase products they don't need or can't afford, but there are most likely many other factors besides the promotion that contribute to their poor decision making.

Ethical questions can also be raised regarding specific messages within some promotions. Many people criticize promotions that give the implication that consumers will be less popular or less successful if they don't own or use a product, or that are misleading about a product's true benefits— although marketers are bound by laws that require truth in advertising. Some fashion promotions may cross the line of good taste as well, using blatantly sexual or sexist images that offend some consumers and may raise questions about the ethical standards of the marketer. Calvin Klein is one company that has frequently been cited for its overtly sexual ads, a few of which have even been banned.

In addition, some who view promotion as an impetus for consumers to over-purchase or purchase unnecessarily also see it as an environmental problem. For example, when promotion creates demand for new products, there is almost inevitably an environmental impact from the manufacturing and distribution of those products. Companies that use direct marketing may also come under fire for the massive amounts of paper and the chemicals of the ink used in frequent catalogue mailings. These are issues marketers must consider and balance against their effectiveness in reaching their marketing goals.

WHAT DO YOU THINK?

What ethical issue in fashion promotion have you recently read about or noticed? How did it make you feel about the marketer? Would you be less likely to purchase the company's products? Why or why not?

FIGURE 12.9 The global marketing of fashion extends to the promotional arena, as fashion shows, advertising, publicity, and other information can now be transmitted instantly over the Internet and mobile devices to consumers anywhere in the world.

Promoting Fashion on a Global Scale

In previous chapters, we've discussed how technology has accelerated the global marketing of fashion. But there is perhaps no area of fashion marketing that can take better advantage of modern technology than promotion, since promotion is all about communications—and the Internet and mobile devices have enabled instantaneous communication between marketers and consumers anywhere in the world.

Each element of the promotion mix has extended its reach globally, even when the marketer might not have specifically set out to do so. Company Web sites can be viewed by consumers with Internet access, wherever they may be, and some marketers even offer access to their site in a choice of languages. News and publicity about a company and its products may also be found online, further communicating information to a global audience. Social media like Facebook and Twitter carry additional items of interest among a marketer's followers and fans globally; and advertising, even when the marketer hasn't purchased air time in a given market, can often be seen on YouTube by consumers in far-flung locales.

At the same time, different countries and cultures may have different standards and values than a marketer's home nation. For example, some European nations have restrictions on advertising aimed at children; in Sweden and Norway, it is actually illegal to advertise to children under the age of 12. Cultural and language differences can also mean that a promotion that is perfectly acceptable to American consumers conveys an undesirable message to consumers in another country. An oft-repeated example (later debunked as an urban legend) involved Chevrolet's rollout of its Chevy Nova automobile in Latin America, with disastrous results, since "*no va*" means "doesn't go" in Spanish. While that particular blunder may not have actually happened, it doesn't lessen the fact that in any planned promotional effort, marketers must be sensitive to words and images that are effective at home but that could have a negative connotation or be offensive to consumers elsewhere. We'll look at these topics further in the following chapters.

summary

Promotion, also called marketing communications, is the final element of the marketing mix, and consists of a variety of activities that are designed to inform and influence target customers about the features and benefits of a product. With the growth of the Internet and mobile communications, promotion is increasingly shifting from primarily impersonal mass communications to more personalized messages to smaller, more narrowly targeted groups. The goals of promotion are sometimes broken into four steps known as the AIDA model, leading consumers through attention, interest, desire, and action. Among the key ways in which marketers use promotion are to introduce a new product, to gain new customers, to increase sales, and to reposition a brand.

There are five elements of promotion: advertising, public relations, sales promotion, personal selling, and direct marketing. The combination of elements a marketer chooses for a specific promotional effort is called the promotion mix. A number of factors influence the promotion mix, including a marketer's available budget, the characteristics of the product being promoted (including price, type of buying decision, and stage in the product life cycle), and the characteristics of the target market. The promotion mix also is influenced by whether the marketer is employing a push or pull strategy, promoting a product only to the next level in the supply chain or creating consumer demand to pull it through.

Fashion companies are increasingly using integrated marketing communications to create a consistent and coordinated approach among all elements of their promotion mix.

Fango Pushes the Envelope in Promotional Campaign

To celebrate the 25th anniversary of its Fango brand mineral-enriched mud mask (officially Fango Active Mud), Borghese created a promotional campaign designed to raise awareness of the product as well as remind long-time fans to replenish their supplies. The campaign—with an estimated budget of more than $2 million and a theme of "Do you Fango?"—featured women, the traditional market for Fango, and men, to signal to them that they too could benefit from slathering the product on their skin, hair, and scalps. It included print advertisements in magazines like *Allure*, *Elle*, *InStyle*, *Marie Claire*, and *Vogue*; posters on taxis, phone kiosks, and buses; ads on electronic signs in Times Square; plus ads on the Borghese Web site and a presence on Facebook and Twitter.

Nothing too unusual in the strategy so far, right?

But here's where the campaign got creative: To help draw attention to the ads, the models wore nothing other than Fango, applied to their chests, arms, legs, and backs, with the photos discreetly cropped to avoid causing an issue with those easily offended.

The campaign was clearly indicative of efforts by marketers to stand out amid the clutter by using copious amounts of bare skin, a tactic consumers seem to accept more readily from marketers of fashion and beauty brands than they would from other types of companies. And according to Neil Petrocelli, vice president for marketing at Borghese in New York, everyone who had seen the campaign so far had "responded positively to it," because "they see the fun." The smiles on the models' faces "are happy instead of sexy," he added.

According to Petrocelli, the goals of the campaign were twofold, the first being to celebrate the Fango customer and reaffirm her decision to use the product and continue to do so. The second aim was to make the product feel more contemporary, using the eye-catching visuals to address a younger audience than the brand had been targeting.

Along with the advertising, the Fango campaign included a public relations effort and events including a reception at the home of Georgette Mosbacher, Borghese's chief executive, where guests were promised they could learn more about "the mud that helps you shine from the inside out." An equally important facet of the campaign was to drive consumers to the Web site as well as to stores to make a purchase, since e-commerce is playing an ever bigger role in the beauty and cosmetics category.

Adapted from: Stuart Elliott, "Here's Mud on Your Skin," *New York Times*, July 6, 2010, www.nytimes.com/2010/07/06/business/media/06adnewsletter1.html?ref=advertisingemail&nl=business&emc=ata1 (accessed March 6, 2012).

QUESTIONS

1. What do you think of the strategy that Borghese used in promoting its Fango mud mask? Do you think the company was successful in using integrated marketing communications to convey a consistent message? From what you read, do you believe the company accomplished its promotional goals? Why or why not?

2. How easy would it be for other fashion marketers to adopt the theme of this promotional campaign? What would be the drawbacks?

3. Do you think the nature of the Fango promotional campaign raised ethical issues that could detract from the results? Even if you found nothing offensive in the images, do you think other consumers might? Should that risk influence whether the company carried out the campaign? Explain your answer.

KEY TERMS

advertising

AIDA model

direct marketing

integrated marketing communications

mass communication

mass media

personal selling

product publicity

promotion

promotion mix

public relations (PR)

pull strategy

push strategy

sales promotion

REVIEW QUESTIONS

1. What is the main purpose of promotion as it relates to the other elements of the marketing mix?

2. Name the four steps of the AIDA model for promoting a product, and give an example of how each step might be accomplished.

3. What are the five elements of a promotion mix? Define each element and state one of its advantages.

4. What are three factors that affect how a fashion marketer develops a promotion mix?

5. Explain why it is important for a company to use a strategy of integrated marketing communications.

DISCUSSION ACTIVITIES AND PROJECTS

1. Choose a fashion product to market, and write a brief promotional message about it, incorporating each of the four AIDA communication tools.

2. In a class discussion, describe a magazine or television ad that you find memorable. It may be recent or not. Refer back to the Marketer's Insight feature called "Key Uses of Promotion", and decide what goal or goals the marketer was trying to accomplish with the promotion. Do you think it was successful? Why or why not?

3. You and a classmate partner have decided to design and market your own line of accessories through the small boutique you own. Explain how you would apportion your promotional budget among the five promotional elements. Write a brief report stating the percentage of your budget you would devote to each element. Explain your reasoning.

4. With a partner or small group, choose a fashion product currently on the market and try to discover how many different ways it is being promoted by searching for examples of advertising, public relations, sales promotion, personal selling, and direct marketing. You can look online, through newspapers and magazines, in stores, and on television. Make a chart with each element as a header, and list the examples you found underneath. What does your chart tell you about the marketer's promotional strategy? Share your results with the rest of the class.

5. Go to the L'Oréal Web site (www.loreal.com) and look for ways in which the company uses the site to promote its products to international customers. Next, explore the site for information about the company's ethics and social responsibility initiatives. Write a paragraph on each of those topics, describing how effectively you think the company conveys its global and ethical marketing messages.

DEVELOPING YOUR MARKETING PLAN

The final element to add to the marketing mix for your plan is promotion. Keeping in mind all other elements of your marketing plan, determine an overall strategy for promotion, discussing how each of the five elements will be used. In Chapters 13 and 14 you will have an opportunity to expand on specific elements in your promotion mix.

1. Write a paragraph outlining the promotional goals of your product or company.
2. Describe the elements of promotion, and write a sentence or two on the role that each will play in helping reach your marketing goals.
3. Explain how the elements will be combined into an integrated marketing communications plan.

Refer to the Marketing Plan Outline, Table 1.2, provided at the end of Chapter 1, as well as Appendix A: Sample Marketing Plan.

REFERENCES

1. Aaron Smith, "Super Bowl Ad: Is $3 Million Worth It?" CNNMoney.com, February 3, 2011, http://money.cnn.com/2011/02/03/news/companies/super_bowl_ads/index.htm (accessed November 29, 2011).

2. Condé Nast Media Kit, 2011 General Rates, http://www.condenastmediakit.com/vog/genrates.cfm (accessed on January 31, 2012).

3. Dan Caesar, "Super Bowl Draws Record Audience, But Not Rating," STLToday.com, February 7, 2011, http://www.stltoday.com/sports/football/professional/article_29c5181a-3315-11e0-808c-00127992bc8b.html (accessed November 28, 2011).

CHAPTER 13

Promoting Fashion through Personal Selling and Direct Marketing

This chapter first explores personal selling as a promotional tool, explaining the nature and types of selling, as well as outlining the selling process. It then turns to direct marketing, presenting its benefits to fashion customers and marketers, and describing the variety of media that fashion companies use in their direct marketing efforts on both a local and global scale.

WHAT DO I NEED TO KNOW ABOUT PERSONAL SELLING AND DIRECT MARKETING?

- The roles of personal selling and direct marketing in the promotion mix
- The key steps in the personal selling process
- The benefits of direct marketing to both fashion marketers and consumers
- The various types of direct marketing vehicles used globally, both online and offline
- Ethical issues that may arise in personal selling and direct marketing

FASHION MARKETING IN FOCUS:
Personalizing the Sale

Imagine this: You're going on your first skiing trip with a group of friends, and you need to buy the perfect ski jacket—something that's warm but not bulky, that has zippered pockets to securely stow your cell phone and iPod, and that ideally has navy blue trim to match the ski pants you already bought. Also, you don't want to spend too much money, since the trip itself is already taking a bite out of your savings.

In one scenario, you go to a sporting goods store downtown that specializes in ski apparel and equipment. As you begin scanning the racks, a friendly sales associate approaches to ask if you need help finding something. You explain your quest, and the salesperson immediately leads you to a jacket he thinks might meet your needs. While you're examining it, he brings two others over for you to look at and compare. He fills you in on what features make the three jackets different, answers your questions about the quality and reputation of each brand, and informs you that one is on sale that week. Once you've tried them on and decided which you like best, the sales associate proceeds to show you some coordinating hats and gloves, makes sure there's nothing else you need, and asks if you're ready for him to ring up the sale. Afterward, he writes his name on the receipt and invites you to ask for him if you need anything further.

In an alternate scenario, you return home from a class to find a catalogue devoted to ski gear in your mailbox—for the same company from which you ordered your ski pants online. You sit down and begin flipping through the pages, and see three different jackets that coordinate with the pants you bought. Each jacket is described in detail, including its warmth ratings in different winter temperatures, its features including number and type of pockets, and other key information such as size guidelines, shipping and return policies, and price. You notice that if you place an order within 15 days, you get a 20 percent discount as a thank you for your previous purchase, and you can order by phone, mail, or online, using a personalized code on the back page of the catalogue.

ach of the scenarios in this chapter's Fashion Marketing in Focus, "Personalizing the Sale," illustrates a different element of the promotion mix: personal selling in the first and direct marketing in the second. These are the topics we'll examine more closely in this chapter. As you'll recall from Chapter 12, personal selling is a one-on-one interaction between a salesperson and a potential buyer with the goal of producing a sale; and direct marketing is any communication targeted directly to an individual customer and designed to cultivate a relationship and generate a response.

For time-starved consumers and for profit-seeking fashion businesses, both of these promotional elements have merit and a distinct role in the promotion mix. Salespeople involved in personal selling strive to establish relationships with customers or clients and present them with solutions to their fashion needs; and direct marketing targets carefully selected potential customers with offerings meant to satisfy their specific fashion needs or desires. Both of these more personalized types of promotion key in to the accepted fact that marketers generally earn more of their sales and profits from repeat purchases by loyal customers than from first purchases by new ones, and therefore both are meant to increase customer loyalty.

The Personal Selling Process

To discuss the marketing tool of personal selling, it helps to have a clear understanding of **selling** in general—which we can define as presenting

FIGURE 13.1 Both personal selling and direct marketing target individual customers, presenting products that marketers believe will fulfill those customers' specific needs.

FIGURE 13.2 Key aspects of personal selling include identifying what the customer wants and needs, and suggesting appropriate products that meet those needs and offer value.

information about a product or service to a customer with the goal of motivating the customer to buy the product. Personal selling takes that activity further by involving a two-way exchange of information between the buyer and seller that is meant to build trust and enable the salesperson to provide a product that solves a customer's problem or need, helping to create a longer-term relationship beyond the current sale. When a boutique owner helps you select the perfect formal outfit for your style, when the cosmetics counter adviser leads you to a great new look for yourself, when an electronics store's sales associate provides

you with expert advice about putting together a home entertainment system, or when an interior designer works with you to create a harmonious décor for your home, you are experiencing and benefitting from personal selling.

Personal selling relies on communication in order to identify customer needs, present appropriate solutions, and help customers make value-driven buying decisions.

1. *Identifying needs*. A salesperson determines what a customer needs both rationally (size, features, price points, delivery requirements) and emotionally (social concerns, esteem, and self-actualization), aspects of consumer behavior discussed in Chapter 3. For example, suppose that you spend $175 on a pair of black, size 7B, Italian leather dress shoes for an important job interview; these are rational needs. If a salesperson steers you to consider a pair of Prada dress shoes that cost more than twice as much, the salesperson is addressing your emotional wants, such as your social concerns (fitting in with your peer group) and your ego/esteem (recognition for your stylish choice of shoes).

2. *Discussing appropriate solutions*. A salesperson suggests products that work for the specific customer. For example, the last time you bought jeans, you undoubtedly wanted a pair that flattered your shape and maybe that also flattened your tummy. The salesperson may have guided you to a couple of brands or styles that incorporated a front panel to give a slimming look.

3. *Making value-driven decisions*. A salesperson ensures that the product solution makes the

best use of the customer's resources, including money, time, effort, and usage. For example, you could buy a $20 basic white T-shirt or spend $70 on a trendy name brand. The professional salesperson helps you consider multiple factors, such as your budget, the construction and style of each brand, and how many times and where you will wear it, to make sure you're getting the best value.

THE NATURE OF SELLING

Selling is both a science, in that there are fundamental concepts and steps in the process, and an art, in that those who are selling need the talent to adapt to people, cultures, and personalities in order to impact buyers' senses or emotions. While it may seem simple enough—all it takes is to reach enough people who make the buying decision, then say the right things to persuade them to buy, and, of course, do it consistently—in reality, it's far from simple.

Let's first discuss two types of selling: transactional selling and relationship selling. Selling that focuses on the sale at hand but is not about nurturing a long-term relationship is called **transactional selling**. It generally deals with one need at a time, the immediate one. It could be any basic or staple item, where there is not really much difference between what various sellers offer; the customer does not undertake too much research in preparation for the buy, and the salesperson simply rings up the purchase without much interaction with the customer. Examples include many convenience, impulse, or relatively low-priced products such as nail polish, athletic socks, and plastic tableware.

On the other hand, **relationship selling** presumes that the salesperson takes the time to know, understand, and appreciate the buyer's wants and needs, and then provides appropriate solutions and follow-up service. In short, it creates added value beyond the sale itself. In turn, this ongoing relationship makes the purchaser more trusting and comfortable with the salesperson. Relationship selling is frequently found in marketing goods such as designer apparel, fine jewelry, and home theater systems. When relationship selling is successful, repeat sales, customer referrals, and purchase loyalty from the buyer flow naturally. Think about it: You'd probably return to the hairdresser or boutique owner who takes the time to listen to your needs and desires, suggests viable product or service solutions, provides objective advice, then follows up to see how those solutions worked. That's relationship selling—and the primary concept of personal selling.

TYPES OF SELLING

Some salespeople are called **order takers**, those who collect and process orders initially begun by the buyer; they merely note buyers' specifications and provide what is requested. A retail store counter clerk, a backroom manufacturing representative transcribing a vendor request, and the phone attendant taking your pizza order are examples. On the other hand, a *missionary salesperson* promotes a company's products by discussing their benefits and invites potential buyers to consider future purchases, but does not actually take the order. The salesperson from a medical products or pharmaceutical company who visits physicians' offices, explaining new products and leaving samples, is one example of a missionary salesperson. The samples might include nurses' tunics, orthotic shoes, or ID bracelets.

The most sophisticated and highest-paid salespeople are those who seek out new customers for relatively complex and costly products. Called **order getters**, these salespeople initiate and develop business relationships and use creative selling techniques to assist customers with purchase decisions. These salespeople uncover customer buying needs and—through problem-solving methods—offer appropriate solutions to customer buying dilemmas. Order getters demonstrate how certain product solutions differ from the others, and help customers envision themselves using and enjoying the product. If customers personalize the value, they are more likely to buy the product. Consider the fashion designer who works with boutique or chain store buyers to get them to carry his or her designs, or the personal shopper who calls clients when a new collection by their favorite designer arrives in the store. Order getters promote sales, gain customer support, and bridge the **sales gap**, the difference between the benefits of products the consumer currently owns and those that other products offer. Sometimes order getters work alone and sometimes with other sales personnel. The latter situations are known as *team selling*, referring to a group of specialists who work together in devising and delivering appropriate sales solutions. New car dealers traditionally use selling teams in negotiating vehicle sales, and wedding planners, as another example, have relationships with florists, caterers, and other key businesses in order to sell an entire event package.

THE ROLE OF PERSONAL SELLING

The interactive, one-on-one process of personal selling works particularly well for situations in which there are product, pricing, or trade-in negotiations or customized items, and that involve more detailed, technical, or expensive goods and services. People knowledgeable about customer needs and selling solutions work in planning parties and events, marketing fine jewelry and gemstones, and designing home and office interiors. As a salesperson creates value for the customer, the company benefits from that sale and potential future transactions.

Incorporating Push Strategy

Personal selling also occurs frequently when the goal is to move the product through the distribution channel, known as a *push strategy* (see Chapter 12), instead of waiting for customers to come to the seller. For example, a food manufacturer may produce a fashionable new frozen dessert and want supermarket chains to stock it. The manufacturer's wholesale sales representative visits the supermarket headquarters with samples to encourage the grocery chain to put the product in the freezer case. As a bonus, these intermediaries in the field also obtain firsthand feedback about company products, competitors, and marketplace trends. This information helps organizations improve product offerings. In comparison, advertising, public relations, and sales promotion—the promotion mix tools we'll discuss in the next chapter—use nonpersonal, one-way messages to focus on specific target groups.

FIGURE 13.3 Fashion marketers' sales representatives are order getters, developing relationships with retail buyers and working closely with them to make sure the store carries the merchandise most suited to its customers.

Utilizing the Sales Cycle

The time period between when a customer starts thinking about buying and the actual purchase date is known as a **sales cycle**. During sales cycles, marketers work to influence buyers through a combination of personal selling, advertising, sales promotion, and public relations strategies. Think of all the consumer ads you see online or the positive information you read and hear about as it relates to what companies are doing to help the public—that is, demonstrating corporate social responsibility. One company promotes the sustainability of its products or retail environment, another states that it offers only fair trade goods, and a third explains what it is doing to help fight drug abuse and AIDS. These corporate efforts appeal to customer confidence and loyalty because customers want to patronize those businesses they admire and trust. Because marketers want to understand, communicate with, and influence consumers, personal selling is a strong promotion mix tool. However, because the cost factor for sending a personal representative is high, the results must justify not using less expensive, targeted promotional messages—multimedia ads, billboards, or social networking events.

KEY STEPS IN THE SELLING PROCESS

Gaining a competitive advantage necessitates understanding the "how to" of personal selling and then adapting the fundamentals to each customer and marketplace. A systematic approach to the sales process includes the key steps that follow, which are recapped in Table 13.1.

Prospect and Qualify

A **prospect** is a possible buyer who is not yet a customer. In the sales process, then, *prospecting* involves identifying possible customers. In some cases, prospects come to the salesperson—as when a consumer walks into an apparel boutique or calls a caterer for information. In other situations, the salesperson must develop leads on prospects from multiple sources: commercial, residential, membership, or governmental directories; the company's inactive client lists; trade shows; referrals from existing customers of their friends, family, or other peer groups; marketing databases; ongoing company advertising efforts; and social or Internet networking.

Deciding which prospects are viable ones worth pursuing is important to saving both time and money that would be wasted by contacting just anyone and everyone. Think of old movies you've seen where people would prospect for gold. They had a better chance for success if they looked in the right areas. Likewise, when looking for new potential buyers, it's important to look in the right areas and for the right buyer characteristics; that is, it's important to **qualify** the leads, determining which are most likely to become actual customers. A salesperson will ask what level of interest might this person or group have in our product? Do they have access to funds and the authority to make the purchase? Suppose you are a manufacturer's representative selling children's wear to retail stores. Using the Internet, you consult government and business directories to find where potential stores are located, and sift through the lists to find appropriate retailers.

Preapproach

Before making a blind phone call or seeing a potential buyer, a good salesperson will develop additional key information about the prospective buyer, make a plan, and set some call objectives (what the salesperson realistically wants to accomplish). This research might include buyer preferences, previous suppliers, buying styles, association memberships, company information, or knowledge of other key decision makers. Checking company Web sites, publication directories, or social or professional business

FIGURE 13.4 Salespeople can find potential customers, or prospects, through a variety of means, including at trade shows.

TABLE 13.1 Important Sales Steps

Sales Step	Explanation	Example: Selling your fashion design (scarves)
1. Prospect and Qualify	Locate and prioritize list of potential buyers.	List potential channels (boutique/retail chain /Internet); identify and prioritize a list of potential buyers.
2. Preapproach	Research these buyers and decide how to approach them.	Study the organization, customer base, and corporate buyer to become familiar with their needs, reputation, buying preferences, and current suppliers. Draft quality questions for the sales meeting.
3. Approach	Communicate with the prospects. Make a strong first impression.	Contact the buyer; act professionally as you initiate the relationship. Ask key questions to understand the buyer's goals.
4. Make the Sales Presentation	Discuss your personalized product solutions. Show value-added benefits.	Explain how and why your scarves will sell well, and help the buyer achieve stated goals. Show evidence to support your statements.
5. Resolve Objections	Identify and clear up any buyer questions/barriers to a purchase.	Find out and deal with whatever issues might prevent the buyer from making an order.
6. Close the Sale	Get a favorable decision and commitment to buy.	Get an order for your scarves.
7. Follow Up	Tie up loose ends: terms, delivery specifics, payment. Stay in touch to ensure the customer and stakeholders are satisfied.	Review the details; make sure everything goes smoothly at all levels. Nurture this new relationship; it may lead to repeat business or customer referrals.

networking sites, or asking friends and business acquaintances can provide a strong foundation of data. Another source is the company's own database, which usually includes lists and contact information for current and past customers and prospects. Going back to the children's wear example, your preapproach for a specific store would include finding out what other children's apparel lines are carried, what age range the retailer targets, who is responsible for buying different categories, and so on.

Approach

Once this data is organized, the salesperson will focus on identifying how and when to make contact. In other words, after planning their work, salespeople work their plan. This is the approach phase, and it involves speaking to or meeting the prospect, with the goal of making a dynamic, professional first impression. In a retail or other setting where the prospect has made the initial contact, this is where the selling actually begins. The idea is to get buyers' attention and whet their appetites about the company and its product. Good salespeople will ask discerning questions designed to uncover key needs and wants (using the background information they learned when they conducted preapproach research), all the while conveying their industry knowledge and expertise. With the children's wear example, you might ask questions about the style preferences of the store's customers (both children and parents), as well as price ranges the store wants to carry, and communicate how your garments complement those the store already carries.

Make the Sales Presentation

The next step is for a salesperson to make the actual sales presentation—that is, to propose and explain the company's product solutions with evidence that the buyer understands, using product samples if possible, along with supporting information and data via whatever technology works best: netbook, iPad, laptop, cloud computing, handouts, or handheld charts. In a high-end apparel retail setting, the presentation might include a private showing of gowns or suits on models. For home theater equipment, it might involve a demonstration in a living room-type setting. In our children's wear example, you would have a trunk of samples with you in order for the prospective buyer to see the styling and colors, touch the fabric, and notice the construction of the garment. This is the point at which the customer must identify with and find value in your product.

Resolve Objections

Objections are often really requests for more information. A salesperson's positive attitude here is important because objections suggest that the customer is conscious and interested in at least hearing the response. Objections are either practical, real, logical reasons why the product might not work (price, delivery schedule, existing commitment) or psychological (predetermined beliefs, fear of making a bad decision, resistance to the salesperson). A skilled salesperson should anticipate and address these concerns (objections) in a professional manner, showing the customer that the goal is to help the buyer make a smart decision, not just sell the product. If the sleeves on a jacket are too long, the retail salesperson might offer to call the store's tailor to discuss an alteration. Or a car salesperson might resolve a price issue for a customer by offering a special financing package. An objection of the children's wear store buyer might be concern about receiving complete shipments on time, and you would assure her that the company prides itself on its on-time deliveries.

Close the Sale

When salespeople **close** the sale, they are obtaining a commitment to buy, a sales step called the *close*.

It is often expressed as a decision-asking question requiring a yes or no response from a buyer. Buyers may make multiple positive or negative decisions during the approach and sales presentation steps; for example, during approach, the buyer decides to continue listening or not, or agrees to a second meeting or not. Think of the last time you were at the store and the salesperson asked you if you wanted to use the fitting room. You answered yes or no, didn't you? That's a preliminary closing question. Some salespeople never ask closing questions because they fear rejection. They hope the buyer

officially states the positive answer in advance. The salesperson who gets the customer making small "yes" answers along the way and keeps that momentum going generally succeeds in getting the commitment. No commitment means no sale. To close the children's wear sale, you might reach an agreement with the buyer as to specific items in the line that will be tested for consumer reaction at the store, and the most convenient delivery dates for the order.

It is much easier to add on to a sale to an existing customer than to start working with a new customer. Perhaps you remember when you bought a pair of summer shorts and the sales associate suggested a belt, a coordinating shirt or two, and perhaps a jacket. Or maybe you put an MP3 player in your shopping cart at an online store and the site opened a pop-up window suggesting a stylish carrying case or docking speaker. When you saw the other products and realized how well they went together, you decided on another item or two. This is an example of *suggestion selling*, which, when well done, can be a real advantage to the customer, adding to the functionality of the original purchase. Unfortunately, suggestion selling is often forgotten or, worse yet, poorly executed. With training and experience, suggestion selling can be handled deftly and is of benefit to both the customer and the salesperson. As the children's wear sales representative, you might alert the store buyer to an upcoming preseason sale of children's coats and obtain an order for those goods as well.

FIGURE 13.5 Suggestion selling is a way for a personal seller to persuade customers to make a logical addition to their current purchase, such as a tie to go with the new shirt, or a carrying case to go with the new laptop computer.

Follow Up

Once the buyer makes the purchase commitment, the initial follow-up refers to the final details needed

MARKETER'S INSIGHT:
PERSONAL SELLING IN THE AGE OF E-TAILING

If one knowledgeable salesperson at a customer's beck and call is a good thing, imagine a retail floor teeming with hundreds of associates ready to offer expert recommendations on products. While that's certainly not practical in a brick-and-mortar retail setting, it is completely possible in the world of e-commerce— thanks to state-of-the-art recommendation technology, which can, in essence, turn every person visiting a Web site into a salesperson.

Just ask Bluefly.com, an e-tailer specializing in designer trends at 20 to 75 percent off. After deploying new "collective intelligence" recommendation technology on its site, the company enjoyed a 300 percent increase in sales from recommendations in just the first three months.

Previously, Bluefly had used a recommendation engine that required the company to manually send transaction and product data to its vendor once a week—a process that meant recommendations were quickly out of date. Because Bluefly specializes in cutting-edge trends from famous designers, and because

its inventory can be extremely thin on certain items, timeliness was critical. What's more, the old system only provided data on what customers purchased, even though the retailer knew that it could learn valuable information about customers' interests from knowing what items they looked at or even put in their shopping cart but didn't buy.

Bluefly's new recommendation platform, purchased from software-as-a-service provider Baynote, is based on behavior patterns, or what Baynote calls *collective intelligence*. The technology silently observes everyone visiting the site, instantly groups users with like-minded peers based on similar behaviors, and begins delivering recommendations in real time. Those recommendations are presented to shoppers at three key points: the department and product pages, which generate "most wanted" lists, and when an item is placed in a shopping bag. That final spot is a pop-up that shows recommendations for that specific item, sometimes a coordinating piece, sometimes a competing one.

Adapted from: Sandy Smith, "Power of the People," *Stores*, April 2010, www.stores.org/stores-magazine-april-2010/power-people (accessed March 6, 2012).

to ensure that the transaction proceeds smoothly. For example, a salesperson might verify the payment method, how the item is to be packaged, or how delivery to branch stores is to be handled. The

longer-term follow-up relates to the newly established customer relationship. The salesperson who nurtures this bond (via service calls or special sales opportunities) may receive repeat sales or business referrals. Do you recall receiving a follow-up contact from a salesperson after making a purchase? How did it make you feel? As a children's wear sales representative, you phone or e-mail the retail store buyer to confirm delivery of the goods, make sure the merchandise is satisfactory, and keep your customer apprised on an ongoing basis of upcoming market weeks and store visits.

READING CUSTOMER SIGNALS

A salesperson works to identify with and understand the customer. As such, reading and adapting to customer signals is important because it builds the relationship and can lead to repeat purchases or new business referrals.

Successful salespeople understand that the keys to selling include garnering customers' attention and interest, providing solutions, and knowing how and when to close the deal. All of those are more easily accomplished when salespeople incorporate **360° listening**—using their ears, eyes, and intuition to pick up on subtle cues that the customer is leaning toward or away from making a purchase. To put it in more personal terms, for example, when a friend tells you "everything is fine," you may notice a slight tremor in her voice, or perhaps catch a look in her eye, or simply have a "gut feeling" that everything is not really fine. The practiced sales professional who can match a customer attitude with the corresponding sales level (as shown in Table 13.2) is much better able to muster the appropriate sales tools to stay in sync with the customer than a salesperson listening only to a customer's words.

Who is the best fashion salesperson you know? How do you account for that person's expertise? What personal and professional characteristics contribute to that person's success in sales?

Direct Marketing

While personal selling is the direct, personal interaction of a salesperson with a customer, direct marketing is just a step removed, allowing marketers to pinpoint key customers and prospects and present them with a variety of communications that are targeted to their lifestyle or needs. Think of the scenario at the beginning of this chapter where the ski apparel marketer used a purchase of ski pants to target you as the customer with a catalogue for other skiwear. Whenever you get a mobile text or e-mail message from a retailer, a catalogue in the mail, a product offer with your credit card bill, or a telephone sales call—or whenever you watch an infomercial on TV or online or view a home shopping network segment—you are receiving direct marketing communications.

Just as marketers engaged in personal selling need to prospect and quantify their leads, companies that conduct direct marketing must also ensure that they are spending their time and money effectively in reaching the correct customers. A family with no young children probably has no interest in receiving catalogues for baby clothes, and a grandparent who bought a videogame one time as a birthday gift for a grandson would not need ongoing e-mail alerts about new

TABLE 13.2 Customer Signals Checklist

Sales Approach Step	Attention	Interest	Solution	Desire	Close
Customer attitude	Preoccupied; not paying attention	Not interested	Skeptical; doubts things	Seems to hesitate or put things off	Anxious; shows buyer remorse
Customer thinks:	"I have better things to do."	"I don't need or want it."	Product/ service does not work; salesperson may not know enough.	"Let me delay my decision;" bad timing	"I'm scared to make a bad decision;" others might not agree.
Actions by salesperson	Connect; schmooze; get the other person talking	Ask questions; find out both logical reasons and emotional reasons for customer to buy. People buy emotionally and justify logically.	Use evidence; prove/support what you say; show that it works, it's worth it, and others support it (not just the salesperson).	Create a word picture that helps the buyer see him- or herself enjoying its usage; use present tense action verbs; be realistic; keep it simple.	Get agreement; get the other person saying/ thinking "yes."
What the salesperson is trying to sell	Him/herself	A need	A product, service, and/or brand	An immediate want	A purchase decision

game releases. That is why marketers use **targeted databases**, lists of qualified consumers who are most likely to actually make a purchase of their product. Once a direct marketing initiative is undertaken, companies then analyze the *response rate*, or the percentage of people reached who take some kind of action based on the communication, either by calling, e-mailing, going to the Web site, or showing up at the store. From there, marketers also analyze and determine the *conversion rate*, or percentage of customers who actually buy. The more accurate a marketer's targeted database is,

FIGURE 13.6 A wide variety of fashion companies promote their products through direct marketing, using targeted databases to ensure they are reaching the right customers.

the better chance that response and conversion rates will be consistently high. To the company, this means increased sales.

BENEFITS TO FASHION CONSUMERS AND MARKETERS

Fashion companies are drawn to direct marketing as a promotional tool by more than simply the possibility for increased sales. Sellers benefit from the ability to reach qualified buyers very effectively,

wherever they may be and at whatever time they are available to receive the communications. Companies can also profit from direct marketing to minimize overhead expenses, reduce the sales cycle, nurture existing business relationships by rewarding customers, and establish new relationships using value-added promotions.

Incorporating digital and mobile communications into this process can further enhance the effectiveness of direct marketing. For example, a process called Web morphing enables Web sites to automatically adjust content and visual displays to favor the individual ways that people perceive, process, and remember information. This means that potential buyers screening the same product at the same time using separate Web-enabled devices will view the promotional data differently. A person who processes information more logically or analytically (left brain) may see more detailed, data-driven material. Another person who uses a subjective, intuitive style (right brain) would view and absorb more creative visuals and emotional descriptors.[1]

But it's not just sellers that benefit from direct marketing. The promotional tool also holds advantages for fashion consumers, providing them with product information that is tailored to their lifestyle or needs, along with an easy mechanism for making a purchase. Think of it this way: When you consider buying something, isn't it nice to have information at your fingertips, easy access to a variety of suppliers (both domestic and global), the ability to communicate with the seller, and then the ability to complete the process on your own time and in the setting of your choice? For instance, it's 11:30 at night and you're at home going through your mail. When you open the credit card bill from your

MARKETER'S INSIGHT:
TARGETING CATALOGUE CUSTOMERS BY ZIP CODE

In recent years, direct marketers from L.L. Bean to Neiman Marcus Group have looked for ways to cut back on catalogue mailings in the face of higher paper and postage costs, coupled with sluggish consumer spending. Williams-Sonoma not only found a way to cut its costs, but to better target potential buyers at the same time—by using data collected about zip codes as one means to help eliminate mailings to unlikely customers.

Williams-Sonoma—whose six catalogues include Pottery Barn, West Elm, and the eponymous Williams-Sonoma books—is a pioneer in the use of aggregated data about zip codes, including declines in home prices and credit scores, to weed out people who probably won't buy its home goods. The company, which mails well over 300 million catalogues each year, recently made a plan to cut circulation by 10 to 15 percent for a savings of $35 to $45 million, but without hurting its sales.

While most catalogue mailers base their decisions on the purchasing history of particular households, and sometimes additional data such as second-home ownership and magazine subscriptions, most are leery of using financial data for fear that consumers might see it as an invasion of privacy. Williams-Sonoma defends its strategy, however, noting that it uses only aggregate data about a zip code, and not data about individuals. The company also looks at other variables including the percentage of European automobiles in an area and the percentage of the population that is 4 years old or less.

Williams-Sonoma also applies its economic screen only to those people it has already deemed unlikely to buy—for instance, those who haven't made a purchase from one of its stores or from similar catalogue merchants, or who haven't browsed one of its Web sites in at least a year.

Adapted from: Jennifer Saranow, "A ZIP-Code Screen for Catalog Customers," *The Wall Street Journal*, June 24, 2008, http://online.wsj.com/article/SB121426761450198531.html (accessed March 6, 2012).

favorite store, you find a colorful brochure showcasing a 60 percent discount on your favorite brand of jeans—jeans you'd purchased at that store a few months ago, using your store card. The brochure says that you can take advantage of this discount if you place an order for the jeans online within a week. You put the statement with your checkbook to take care of later, and go online to check the deal. It's too good to pass up, so you buy two pairs. Without the direct marketing vehicle you received, you would not have had the opportunity to take advantage of this special buy.

TYPES OF DIRECT MARKETING

There are a number of different media that fashion marketers have available for their direct marketing communications. These can be used alone or in strategic combinations, depending on the marketing goals.

Catalogues

A traditional catalogue is a hard-copy (printed on paper) collection of product information and illustrations or photos generally displayed in organized categories and subcategories. Retail and specialty department stores, consumer electronics companies, vacation service organizations, and other fashion marketers use catalogues to generate interest in their offerings and to generate sales. Catalogues sometimes have an extended reach beyond the initial recipient because they end up on someone's desk or are shared with friends or other family members. Check your mail this week and you may well find several. Many marketers re-create their paper catalogue on their Web site for customers who like to browse the pages on the couch but place an order online. In addition, some companies are creating special versions of their catalogues specifically for viewing on an iPad or other tablet computer, or on a smartphone. Web sites that include multiple online

FIGURE 13.7 Direct marketing allows consumers to take advantage of personalized offers they receive, and to shop at their convenience. Do you sometimes get e-mails or text message alerts from a favorite store or brand, alerting you to a special sale? That's direct marketing.

catalogues or shopping opportunities are called **virtual malls**. (See Chapter 11 for more information on catalogues.)

Direct Mail

If you ever received a letter, postcard, brochure, CD, DVD, thumb drive, or any form of personalized marketing offer via mail or e-mail, you were included in a direct mail campaign. While some people refer to it as "junk mail," when direct mail is properly targeted to a qualified consumer, it can provide valuable information and purchasing opportunities to the customer, and additional sales for the marketer. Some tools used in direct mail to attract consumers' attention include colorful words and images, interactive media links, personalized messages, or animation. Both for-profit and not-for-profit organizations use this method to solicit or sell.

WHAT DO YOU THINK?

What kind of direct mail pieces get your attention? What factors influence you to open up one piece of mail but throw away other direct mail pieces?

Kiosks

Kiosks are freestanding, sometimes movable booths or stands used for selling or to provide marketing information directly to consumers. They may be staffed by an attendant or equipped with an Internet-connected touch screen to function as a self-service, cyber-salesperson. A consumer gets the data and orders or receives the product.

Any business, whether small or large, might open a kiosk in a mall or other high-traffic location to save the overhead expenses of a traditional store space, since the rental, employment, and merchandising costs are far lower for a kiosk. Redbox, for example, places its movie rental kiosks in supermarkets, convenience stores, fast-food restaurants, and other locations that make it convenient for consumers to pick up a DVD, Blu-ray disc, or video-game while completing other shopping. In shopping centers, kiosks often offer items such as sunglasses, jewelry, scarves, small electronics, decorative home accessories, and other goods. Other types of kiosks market photo services, hotel reservations, car rentals, and airline ticketing directly to consumers.

Some kiosks are pop-up or temporary outlets geared to a season, providing book bags, T-shirts, and caps for back-to-school; masks for Halloween; or decorations for Christmas. Trade show kiosks offer convention information, maps, and tickets to special events. Customers making a purchase may pay with credit and smart cards, smartphones, and in some cases checks or cash.

Direct Response TV (DRTV)

Direct response TV (DRTV) is a programming selling message that replaces the traditional store experience with televised electronic marketing. The form may be 30- to 60-minute infomercials, short advertising commercials, or home shopping network programs that showcase products through demonstrations and testimonials. (See Chapter 11 for more on television home shopping.) This method is cost-effective in reaching a mass audience, is easily measured, and encourages impulse buying, often encouraging consumers to "act now." Also, because phone numbers or Web sites are shown when the selling call-to-action is made, companies receive

FIGURE 13.8 With direct-response TV, consumers are encouraged to "buy now," making it easy for marketers to quickly measure the effectiveness of their promotion.

immediate feedback about the effectiveness of their direct marketing, and can make rapid adjustments or improvements to the programming. You have probably viewed such programming, or maybe even made a purchase of the products, which might include beauty products, jewelry, kitchen appliances, diet and health-care items, fitness equipment, self-defense or self-improvement DVDs, music, or digital equipment.

Telemarketing

Telemarketing is the use of the telephone to make direct contact with a customer. Business-to-consumer (B2C) telemarketing refers to marketing by companies that call consumers at home or on their cell phone. Portrait studios, magazine subscription agents, and carpet cleaners are among those businesses using telemarketing. Business-to-business (B2B) telemarketers include furniture, jewelry, clothing, office products, and other manufacturers or organizations contacting retailers to carry their line. Outbound callers (order getters)

try to sell, whereas inbound calls are serviced by order takers. If you have ever sold or bought an item from another person (not a business), the term customer-to-customer (C2C) applies; perhaps you've called several friends to see which one might like to buy the Green Day concert tickets you can't use and are trying to sell. Even though the government enacted a national Do Not Call Registry in 2003, providing an enforceable means for consumers to remove their phone numbers from telemarketers' lists, nonprofit organizations and companies with which consumers have previously conducted business are exempt from the restriction. And because it can be an effective sales tool, telemarketers continue to develop creative selling strategies to entice prospects with value-added offers and important information. On occasion, certain targeted consumers invite these callers to contact them.

Whatever direct marketing tools are used, the objectives of a direct marketing campaign include getting a consumer response, nurturing a business relationship, enhancing a brand and image, and making a sale. When a company organizes and coordinates the various media so that they complement each other and enhance the total effort, the process is called integrated direct marketing. This means there is a centralized, strategic direct marketing plan, like the hub of a wheel, and each "spoke" is the type of direct marketing used. (See Figure 13.9.) The objective is to increase the customer response ratio, which in turn should lead to an increase in sales. For example, systematically adding direct response TV and an interactive Web site to an initial direct mail campaign may raise the response rate from 2 percent to 30 or 40 percent.

DIRECT MARKETING TO GLOBAL FASHION CONSUMERS

The use of the Internet and other electronic methods of communication for direct marketing has become increasingly popular among fashion organizations because of the variety, flexibility, immediacy, and global reach. Through online or mobile direct marketing, customers in Denver, Dubai, and Dublin can order outfits from designers and fashion marketers in New York, Paris, Tokyo, and many other places worldwide. The tools of electronic direct marketing are evolving as technology continually evolves, and encompass a range of vehicles including blogs, Twitter, e-mail, social networks, mobile applications, and widgets.

Blogs

Blogs (short for "Web logs") are Web sites where marketers (and others) can communicate and share news and opinions about products, fashion trends, and any other information they desire. While some blogs may offer goods for sale, others are not involved in direct sales, but might provide information or links to other sites where customers can purchase the fashion items being discussed.

Fashion blogs include critiques of the fashion scene, suggestions on finding up-to-the minute trends, and fashion information from various countries. Some of the fashion blogs found online in recent years include Fashion Copious (http://fashioncopious.com/), which focuses on trends, and Pirabalini (http://pirabalini.blogspot.com), which calls itself the ultimate fashion bible. Trendy Japanese fashion, including Harajuku street styles, is featured on La Carmina (http://www.lacarmina.com/blog/).

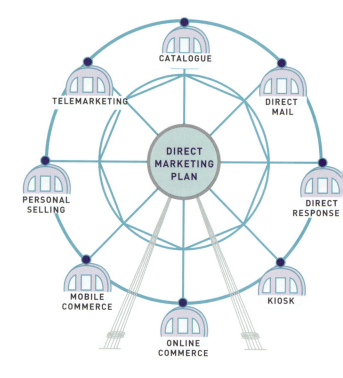

FIGURE 13.9 In an integrated direct marketing program, marketers coordinate different types of direct marketing to work together and increase customer response. BY VANESSA HAN AND ALICIA FREILE

Twitter

Even those who don't use it are most likely very familiar with Twitter, a micro-blogging social networking service that permits organizations and individuals to send continual messages, or "tweets," to their followers, provided the messages consist of no more than 140 characters. An apparel retailer can use Twitter to inform customers of a flash sale on dress shirts, for example.

E-mail

E-mail enables marketing organizations to send direct marketing messages to customers on a regular or occasional basis, usually when consumers

MARKETER'S INSIGHT:
DIRECT MARKETING TAKES FUTURE TWIST

Even with the wealth of media competing for consumers' attention, there is still nothing more critical than television for establishing a brand's presence. But innovations in direct response TV are poised to take this direct marketing vehicle to a whole different level—as new technologies are being employed to make impulse buying even faster and easier.

It used to be that television pitchmen for quirky products like Pajama Jeans and lighted slippers tried to get viewers to place orders by telephone. They then shifted to getting products into retail outlets with labels that screamed "As Seen on TV." Now, the new owner of AsSeenOnTV.com is embracing technologies that use cell phones and remote controls to enable purchases directly from a TV set.

As part of the company's new direction, daily Web videos with product demonstrations are being produced, and Facebook pages where users can buy products directly are set to roll out. In addition, the company plans to push the videos out by e-mail to subscribers to the site.

But streamlining the way consumers buy the products—including a high-end set of wireless, over-the-ear headphones promoted by 50 Cent—is a central goal, eliminating the need for television viewers to jot down an 800 number or go to a Web site. As a result, the company is rolling out technology it calls audio fingerprinting, which will enable cell phones to decipher which infomercial a user is watching after the phone is held up to the TV. The user will then be sent to a mobile Web site where the product can be bought through the cell phone.

Another development will let viewers use ordinary remote controls to buy products off a TV screen by clicking a button that opens a purchase window. Advertisers will also be able to track which commercials elicited purchases.

Adapted from: Tanzina Vega, "Impulse Buying on TV Enters an Even Faster Phase," *New York Times*, June 29, 2011, http://www.nytimes.com/2011/06/30/business/media/30adco.html (accessed March 6, 2012).

---

have made a purchase and provided their e-mail address, or they have "opted in" to receive promotional e-mails. Fashion organizations such as Neiman Marcus, Macy's, Lafayette 148, Frette linens, Shoebuy.com, and many others, as well as museums, theaters, and other entertainment venues use e-mail messages to alert customers to new product offerings or special sales and promotions.

Social Networks

Social networks, such as Facebook, Pinterest, and LinkedIn, are Web-based venues designed to make it easy for people to communicate and share personal

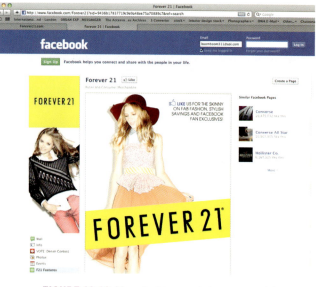

FIGURE 13.10 Many fashion marketers use social networks such as Facebook to convey direct marketing messages to their target customers.

information, news, and opinions with friends and colleagues. Fashion marketers such as Forever 21, Neiman Marcus, and Nordstrom, among many others, maintain Facebook pages, encouraging consumers to "like" their brand so that they may update them with information on new products, events, and trends.

Mobile Applications

Better known as "apps," mobile applications are marketing programs that can be sent to portable devices such as smartphones and iPads to encourage buying. Some retailers offer redeemable points for viewing store window displays, and more points for trying on merchandise. Target has a Gift Finder app, permitting users to search for gifts by entering the gender, age, and personality of the intended beneficiary. Combined with GPS technology, mobile apps

can sometimes pinpoint a consumer's current location as being in the vicinity of a particular marketer and send a text coupon or offer to encourage the consumer to stop in right away.

Widgets

Widgets are applications that offer live updates to a Web site. Widgets may be set up on computer desktops, on some broadband-equipped televisions, or on mobile devices. Pizza Hut has a desktop widget, Pizza Hut Shortcut, which enables viewers to scan the latest menu and order from their computers.[2]

WHAT DO YOU THINK?

What is your preferred way of receiving digital marketing messages? Why? If you owned a boutique, which electronic methods would you use to send out your messages? Why?

Ethical Issues in Personal Selling and Direct Marketing

Of all the elements in the promotion mix, personal selling and direct marketing are the most individualized—they rely on at least some knowledge of consumers' personal information, needs, desires, and lifestyle in order to successfully target the right audience and find the right fashion solution for each customer. Because of that, marketers must always be aware of privacy concerns, and be careful not to cross an ethical line when requesting or using personal data in their sales and marketing activities.

Another question of ethics may arise when consumers feel they are being pressured by an overly zealous salesperson or are being bombarded by too many unsolicited direct marketing communications. A too-pushy salesperson—typically one who lacks the skills and talent for picking up on customer cues that the more skilled, and generally more successful, professional salespeople possess—can aggravate customers and give a bad name to others in the profession. A reputable marketer will most likely become aware of the problem relatively quickly and replace the salesperson with someone able to build a better rapport with customers. As for unsolicited or excessive direct marketing communications, there are a number of mechanisms in place through which consumers can inform a company that they do not wish to receive as many, or any, further contacts. Placing a phone number on the "do not call" list, contacting a catalogue company to have it discontinue mailings, and clicking the "unsubscribe" link on a marketing e-mail are just some of those methods. Because not all customers are aware of these options or willing to take the time to notify marketers, a company with good customer relationship management will try to be conscientious and considerate in its communications and their frequency.

summary

Personal selling and direct marketing are the elements of the promotion mix that are personalized to individual consumers. Both have a goal not only of obtaining a sale but also of addressing target customers' needs and establishing a relationship that builds customer loyalty.

Personal selling relies on two-way communication between the salesperson and customer. It generally involves relationship selling, which presumes that the salesperson takes the time to learn about the customer's needs, provides appropriate solutions, and follows up to ensure customer satisfaction, thereby creating value beyond the sale itself. Personal selling works particularly well for sales situations involving negotiations, customization of products, or more detailed, technical, or expensive products.

The key steps in the selling process are: prospect and qualify, preapproach, approach, make the sales presentation, resolve objections, close the sale, and follow up. Suggestion selling involves offering items that are complementary to the chosen purchase in order to solicit add-on sales and add value for the customer. Throughout the process, successful salespeople use 360° listening to pick up on cues about the customer's attitude.

Direct marketing involves a variety of communications to selected customers based on their likelihood of buying the marketer's products. Companies using direct marketing rely on targeted databases in order to maximize their response rate, or the percentage of customers who take some action based on the communication, and their conversion rate, or the percentage of customers who actually buy. Marketers benefit by being able to reach qualified buyers in a convenient manner and with less overhead than at a physical location. Fashion consumers benefit from the flexibility and convenience of shopping by whatever means, and at whatever time, suits them. Types of direct marketing include catalogues, direct mail, kiosks, direct response TV, and telemarketing.

Using the Internet and other electronic communications vehicles for direct marketing has provided fashion companies with instant global reach. Among the technologies being used by marketers include blogs, Twitter, e-mail, social networks, mobile applications, and widgets. The major ethical issues relating to personal selling and direct marketing involve privacy concerns for consumers, overly pushy salespeople, and an overload of marketing communications.

Bon-Ton Finds Key to Selling Beauty

There is perhaps no other fashion product that requires more trust between a customer and a salesperson than cosmetics. After all, the sales staff at a cosmetics counter is regularly required to get "up close and personal" with consumers—meaning the best cosmetics sales associate must be not just a pretty face, but someone who can build relationships, problem solve, and be creative to get the job done.

That was a fact that hit home for The Bon-Ton Stores, which noticed that its roughly 3,650 "beauty advisers," supporting 13 different cosmetics lines, had a higher turnover rate than associates in other parts of the stores. As Denise Domian, Bon-Ton's senior vice president, human resource operations, noted, "In the cosmetics area, there's a greater degree of customer interaction and actual selling that goes on," adding that based on feedback from the stores, "we discovered that perhaps we were not capturing the best candidates."

As a result, the department store chain—in conjunction with Kenexa, a global provider of business solutions for human resources—began developing a new assessment tool specifically for cosmetics department hiring. The process began with five key areas that have been shown to predict individual performance and potential: experience, skills, abilities, personality, and judgment. Also included were mathematical questions to assess candidates' cognitive ability, which was found to be the number-one predictor of success for cosmetic counter employees. "It's about being able to think on your feet and respond to customer needs," Domian said.

Since the retailer began using the new assessment as part of a comprehensive strategy for beauty adviser retention, it found that the newly hired associates achieved an average 2.1 percent increase in total sales per hour versus previous employees hired without the assessment. The turnover rate for beauty advisers also declined—so much so that it dropped below the turnover rate for associates in other parts of the company's stores.

In the end, Bon-Ton has benefitted from higher employee retention and increased sales, and customers have benefitted from working with sales associates who can be trusted to intuitively meet their individual skincare and makeup needs.

Adapted from: Fiona Soltes, "Grooming Great Salespeople," *Stores*, April 2011, www.stores.org/STORES%20Magazine%20April%202011/grooming-great-salespeople (accessed March 6, 2012).

QUESTIONS

1. Why do you think cosmetics requires a higher level of personal selling than some other fashion products?
2. How would hiring better qualified sales associates result in better retention of staff for the cosmetics department? Why would that be important to Bon-Ton?

KEY TERMS

360° listening

close (a sale)

order getter

order taker

prospect

qualify (a lead)

relationship selling

sales gap

sales cycle

selling

targeted database

transactional selling

virtual mall

REVIEW QUESTIONS

1. Explain the difference between transactional selling and relationship selling. Which is more important in personal selling as a promotion tool?

2. List the key steps in the selling process. What does each one entail?

3. Explain why direct marketers use targeted databases, and list three ways to develop such lists.

4. What are four of the different types of direct marketing? Give an example of each.

5. Name three electronic methods of direct marketing. Why is electronic direct marketing important to marketers trying to reach a global customer base?

DISCUSSION ACTIVITIES AND PROJECTS

1. Interview a salesperson who sells B2B to discover how that person prospects and qualifies possible buyers.

2. Identify two salespeople you know, and discuss how one of them presents him- or herself more professionally in terms of relationship selling.

3. Create a selling scenario and explain how you might utilize the Customer Signals Checklist (Table 13.2) to get in sync with your customer.

4. Contact a fashion marketer and inquire what types of direct marketing tools discussed in the chapter are most used. Explain the product and target market involved.

5. Survey five people (classmates, family, others), and ask them what direct marketing communications they remember receiving in the past few weeks. For each person, make a chart to track how many of each type they received (catalogue, direct mail, e-mail, text message, etc.), including what marketers sent them. Did some receive multiple communications from the same company? Ask if they are already customers, whether they take action in response to the marketing, and which forms of communication they respond to most. Prepare a brief oral report on your findings to the class.

DEVELOPING YOUR MARKETING PLAN

As you continue to develop the promotional aspect of your marketing plan, consider the ways in which you will use personal selling and/or direct marketing. Here's what you need to do:

1. Decide whether your product would benefit from personal selling. Do its features or benefits require in-depth explanation? Is it a high-priced product that would benefit from a salesperson persuading customers to make a purchase? Providing details on specific product attributes and your target customers, explain why you would or would not include personal selling as a promotional tool in your plan. If you would use personal selling, list the top three benefits you would stress in your sales presentation. What are one or two objections you could envision having to resolve? How would you address those to close the sale?

2. Review your target market to determine what type(s) of direct marketing would be appropriate for your product. Based on who your target customers are, which direct marketing vehicles would you use in order to reach the desired audience? Write a description of your direct marketing plan, including what vehicles you would use, how they would complement each other, and how you would track results of the effort.

Refer to the Marketing Plan Outline, Table 1.2, provided at the end of Chapter 1, as well as Appendix A: Sample Marketing Plan.

REFERENCES

1. Tim Greene, "MIT Researchers: Morphing Web Sites Could Bring Riches," *Network World*, May 22, 2008, http://www.networkworld.com/news/2008/052208-mit-researchers-morphing-web-sites.html (accessed November 15, 2011).

2. "Digital Handbook," *Marketing News*, April 30, 2009.

CHAPTER 14

Fashion Advertising, Sales Promotion, and Public Relations

This chapter describes the nature of advertising as a promotional element, explores the different types of advertising, and explains how fashion marketers create and implement an advertising campaign. It goes on to discuss sales promotion as a fashion marketing tool, and then describes the role and goals of public relations as part of an integrated marketing communications strategy.

WHAT DO I NEED TO KNOW ABOUT FASHION ADVERTISING, SALES PROMOTION, AND PUBLIC RELATIONS?

✱ The role of advertising, sales promotion, and public relations in the promotion mix

✱ The nature and types of advertising

✱ The steps in creating an advertising campaign

✱ The purpose of sales promotion in fashion marketing

✱ The goals and uses of public relations in marketing fashion goods

FASHION MARKETING IN FOCUS:
Fashion and Marketing in the World

You're at home, relaxing in front of the television after a busy day of classes and work. Or perhaps you're riding a bus downtown on your way to the dentist, or are already at the dentist's office and flipping through the pages of a magazine you picked up in the waiting room. Then again, you could be browsing in your favorite store, or surfing to your favorite Web site. Wherever you are, and whatever you're doing (other than sleeping), chances are you have received—even if you weren't paying much attention—at least one message being conveyed by a fashion marketer.

Did you glance at a poster for Nike running shoes on the side of the shelter at the bus stop? Did you stop and read a magazine article about young designer LaQuan Smith and the custom pieces he created for Lady Gaga and Rihanna? Maybe you found yourself humming along to the tune in a Target commercial, or lingered at the Clinique counter to see what was in the gift-with-purchase "goody bag." These scenarios reflect just some of the types of communications that fashion marketers hope you'll notice as part of your daily life, even when they're not specifically addressed to you as an individual.

As stated at the opening of Chapter 1, fashion and marketing surround you virtually all the time and wherever you are, and the marketing communications elements of *advertising*, *public relations*, and *sales promotion* are often the most visible aspects of that fact. Fashion marketers go to great lengths to place their product and brand messages where customers will be most likely to notice them and view them favorably. By using these three impersonal promotional tools—those that, unlike *personal selling* and *direct marketing*, are not tailored to individual consumers—they are able to reach the broadest possible audience of customers and potential customers with information or news of general interest about their company and its products.

As you'll recall from Chapter 12 and our discussion about integrated marketing communications, a company's advertising, sales promotion, and public relations efforts are most effective when they are coordinated with each other—and with whatever direct marketing or personal selling is being conducted—to convey a clear and consistent message to consumers. In this way, marketers can achieve the greatest impact for the budget and resources they have available. Just think: If you watch an apparel company spokesperson on a talk show segment describing the company's clothing line as perfect weekend casual attire for twenty-somethings, then notice a magazine ad showing models in their forties wearing the clothes in a business setting, you're receiving mixed messages, and won't have a clear idea of who the company is trying to target or how it truly means to position its clothing in the marketplace.

In an integrated marketing communications strategy, a fashion company plans its promotional elements of advertising, sales promotion, and public relations to seamlessly blend, complement, and enhance each other. Say that a designer organization like Stella McCartney is getting ready to promote a new apparel collection. Every promotional element will work hand in hand with the others to build a cohesive overall impression:

▶ The designer's staff might organize fashion shows in key markets in Europe, Asia, and the United States, making sure that the important fashion editors and bloggers are present to review the line. Selected retail buyers might receive an invitation with a sales promotion offer involving

FIGURE 14.1 Marketing messages are conveyed through a variety of media, with advertising, public relations, and sales promotion reaching us almost anywhere, even when we're not necessarily aware of it.

special purchase terms on orders placed within a week of the show.

- Coinciding with the collection's launch, the company might place advertisements in fashion magazines such as *Vogue* and *Harper's Bazaar*. At the same time, it would contact editors of key magazines or producers of appropriate television programming with information about the line or perhaps the offer of an interview about the collection with McCartney herself.
- To further promote the collection, the designer's staff would position the new apparel prominently on the company's Web site, as well as on the Web sites of retailers that agreed to participate in the launch.
- On a local level, Stella McCartney sales representatives might hold trunk shows in retail stores such as Neiman Marcus, working with the retailers to

create ads, press releases, displays, and additional promotional material that reinforces the designer's own messaging in tone and image. They might also send personal invitations to key customers who have purchased the designer's apparel, or similar collections, in the past, offering a special gift to customers who purchase a minimum dollar amount of the clothing.

In short, integrated marketing communications accomplishes a company's goal when the promotional message is clear, coordinated, consistent, and persuasive in eliciting a positive consumer response. Let's look at the ways in which each of our remaining promotion mix elements has its own character and function within an integrated marketing communications plan, starting with advertising.

FIGURE 14.2 Fashion marketers coordinate their advertising, public relations, and sales promotion to complement each other and create a bigger impact.

The Nature of Advertising

A major part of the promotion mix is advertising. As you will recall from Chapter 12, advertising is the placement of a paid, nonpersonal message in any of the mass media in which the sponsor is clearly identified and is seeking to inform or influence the audience. The broad purpose of advertising is to present a favorable image of a product or organization, but individual advertisements may also have a more specific goal they are hoping to accomplish, such as to announce the grand opening of a new store and draw a large crowd to the event.

ADVERTISING OBJECTIVES

A marketer's objectives for its advertising efforts are always aligned with its overall promotional objectives. These are threefold: to inform, to persuade, and to remind. When fashion marketers participate in a trade show, their displays, brochures, and catalogues inform retail store buyers of new products, as well as provide information on pricing, ordering, and shipping. Ads on Web sites and in fashion magazines explain new product features and benefits, such as improved fabric or embellishments. Fashion marketers' Facebook pages often

TABLE 14.1 Possible Objectives of Advertising

Advertising Type	Key Objectives
Informative advertising	■ Telling consumers about a new product ■ Presenting new uses for an existing product ■ Explaining or demonstrating how a product works ■ Announcing a price change ■ Correcting misinformation ■ Reducing consumer fears or misgivings ■ Building a positive company image
Persuasive Advertising	■ Encouraging consumers to switch to a brand ■ Nurturing brand preference ■ Giving reasons for consumers to purchase now ■ Changing customers' perception of a product or its attributes ■ Persuading customers to accept a sales call
Reminder advertising	■ Maintaining a relationship with customers ■ Reminding customers that they may need the product soon ■ Reminding customers where to buy the product ■ Keeping the product or company top-of-mind during off-seasons

Source: Gary Armstrong and Philip Kotler, *Marketing: An Introduction*, 10th edition (Prentice Hall, 2011).

contain persuasive advertising, pointing out how a product's unique features will benefit a consumer, or highlighting the brand's use or endorsement by celebrities. Persuasive advertising is also part of fashion presentations in television commercials and magazines. The goals of reminder advertising are to reinforce brand awareness, maintain customer loyalty, and let customers know where they may buy the product. Direct mailers, banners on Web sites, and catalogues are some of the media used in reminder advertising.

TYPES OF ADVERTISING

Depending on their objectives, fashion marketers may use one or more of three major types of advertising: **product advertising**, which promotes the benefits of a given product; **institutional advertising**, which promotes the marketing organization and its image; and **advocacy advertising**, which promotes an organization's social or political views. In some cases, all three objectives might be accomplished in a single ad. For example, environmental responsibility is so completely ingrained in every aspect of Patagonia's operations, an advertisement for its apparel might well highlight not only the outdoor clothing but the company's sustainability practices and overall support for environmental causes as well.

Product Advertising

Take a look at a recent issue of a fashion magazine such as *Elle* or *InStyle*. Most of the ads you will see by companies such as Ralph Lauren, Estée Lauder, Tommy Hilfiger, and others are examples of product advertising. A large proportion of television

FIGURE 14.3 Product advertising can help reinforce the marketer's brand image.

advertising is also product advertising, such as commercials for a new model of Volkswagen, a new formulation of Cover Girl makeup, a Citizen watch, a Toshiba 3D TV, or the latest spring fashions from Macy's. The purpose of product advertising is to introduce new styles, looks, models, or technologies; persuade customers to buy them; and/or remind them of the brand so they will think of it the next time they are shopping for that type of product. Product ads generally aim to promote the uses and benefits of the advertiser's product to target customers, even when the benefit is intangible, as in raising a user's self-confidence or social status.

Sometimes product advertising offers reasons why the product is superior to that of the competition. When a product advertisement includes a comparison—either direct or indirect—to one or more competing products, it is called **comparative advertising**. One example of a recent comparative advertising campaign you probably remember was the humorous series of "I'm a Mac/I'm a PC" commercials that Apple produced to persuade consumers of the advantages of their computers over competing Windows-based models. When a brand is well known and a product has been on the market for a while, marketers may use reminder advertising more than persuasive advertising, simply to keep the product name in the front of consumers' minds. You've doubtless seen an ad featuring a single bottle of perfume labeled "Chanel No. 5" and nothing more on the page. Or perhaps you've noticed an ad showing only a handbag covered with the Gucci label. These are examples of reminder advertising for a product.

WHAT DO YOU THINK?

Can you remember seeing an example of comparative advertising recently? What was the product being advertised? Did the marketer use direct or indirect comparison to the competing product? Did you find the comparison to be compelling? Why or why not?

Institutional Advertising

Organizations use institutional advertising to build or maintain a certain image. During the holiday season, for instance, fashion retailers may put ads in the local newspaper to reinforce the good will of the store, such as "Lord & Taylor wishes you a happy Thanksgiving." A fashion marketer's Facebook page may tout that its imports come only from organizations engaged in fair trade practices, or that it uses only 100 percent recyclable packaging. Occasionally, marketers use institutional advertising to respond to an event or negative publicity that has affected the company. A few years ago, when Toyota was faced with a barrage of investigations regarding mechanical and engineering issues in several of its popular model cars, the company bought advertising to reassure the public that it was committed to ensuring the quality and safety of its vehicles. Institutional advertising is geared not only to customers but also to other groups such as employees, stakeholders such as suppliers and corporate shareholders, federal and local governments, and the general public.

Advocacy Advertising

Sometimes considered a segment of institutional advertising, advocacy ads are used by marketers to take a stand on social, environmental, or other issues that are meaningful to them, and by extension, to their customers. Because of the worldwide devastation wreaked by AIDS, the fashion industry undertook a campaign for HIV awareness and AIDS prevention. The Council of Fashion Designers of America (CFDA) raises funds and promotes this cause, as well as that of breast cancer research, through advocacy ads in fashion trade papers and magazines. Other fashion organizations promote the importance of controlling substance abuse and encouraging healthy lifestyles. Advocacy advertising is popular in promoting many kinds of issues such as climate change, tolerance and nondiscrimination, alternative energy sources, and candidates for public office, among other matters.

Creating an Advertising Campaign

In order to create advertising that reaches its intended audience effectively and persuasively, marketers develop an advertising campaign. An **advertising campaign** is the group of advertisements and related promotional materials and activities that are employed during the same period of time as part of a coordinated plan to reach a designated target audience and to meet a marketer's specified advertising objectives. Creating an advertising campaign involves a series of steps: (1) identify the target market; (2) define the campaign's objectives; (3) determine the advertising budget; (4) plan the campaign strategy; (5) implement the advertising campaign; and (6) evaluate the campaign's effectiveness.

IDENTIFYING THE TARGET MARKET

Fashion marketers want to focus their advertising as much as possible on those consumers who are most likely to buy their products. Only after analyzing the demographics, psychographics, lifestyles, and buying behavior of desired consumer groups are marketers able to create the kinds of advertising these groups would find most persuasive, and place it in the media their customers access most.

For example, Mary-Kate and Ashley Olsen have determined their best customers are sophisticated girls and young women in their late teens through their twenties who are interested in well-designed, fashion-forward looks. Advertising for their merchandise lines, such as The Row, is then created to address this target customer base. Mattel's American Girl collection of dolls (plus outfits, accessories, furniture, and books), with background stories from different time periods, is aimed toward more than one target market. While the ultimate consumers of American Girl products are girls ages three to 13, the customers for these goods are parents, grandparents, and other adults. In its advertising, American Girl targets both groups through a colorful Web site, engaging catalogues, and realistic in-store displays—emphasizing the dolls and their stories to appeal to girls, and focusing on how the dolls help girls develop a positive self-image through creative play in order to appeal to adults.

DEFINING CAMPAIGN OBJECTIVES

In creating an advertising campaign, marketers need to establish what results they want to accomplish. This means developing their *campaign objectives*, or the specific communications tasks and goals that are to be accomplished within a certain time period. Typical objectives may be to increase sales of a product or line, to increase market share, or to introduce a new brand.

To help develop a campaign's goals, marketers may apply a measurement based on their current figures before the campaign. For example, if the overall campaign objective were to increase market share, a shoe company might further define it by saying, "Our goal is to increase our market share of men's athletic shoes from 7 percent to 12 percent in the next six months." When introducing a new product, since there are no current sales figures to serve as a benchmark, management might decide

MARKETER'S INSIGHT:
EDUN FOCUSES AD MESSAGE ON MEN

From its inception, Edun, the fashion brand started in 2005 by Ali Hewson and Bono, was built on a message of social responsibility, encouraging trade in Africa and promoting fair trade practices and sustainability. But in fall 2011, the company decided to take its message to a new audience—men.

After hearing from retailers that it needed to define for them who the "Edun guy" was, the company created its first-ever digital-only advertising campaign promoting its men's wear line. The idea was to feature a line-up of well-known men and highlight them as "Edun Pioneers," or men who are doing charitable work or pioneering new ideas in areas like food or business. Among the 11 men spotlighted in the ads were Marcus Samuelsson, owner of

the Red Rooster restaurant in Harlem; Sean Carasso, founder of Falling Whistles, a nonprofit organization that promotes peace in the Congo; and Blake Mycoskie, founder of TOMS shoes.

The campaign included digital banner ads appearing on Web sites like Refinery29.com and foodrepublic.com, on the Edun Web site, and on the Web sites for each of the men featured. Videos related to the campaign were featured on the Edun Facebook page, and the company hosted a reception for the men's collection at Samuelsson's restaurant. In addition, as part of the online sales promotion, Edun highlighted one item of clothing worn by each man and donated a percentage of the proceeds of sales of that item to charity. Customers were also given a gift code for 25 percent off clothing bought at Edun.com.

Adapted from: Tanzina Vega, "A Fashion Brand Introduces 'Edun Pioneers,'" *New York Times*, September 5, 2011, http://mediadecoder.blogs.nytimes.com/2011/09/05/a-fashion-brand-introduces-edun-pioneers/?nl=business&emc=atb2 (accessed on March 6, 2012).

on a campaign objective to increase product awareness from 0 to 28 percent in three months, or to set a minimum sales volume to reach within that time frame, based on the size of the target market, the price of the product, and the breadth of distribution the company has established. Later, when evaluating campaign effectiveness, these measurements give managers information useful for planning additional or follow-up campaigns.

DETERMINING THE ADVERTISING BUDGET

Advertising, by its nature as a paid vehicle, requires money to be spent. Working within their total marketing budget, fashion marketers can use one of several methods to calculate the amount they are prepared to spend on an advertising campaign. One of the most potentially successful is the **objective-and-task method**, which bases the advertising budget on the goals the company wishes to accomplish. Management determines the tasks required to reach the goal, estimates the combined cost of those tasks, and allocates the resulting amount to the advertising campaign. The biggest drawback to this method is that it is very difficult to know with certainty how well each task will achieve the desired goal and therefore how much funding will be needed. For example, in the men's athletic shoe situation above, the marketer has to try to calculate just how much advertising, and in what forms, it will take to increase its market share by the desired percentage.

FIGURE 14.4 Mary-Kate and Ashley Olsen identify their customers for The Row apparel as sophisticated, fashion-forward young women, and target their advertising to that audience.

Many fashion marketers find that budgeting for an advertising campaign based on sales numbers is the simplest method to apply. Known as the **percent-of-sales method**, this tactic involves allocating advertising expenditures as a fixed percentage of sales. Sometimes the advertising allotment might be calculated based on a percentage of the unit sales price for a product being advertised. In other cases, a company uses past or current sales numbers, or may forecast the direction sales are headed to arrive at a figure on which to base the percentage. While easy to calculate, one problem with this method is that in a sales decline, when added promotion might well encourage increased sales, less money will have been allocated for advertising.

Sometimes fashion marketers need to react to the promotional activities of their competitors and therefore work to match the advertising spending of their rivals. Businesses using the **competitive-parity method** try to determine or estimate the dollar amount or percent-of-sales amount that their competitors are spending on advertising, and allocate a similar amount themselves. Fashion businesses make use of the competitive-parity method on the national and local levels. For example, large national fashion marketing organizations such as VF Corporation or Levi Strauss can easily track each other's broadcast and print advertising expenditures for jeans, as these figures are available through advertisers' trade associations and other sources. Regionally and locally, department and specialty stores, discounters, and fast-fashion retailers, particularly those in close proximity, observe each other constantly and plan their campaign expenditures accordingly, in order to capture, or recapture, consumers' attention away from the competition.

FIGURE 14.5 Fashion marketers monitor their competitors' advertising and often try to allocate a similar budget for their own campaign.

In certain cases, one individual may closely control the business aspects of an organization—as for years Pierre Bergé did when pulling the strings of the Yves Saint Laurent enterprise—and as a result, that person can determine the entire marketing budget, including advertising expenditures. When a top-level executive establishes the amount to be allocated for an advertising campaign, he or she is using the **arbitrary method** of budgeting. Because the arbitrary method is subjective, and usually not based on thorough analysis, it can mean spending either too much or too little on the campaign for it to reach its goals. Whatever method is used, determining the most productive and cost-effective campaign budget is essential. If the budget is too large, funds are wasted; if it is too small, the goals of the campaign may be unreachable

PLANNING THE CAMPAIGN STRATEGY

Planning an advertising strategy consists of two parts: *creating the advertising message* and *selecting the advertising media*. Both are dependent on what group or groups the marketer has chosen as its target market, because, as stated previously, fashion marketers want to reach the consumers most likely to buy their products. Therefore, the message—both in words and images—used throughout the advertising must be one that is both attractive and

MARKETER'S INSIGHT:
CELEBRITY POWER: NOT WHAT IT USED TO BE

According to popular wisdom, getting a celebrity endorsement is a tried-and-true, simple-to-implement way to maximize advertising effectiveness. It may be expensive, but celebrities always yield stronger ties with viewers and, ultimately, greater sales. Or do they?

A recent study stands that supposition on its head, finding that with rare exception, celebrity endorsements were largely ineffective and failed to yield the benefits that popular wisdom promises. After looking at every nationally televised ad for the first 11 months of 2010, the study showed that fewer than 12 percent of ads using celebrities exceeded a 10 percent lift—and one fifth of celebrity ads actually had a negative impact on advertising effectiveness.

Have celebrities lost their pizzazz in influencing consumers? In a word, yes, based on the study. Today's consumer is a totally different animal than the consumer of even five years ago, and is more likely to be influenced by someone in his or her social network than a weak celebrity connection. Today's consumer is informed, time-compressed, and difficult to impress, and is only influenced by ads that are relevant and provide information. Simply adding a celebrity to an ad with a poor creative message makes the message even less effective—the bottom line being: Good ads stand on their own.

Adapted from: Peter Daboll, "Celebrities in Advertising Are Almost Always a Big Waste of Money," *Advertising Age*, January 12, 2011, http://adage.com/cmostrategy/article?article_id=148174 (accessed March 6, 2012).

persuasive to customers the company wants to address; and the media carrying the message must be those that the target customers read or view on a regular basis.

A large portion of advertising is done through mass media, which (you'll recall from Chapter 12) consists of the various channels by which information can be communicated to a large number of people all at one time—such as newspapers, magazines, television, radio, the Internet, and outdoor advertising. Advertising media in general are expensive, so to make the most effective use of the campaign budget, marketers identify and analyze the best means to reach as many people in their target audience as possible. Part of their analysis is to determine the reach and frequency of each of the media possibilities, and optimize both within the confines of the advertising budget. **Reach** refers to the percent of the target audience that sees or hears a given advertisement in a certain time period. **Frequency** is the number of times the audience is exposed to an advertisement.

Creating the Advertising Message

The first consideration in planning an advertising campaign strategy is to create a message that will resonate with the target audience. The message clearly must relate to the product being advertised, or whatever objective has been set for the campaign. In addition, fashion marketers study consumer buying behavior as well as the age, interests, occupations, and buying power of their target markets in order to create an appropriate and persuasive message. Forever 21, for example, closely follows the purchasing habits of its young fast-fashion customers in order to provide, and promote, the next trends to which these consumers will be drawn. Levi's Dockers, tracking middle-age consumers looking for comfort over fashion, offers new lengths and widths in pants just before customers begin to ask for them, and promotes those features in its advertising messages.

In general, advertisers want to spotlight the unique characteristics of their product, conveying the ways in which the product's features become

customer benefits. An ad for a new smartphone might picture the device's stylish new color and innovative design, with a description underneath informing readers that the phone offers 4G capabilities, slide-out QWERTY keyboard, and other desirable features. The message of an ad for a face lotion might tout the way it minimizes fine lines and wrinkles with an exclusive collagen formula, or protects against damaging UV rays from the sun while imparting a sunless bronze glow to the skin.

Wherever an advertising message appears, it contains many of the same elements, adapted for the specific media. These include a headline, illustration, copy, and signature. The *headline* is often the first thing to grab consumers' attention, whether it's a word or phrase in large, bold type on a printed page or Internet banner, or a spoken statement or sound on a TV, radio, or YouTube commercial. An ad's *illustration* shows the product, or tells a story about the product; television or other video has the advantage of being able to show the product in action. The written or spoken message in an advertisement is called the *copy*. The features and benefits of the product for the target audience are described here. The *signature* identifies the company paying for the ad.

The objectives of the campaign influence the chosen advertising message, along with the way the message is conveyed to the audience. If the objective is to introduce a new product, repetition is important in order to place the name firmly before customers. That is why you may feel as if you see the same television commercial over and over again, every time you sit down to watch. Dolce & Gabbana, in introducing the fragrance Blue, placed the same ad in four fashion magazines in one month. Some automobile marketers buy the same inside cover of

FIGURE 14.6 Advertising uses a headline, illustration, copy and advertiser's signature to convey a clear message.

a particular magazine 12 months a year, to reinforce their message with consistency. If the objective is to increase market share, a marketing organization would place ads in a number of media to reach as broad an audience as possible. Recent ads for Calvin Klein underwear, besides appearing in fashion magazines across the board as well as on Web sites, were placed on city billboards, buses, and subway station posters, among other media.

Selecting the Advertising Media

In conjunction with creating a message, marketers need to select the appropriate media for disseminating that message. In the past, the options open to marketers were primarily print media (newspapers and magazines) or broadcast media (television and radio), or a combination of the two. Today, fashion marketers have a large and growing number of potential advertising media from which to choose, including a range of "new" media, or digital formats including Web-based or mobile marketing media. Armed with information on fashion consumer behavior, marketers try to select those media most likely not only to reach the most potential customers but also to convey their fashion message with the greatest impact.

Traditional Media Fashion marketers employ three types of traditional media: *print*, *broadcast*, and *outdoor media*, such as billboards, posters on mass transit, electronic signs, and other advertising spots found on streets, highways, and other public sites. Print media includes newspapers, magazines, catalogues, flyers, mailers, theater playbills, and other printed materials. Fashion apparel and accessories marketers often show new seasonal

FIGURE 14.7 Network television advertising is the most expensive for marketers, but it is effective in reaching a vast audience, especially for holiday selling. Celebrities are sometimes used to capture more attention, such as when Macy's featured Queen Latifah in its holiday ads.

collections in fashion magazines, which are found worldwide. *Vogue* has British, French, and Italian editions. Companies in Japan, Eastern Europe, Russia, and Brazil, among other nations, regularly produce fashion publications for local consumption. The glossy paper, high-quality photographs, and attention to written content give fashion magazines a long "shelf life," and readers may return to them multiple times or share them with others. Newspapers, on the other hand, have a short life span, usually being read once and then recycled. Nevertheless, because of their immediacy, fashion retailers find them highly useful in promoting styles that are currently in stock as well as items bought for special sales. Catalogues, while serving a direct-marketing purpose as selling vehicles (see Chapter 13), are also a form of advertising.

Broadcast media include radio, network and cable television, and movie commercials. Fashion marketers do not use radio as frequently to advertise their goods, in large part because the medium appeals to only one sense, hearing, while most fashion items need to be seen in order to attract customers. Automobiles are one exception, and from time to time you may hear an ad about a fashion retailer's special event or sale. Television, on the other hand, is ideal for advertising fashion goods because it can not only picture a fashion look and describe its features in words but also show it in action. The drawback is that television advertising can be quite expensive.

There are two types of television advertising: *network* and *cable*. Network advertising refers to commercials running on the major television networks, including ABC, CBS, NBC, and Fox, which air nationwide. Because of its national reach, network television air time is the most expensive, so all but the largest fashion marketers may limit its use to special occasions, such as Christmas or back-to-school. Major brands such as Estée Lauder and L'Oréal, and national retailers such as Macy's and JCPenney advertise on network television because of the large audience these media attract. Cable television, on the other hand, is often local, far less expensive, and a frequent choice for fashion retailers in smaller cities and towns. They can advertise to announce new merchandise arrivals, sales events, or other special promotions, or just remind shoppers of their presence.

New Media Fashion marketers are increasingly using newer forms of electronic and digital media both for advertising and direct selling. Most large and small fashion marketing organizations, such as Net-a-Porter, Hermès, and Nordstrom, maintain Web sites, where they can both advertise and market their goods directly or, in some cases, point customers to retailers that sell their products. A growing number of fashion marketers maintain a brand page on Facebook, where they can engage regularly with customers and inform them of new merchandise and special promotions, as well as provide links to their Web site.

Fashion companies are also extending their advertising reach through media such as Twitter, YouTube, text messaging, and mobile apps. For example, Macy's recently developed an app that enables viewers to go behind the scenes to view preparations for its annual Thanksgiving Day parade, or to see short videos of fashion designers discussing their products. French Connection, Diesel, and Marks & Spencer have placed fashion videos on YouTube that accounted for a 26 percent increase in sales in Europe. Sears has an app that lets a viewer send a picture of an item to a personal shopper who locates the product and tells the customer where it is available. Fabergé has an online store that includes Skype video, instant messaging, and telephone service, giving viewers throughout the world access to its fashion goods.[1]

WHAT DO YOU THINK?

Have you ever visited a fashion company's Facebook page? What kinds of information do you expect to find there? Do you think you relate better to an advertising message on Facebook than to a commercial for the same company on television?

Identifying Customers' Media Preferences

The growth of potential media through which marketers can advertise presents both opportunities and challenges. To a greater degree than ever before, marketers must not only devise an advertising message that will capture the attention and fancy of target customers, but they must also disseminate that message through the media those target customers are most likely to access.

Old Navy offers a perfect example. The discount clothing chain recently ran a campaign under the theme of "Old Navy Records. Original hits. Original styles." Designed to appeal to "Jennie," its 25- to 35-year-old target customer seeking trendy but well-priced fashion for herself and her family, Old Navy's campaign reflected the fact that the retailer's core customer loves music. Each commercial featured an original song—performed by a group of singers and dancers presented to look like an actual band with names such as Audio Threadz—and tied in with store merchandise and promotions, such as a sale on jeans. To get consumers' attention that a new campaign was coming, Old Navy uploaded a video clip "teaser" to YouTube. In addition, the retailer partnered with Shazam, the song-identifying app, enabling consumers to connect the music with actual product: When consumers used the app to identify any of the Old Navy songs, they gained access to the looks featured in the commercial, styling tips, and special deals. They could also download the song, watch the video again, or learn more about the musicians. The app worked whether a consumer was watching the video on TV, Facebook, YouTube, or in an Old Navy store; and if consumers were watching on TV or in the store, they had the option of immediately buying the clothing on the Old Navy Web site. As Amy Curtis-McIntyre, Old Navy's senior vice president of marketing, stated, "Music is synonymous with fashion for Jennie. What she listens to is as important as what she wears and we are always looking for new and culturally relevant ways to engage with her. By integrating music with Old Navy's on-trend looks, we build more energy between Jennie and the brand."[2, 3, 4]

IMPLEMENTING THE ADVERTISING CAMPAIGN

Executing an advertising campaign means calling on a variety of resources, some of which may be within the marketer's own organization and some of which may be outside firms, agencies, or consultants. Numerous specialties come into play to handle the various tasks a campaign involves; among the professionals contributing their skills might be photographers, copywriters, graphic designers, models or actors, video producers, printers, researchers,

FIGURE 14.8 Blending traditional and new media is increasingly commonplace for fashion advertisers. Old Navy created original music videos and used a mobile tie-in with Shazam to let consumers both identify the Old Navy song and connect with the actual product, styling tips, and deals.

media buying specialists, and more. Some marketers, including large manufacturers, designers, and retail chains, maintain their own advertising department, but even when they have in-house staff, most also use an outside **advertising agency**, a marketing services company that specializes in assisting its clients in the planning and execution of advertising campaigns. An advertising agency generally employs or has associations with experts in all the disciplines required to develop and implement a campaign, taking a large burden off the client's shoulders. Some agencies go beyond just advertising and assist clients in other aspects of marketing and marketing communications as well, such as public relations and sales promotion.

EVALUATING THE CAMPAIGN'S EFFECTIVENESS

Whether planned and executed in-house or by an outside agency, an advertising campaign cannot be considered effective unless it meets its objectives. To help ensure that a message will "break through the clutter" of all the other advertising to which consumers are constantly exposed, and to be sure that target customers "get" the message, marketers often *pre-test* an advertising concept or portions of a campaign before the campaign is launched. This might be done through focus groups or other marketing research vehicles, presenting a possible ad or several versions of an ad to consumers and gauging their response to the message. The information gleaned from pre-testing can then be incorporated into the final form of the campaign. For example, adidas might pre-test ads for sports apparel using a new

high-performance fabric, with one ad concept focusing on the technical aspect of how the fabric breathes and wicks moisture away from the body, while another stresses the sleek styling the fabric gives the apparel. If target customers respond more positively to the styling message, adidas might make that the more prominent feature of its campaign, with the technical information secondary.

Once a campaign is underway or over, marketers continue to evaluate the effectiveness of the message and the media. In some cases, a built-in response mechanism can provide instant feedback on consumers' reaction to an ad—such as when someone clicks on a banner ad on a Web page and is linked to the marketer's site, or when consumers listening to a radio commercial contact the marketer and give a code word mentioned in the ad to receive a special offer. In other cases, marketers may turn again to research, perhaps conducting or commissioning a survey that asks consumers whether they recall a particular ad, where they remember seeing or hearing it, and other details to help gauge the ad's impact. The most concrete measurement of an advertising campaign's effectiveness, however, is how many consumers it propels to take action, as in making a purchase of the advertised product. Although this data might be difficult to determine with certainty, since every sale may not be the direct result of someone seeing an ad, marketers can obtain at least some idea by tracking sales numbers for a product before, during, and after a campaign has taken place to see if the numbers show a positive uptick during the campaign's time frame.

Sales Promotion

In Chapter 12, you learned that sales promotion includes marketing communications activities that take place for a predetermined, limited time with the purpose of increasing demand and stimulating sales. Marketers use sales promotion to give an instant boost to sales of an existing product. If well-planned, the promotion mix tool will do just that—at least during the length of the promotion. Often, however, once the promotion is over, sales go back to the original level. Nevertheless, when stiff competition exists, as in the cosmetics industry, sales promotions can encourage customers to buy the promoted brand over competitive products. In addition, because there is less risk than there would be if they bought it at its regular full price, sales promotion can be effective in getting consumers to try a new product. Marketers know that product trial can lead to acceptance; once consumers sample

a new product and like it, they'll be more likely to continue to purchase it after the initial promotion has ended. That potential for building sales and customer loyalty can more than balance the initial cost of the sales promotion.

All of the large fashion brands and many smaller ones have periodic sales promotions. Among the most prevalent types among cosmetics companies is a **gift-with-purchase (GWP)** promotion, in which customers buying a specified minimum dollar amount of the brand receive a gift of sample cosmetics from the line. Estée Lauder, Clinique, and Lancôme regularly include sample-sized moisturizers, lipsticks, makeup removers, and other products in a reusable cosmetics case as part of their gift-with-purchase sales promotions. A similar sales promotion vehicle is the **purchase-with-purchase (PWP)**, in which a company offers a specially priced or sometimes exclusive item for a small additional price when customers make a purchase at or above a certain dollar amount or buy a specific product. Fashion marketers such as Calvin Klein might offer a distinctive umbrella or duffel bag for $20 when a customer purchases $100 of products from a particular collection. These purchase-with-purchase products are generally obtained by the marketer at a low cost, so the company doesn't necessarily make or lose money on the item itself, but stands to generate higher sales of its regular merchandise being offered with the PWP.

The most frequently used types of sales promotions are temporary price reductions, or sales. Popular-priced fashion marketers such as Kohl's may conduct this type of promotion on a weekly basis, each time changing the products and brands that are offered at the reduced price; and

FIGURE 14.9 Gift-with-purchase is a widely used form of sales promotion in the cosmetics industry and other fashion businesses.

even high-end fashion companies promote sale prices from time to time. Fashion marketers such as Eddie Bauer and Nordstrom frequently lower prices at the beginning of a fashion season for a couple of reasons. One is to interest customers in the new merchandise and entice them into the store or to buy online. The other is to give the company an early idea of which items might be most popular and become candidates for prompt reorders. In addition to temporarily lowering the price on selected merchandise for all shoppers, some marketers also offer coupons or discount codes that consumers can clip, click, or enter online to receive a lower price on a specified item or total purchase. Bass and Izod are among a growing number of fashion marketers using text messages to send consumers instant coupons for limited-time promotions. The customer simply mentions the promotion code number to the salesperson to receive the discounted price. Games and contests are other sales promotion tools that fashion marketers turn to from time to time to capture consumers' attention and spur sales.

Sales promotion methods are also a way of doing business throughout the marketing channel. Suppliers may offer retail store buyers small gifts, known as *premiums* or *incentives*, such as pens or golf umbrellas printed with the company's name, as an enticement for a purchase, or they may offer discounts on purchases when buyers place orders above a certain level or by a certain date. They may also provide discounts or money back to retail partners to compensate them for advertising expenditures promoting the company's products (called an *advertising allowance* or *co-op advertising*) or for special in-store displays that prominently feature the line

(called a *display allowance*). With fashion apparel, marketers might also arrange for a trunk show to be presented at their top retailers' stores. Sales representatives are also targeted with sales promotion methods such as contests for achieving the highest sales volume, or with *premium money* offers of additional compensation in exchange for pushing a line of goods to customers.

Public Relations

As you'll recall from Chapter 12, public relations is the marketing communications function whose aim is to generate goodwill and build a positive image for the marketer and its products among all its various publics. Every company wants to create and maintain a favorable image in the public eye, as well as maintain positive relationships with its stakeholders—which include not only customers but also employees, suppliers, shareholders, the media, government, and the general public. This broad task, along with a number of more specific functions, is the goal of public relations.

Among the key functions that fall under the public relations purview are the following:

▶ *Media relations*. Developing professional relationships with reporters/editors on behalf of the company in order to obtain ongoing coverage of company news, events, and other information.

▶ *Product publicity*. Disseminating information about specific products to garner news stories/articles and other media coverage.

▶ *Investor relations*. Providing shareholders with current information about the company's products, activities, and financial condition.

▶ *Public affairs.* Working with consumer and governmental agencies, representing the company to the greater public, and maintaining the marketer's positive image on a national and/or local community level.

▶ *Events and sponsorships.* Developing and executing special programs, sometimes tied to public events or figures that coordinate with other PR activities to promote the company and enhance its image.

MEDIA CONTACT

One of the primary functions of public relations is the dissemination of information to the media in order to reach a variety of audiences. As with advertising, the approach of public relations is to create a compelling message about a product or company and to place it in the media most likely to be

accessed by the target public. The main difference is that, because public relations does not buy space or time in the media, PR professionals must make sure their information is newsworthy and appropriate for a given media outlet, offering them the best chance that the information will be used. PR professionals work hard to develop and nurture contacts in key media to better understand their needs and interests—sometimes working with an individual editor or producer to find a different angle or twist on a story that will be exclusive to that publication or program. In addition, PR professionals try to establish themselves as a reliable source of information not only about the company they represent and its products, but often about broader trends in the product category or industry, so that the media will turn to them for input. Having good relationships with the media can be even more important if public relations is called on for *crisis management*, or the need to counteract negative publicity. When Christian Dior's star designer, John Galliano, was caught on video making anti-Semitic remarks, public relations executives for the design house undoubtedly leapt into action to advise Dior's chief executive and to make appropriate statements to the media regarding the company's condemnation of the comments, and subsequent firing of Galliano.

In "pitching" a product or story idea to the media, the most common PR tool used is a **press release**, a written document that presents news or other timely information in a manner designed to promote the company or its products. A fashion marketer might disseminate press releases about the launch of a new collection, the hiring of a new designer, an increase in sales over the previous quarter, the endorsement of its line by a celebrity,

UNIQLO'S "TWEET" SALES PROMOTION

When Uniqlo had to temporarily shut down its website in the United Kingdom for an e-commerce migration, it didn't want to lose contact with its customers. So the Japanese fast-fashion retailer found a way to boost its Web presence and brand recognition all while conducting a novel sales promotion: Every time a customer tweeted about a clothing item, the company dropped its price on that item.

The "Lucky Counter" promotion was featured on a dedicated Web page showcasing ten different apparel pieces from the retailer's line, and users could choose which of the pieces they wanted to see discounted on the Uniqlo e-commerce site when it relaunched. Clicking on one of the apparel items brought up a prewritten tweet using the hashtag #luckycounter, to which users could add their own message before sending it. The more tweets sent about a particular item, the lower the price would go. Two days before the website relaunch, one of the items—a gray crewneck, long-sleeved T-shirt—had hit its target price of nearly 60 percent off, meaning it would go on sale online at $4.60 instead of $10.70.

Uniqlo relied solely on users to spread the word about the promotion on Facebook and Twitter, as opposed to paying for promotional tweets, and also trailed the promotion heavily on its website, which was otherwise closed for business. Tweets were sent largely by people taking part in the promotion as well as those who told their followers about Uniqlo's unusual social media experiment. Said Amy Howarth, head of marketing at Uniqlo in the United Kingdom, "The campaign has been really successful and we've been delighted with the response. Customers seem to really want to engage with us, and it's great as the campaign is so transparent and immediately dynamic, so they can see their tweets actually making a difference."

After the new e-commerce website went live, Uniqlo planned to promote it further with an online pinball game called "Lucky Machine," offering a cash prize and discount codes.

Adapted from: Jennifer Whitehead, "Uniqlo's U.K. Twitter Campaign Looks to Be a Perfect Fit for Retailer," *Advertising Age*, September 7, 2010, http://adage.com/globalnews/article?article_id=145769 (accessed March 6, 2012).

or other topics for which the company would like media coverage. In some cases, such as when a company is introducing a number of new products at one time, or is presenting a topic that requires additional background, it will create a compilation of press releases, sometimes along with related materials and photos, and occasionally samples, in a **press kit**. For example, if a fashion retailer and designer negotiate an arrangement for an apparel collection to be carried exclusively by that retailer, a press kit might be developed that would include one press release announcing details of the partnership and another release describing the apparel, plus biographical information on the designer, background on the retailer, and photos of representative pieces in the collection. When it is deemed helpful to securing coverage, public relations staff may send actual products for their media contacts to try or review and either keep or return, depending on the type and cost of the product. A sample of a new BlackBerry "skin" made out of a unique material might be given to technology editors to keep, whereas a new touch screen video MP3 player might be loaned for a couple of weeks for an editor to use and then return.

In the case of a particularly important announcement, or news that the marketer feels could attract major media attention, the company might hold a **press conference**, an event in which appropriate media are invited to learn specific news in person, usually through a planned presentation by one or more company executives or others involved in whatever is being announced. Apple, for instance, knows that its new technology introductions garner widespread attention in the media, so the company generally introduces new products, such as its iPad, at a press conference. Media representatives attending a press conference are given a press kit with full details and background on the topic, and may have the opportunity to try out or examine a product firsthand, as well as ask questions of company spokespeople, either the public relations staff or executives, or both.

ANNUAL REPORTS

For large, publicly held organizations such as Walmart, Macy's, Ralph Lauren, and Gap, another key public relations instrument is the company annual report. Required by law, the annual report contains a letter from the chief executive describing the year's activities, such as new products that were introduced or new markets that were entered, and plans for the coming year. The annual report also contains detailed financial information for the year, usually with breakdowns for each division the company may have. For example, the Disney Company's annual report has separate sections to describe activities, sales, and profits for its film, television, amusement parks, stores, and licensed products divisions, among other areas.

EVENTS AND PRODUCT PLACEMENT

Sometimes as part of their public relations program, fashion marketers sponsor events, such as a concert or sporting event, or participate in a benefit, such as a fashion show to raise money for a local hospital. Another aspect of PR may be **product placement**, an increasingly widely used marketing tool whereby companies arrange to have their product or company name appear in a movie, TV show, magazine photo shoot, or even videogame, or be featured prominently at a public event. Have you ever noticed a favorite television character working on a laptop that clearly says "Dell" on the cover? Or maybe you noticed the Nike swoosh on a cap worn by an on-screen player in your Wii

FIGURE 14.11 Communications with shareholders, including creation of an annual report, is part of public relations. Notice how these cover designs for Tiffany's annual report maintain the brand image.

golf game. In all likelihood, it is not a coincidence that the brands were positioned in plain sight, but rather a planned product placement by the marketer to gain additional exposure for the product and the brand.

WHAT DO YOU THINK?

How do you feel about product placement in TV shows and movies? Do you think marketers are being "sneaky" and trying to manipulate the audience, or do you think it's a legitimate way to increase exposure for a product or brand?

BLURRING THE LINES BETWEEN PROMOTIONAL MIX ELEMENTS

As we discussed in relation to advertising, the proliferation of new media is also impacting the field of public relations, creating a plethora of additional outlets through which publicity and other coverage may be obtained. It is also increasingly blurring the lines among the different elements of the promotion mix, as companies struggle not only to keep up with the media their customers are using and prefer, but also to determine which marketing communications discipline will take the lead for each medium. For example, should a Facebook brand page be maintained by public relations or by advertising? Who should handle monitoring and updating the company's Twitter feed? A host of questions such as these are still being debated and hashed out within many organizations' marketing departments. But whatever division of responsibilities each decides to implement, it underscores

even more emphatically that promotion is most successful when it is coordinated as an integrated marketing communications strategy, with all aspects conveying the same clear, consistent message to customers and the public.

Ethical Issues in Fashion Advertising, Sales Promotion, and Public Relations

Within the promotional elements of advertising, sales promotion, and public relations, a number of legal or ethical issues may arise—particularly with regard to advertising. Some of these issues are addressed by laws and regulations in the United States, and often by differing regulations in other countries. The U.S. Federal Trade Commission, for example, enforces the nation's **truth-in-advertising laws**, which require marketers to create advertising that is truthful and to be able to support any claims about a product with reliable, objective evidence. In Britain and France, lawmakers have proposed legislation that would require disclaimers to appear on ads containing altered photos of models, or to ban altered photos entirely in ads aimed at children under 16.[5] In addition, when the U.K. recently lifted its ban on product placement in television shows, it required that broadcasters show a letter "P" for three seconds at the beginning and end of each program in which the promotion technique is used.[6]

The use of racy or off-color images has long been an ethical issue for advertisers as well. While the practice is rationalized as a way to break through

SOCIAL MEDIA SPARKS A GROWING ROLE FOR PUBLIC RELATIONS

Not too many years ago, some marketers looked at public relations as purely tactical: Announce a new product or service, knock out a press release, work the wire services, and follow up with media reps in the hope of landing some coverage. While those tactics are still integral to any marketing campaign, the mandate for PR is broadening—and the reason is the rise of social media and its move to center stage in marketers' efforts to get their messages out.

In a Web 2.0 world, cultivating relationships with consumers requires an organic approach, which is built into the DNA of PR. Indeed, the core strengths of public relations—namely the ability to tell a story and spark conversation—play into the nature of social media such as blogs, Facebook, Twitter, YouTube, and forums. As a result, some see a new blending of public relations and marketing, with some brands putting PR executives on an equal footing with their advertising and marketing colleagues when it comes to creating campaigns and measuring their returns. Noted Gary Stockman, CEO of Porter Novelli, a public relations agency whose clients include megabrands Hewlett-Packard and Procter & Gamble, "No marketing discipline can operate in a vacuum anymore. PR, in many respects, takes the most holistic approach to the brand and reputation management."

One example is the way public relations played a key role in the marketing campaign for Sony's VAIO P-series notebooks when they debuted during New York's Fashion Week a couple of years ago. To highlight the sleek, lightweight PC, Sony stopped traffic in Grand Central Terminal by having ten "live mannequins" stand frozen, each holding a VAIO PC. Public relations supported the campaign with a separate blog, a YouTube channel featuring 12 videos that got more than 22,000 views, and a Flickr page that captured more than 38,000 views. The campaign also got exposure on CBS' *Early Show*, NBC's *Today* show, and ABC's *Good Morning America*. In all, the campaign garnered more than 30 million impressions on blogs, Web sites, magazines, newspapers, and broadcast news channels.

"The majority of what was involved in the campaign was taking what PR had been doing in isolation in the past and now having all of those tools work holistically in executing the campaign from start to finish," said Stuart Redsun, Sony's senior vice president of marketing. "You would be hard-pressed to find a good marketer who hasn't combined PR and marketing communications all in one. Since the end user only sees one brand, we need to be consistent at all touchpoints."

Adapted from: Matthew Schwartz, "New Influence: Thanks to Social Media, PR Is Playing an Increasingly Important Role in Marketing Communications," *The PR Factor: Pushing Marketing to the Next Level*, Special Advertising Section of Advertising Age, October 26, 2009, p. S4.

the media clutter to capture consumers' attention, in some cases the public may feel an advertiser goes too far, so marketers must weigh the pros of catching people's eye against the cons of the risk of offending some customers. To help marketers make appropriate decisions, the Institute for Advertising Ethics, an independent body administered by the American Advertising Federation and the Donald W. Reynolds Journalism Institute at the University of Missouri, recently released a new ethics code. The non-binding code outlines eight advertising principles on issues ranging from the blurry line between advertising, editorial, and entertainment content to behavioral targeting and disclosure of compensation for social media endorsements.[7]

summary

The promotion mix elements of advertising, sales promotion, and public relations are impersonal tools that are not tailored to individual consumers, but that work together with personal selling and direct marketing in an integrated marketing communications strategy.

Advertising has the objectives of informing, persuading, and reminding, and falls into three types: product advertising, institutional advertising, and advocacy advertising. Product advertising is created to introduce or promote a specific product or line. Institutional advertising is meant to build or maintain the company's image in the public eye. Advocacy advertising is used by marketers to convey a position on social, environmental, or other issues that are meaningful to them and their customers.

Marketers use an advertising campaign to accomplish specific objectives. Creating a campaign involves a series of steps, beginning with identifying the target market to be reached, defining the objectives, and determining the advertising budget. The next stage, planning the campaign strategy, involves creating the message and selecting the media from among the broad range of traditional and "new" media that consumers access. Implementing the campaign comes next, followed by an evaluation of the campaign's effectiveness.

Sales promotion is employed by fashion marketers on a limited-time basis to give an immediate boost to sales. Gift-with-purchase (GWP) and purchase-with-purchase (PWP) are two commonly used sales promotion tools in the fashion industry, along with temporary price reductions, or sales. Coupons, games, and contests are other forms of sales promotion.

Public relations is designed to generate goodwill and build a positive image for the marketer and its products with customers and other publics. Among the key functions of public relations are media relations, product publicity, investor relations, public affairs, and events and sponsorships. Public relations professionals convey information to the media though press releases and press kits, and may hold press conferences to make important announcements. To communicate with shareholders, PR staff creates annual reports, outlining activities and financial results for the company for the year. Product placement is another public relations tool, in which marketers arrange to have their product or brand featured in movies, TV shows, and other publicly viewed spots.

Old Spice Campaign Makes a Viral Splash

There's no question that the best promotional campaigns are the ones that get people talking and also sell products. One recent integrated marketing communications campaign that did both those things went so far as to achieve pop icon status, breaking all previous viral video records in the process. We're talking about the promotion for Old Spice body wash starring actor Isaiah Mustafa as "The Man Your Man Could Smell Like."

The campaign began in February 2010 with a TV ad featuring the sotto voce humor of Mustafa and production wizardry of Wieden+Kennedy, the advertising agency working with Old Spice, a 75-plus-year-old brand of men's grooming products now owned by Procter & Gamble. The initial ad won the Film Grand Prix at the International Advertising Festival at Cannes that June—and the moment it aired, Old Spice began to reverse the losses in share of market it had been experiencing. But that was just the beginning.

In July, a team of creatives, tech geeks, marketers, and writers gathered in an undisclosed location in Portland, Oregon, to add an unprecedented digital dimension to the campaign. In recognition of the massive appeal of Mustafa's character, various social networks were seeded with an invitation to ask questions of the "Old Spice Guy," and in a well-orchestrated plan, the most interesting questions from fans of the commercials or from high-profile people—including Demi Moore, Alyssa Milano, and George Stephanopoulos—were selected for a direct response by name in short, comedic YouTube videos. Over the course of 48 hours, some 186 videos in all were written, produced, and posted in real time.

The response was overwhelming, with Old Spice garnering more than 1.5 billion impressions between February and mid-August, including 130 million video views. Twitter followers were up 3,200 percent; Google searches were up 2,200 percent; Facebook interactions were up 800 to 1,000 percent; and traffic to the Old Spice Web site was up 350 to 500 percent. Equally impressive, the impact of the advertising campaign, coupled with a national sales promotion of buy-one, get-one-free coupon offers, pushed sales of Old Spice body wash up by more than 100 percent in July alone. Although sales retreated from their dramatic highs after the height of the promotion, a year later they were still up more than 50 percent over the year prior to the campaign.

Sources: Marshall Kirkpatrick, "How the Old Spice Videos Are Being Made," *ReadWriteWeb*, July 14, 2010, www.readwriteweb.com/archives/how_old_spice_won_the_internet.php##comments (accessed March 6, 2012); E.B. Boyd, "The Old Spice Campaign, By the Numbers," *Mediabistro.com*, August 19, 2010, www.mediabistro.com/agencyspy/the-old-spice-campaign-by-the-numbers_b7236#more (accessed March 6, 2012); Jack Neff, "How Much Old Spice Body Wash Has the Old Spice Guy Sold?," *Advertising Age*, July 26, 2010, http://adage.com/article?article_id=145096 (accessed March 6, 2012); and "Old Spice Is Killing It on YouTube Again, But Sales Are Down Double-Digits," *Advertising Age*, August 4, 2011, http://adage.com/article/viral-video-charts/spice-killing-yotube-sales/229080 (accessed March 6, 2012).

QUESTIONS

1. Why do you think Old Spice chose to use both traditional and digital media in its advertising campaign? Do you think the brand reached different target customers with each? What was the benefit of producing the videos that responded directly to individual questions?

2. How important was the coupon promotion in the overall campaign? Do you think sales would have increased as much without the coupons?

KEY TERMS

advocacy advertising

advertising agency

advertising campaign

arbitrary method

comparative advertising

competitive-parity method

frequency

gift-with-purchase (GWP)

institutional advertising

objective-and-task method

percent-of-sales method

press conference

press kit

press release

product advertising

product placement

purchase-with-purchase (PWP)

reach

truth-in-advertising laws

REVIEW QUESTIONS

1. Name the three major objectives of advertising and the three major types of advertising, and explain each.
2. List and describe the seven steps involved in creating an advertising campaign.
3. What are three examples of traditional media? What are three examples of new media? Why would marketers use a combination of the two types?
4. Give two examples of sales promotion techniques that target consumers and two examples that target retail buyers.
5. What are three key functions of public relations?

DISCUSSION ACTIVITIES AND PROJECTS

1. Look through recent issues of several magazines or newspapers and find a fashion (or other) example of each type of advertising: product advertising, institutional advertising, and advocacy advertising. Examine each ad to analyze how the message is being conveyed, whether through its headline, illustration, copy, or all three. Can you determine what audience each marketer is targeting with its ad? Share your results with the class.
2. Choose a current fashion product and imagine you're responsible for planning an advertising campaign that will increase its market share over the next six months. First write a sentence or two to identify who the target customer base is, and then make a list of the media that you think will be most effective in reaching those customers. Explain your choices.
3. Create a questionnaire asking about different types of sales promotion vehicles (gift-with-purchase, purchase-with-purchase, sale pricing, coupons, etc.), designed to discover how influential each is in the purchase decision. You might ask, for example, "How likely would you be to switch from a favorite brand if

another brand offered a gift-with-purchase?" Use the questionnaire to conduct a survey among 10 or 12 friends to determine what sales promotion tools are most effective among your peer group. Summarize the results in a written paragraph, and create a graph to show the relative strength of the different sales promotions.

4. Do an online search for news of one of your favorite brands or designers, and make a list of at least five of the results. For each news item, identify whether you think it is a result of a public relations effort, and if so, from what function it arose (media relations, product publicity, investor relations, public affairs, or events and sponsorships).

DEVELOPING YOUR MARKETING PLAN

The final piece of your marketing plan involves advertising, sales promotion, and public relations for your product or company. Keeping in mind the overall promotional strategy and goals you developed for your product in Chapter 12, detail how these last three elements will be employed:

1. Create an outline for a three-month advertising campaign, using the six steps described in the chapter as a guide. Make sure to include what the campaign's objectives are, what audience(s) you are trying to reach, and what media you will employ. What is the campaign's main message? Will the campaign involve product, institutional, or advocacy advertising? What method will you use to determine your budget? Are you primarily looking to inform, persuade, or remind? How will you evaluate the campaign's effectiveness?

2. Determine whether sales promotion is an appropriate promotional tool for your product or company, and if so, describe what type of sales promotion you would run and what it would be designed to accomplish. Would it tie in with your advertising campaign? If you don't think sales promotion would be effective for your product, explain why not.

3. Describe three ways in which you would use public relations to promote your company or product.

Refer to the Marketing Plan Outline, Table 1.2, provided at the end of Chapter 1, as well as Appendix A: Sample Marketing Plan.

REFERENCES

1. "WWD Digital Forum," *Women's Wear Daily*, June 15, 2011, pp. 10, 11.
2. Kiran Aditham, "Shazam, Fakeass Black-Eyed Peas Help Reposition Old Navy," *Mediabistro.com*, February 17, 2011, www.mediabistro.com/agencyspy/shazam-fakeass-black-eyed-peas-help-reposition-old-navy_b14467 (accessed November 29, 2011).
3. Natalie Zmuda, "Old Navy Retires 'Supermodelquins,'" *Advertising Age*, February 17, 2011, http://adage.com/article/news/navy-retires-supermodelquins-music-centric-ad-push/148908 (accessed November 29, 2011).

4. Stuart Elliott, "Old Navy Replaces Mannequins with Music," *New York Times*, February 17, 2011, http://mediadecoder.blogs.nytimes.com/2011/02/17/old-navy-replaces-mannequins-with-music/ (accessed November 29, 2011).

5. Eric Pfanner, "A Move to Curb Digitally Altered Photos in Ads," *New York Times*, September 27, 2009, www.nytimes.com/2009/09/28/business/media/28brush.html?8ad&emc=seiab1 (accessed November 29, 2011).

6. Emma Hall, "U.K. Proposes Product Placement Alert," *Advertising Age*, June 30, 2010, http://adage.com/globalnews/article?article_id=144751 (accessed November 29, 2011).

7. "Ad Industry's New Ethics Code Takes on Brand Integration, Social-Media Disclosure," *Advertising Age*, March 17, 2011, http://adage.com/article/news/advertisers-agencies-ethics-code-review/149464/ (accessed November 29, 2011).

APPENDIX

SAMPLE MARKETING PLAN

Marketing Plan for Glamour Gifts

This marketing plan for Glamour Gifts, a fictitious company, points out some of the major elements of the marketing process and could serve as a sample in creating a term marketing plan project. It contains the following components:

EXECUTIVE SUMMARY

Glamour Gifts is a private corporation, owned and managed by three graduates of a well-known fashion design and marketing college (the founders), and is in its first year of operation. Each of the founders brings to the corporation several years of fashion design and marketing experience through previous employment with design and marketing organizations.

The three formed the company in order to offer consumers a variety of fashionable apparel, accessories, and household and gift items that would appeal to particular target markets. Those markets, consisting of men and women ages 20 to 45, middle- to upper-income urban and suburbanites, are similar in that they all possess a strong sense of fashion.

The products would be not-previously-available designs created by artists and craftspeople from both the United States and overseas. Glamour Gifts plans to market its unique lines in its own Seattle retail store, via its Web site, and through seasonal catalogues.

ENVIRONMENTAL ANALYSIS

Although the economy is not at its peak, research has shown that the intended target market has disposable income for well-styled fashionable wearing apparel and decorative household goods. Among the competition, Sundance, which features western wear and home items, seems to limit itself to niche markets; catalogue company Uno alla Volta (One at a Time) caters to a different niche market, emphasizing Italian imported jewelry and leather goods, as well as scarves, shawls, and art objects. Political influences are few to date and exercise minimal influence on the target market. Legal and regulatory influences on imports are strict but knowable, while potential domestic postal and Internet regulations have an effect on all marketing organizations, so will be monitored closely. Technological advances in order processing and product delivery can enhance distribution, improving customer service. Market research shows an increasing number of consumers are becoming interested in unique styling for apparel and home décor, as well as in distinctive gift items.

TARGET MARKETS

After thorough market segmentation analysis, Glamour Gifts selected a target market of women and men, ages 20 to 45, having middle- to upper-range incomes, and living in urban or suburban locations. Consumer research reveals that both external and internal influences on these target customers are contributing to an increasing number of consumers interested in unique and one-of-a-kind fashion goods. Target consumer demographic studies, such as age group, income, and occupation, as well as lifestyle research, indicate the markets are substantial enough to support a business of this kind.

CREATING A COMPANY STRATEGY

Before developing a company strategy, Glamour Gifts conducted a SWOT analysis. Strengths include the design and marketing expertise of its founding team, adequate funding to operate the business during start-up years, and a suitable headquarters location in its initial retail store. Among the weaknesses are a limited number of merchandise sources and unfamiliarity with distribution logistics. Opportunities include occasions to network at wholesale apparel and gift shows and possible partnerships with vendors. Threats come from competition as yet unknown.

MARKETING OBJECTIVES

The marketing objectives stem from the company's mission, and they incorporate business unit marketing strategies. The mission is to provide fashion-oriented apparel and home furnishings produced in a fair-trade environment for target consumers who appreciate the style and quality of the product offerings. Eventually there will be three separate business units (SBUs): fashion apparel for men, fashion apparel and accessories for women, and decorative home and gift items. Initially, one marketing strategy is in effect covering the entire company. During the first year, the company expects to realize sales of between $500,000 and $750,000, with extensive CRM strategies in effect to build significant repeat business and for the business to grow. The Web site is expected to bring in 10 to 15 percent of the sales the first year, anticipating future growth through expanded service and reward plans. The catalogue is estimated to contribute a similar amount, with the Seattle retail store accounting for the rest.

MARKETING STRATEGIES

Marketing objectives are to be reached by carefully focusing the marketing mix on the target market. That market includes affluent urban women and men purchasing distinctive apparel, home furnishings, and gift items. The products offered include shirts, jackets, wraps, hats, neckwear, hosiery, and hand-crafted jewelry. Home and gift items include art objects such as vases, bowls, candle holders, small statues, and carvings; hanging wall art such as paintings and tapestries; and other items. Each will be selected for its inherent artistic features. Prices will reflect the uniqueness of the merchandise yet be consistent with market conditions and consumer expectations. Style and fair-trade policies will have the effect of positioning products as near-luxury items. Distribution will be direct from the manufacturer to the consumer except for the retail store, where an inventory will be maintained. The retail store, located in downtown Seattle, will also serve as company headquarters. Promotional activity will include sophisticated Web site design with frequent merchandise changes, advertising in local Seattle art papers and cable television, gala receptions to meet the artist vendors at the store, public relations efforts with local and online media to increase awareness and name recognition, and well-designed artwork for the seasonal catalogues.

MARKETING IMPLEMENTATION

Because the purpose of the organization is to serve its customers' design needs, all company personnel will be educated in CRM, including extensive training in consumer behavior, product details and benefits, and salesmanship. The founders will work in their individual areas of expertise: identifying fashion trends desired by the target markets, sourcing products from domestic and overseas vendors, and relating new style benefits to customers.

EVALUATION AND CONTROL

The founders will evaluate the progress of the business, first weekly, and later monthly and quarterly. They will analyze sales trends, sales versus costs, and customer satisfaction, among other elements, revising estimates as necessary. In addition, they will analyze the marketing plan for its overall effectiveness and create new plans for coming years.

GLOSSARY

360° listening Technique in which salespeople use their ears, eyes, and intuition to pick up on subtle cues that a customer is leaning toward or away from making a purchase. (13)

administered marketing system A type of vertical marketing channel in which one member of the marketing channel wields more power than the others. Example: Walmart's influence due to its size. (10)

advertising The placement in any of the mass media of paid, nonpersonal announcements or messages in which the sponsor is identified and is seeking to inform and/or influence the audience about its products or organization. (12)

advertising agency A marketing services company that specializes in assisting its clients in the planning and execution of advertising campaigns. (14)

advertising campaign The group of advertisements and related promotional materials and activities that are employed during the same period of time as part of a coordinated plan to reach a designated target audience and to meet a marketer's specified advertising objectives. (14)

advocacy advertising Type of advertising that promotes an organization's social or political views. (14)

agents See *agents and brokers*.

agents and brokers Marketing channel intermediaries who do not own the goods they sell. (10, 11)

AIDA model A concept used in promotion that delineates four steps—*attention, interest, desire,* and *action*—through which a marketing message should lead consumers in order to achieve the intended result. (12)

analysis A detailed examination of specific data that yields key strategic insights. (4)

arbitrary method Budgeting method for an advertising campaign in which a top-level executive establishes the budget subjectively, usually not based on thorough analysis. (14)

attitude scale A type of survey question designed to capture the level or degree of a respondent's feelings about something. (5)

barter In an exchange, using substitutes for money, exchanging product for product. (9)

brand The name, term, design, or symbol that identifies a product. (7)

brand equity The marketing and financial value associated with a brand's strength in the market. (7)

brand extension The practice of a company placing its brand name on an entirely new category from its existing product mix. Example: Ralph Lauren placing its name on home furnishings, a new category in addition to apparel and accessories. (7)

brand licensing An agreement between the owner of a brand and a manufacturer to provide related brand-name products in exchange for a royalty fee. Example: Luxottica licensing the brand names of designers such as Ralph Lauren for eyeglass frames. (7)

brand loyalty A customer's favorable attitude toward a certain brand. (7)

brand mark The part of a brand that is a symbol or figure, such as the Nike "swoosh." (7)

brand name The part of a brand that can be spoken. (7)

brand personality An image of a product endowed with human characteristics that coordinate with the self-image of intended customers. (7)

branding The creation by marketers of a personality for their products that is meant to relate to the personality characteristics of their target market. (3)

break-even analysis Determining the point at which the costs of manufacturing a product equal the revenue from marketing it. (9)

brokers See *agents and brokers.*

business cycle Movement within an economy typically consisting of four stages: prosperity, recession, depression, and recovery. (2)

business products Products that are incorporated in other manufacturing processes to create an end product or that are resold to other organizations. (8)

business-to-business (B2B) markets Business organizations buying from or selling to other businesses including producers, resellers, governments, and institutions. (3)

buying center A permanent group of people designated by an organization to approve its purchase orders. (3)

buying power The amount of money consumers are willing and able to spend at a given time. (2)

cash discount A price reduction retailers may receive by paying on time for their purchases. (9)

chain stores Multiple retail outlets owned and managed by one organization. (11)

channel conflict Disagreements over the responsibilities of members of a marketing channel and how they should be compensated. (10)

channel of distribution See *marketing channel.*

close (a sale) Obtain a commitment to buy from a potential customer. (13)

co-branding The placement of two brand names on the same product to increase customer reach and impact. Example: Dell computers with "Intel inside." (7)

cognitive dissonance Also known as *buyer's remorse*, a feeling of discomfort that can occur in a customer when reevaluating the features of a product just purchased. (3)

comparative advertising A product advertisement that includes a comparison—either direct or indirect—to one or more competing products. (14)

competitive advantage Superiority in a marketing offer to a competing organization's offer. (6)

competitive-parity method A method of determining an advertising budget in which businesses estimate the dollar or percent-of-sales amount that their competitors are spending on advertising, and allocate a similar amount themselves. (14)

computer-aided design (CAD) An electronic, software-based design process that allows designers to create and change designs easily on a computer. (2)

computer-aided manufacturing (CAM) Method of production that incorporates computer processing into manufacturing equipment including patternmaking, cutting, and sewing machines. (2)

computer-integrated manufacturing (CIM) Manufacturing process that links many computers within a company in order to streamline and coordinate production from design through finished product. (2)

consumer behavior The decision-making processes and actions of buyers as they recognize their desire for a product and engage in the search, evaluation, use, and disposal of a particular item. (3)

Consumer Goods Pricing Act A federal law that prohibits vertical price fixing. (9)

consumer products Goods and services intended for consumption by individuals and families. (8)

contractual marketing system A marketing channel created through written agreement between a manufacturer and intermediaries. (10)

containerization The shipping of goods in standard containers (up to 80 feet long) that do not need to be opened from point of origin to destination, thus avoiding the possibilities of damage or theft. (10)

convenience products Goods and services that consumers buy often, that are usually inexpensive, and are found in many places such as food, drug, and discount stores. (7)

conventional marketing channels Marketing channels made up of independent manufacturers and intermediaries working for their own organization's benefit, without coordination or leadership. (10)

corporate brand See *manufacturer's brand.*

corporate social responsibility (CSR) A business strategy that incorporates issues of public interest into corporate decision making, in the belief that responsible labor and environmental practices will benefit both the company and society as a whole. (2)

corporate vertical marketing system A marketing system in which the entire marketing channel operates under the ownership of one organization. (10)

corporation An organization of individuals authorized by law to act as a single entity. (11)

cost-plus pricing Setting a price by adding a certain dollar amount or percentage to the cost of an item. (9)

cross-sectional study Research in which data is collected once from a random sampling of people to provide a "snapshot" of statistics or opinions at a particular point in time. (5)

cultural branding Creating a brand that conveys a powerful myth that consumers find useful in cementing their identities. (7)

culture The set of learned values, norms, and behaviors that are shared and practiced by members of a group or society. (2)

customer experience management (CEM) Business function by which companies manage the overall experience that a customer has with them as a supplier. (6)

customer relationship management (CRM) The overall process of building and maintaining profitable customer relationships through providing superior customer value and satisfaction. (1) (6)

customer retention management The process of consistently coordinating important elements of the customer experience when delivering products or services in order to maintain or improve customer loyalty and business growth. (6)

demand The quantity of a good or service that customers want at a given price. (9)

demand curve A graph showing the relationship between demand and price. (9)

demographics The statistical analysis of a population, especially with reference to its size and density, distribution, and vital statistics. (2)

department store Retailer that offers a wide selection of apparel and accessories for women, men, and children, as well as cosmetics, home furnishings, and other items, organized by department. (11)

depth interview A one-on-one qualitative research method in which a researcher elicits thoughts and opinions from a single respondent on a product, service, or other marketing-related topic. (5)

direct marketing A promotional strategy in which the seller initiates direct contact to carefully chosen individual customers by one or more channels in order to cultivate a relationship and solicit a response, usually in the form of a purchase. (12)

direct marketing channels Marketing channels that involve no intermediaries, with the marketer selling directly to consumers. (10)

direct relationship A situation in which the factors of value and perceived cost move in the same direction, either both up or both down. (6)

direct sellers Fashion retailers that use sales representatives to sell apparel, accessories, and other fashion goods directly to consumers. (11)

discontinuous innovations Products that are unlike anything that existed prior to their introduction and that can change the way we live or function. (8)

discount store Retailer that offers a broad assortment of budget-priced merchandise, ranging from apparel, accessories, and household items to automotive and garden supplies, and food. Sometimes known as discount department stores. (11)

discretionary income The amount of income left after meeting all required and necessary expenses; money to spend as one wishes. (2)

disposable income The amount of income left after paying taxes. (2)

durable goods Goods that are generally kept for many years that are not used up or worn out quickly. (8)

elasticity of demand A measure of the extent of consumer sensitivity to the change of prices. (9)

electronic data interchange (EDI) An electronic system that enables companies to share real-time information with suppliers to help in production planning and timely delivery of goods. (2)

e-tailers The name given a retailer that engages in e-commerce ("e-" meaning "electronic"), conducting sales over the Internet. (11)

ethics A system of moral values or set of principles that define right and wrong. (1)

ethnographic research A type of observational research involving the study of consumers in the natural context of their activities. (5)

exchange In marketing, any activity such as buying and selling in which one party receives something by voluntarily giving something in return. (1)

exclusive distribution A marketing strategy using one or a very few retailers to handle the producer's goods in order to maintain prestige. (10)

expanded benefits The extra value follow-up features of a product that go beyond the product essence and real product to contribute to its benefit package for customers. (8)

experimental research A type of study whereby researchers set up a situation in which they can change one key element while keeping all others constant, and gauge the different results. (5)

exporting The marketing of a company's products in other countries. (10)

extended problem solving A buying process calling for complex decision making, seeking information, weighing alternatives, reaching a decision, and evaluating the choice. Usually associated with high-involvement buying situations. (3)

family brand A branding situation in which all of a company's products carry the same name. Examples: Tiffany, Banana Republic, and Totes. (7)

fashion Any designed product that is currently popular and that people consider desirable and appropriate at a given time. (1)

fashion marketing The application of marketing processes and activities to currently popular, designed products. (1)

fashion retailing The business of sourcing and selling apparel, accessories, and other designed products to individuals and households. (11)

fashion product Anything that is popular at a given time. (8)

Federal Trade Commission Act Legislation developed to counteract the possibility of deceptive pricing, and the basis for the establishment of the Federal Trade Commission. (9)

fixed costs Costs that do not change with the quantity of goods sold, such as rent, insurance, and executive salaries. (9)

flash sale An online, limited-time (usually 36- or 48-hour) discount on high-end brand merchandise offered by a retail store or a Web site specializing private sales. (11)

focus group A form of qualitative research in which approximately 8 to 12 consumers share their opinions of a product, service, or other marketing-related topic, guided in their discussion by a moderator. (5)

forecasting A process in which professional observers of culture and cultural shifts provide calculated predictions about the likely direction in which design and other consumer preferences are moving. (5)

franchise An agreement between a large, well-known marketing organization (franchisor) and a local business (franchisee) to market the franchisor's product exclusively. (10)

frequency The number of times a target audience is exposed to a given advertisement. (14)

gift-with-purchase (GWP) Promotion in which customers buying a specified minimum dollar amount of the brand receive a gift from the line. (14)

global brand A brand that is marketed with the same name and according to the same strategic principles in every part of the world. Examples: Coca-Cola, Disney, and McDonald's. (7)

goods Tangible items such as coats and hats, computers, and furniture. (1)

gray market goods Also known as parallel goods, items not intended for sale in the country where they are being offered. (9)

green marketing A business approach that is focused on protecting the environment throughout the development and marketing of the company's products. (1)

G-PESTELC A situational analysis of the macroenvironment in which the marketer operates. (4)

impulse item A product that consumers purchase without previous thought. (3)

independent retailers Retail businesses owned by a single person (sole proprietor), by a partnership, or by a private corporation. (11)

indirect marketing channel A marketing channel that contains one or more intermediary. (10)

individual brand Products from the same company that are marketed under separate names. Examples: Cadillac's Escalade or Levi's 501 jeans. (7)

innovation Product or service that is perceived as new by consumers. (8)

institutional advertising Type of advertising that promotes the marketing organization and its image. (14)

integrated marketing communications
A strategy in which all elements of promotion are carefully coordinated in order to deliver clear and consistent information across all channels. (12)

integrated marketing system Business situation in which all four elements of the marketing mix are planned, coordinated, and targeted, and ideas and strategies to reach customers are continuously shared within the marketing organization. (3)

intensive distribution A marketing strategy generally used for frequently purchased and relatively inexpensive products by making them available in many locations. (10)

intermediaries Also known as middlemen or resellers, those who work with manufacturers, other intermediaries, and/or consumers to buy and sell products. (10)

intermodal transportation The use of a combination of one or more types of carrier (e.g., train and truck) in moving goods along the supply chain. (10)

inverse relationship A situation in which the factors of value and perceived cost move in opposite directions of each other. (6)

Likert scale A research survey question that presents a statement and asks respondents to indicate how much they agree or disagree. (5)

limited problem solving Buying process that calls for some degree of decision making, as when selecting a raincoat from among several choices. (3)

longitudinal study Research in which data is collected over time or at a series of specific points in time to provide information on trends in the marketplace and changes in consumer behavior and attitudes. (5)

m-commerce Selling to consumers via a mobile device. (11)

macroenvironment The set of uncontrollable forces and conditions that face a company, including social, technological, economic, competitive, political/legal, and natural forces. (2)

manufacturer's brand Also known as a corporate or national brand, a brand carrying the name of its manufacturer or designer. Examples: Avon, Levi's, Amazon.com. (7)

market (a) A group of actual and potential customers who have both an interest in and the ability to buy a company's product. (1)
(b) A venue where manufacturers and wholesalers selling the same types of products have a significant presence and retailers can see and order new goods. (11)

market research A process used to define the size, location, and/or makeup of the market for a product or service. (5)

market segment A group of consumers displaying similar needs, wants, values, and buying habits. (1)

market segmentation Defining smaller, more homogeneous customer groups based on similar customer characteristics. (1)

market share The percentage of a total industry market that a particular product or company holds. (6)

market weeks Times designated by the fashion industry to show retailers new merchandise for the coming season. (11)

marketing An organizational function and a set of processes for creating, communicating, and delivering value to customers and for managing customer relationships in ways that benefit the organization and its stakeholders. (1)

marketing channel Also known as distribution channel. A set of independent business organizations (called channel members) that help make a product available to customers. (10)

marketing environment The diverse internal and external forces that can affect the way a company reaches its goals. (2)

Marketing Information System (MIS) A set of procedures and practices a company puts in place in order to analyze, assess, and distribute the marketing information being gathered

continuously from sources inside and outside of the firm. (5)

marketing intelligence A systematic collection and analysis of publicly available information about competitors and developments in the marketplace. (5)

marketing logistics Also known as physical distribution. The activities involved in making certain that products are ready, shipped, stored, and made available when, where, and in the quantity that customers demand; includes planning, initiating, and controlling the physical flow of products from producers to consumers. (10)

marketing mix The combination of marketing tools—product, place, price, and promotion—that a firm uses to offer its customers value and to pursue its own sales and profitability goals.(1)

marketing plan Written document that is the roadmap by which a company assesses its marketing objectives, determines what marketing strategies will help customers understand its product's value, and establishes how it will go about reaching its marketing goal. (4)

marketing research Process by which businesses collect and analyze information specifically related to a marketing question, problem, or opportunity. (5)

marketing strategy A plan of action designed to identify the target market and shape the marketing mix in order to satisfy target customers' needs and propel the marketer toward its goals. (4)

markup A dollar or percentage amount added to the cost price of an item before its resale. (9)

markup pricing A cost-based pricing strategy adding a certain percentage to a product to arrive at the retail price. (9)

mass communication The delivery of impersonal messages to a general public utilizing communications vehicles that reach a broad audience. (12)

mass marketing An undifferentiated targeting strategy focusing on an entire market universe. (6)

mass media The various channels by which information can be communicated to a large number of people all at one time. (12)

masstige marketing The strategy of designers creating goods at lower prices and available in more accessible locations than their prestige lines. Example: Vera Wang creating designer apparel for Bergdorf Goodman as well as lower-priced fashion goods for Kohl's. (2)

merchant wholesaler A business intermediary that owns the goods it sells to other intermediaries such as retailers or wholesalers. (10)

microenvironment The forces close to an organization that have a direct impact on its ability to serve its customers, including the company itself, its suppliers, customers, competitors, and the general public. (2)

mission statement A declaration that concisely conveys, in a big-picture perspective, the overarching goals of a company. (4)

modified rebuy A slight change in the reorder of merchandise originally purchased. (3)

multi-channel marketing The use by marketers of a variety of channels in order to reach a wide range of customers. (10)

multi-channel retailing The strategy of selling to consumers through multiple-store and/or non-store means. (11)

multiple selves The various roles in life that each person has—for example, student, daughter or son, employee, friend. (3)

national brand See *manufacturer's brand*.

need Something a person cannot do without. (1)

new products Innovative product solutions developed to satisfy customer wants and needs. (8)

new task buying A new buying situation in which the buyer is seeking goods not previously purchased. (3)

niche marketing Targeting specialized market sub-segments within a larger group. (6)

nondurable goods Products used up relatively quickly. (8)

nonprobability sample A research study group selected with little or no attempt to get a representative cross section of the population. (5)

non-store retailing Selling to customers through means other than an actual brick-and-mortar store. (11)

objective-and-task method A method for determining an advertising budget that is based on the goals the company wishes to accomplish. (14)

objectives (research) The specific information identified by marketers as what want to learn through a research study. (5)

observational research A method of research based on watching people to determine their actions or to gain other knowledge based on visible cues or behavior. (5)

off-price stores Retailers that sell brand-name merchandise at the peak of its life cycle, buying goods late in the season at below the wholesale price and offering them at a low retail price. Example: T.J.Maxx. (11)

order getter A salesperson who initiates and develops business relationships and uses creative selling techniques to assist consumers in buying a product. (13)

order processing Receiving and transmitting information concerning merchandise orders, such as style, quantity, and price. (10)

order taker A salesperson who records buyers' specifications and provides what is requested. (13)

outsource Assign jobs, such as manufacturing, to a business entity or individual outside of one's company. (8)

partner relationship management (PRM) The methods used by a company in dealing with its supply chain partners. (6)

penetration pricing Strategy of introducing a new product at a price lower than the competition in an attempt for the company to gain a foothold in the marketplace. (9)

perceived value A customer's internal calculation as to whether or not a product is worth its cost. (1)

percent-of-sales method A method of determining an advertising budget by allocating advertising expenditures as a fixed percentage of past, current, or forecasted sales. (14)

perceptual map A visual display of data shown in graph form, used to analyze data, spot trends, and provide foundations for appropriate decision making. (4) (6)

personal selling A one-on-one, often face-to-face interaction between a marketer's representative and an individual or small group of customers with the goal of generating a sale. (12)

personal shopper A salesperson who works to meet the fashion needs of select customers, referred to as clients, by supplying fashion information and choosing merchandise tailored to them in their business and social lives. (11)

plan Steps on which someone acts to reach his or her goals. (4)

pop-up stores Temporary shops that open in a major city or mall for a few days or weeks and then disappear. (11)

positioning Using the various marketing mix tools to determine and communicate how a product fits within the marketplace and in relation to other products, and to influence how consumers in specific segments experience the product. (4)

press conference Event in which media are invited to learn specific news in person, usually through a planned presentation by company executives. (14)

press kit A compilation of press releases, photos, and other related materials to provide the media with information on a major introduction or announcement. (14)

press release A written document that presents news or other timely information in a manner designed to promote the company or its products. (14)

price The amount one pays in exchange for a product. (9)

primary data New information developed from original research. (5)

primary research Original research undertaken to glean previously unavailable information. (5)

private labels Goods that are available only from a certain retail organization. Example: JCPenney's Arizona Blue. (7)

probability sample A research study group chosen so that each member of the survey population has a known and equal chance of being selected, and sampling is random within the defined population. (5)

product Any offering presented to target markets, including goods, services, ideas, and people. (1)

product adoption The process potential buyers go through as they learn about and decide to use or reject a product. (8)

product advertising Type of advertising that promotes the benefits of a given product. (14)

product essence The basic benefits received from using a product. (8)

product life cycle The cycle that takes products from introduction through obsolescence. (8)

product line A group of closely related products selected to appeal to the same customers, marketed through the same channels, and within the same price range. Example: Gap's shirts, jeans, and sweaters. (7)

product placement Marketing tool whereby companies arrange to have their product or company name appear in a movie, TV show, magazine photo shoot, or videogame, or be featured prominently at a public event. (14)

product publicity The placement of unpaid articles or announcements about a product in the media to gain positive exposure. (14)

product mix All of a company's product lines together. Example: All the products in Gap's Banana Republic, Gap, Old Navy, and other lines. (7)

profit The amount of money a business retains when its revenues exceed its costs and expenses. (9)

promotion The variety of activities that are designed to inform target customers about the features and benefits of a product and to persuade those customers to buy. Promotion can also inform the public about a company or brand, enhance its image, and create positive relationships between a company and its various publics. (12)

promotion mix The combination of techniques—including *advertising, public relations, sales promotion, personal selling,* and *direct marketing*—that a marketer uses to achieve a specific goal. (12)

prospect A possible buyer who is not yet a customer. (13)

psychographics Lifestyle preference descriptors, such as individuals' attitudes, values, and interests. (4)

public Any group that has an interest in a business or organization. (2)

public relations (PR) The marketing function whose aim is to generate goodwill and a positive image for the marketer and its products among all its various publics, including consumers, shareholders, government, and the media. (12)

pull strategy A promotional strategy in which marketers focus the promotion mix on the end consumer, with the goal of stimulating consumer demand and in turn generating orders from retailers and wholesalers. (12)

purchase involvement The level of a customer's interest in buying a product, as seen in that person's need for the product. (3)

purchase-with-purchase (PWP) A special item offered at a slight additional price when a customer buys a certain dollar amount of products in a specified line. (14)

push strategy A promotional strategy in which marketers focus the promotion mix only to the next level along the supply chain. (12)

QR code Two-dimensional bar code that consumers can scan to view Web-based marketing content on their smartphone. (11)

qualitative data Subjective information derived by focusing on people's attitudes, opinions, and feelings about a product or service. (5)

qualify (a lead) Determine which potential customers are most likely to become actual customers. (13)

quantitative data Objective information obtained from research that focuses on numbers and facts that can be interpreted statistically. (5)

quantity discount Reduction in price that retailers may receive for purchasing goods in large amounts. (9)

Quick Response (QR) An electronic system used to record the sale of products simultaneously at the retail and manufacturing offices in order to initiate rapid inventory replenishment. (2, 10)

radio frequency identification (RFID) Technology in which tiny chips, placed on goods at the factory, can be scanned with special equipment to provide detailed information about the product at any point throughout the supply chain. (10)

reach The percent of the target audience that sees or hears a given advertisement in a certain time period. (14)

real product The actual physical components that make up a product and contribute to its package of benefits. (8)

relationship selling Type of selling technique in which the salesperson takes the time to know, understand, and appreciate the buyer's wants and needs, and then provides appropriate solutions and follow-up service. (13)

repositioning Revising a marketing strategy in order to modify the way consumers think about (or perceive) the brand and thereby increase sales. (4)

retailer A business that sells mainly to consumers. (10)

return on investment (ROI) The amount of value (money/time/effort) realized after expenses. (4)

Robinson-Patman Act Federal law created to prevent discriminatory pricing, that is, charging different prices to various customers for similar goods. (9)

routine problem solving The process a customer goes through in selecting a product without seeming to think about the purchase decision, as when buying convenience items like toothpaste or shampoo. (3)

sales cycle The time period between when a customer starts thinking about buying a product and the actual purchase date. (13)

sales gap The difference between the benefits of products the consumer currently owns and those that other products offer. (13)

sales promotion Marketing communications activities that take place for a predetermined, limited time with the purpose of increasing demand and stimulating sales. (13)

sample In research, a subset of the group that will represent the study's larger population as a whole. (5)

seasonal discount A price reduction producers may grant to retailers for buying goods out of season and performing some marketing function such as storing them until the appropriate time. (9)

secondary data Information collected from secondary research. (5)

secondary research The process of exploring existing sources to find desired information. (5)

segment profile Specific customer characteristics within a particular targeted segment that reflect distinctive patterns. (6)

segmenting Dividing the marketplace into groups that share common or similar (homogenous) interests of needs. (4)

selective distribution A marketing strategy of selling products to a limited number of retailers that can explain the product and enable customers to make comparisons. (10)

selling Presenting information about a product to a customer with the goal of motivating the customer to exchange money in order to obtain the product. (13)

services Helpful or professional activities provided to a customer. Examples: hairstyling, wardrobe consulting, or air travel. (1)

Sherman Anti-Trust Act Federal law created to prevent businesses from attempting to fix or otherwise illegally set prices. (9)

shopping products Items consumers want to compare before purchasing. Examples: most apparel and accessories, electronics, and furniture. (7)

skimming pricing A pricing approach whereby marketers introduce a new product at the highest possible price. (9)

SMART objectives Criteria used to quantify and qualify objectives (specific, measurable, attainable and realistic, results-driven, and time-based). (4)

social class Hierarchical groups of individuals belonging to different levels of society, often based on income, education, occupation, and wealth. Members of the same class tend to have similar interests and behaviors. (3)

social forces The factors that have a major effect on what people believe and how they acquire products, such as population demographics and cultural values. (2)

social norms The behaviors a social class expects its members to exhibit. (3)

social responsibility The principle that everyone is responsible for making the world a better place for all its inhabitants. (1)

specialty products Type of consumer products that are unique and expensive, and usually found in limited locations. Examples: BMW automobiles, Tiffany jewelry, and Louis Vuitton luggage. (7)

specialty store A retailer that focuses on a specific type of merchandise, such as apparel, footwear, furniture, or toys. (11)

stakeholders Those people and organizations that have an investment or other interest in a business, including customers, employees, stockholders, suppliers, and government. (1)

store brand Goods labeled with a retailer's brand name. Examples: Brooks Brothers, Forever 21. (7)

straight rebuy An exact reorder of merchandise originally purchased. (3)

strong moral compass A phrase used to describe the intersection of a person's core values with ethical decision making. (8)

subculture A smaller group within a larger society or culture, such as persons of the same age or political beliefs. (3)

supply The quantity of a product available for sale. (9)

supply chain The combination of businesses that perform the marketing logistics activities necessary in moving products from producers to consumers. (10)

supply chain management The coordination of supply sources with market demands. (6)

survey A quantitative research method in which researchers ask people questions in order to obtain facts and information on attitudes, preferences, and buying behavior. (5)

SWOT analysis Examination of quantitative and qualitative areas related to both the internal factors (Strengths and Weaknesses) and the external factors (Opportunities and Threats) that potentially impact a marketing situation. (4)

target market The group of customers deemed most likely to purchase a given product and on whom the company's marketing efforts are focused. (1)

target marketing The grouping of customers according to shared similarities and then delivering products that meet and exceed that group's expectations. (6)

targeted database A list of qualified consumers who are likely to actually make a purchase. (13)

total costs Combined fixed and variable costs. (9)

trade discount A reduction in price a supplier gives a retailer for reselling its goods. (9)

trade show Temporary exhibition organized to showcase to retail buyers products from a wide variety of manufacturers in a particular industry. (11)

trademark The legal designation of brand ownership registered with the U.S. Patent and Trademark office of the federal government. (7)

traits Distinct characteristics of our personalities (such as agreeableness or extroversion) that differentiate us from others and contribute to our behavior. (3)

transactional selling Sales approach that focuses on the sale at hand but not on nurturing a long-term relationship. (13)

truth-in-advertising laws Regulations enforced by the U.S. Federal Trade Commission that require advertisers to create advertising that is truthful, and to be able to support any claims about a product with reliable, objective evidence. (14)

unsought products Goods and services that consumers either don't realize they need, purchase only when a specific problem arises, or don't think regularly about buying. Examples: flood insurance, home alarm systems, or ambulance service. (7)

value proposition The sum of all benefits that marketers offer customers. (1)

variable costs Costs that change with the amount of goods sold, such as raw materials, workers' wages, and transportation costs. (9)

vertical marketing system (VMS) Arrangement in which manufacturers and intermediaries work together to coordinate marketing efforts. Three types of VMS are corporate, contractual, and administered. (10)

virtual mall Web sites that include multiple online catalogues or shopping opportunities. (13)

want Something a person craves or desires, influenced by his or her personality, culture, and society. (1)

wholesale club Also called a warehouse store, a discount operation that offers a variety of low-cost items, such as food, apparel, and home furnishings to member customers. Example: Costco. (11)

wholesaler An enterprise that engages in wholesaling activities, typically buying large quantities of goods from manufacturers and selling them in smaller quantities to resellers, or to institutional or industrial users. (11)

wholesaling All of the activities involved in selling goods that are intended for resale or for business use. (11)

World Trade Organization An international organization consisting of most of the trading nations in the world, one of whose goals is to lower trade barriers among participating countries. (2)

BIBLIOGRAPHY

BOOKS

Armstrong, Gary, and Philip Kotler. *Marketing: An Introduction*. 10th ed. Upper Saddle River, NJ: Pearson Prentice Hall, 2011.

Asacker, Tom. *A Clear Eye for Branding*. Ithaca, NY: Paramount Market Publishing, 2005.

Brenna, Bridget. *Why She Buys*. New York: Crown Business Books, 2009.

Caplan, Ralph. *By Design: Why There Are No Locks on the Bathroom Doors of the Hotel Louis XIV and Other Object Lessons*. 2nd ed. New York: Fairchild Books, 2005.

Easey, Mike, ed. *Fashion Marketing*. 3rd ed. Chichester, U.K.: John Wiley & Sons, 2009.

Flynn, Judy Zaccagnini, and Irene M. Foster. *Research Methods for the Fashion Industry*. New York: Fairchild Books, 2009.

Friedman, Thomas L. *The World Is Flat Release 3.0: A Brief History of the Twenty-First Century*. New York: Picador, 2007.

Holt, Douglas B. *How Brands Become Icons: The Principles of Cultural Branding*. Boston: Harvard Business School Press, 2004.

Kerin, Roger A., Stephen W. Hartley, and William Rudelius. *Marketing: The Core*. 2nd ed. New York: McGraw-Hill/Irwin, 2007.

Lamb, Charles W., Joseph F. Hair Jr., and Carl McDaniel. *MKTG*. 2010–2011 ed. Mason, OH: South-Western, 2011.

Pride, William M., and O. C. Ferrell. *Marketing*. 14th ed. Boston: Houghton Mifflin Company, 2008.

Rath, Patricia Mink, Stefani Bay, Richard Petrizzi, and Penny Gill. *The Why of the Buy: Consumer Behavior and Fashion Marketing*. New York: Fairchild Books, 2008.

Reis, Al, and Jack Trout. *The 22 Immutable Laws of Marketing*. New York: HarperCollins, 1994.

Shoemack, Harvey, and Pat Rath. *Essentials of Exporting and Importing*. New York: Fairchild Books, 2010.

Solomon, Michael R. *Marketing*. 4th ed. New York: Pearson Prentice Hall, 2006.

Solomon, Michael, Greg Marshall, and Elnora Stuart. *Marketing: Real People, Real Choices*. 6th ed. New York: Pearson Education, 2009.

Stone, Elaine. *The Dynamics of Fashion*. 3rd ed. New York: Fairchild Books, 2008.

Trout, Jack. *Repositioning: Marketing in an Era of Competition, Change, and Crisis*. New York: McGraw-Hill, 2010.

Wallace, Margot A. *Museum Branding: How to Create and Maintain Loyalty and Support*. Lanham, MD: Rowman & Littlefield Publishing Group, 2006.

WEB SITES

Advertising Age (http://adage.com/)

American Marketing Association (www.
    marketingpower.com)

BusinessWire (www.businesswire.com)

Ecouterre (www.ecouterre.com)

FashionMag.com (www.fashionmag.com)

The Fashion Group International (www.fgi.org)

Fashion Trends Daily (http://fashiontrendsdaily.
    com)

Financial Wire (www.vimcor.com/financialwire.
    htm)

Harvard Business Review (http://hbr.org/)

National Cotton Council of America (www.cotton.
    org)

New York Social Diary (www.newyorksocialdiary.
    com)

Thinkexist.com (http://thinkexist.com)

The New York Times (www.nytimes.com)

United States Census Bureau (www.census.gov/ipc/
    www/idb/worldpopgraph.php)

The Wall Street Journal (http://online.wsj.com/)

Women's Wear Daily (www.wwd.com)

INDEX

Kors, Michael, 58, 58f, 317. *See also* Michael Kors

L

La Carmina (blog), 418

labeling, 222–23, 222f

Lacoste, 322

Lacroix (brand), 40, 220

Lacroix, Christian, 40

Lafayette 148, 419

Lake, Laura, 104

Lancôme, 210

Landau, John, 121

Land's End, 361

Lauren, Ralph, 59. *See also* Ralph Lauren

laws. *See* legal issues

La-Z-Boy, 354

leader pricing, 296

leads, qualifying, 406

learning, influence of, 85–86

Leduc, Bob, 166

Lee, Kwan Sup, 106

Lee Jeans, 138–39, 141f

legal issues
    laws affecting fashion marketing, 54–55, 54t

in macroenvironment, 53–56

in pricing, 287–88, 297–98, 297f

Lemarié, 330–31

Lettiere, Caren, 270

Levi Strauss
    advertising campaigns, 436, 439

branding, 69, 208–10

sales to foreign tourists in U.S., 89

transportation of goods, 327

wholesaling, 346–47

Levi's Dockers, 439

LG Electronics, 106

LGBT community, 46

Lia Sophia, 362

licensed brands
    as brand choice, 218–19, 219f

Lacroix, 220

product licensing agreements, 317

life cycle of fashion products
    effect on pricing, 281–83

influence on promotional mix, 387, 388f

monitoring, 251–53, 251f

repositioning and, 178–79

stages of, 117, 117f, 282f

lifestyle approach (marketing strategy), 106

lifetime value of customers (LTV), 186

Likert scale, 149, 150f

The Limited, 154

limited problem solving process, 73f, 74

limited-function wholesalers, 347–48

limited-line stores, 356

limited-line wholesalers, 347

line extension, 216

listening, 360°, 411

Liz Claiborne, Inc., 114, 214–15, 308

lobbying, 54

location. *See* place

London Fog, 216, 333

Longaberger, 362

longitudinal studies, 143–44, 143f

"loophole," 255

Lord & Taylor, 331, 352

L'Oréal
    growth strategy, 118

intensive distribution strategy, 322

marketing in China, 9

marketing to Hispanics, 47

television advertising, 441

Louis Vuitton
    expansion strategy, 114–15, 115f

marketing channels, 321–22

non-price competition, 271

pop-up retailing, 363

price levels, 268, 291–92, 292f

LTV (lifetime value of customers), 186

Lucky Brand, 79, 79f, 214, 215

Lucky Goldstar (LG Electronics), 106

Lululemon, 26

Lundgren, Terry, 28

luxury brands
    demand curves, 274, 274f

distribution intensity, 321

economic conditions and, 287

exclusive distribution strategy, 322

personal selling of, 285, 386

M

MacMillan, Ian, 186

macroenvironment, 43–56
    adidas, 51

defined, 43

economic forces in, 52–53, 52f

effect on marketing mix, 36f

legal forces in, 53–56

L'Oréal, 47

natural forces in, 56

political forces in, 53–56

social forces in, 43–49

technological forces in, 49–52

Macy's
    as chain store, 354

direct marketing, 419

exclusive lines, 368

expansion strategy, 114

PHOTO CREDITS

TITLE PAGE: COURTESY OF WWD/YUKIE KASUGA
COPYRIGHT PAGE: COURTESY OF WWD
CONTENTS: PAPER BOAT CREATIVE/GETTY IMAGES
PART ONE: PAPER BOAT CREATIVE/GETTY IMAGES
PART TWO: DIGITAL VISION/GETTY IMAGES
PART THREE: RICHARD BAKER/ALAMY
PART FOUR: RICHARD LEVINE/ALAMY

CHAPTER 1:
1.1 COURTESY OF WWD/YUKIE KASUGA
1.2 © ONOKY - PHOTONONSTOP/ALAMY
1.3 CAR: BRIAN KIMBALL/KIMBALL STOCK; LIVING ROOM: DIANE
AUCKLAND/ARCAID IMAGES; PITCHERS: COURTESY OF WWD; CAKE: ©
EDWARD DJENDRONO/ISTOCKPHOTO; BUILDING: MARTINE HAMILTON
KNIGHT/ARCAID IMAGES; MACARONS: © OLGA KRIGER/ALAMY; DEVIL
WEARS PRADA: 20TH CENTURY FOX/THE KOBAL COLLECTION/WETCHER,
BARRY; SERENA WILLIAMS: KYODO/APIMAGES; MAKEUP: COURTESY OF
WWD/JOHN AQUINO; STORE: COURTESY OF WWD/MATTHEW TEUTEN;
IPAD: © ALLIANCE IMAGES/ALAMY
1.4 ILLUSTRATION BY VANESSA HAN AND ALICIA FREILE
1.5A COURTESY OF WWD/ THOMAS IANNACCONE
1.5B © AGE FOTOSTOCK / SUPERSTOCK
1.5C KRAIG SCARBINSKY/GETTY IMAGES
1.6A © IAN LEONARD/ALAMY
1.6B © ART DIRECTORS & TRIP/ALAMY
1.7A © HUGH THRELFALL/ALAMY
1.7B COURTESY OF WWD
1.7C FILMMAGIC/GETTY IMAGES
1.8 COURTESY OF WWD/STEVE EICHNER
1.9A © KARI MARTTILA/ALAMY
1.9B © JAMES NESTERWITZ/ALAMY
1.9C PHOTO BY JESSICA KATZ
1.10 COURTESY OF PATAGONIA
1.11 ILLUSTRATION BY VANESSA HAN AND ALICIA FREILE
1.12A ASSOCIATED PRESS
1.12B AFP/GETTY IMAGES
1.13 COURTESY OF FASHION AND EARTH

CHAPTER 2:
2.1 ANDREW HETHERINGTON/REDUX
2.2 ILLUSTRATION BY VANESSA HAN AND ALICIA FREILE
2.3 THOMAS BARWICK/GETTY IMAGES
2.4 COURTESY OF WWD
2.5 MAP: JEZPERKLAUZEN/ISTOCKPHOTO; PEOPLE: © LARRY LILAC/ALAMY

2.6 COURTESY OF WWD/JOHN AQUINO
2.7 COURTESY OF WWD
2.8 DAVID MCNEW/GETTY IMAGES
2.9 COURTESY OF WWD/ PETER KNEFFEL
2.10 GRAHAM JEPSON/ALAMY

CHAPTER 3:
3.1 CORBIS SUPER RF/ALAMY
3.2 COURTESY OF WWD/GIOVANNI GIANNONI
3.3A-C COURTESY OF WWD/KYLE ERICKSEN
3.4 COURTESY OF WWD
3.5 ILLUSTRATION BY VANESSA HAN AND ALICIA FREILE
3.6 ILLUSTRATION BY VANESSA HAN AND ALICIA FREILE
3.7 THE ADVERTISING ARCHIVES
3.8 COURTESY OF LUCKY BRAND
3.9 NO CREDIT
3.10 ILLUSTRATION BY VANESSA HAN AND ALICIA FREILE
3.11 NO CREDIT
3.12 NO CREDIT
3.13 RON KIMBALL/KIMBALL STOCK
3.14 THE ADVERTISING ARCHIVES
3.15 ILLUSTRATION BY VANESSA HAN AND ALICIA FREILE

CHAPTER 4:
4.1A CULTURA CREATIVE/ALAMY
4.1B DIRK LINDNER CULTURA/NEWSCOM
4.2 COURTESY OF WWD/ JOHN AQUINO
4.3 ILLUSTRATION BY VANESSA HAN AND ALICIA FREILE
4.4 ILLUSTRATION BY VANESSA HAN AND ALICIA FREILE
4.5 THESTOREGUY/ALAMY
4.6 LAWRENCE LUCIER/FILMMAGIC/GETTY IMAGES
4.7 ILLUSTRATION BY VANESSA HAN AND ALICIA FREILE
4.8A COURTESY OF WWD/ JOHN AQUINO
4.8B COURTESY OF WWD/ANDREA MARTIRADONNA
4.9 LE ROBSHAW/ALAMY
4.10 ILLUSTRATION BY VANESSA HAN AND ALICIA FREILE
4.11 ILLUSTRATION BY VANESSA HAN AND ALICIA FREILE

CHAPTER 5:
5.1A ROSLAN RAHMAN/AFP/GETTY IMAGES
5.1B AP PHOTO/MATT SAYLES
5.1C JIM WEST/ALAMY
5.2 JAMIE GRILL/GETTY IMAGES
5.3 NETPHOTOS/ALAMY